WILLIE

MW00607950

WILLIE STARGELL
A Life in Baseball

Frank Garland

Sandra —

I hope you enjoy reading this as much as I enjoyed writing it.

Frank

McFarland & Company, Inc., Publishers
Jefferson, North Carolina, and London

LIBRARY OF CONGRESS ONLINE CATALOG DATA

Garland, Frank.
　　Willie Stargell : a life in baseball / Frank Garland.
　　　　p.　　cm.
　　Includes bibliographical references and index.

　　ISBN 978-0-7864-6534-7
　　softcover : acid free paper ∞

　　1. Stargell, Willie, 1940–2001.　2. Baseball players —
United States — Biography.　I. Title.
　　GV865.576+　　　　　　　　　　　　　　　　2013009396

BRITISH LIBRARY CATALOGUING DATA ARE AVAILABLE

© 2013 Frank Garland. All rights reserved

*No part of this book may be reproduced or transmitted in any form
or by any means, electronic or mechanical, including photocopying
or recording, or by any information storage and retrieval system,
without permission in writing from the publisher.*

Front cover: Willie unleashes his mighty swing, the one that
propelled 475 balls beyond outfield walls throughout the major
leagues and made him one of the game's all-time great sluggers
(photograph courtesy of the Pittsburgh Pirates)

Manufactured in the United States of America

*McFarland & Company, Inc., Publishers
Box 611, Jefferson, North Carolina 28640
www.mcfarlandpub.com*

This book is dedicated to the biggest influences in my life — my brother, James J. Garland, who instilled in me a love of sports that has only grown over time; my children, Frankie Garland and Gina Garland Wilde, whose caring nature and enthusiasm for life have buoyed me in trying times; my sisters, Tina Blem and Mary Mackay, who have provided emotional support — and the world's best cookies — for decades; and Larry Minner, the best boss who ever lived.

Contents

Preface

A TRIP TO THE National Baseball Hall of Fame is a must for any true fan of the sport. The need to immerse myself in baseball history — and to share that history with my then-18-year-old son — sent me in the direction of Cooperstown, New York, in the summer of 2005. That and the desire to find an old pink house in West Saugerties, New York, where an under-the-radar rock ensemble known as The Band and a legend in hiding named Bob Dylan recorded some of the 20th century's most memorable music. But that's a story for another time.

The Baseball Hall of Fame tour unleashed a torrent of memories of my own boyhood days, when I would idle away the morning hours throwing a tennis ball off our brick house and onto a gravel driveway and trying to field the crazy caroms and unpredictable bounces that only those stones could generate. Afternoons were set aside for playing endless sessions of pickup baseball at Burkett School. Evenings were reserved for "official" Robinson Township Little League games where — as a good-field, no-hit second baseman — I had an unquenchable thirst for gobbling up ground balls. My nights, meanwhile, were spent drifting off to sleep to the melodic tones of Bob Prince, Jack Buck and any other play-by-play voice I could coax out of my sleek, space-age Panasonic radio. Prince, with his unique gravelly voice and his penchant for catchy phrases — "a bloop and a blast," "bug on a rug," and "spread some Chicken on the Hill with Will" were just a few of them — brought Pittsburgh Pirates games to life for a young boy who couldn't make it out to Forbes Field and later Three Rivers Stadium often enough. Buck barked his call of St. Louis Cardinals games over a 50,000-watt blowtorch known as KMOX, which came in loud and clear at night in Pittsburgh — and, as it was in the Central Time Zone, right on cue to bring me the final few innings after the Pirates had finished their nightly eastern time zone battle. Prince, Buck and the other

1

voices weren't just calling big-league baseball games on the radio for a living —
they were performers in an opera of sorts, played out in 162 acts over a six-
month stretch that started with the promise of spring and ended with the chill
of the autumn air. And the start of another school year.

No tour of the Hall of Fame could be complete without a quick stop in
the gift shop or book store. It was there, on that August day in 2005, in that
sea of books, that it dawned on me that the canon of baseball literature was
missing a key element — a look at one of the greatest power hitters the game
has ever seen. Yes, the store did have Willie Stargell's autobiography, written
with his friend and former Pittsburgh Pirates publicist Tom Bird. But the
book was written in Stargell's own voice — his life as he saw it. And while that
certainly proved to be a captivating tale, I felt somewhat deprived, due not
only to the reputation that Stargell had earned over the years as a slugger of
Ruthian proportions (literally and figuratively), but also to the picture of him
as a wise and caring individual, someone who went out of his way to include
others and make teammates — and even some members of the opposition —
feel like they were part of his "family." Yes, I felt fortunate to read Stargell's
story through his own eyes, but I wondered how others saw the special slugger — how did he influence their careers and their lives? How did he cope with
the overt racism that would rain on him during his first years in professional
baseball? How did he cope with the trappings of stardom and reconcile the
glamorous life of a major league ballplayer with that of a husband and father?
Was his reputation as the wise "Pops," cultivated during a splendid 20-year
career but cemented during a memorable and magical championship run at
the advanced age of 39, warranted?

It was there, in that room full of books, that the idea for this adventure
materialized. Over the next five years, I would interview more than 80 people —
Stargell family members, boyhood friends, teammates, opponents, coaches,
managers, general managers, front-office co-workers and fans — to help bring
Willie's story to life. It started with a conversation with former Pittsburgh
Pirates owner Kevin McClatchy in the fall of 2007, just as he was leaving his
post and making way for a new club regime to take over. McClatchy talked
about how rewarding it was to help bring Stargell "home" in the fall of 1997 —
back from a decade in Atlanta, where he had originally gone with Chuck Tanner to learn the coaching ropes with an eye toward one day succeeding Tanner
as manager of the Braves. That plan fizzled, but Stargell found a soft landing
spot in the Braves' front office, working to evaluate and tutor what was rapidly
becoming a system stocked with young stars such as Chipper Jones, Ron Gant,
Ryan Klesko and David Justice.

McClatchy's interview led to another interview and another and another until finally Stargell's story began to take shape. Conversations with boyhood pals such as Nick Cabral and Curt Motton and coaches like George Read helped paint a picture of Stargell as a teenager. Minor-league teammates Ron Brand, Bob Priddy and Dick Doepker recalled the young Stargell, struggling to catch popups at first base and make contact at the plate, but every now and then flashing the power that would make him famous years after he'd left the dusty fields of Texas and New Mexico. Fellow African American teammates such as Bob Veale and Preston Bruce Jr. recounted the horrid conditions minority players had to endure in the late 1950s and early 1960s while America wrestled with race issues that remain unsettled to this day. Big-league teammates such as Steve Blass and Gene Clines told tales of the Pirates of the early '70s — stocked with Hall of Famers Roberto Clemente, Bill Mazeroski and Stargell — while Phil Garner, Ed Ott, Tony Bartirome, Tanner and others brought to life the clubhouse that belonged to the "We Are Fam-A-Lee" Pirates of 1979. Others chimed in. Media members who observed Stargell at work on a daily basis — some for more than a decade — talked about his approach and what he meant to the club. John Schuerholz critiqued Stargell's work as an assistant in the Braves' front office. It was no coincidence that the Braves' unprecedented run of success began during Stargell's tenure there. Cam Bonifay and McClatchy discussed what Stargell brought to the Pirates' front office after he returned in the late 1990s — a stint that likely would have continued had Stargell remained in good health.

Several family members were kind enough to offer their perspective — his sister, Sandrus Collier not only offered her lifelong observations of her famous brother, but also supplied several of the photographs used in this book. Lois Beard Booker, the first of three Mrs. Willie Stargells, talked about the young Stargell and how — despite the dissolution of their marriage — he welcomed and worked to keep in touch with all members of his family. His only son, Wilver Jr., recalled what it was like to grow up with a famous father. Several other family members agreed to be interviewed and related volumes of wonderful material, but ultimately chose not to allow that material to be used in the project, a decision that I of course respect.

In addition to the dozens of interviews, heaping helpings of valuable materials were obtained from the Baseball Hall of Fame, the Pittsburgh Pirates offices, the Heinz History Center and Western Pennsylvania Sports Hall of Fame, and municipal and university libraries in San Francisco, Los Angeles and Davis, California. Court and prothonotary employees in Oakland, California, and Pittsburgh helped uncover key information — such as salary figures — in various documents.

The book is organized largely in chronological fashion, starting with

Stargell's boyhood and working through his minor- and major-league careers before his life in retirement. A separate chapter is devoted to Stargell's long-ball prowess, with that story told through the eyes of teammates, fans and experts in the field — and even a couple of pitchers who served up some of the slugger's longest long balls. Yet another chapter focuses on Stargell's real family — as opposed to the '79 Pirates' "Fam-A-Lee," a crew highlighted in the book's sixth chapter.

Several of the sources who provided priceless material for this book have passed and should be recognized individually — Motton, Tanner, Joe Brown, Nelson "Nellie" King, Ron Santo and Wayne Twitchell. Others who were interviewed for the book were Henry Aaron, Gene Alley, Anthony Arnerich, Tony Bartirome, Steve Blass, Bert Blyleven, Cam Bonifay, Lois Beard Booker, Ron Brand, Greg Brown, Preston Bruce, Ray Burris, Nick Cabral, Gene Clines, Gene Collier, Sandrus Collier, Ron Cook, Dick Doepker, Dan Donovan, David Effron, Lanny Frattare, Robert Freeman, Bob Friend, Phil Garner, Dave Giusti, Jim Grant, Franco Harris, Grant Jackson, Bill Jenkinson, Rex Johnston, Brady Keys, Joe King, Rudy May, Kevin McClatchy, Lindy McDaniel, Roy McHugh, Ron McKee, Joe Morgan, Steve Nicosia, Phil Niekro, Sam Nover, Al Oliver, Ed Ott, Dave Parker, William Patterson, Harding Peterson, Bob Priddy, George Read, Merv Rettenmund, Jerry Reuss, Don Robinson, Jim Rooker, Vic Roznovsky, Stan Savran, John Schuerholz, Joseph Schwantner, Bob Skinner, Bob Smizik, Ned Sokoloff, Willie Stargell Jr., Ron Taylor, Bob Veale and Bill Virdon.

I would also like to acknowledge the use of several online sources — Google News, with its treasure trove of newspaper clippings, enabled me to access key highlights and quotes from game stories during Stargell's 20-year playing career. The archives of several publications — most notably the *Pittsburgh Post-Gazette* and now-defunct *Pittsburgh Press*, but also others including the *Atlanta Journal-Constitution, New York Times, Los Angeles Times, Chicago Tribune, Christian Science Monitor, Beaver County Times, New York Daily News, Sports Illustrated, Pittsburgh Courier, Los Angeles Herald Examiner, USA Today, Wilmington Star News* and *Pittsburgh Tribune-Review* — played major roles in helping fashion this story. Also invaluable were Retrosheet.org and Baseball-Reference.com, both of which featured a wealth of material free of charge that helped me reconstruct specific games and stretches of games.

While dozens of people helped make this project a reality, several deserve special thanks. Eric Compton, a veteran sports journalist who can spin yarns with the best of them, provided much-needed editing help and advice. Sally O'Leary, a longtime Pirate employee who now works with the club's alumni group, supplied contact information for dozens of former players. Jim Trdinich and Dan Hart of the Pirates' media relations department helped open doors to the club's front office, and Dave Arrigo, the team's photographer, provided dozens of photographs. Pat Kelly of the Baseball Hall of Fame also was a major help in terms of acquiring photographs for the project, as was Stargell's sister, Sandrus Collier, and David Coppen at the Eastman School of Music at the University of Rochester. Nick Cabral, the "unofficial" mayor of Alameda, California, took an entire afternoon to show me around the town where both he and Stargell came of age.

The danger in thanking people for their help is that someone is bound to be overlooked. Suffice it to say, this project could not have come to fruition without the help and cooperation of more than a hundred people. It's no surprise that it took that many. Willie Stargell was a big man. And his story is a big story.

Introduction

THOUSANDS OF MEN have carved out careers as major-league baseball players in the nearly 150 years that the game has been played professionally. More than 200 have achieved the ultimate recognition — enshrinement in the Baseball Hall of Fame.

Those honored players earned their place in Cooperstown, New York, by virtue of their playing prowess, compiling statistics that vaulted them to the top of their respective eras. One of them, however, not only managed to amass numbers that placed him among the elite offensive players of all time, but created a magical mystique that prevailed both inside and outside the clubhouse, on and off the field.

Willie Stargell was that player, a one-of-a-kind spiritual leader whose impact left a lasting impression on teammates and rivals alike, not to mention a city that embraced him like virtually no other athlete before him.

Stargell's legacy goes far beyond the 20 seasons he played in Pittsburgh, the 475 home runs he hit, the 1,540 RBIs he collected, the 2,232 career hits he compiled and his seven All-Star game appearances. His legacy is that of a man to whom family meant everything — his actual family as well as his baseball family. He was a man who liked fine things and his talents afforded him the opportunity to experience expensive wines, fur coats and even a Rolls Royce. Yet he could be just as happy cooking up a storm for his family on the grill and mixing up a concoction he called "Purple Passion" for his teammates and friends.

He grew up in an era when racial issues were fracturing the nation. But despite experiencing the horrifying conditions that prevailed in the segregated South during his early days as a professional — even being threatened with a shotgun before a minor-league game during his first season in the minor leagues — he maintained an upbeat attitude and stressed the importance of keeping an even keel. Never get too high or too low in the game, he would caution teammates. But never forget that baseball is a game. One of his favorite sayings was that the umpire says "Play ball"— not "Work ball"— at the start of a game.

He came from humble beginnings and he was proud of his heritage, which included African American and American Indian blood. He experienced a bewildering early childhood stretch that saw him living in Florida with an aunt for several years before he returned to his mother and stepfather in the San Francisco Bay Area, where he came of age in a melting pot community called Alameda. He would play on a high school team that featured two other players who would go on to carve out major league careers and while he was not a high-profile prospect, he had something special that caught the eye of an inexperienced Pittsburgh Pirate scout named Bob Zuk.

Stargell made his way through the Pirates' farm system, methodically climbing the ladder and growing into his large frame and finally exhibiting the power that Zuk envisioned when he first saw Stargell as a 5-11, 170-pound amateur. And after two fairly nondescript seasons to start his big-league career, he began to establish himself as one of the game's great sluggers, both in terms of frequency and distance. He would go on to crush some of the longest home runs ever hit in more than a half-dozen ballparks; he personally accounted for seven of the 16 balls to clear the right-field roof at Pittsburgh's Forbes Field and hit the first two balls — and two of only four total — to leave Dodger Stadium. He hit the longest home runs at Montreal's Olympic Stadium and Philadelphia's Veterans Stadium, sent one into the swimming pool outside Montreal's Jarry Park and deposited four into the upper deck at Three Rivers Stadium. His career total of 475 home runs is somewhat misleading, as he played the first half of his career in mammoth Forbes Field, which some say could have deprived him of another 100 or so round-trippers.

For such a huge and powerful man, one known for feats of heroic strength on the baseball field, Willie's gentle, caring nature seemed to best define him. That, and his interest in the causes that affected those close to him — sickle cell anemia, for one, and an organization created to increase opportunities for African Americans in baseball leadership positions, both on the field and in the front office. Stargell seemed to be decades ahead of his time in seeing the "big picture"— that one could use athletic accomplishments and celebrity as a way to bring about meaningful change in the world. And even though he died in 2001, his name lives on in a foundation that raises money to fund kidney disease research and to support those suffering from the disease.

Those who knew Stargell talked freely about his leadership qualities, and the fact that he never sought to be a leader, but rather the role just seemed to come naturally to him. And he embraced it, setting the tone as a youngster in Alameda and then later in the raucous clubhouse in Pittsburgh's Three Rivers Stadium through the magical decade of the 1970s. It wasn't only teammates who admired his leadership qualities; word spread of his special gifts around the major leagues until it was understood that Stargell was one of the finest teammates a big-league player could have. One of fellow Hall of Famer Joe Morgan's few regrets in baseball was that he never had a chance to play on a team with Stargell.

He would star for the better part of two decades for the Pirates, evolving into one of the most iconic sports figures in a city blessed with numerous sports heroes. When his playing career ended, he remained tethered to the game, hovering in the broadcast booth for a year, before eventually agreeing to work as a special assistant in the Pirates' front office. He was elevated to a coach under Chuck Tanner, and then when new Pirates ownership came in and dismissed Tanner, Stargell followed his old manager to Atlanta, where he started a new chapter in his life. Although things didn't work out as planned — Tanner wanted to groom Stargell to take over as field manager when Tanner himself moved up to become general manager — Stargell earned a position in the Braves' front office and spent most of a decade helping to teach the club's prospects about hitting. And winning. Those who worked with him in the front office acknowledged his influence over an organization that went from being one of the worst in baseball to a team with an unprecedented run of 14 straight division titles.

That wasn't all he did. In 1988, he became the 17th player to be elected to the Baseball Hall of Fame in his first year of eligibility. He remained active, taking on speaking engagements at colleges and universities. He found time to indulge in several hobbies — computers, photography, deep sea fishing for blue marlin and using his compound bow. He also spent time shortly after retiring from the game touring with the Eastman Philharmonia and starring in a production known as *New Morning for the World — Daybreak of Freedom,* written by Pulitzer Prize–winning composer Joseph Schwantner and featuring the words of Dr. Martin Luther King Jr. He received rave reviews and would go on to narrate other musical works in the years to come.

After a decade-long hiatus with the Braves in Atlanta, Stargell was asked to return to Pittsburgh and work with the Pirates in 1997. Overjoyed, he jumped at the chance and became one of the club's trusted advisers. His failing health curtailed his activities but he managed to be on hand in the fall of 2000 when the Pirates announced that a 12-foot statue would be built to honor Stargell at the new PNC Park, set to open for business the following spring. He was moved to tears by the gesture. He stayed in town to see the club drop the curtain on his own personal power playground, Three Rivers Stadium, as the 2000 season wound to a close. By then, appearing gaunt due to his health issues, he received one final salute from the fans while surrounded by teammates and his old field boss, Tanner.

Then in early April, word filtered into the city that the mighty Stargell had passed — on the very day that the Pirates were prepared to make their debut in sparkling new PNC Park. If ever there was a day of mixed emotions, April 9, 2001, was it for Pirates fans young and old alike.

Willie Stargell has been gone for more than a decade now, but his story resonates with as much life today as it ever did. His on-field exploits guaranteed him immortality in the game of baseball; his numbers and upper-deck bombs ensure that he will remain front and center in any conversation pertaining to the game's elite power hitters. His ability to lead, to steady and to inspire guarantees that any discussion of baseball's most beloved and effective leaders will include mention of his name — and prominent mention at that.

His legacy will live on forever not just with teammates, opponents and fans of the game he so dearly loved — playing baseball was all he ever wanted to do for a living — but those who lived with him and loved him. The same inspiration and even keel that he offered his clubhouse mates, he provided for his five children and his grandchildren, and no doubt would have been a constant flowing source of love had he remained alive today.

Willie Stargell was not perfect, as his story will make clear. He was, however, perfectly human.

CHAPTER 1

In the Beginning

S O MANY VARIABLES go into making a man. In no way does the process resemble a mathematical equation, all parts logically fitting together and yielding a sensible walking, talking sum. It's not a chemical formula, where each element can be scientifically extracted and scrutinized, weighed and measured, and assigned a certain value. A man's makeup consists of elements, but putting a chemical or numerical value to each would be a fool's task. Genetics plays a major role, as does the environment into which he is born and raised. Friends, family, co-workers and even adversaries mold and shape. Passions and interests help smooth out the rough edges and fill the gaps.

Wilver Dornel Stargell was a complex man — a man of wisdom and grace. A man of enormous strength and power. A prankster. A kind soul. A man to whom family and friends meant virtually everything. Above all, he was human. As a member of baseball's hallowed Hall of Fame, he displayed feats of superhuman skills and coordination, yet displayed the same lapses in judgment and the same character flaws that the vast majority of humanity shows in its weaker moments. He was a real man, whose impact on the game of baseball and on those who had the pleasure of knowing him will only grow in time.

Coursing through the veins of this real man was the blood of two proud and largely misunderstood races — the black man and the American Indian, both of which he believed largely made him the man he ultimately became. Born in rural Oklahoma and reared for part of his childhood in the deep south of Florida, he came of age in the racial melting pot of the San Francisco Bay Area, largely protected by a unique environment while the turbulence of the 1950s swirled outside. Later, he used his notoriety to help raise awareness of a disease that affected scores of blacks as he pushed against the steely resolve of baseball's establishment for more minority representation in places of power both on and off the field.

11

A genealogical record of Stargell's life, contained in the Pittsburgh Pirates' files, indicates that Stargell's mother's maiden name was Gladys Vernell Hunt and that his paternal grandfather was a Seminole light-horse brigade member named Tecumseh Bruner. The sketch maintained that Stargell's paternal grandmother — Nora May Bruner — was the daughter of Eugene Walker and Dinah Walker and that both families were found in the Indian Territory in the Seminole County in the 1900 census.

According to the Pirates genealogical record, Stargell's great-grandfather, Henry Stargell, moved from Georgia to Oklahoma around 1908. Georgia census records show the Henry Stargell family in Meriwether County, Georgia, in 1900 and 1880, and these accounts list 12 children born to Henry by his first wife, Victoria. In 1899, Henry was remarried to Dora Mitchell, and the two were shown to be living together in the 1900 census.

Although official baseball records place Stargell's place of birth as Earlsboro, Oklahoma, there is some question about the day and year. The National Baseball Hall of Fame lists his birth date as March 6, 1940, but other sources list the year as 1941 and even 1942. Stargell maintained that March 6 was the day that his mother, Gladys Stargell, went into labor — but that he was not born until the following day, March 7. But Stargell held that the year was 1941 — not 1940. However, his half-sister Sandrus said Stargell's birth year was 1940. His unusual first name, Wilver, was a combination of his father's "William" and his mother's middle name, "Vernell."

William Stargell left his wife, Gladys, before young Wilver was born, but the Stargell clan welcomed mother and son with open arms. And there, the first major male influence in Stargell's life surfaced — his paternal grandfather, Wil, who served not only as a father figure to young Wilver but also to his young mother.

The Stargells, like most Depression-era families, struggled to get by financially. In 1942, Gladys married a soldier named Lesley Bush, and two years later the young family — looking to take advantage of wartime job opportunities out West — followed Bush's family to California. Gladys's marriage to Lesley Bush dissolved in 1945, and she and her son moved in with a stepaunt in the housing projects of Alameda. Gladys found work as a cleaning lady and in 1946 married a sailor-turned-truck driver named Percy Russell. But the young family's life would be upended by an unexpected visitor — one of Gladys's older sisters, Lucy, arrived from Orlando, Florida, and stayed with the family for almost a month. Sensing the young couple could use some time to regroup, Lucy talked Gladys and Percy into allowing her to take 5-year-old Wilver back to Florida for a spell. They agreed on a one-year maximum stay, and soon Wilver and Lucy were on a train and bound for Florida.[1]

One year turned into six, and young Wilver spent much of his time doing chores for his aunt. But he managed to find opportunities to hone his nascent baseball skills, tossing stones to strengthen his throwing arm and using those same stones — as well as bottle caps — to develop his trademark hitting stroke. The youngster would simply toss them in the air and blast them with sticks — a pastime he would indulge in for years to come.

Not much is known about Stargell's six-year stay in Orlando, other than what he conveyed in his autobiography. Eventually, however, Gladys — with young Sandrus in tow — boarded a train in California, bound for Florida, and reclaimed her son. By then, at age 11, Stargell believed he had been strongly influenced by his racial makeup. In fact, he maintained that as part black and part Seminole Indian, he was bred as an "outcast." As a Seminole, Stargell wrote, he had never experienced life in a conventional family, and

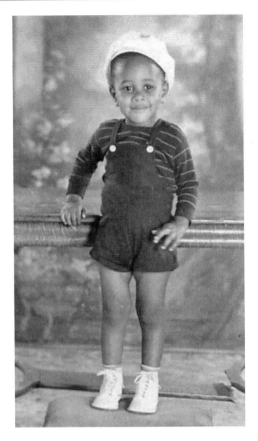

Willie Stargell, posing for a family photograph, at 26 months of age (courtesy Sandrus Collier).

being black, he felt "trapped within the confines of societal prejudice."[2]

He also felt significant influence from his generation, one that emphasized togetherness. Even at a young age, he valued nothing more than friends and family. But baseball was a close third. He looked for every opportunity to improve his skills, even if conventional games or practices weren't often in the offing. He even recalled swinging at imaginary pitches on the train ride from his Aunt Lucy's place in Florida back to the Bay Area and his new home. There, in the island city of Alameda, the reconstituted Stargell family — Wilver, Sandrus, their mother Gladys, and Percy Russell — lived in a one-bedroom apartment in a low-income housing project originally built for government workers who flocked to the Bay Area to fill hundreds of wartime jobs. Gladys toiled at a cannery and moonlighted as a beautician on the side, working out of the family apartment. Percy, meanwhile, provided the discipline and strength the young family needed. And as an added bonus, he shared with young Wilver a love for baseball that went back to his Alabama roots.

Stargell's new neighborhood, known as the Encinal project, provided a safe, loving environment colored by its many races and nationalities. Because everyone was in the same financial boat, no discernible prejudice existed within the housing project. "We all struggled together," Stargell wrote. "My mother termed our neighborhood 'the family'—different households were that close with one another."[3] More than 40 years later, it would be another "family"— the 1979 Pittsburgh Pirates—that would become synonymous with Stargell.

Nick Cabral, who befriended Stargell at a local Boys Club before they were teenagers and later attended Encinal High School with him, remembered Alameda as a wonderful place to grow up. "In the mid–1950s, with all this racial strife and changes, we were in our own little cocoon, contained on this island," he said. "It was this perfect little nest. It was amazing. We were so protected by this community—we had a wonderful time growing up. Our high school was so diverse. One year we'd have an Anglo running for student body president, then an Asian, then a Hispanic, then a Hawaiian. It was a melting pot of a high school. It was special and it's not a surprise that Willie came out of that environment. We were diverse with friends so young. We knew no different. We thought the whole world lived like this."[4]

Willie, dressed as a young sailor, at 4½ years of age (courtesy Sandrus Collier).

The melting pot that was the Alameda projects and the lack of prejudice that prevailed would stand in stark contrast to the world Stargell would inhabit just a few years later. But in the meantime, he lived what appeared to be a rather typical young teen's life — playing sports, spending time with friends and getting into a little mischief now and then.

Stargell found a haven of sorts at a local Boys Club, which was located in the west end of Alameda. Joe King, the Boys Club director, recalls Stargell joining the group at the age of 12 or so. In those days, no one referred to Stargell as Willie — it was always by his given name, Wilver. "In fact we'd always call him 'Wil-i-ver' — we'd put that extra vowel in there," King said.[5]

At the age of 13, Stargell and Cabral played on a Boys Club team that ultimately battled for the Bay Area Boys Club championship, against Columbia Park of San Francisco, at Seals Stadium, which was to become the first home of the San Francisco Giants after they relocated from New York in time for the 1958 season. "I can't tell you what Stargell did but he must have done well because we won 8–1," King recalled. "And Nick had a no-hitter going for six innings." That would be the only year that Stargell would play for the Boys Club team; the next year he was off to Encinal High School, where he started playing as a freshman.

Cabral said the Boys Club was the center of life for boys ages 10 to 14 in the Oakland area. In addition to baseball and basketball, the club offered escapes that weren't often available to inner-city youth like those who lived in Alameda's Encinal, Estuary and Webster housing projects. "We'd walk over there to the club and pick up eight or nine kids along the way — and we'd stay all day," Cabral said. On Tuesdays, youngsters would take field trips, one of which stood out in Cabral's memory. "We had a doctor in Alameda who had a cabin up in the Oakland Hills. It was still urban — it was right in the city — but we thought we were in Yellowstone. These little black kids didn't know where they were. Giant Oak Knoll Hospital was right down the road from the cabin — you could look down from the porch and see the hospital — but we thought we were in the wilderness. That was our life. It was a Norman Rockwell life."

Throughout his pre-teen and early teenage years, Stargell's love for baseball grew stronger, and despite the fact that only a few black ballplayers by that time had reached the major leagues, he was convinced he could make a career of it. Although he had moved from rocks and bottle caps to rubber balls and tennis balls to improve his batting eye, he wasn't above hitting stones in a pinch. Curt Motton, who grew up in the Alameda projects and became Stargell's teammate at Encinal High School — and ultimately played in the major leagues with Stargell and another fellow Encinal alum, Tommy Harper — recalled he and Stargell hitting pebbles with a stick on more than one occasion. "We wouldn't do it religiously, but I know we used to do it," said Motton, who died in 2010. Motton said Stargell apparently picked up the exercise from an older neighborhood player named Joe Wilson. "Joe gave him this technique — if you hit this pebble like this, this is what would happen," Motton said. "One person would throw and the other person would hit. I can recall Stargell mentioning to me later that he thought that exercise had a lot to do with helping him develop into the hitter he became."[6]

Motton first ran into Stargell when the two were about 12 years old, when Motton was delivering newspapers to Percy and Gladys Russell's apartment in the Encinal Project. "One day I came to collect and when Stargell answered the door, he said, 'My mama ain't gonna pay you.' He was just pulling my leg. That's how we met."

It wouldn't be the last time Stargell pulled Motton's leg. In fact, Stargell was perennially upbeat; at least that is the way Motton remembered him. "He seemed to be a guy who was always happy," he said. "The people that he liked, whenever he saw you, his face would just light up. He liked to have fun. He was an easy person to like — outgoing, pleasant to be around. Even after he became quite successful, he didn't change. Whenever we would bump into each other, it was always a pleasant surprise if we weren't expecting to see each other. If I had gone to sleep for a long time and woke up and didn't know he'd done the things he'd done in baseball, I'd think he was pretty much the same guy."

When he wasn't hitting rocks, Stargell was working on his game at nearby Washington Park. Those who played with and against Stargell can remember a few of the long balls he hit. "He was around 12 years old and he was hitting the ball 400 feet-plus," said Robert Earl Davis, a teammate of Stargell's at Encinal High School and the school's best all-around athlete in Stargell's estimation. "When he was hitting them, he was hitting them over the fence."[7] And occasionally through a window. "There was this house with blue glass," remembered Cabral, "and he just knocked it out."

Motton, who was the leading hitter on the Encinal Jets team during the trio's senior year of high school in 1958, said Willie's scorebook featured no cheap hits. "As youngsters, we tended to evaluate ourselves based on our batting average. Looking back, Willie might have hit .400 and I would have hit .420 and Harper would have hit .480 or .500. If I got 25 hits, eight or nine of them were because I could run. Every one of Stargell's hits was legitimate. If I played against good infielders, my batting average would have gone down. Willie could have played against the best infielders and outfielders and his batting average wouldn't change. When he hit the ball, he really hit it hard and the ball really carried. He used to hit the ball over the fence in high school. I don't recall him hitting any really long home runs — balls that would make my mouth drop, like he did when he got to the big leagues. But I do remember that he got the longest base hits. He didn't run very well, so he would hit a single and it'd be longer than any ball I hit. It would be a long line drive."

Although Stargell ultimately became the most successful player ever to come out of Alameda, during his days at Encinal, he wasn't even the best on his team. That honor went to Harper, who not only stood out in baseball but was an accomplished basketball and football player. "Tommy Harper was an adult man at 17," Cabral said. "He didn't fuck around. He was quiet — he was focused at a very young age. He was the same guy at 10 as he is today — very focused."

Anthony "Lil" Arnerich, who ran the Alameda Recreation and Parks system when Stargell, Motton and Harper were growing up, said Harper — who would go on to play for 15 seasons in the major leagues — was the best all-around player and athlete of the bunch. "He was a good baseball player, a very good football player and a good basketball player," said Arnerich, who himself advanced to the highest rung of minor-league baseball before ending his playing career and then watched dozens of top-rate players come up through the Alameda parks system. "Willie was not what you would call a great or even very good high school baseball player. He was an average player for high school."[8]

But William Patterson, the director of the Brookfield Recreation Center in nearby Oakland during Stargell's teenage years, recalled Stargell as an outstanding athlete with very good body control. "He was a little shy around the girls," Patterson said. "But playing baseball or something like that, he had no problems." Patterson said he was friends with Gladys and Percy Russell, and it was Gladys Russell who encouraged Willie to frequent the Brookfield club on occasion. Patterson remembers Stargell as a well-behaved youngster. "When he was with the guys alone, he might have been different," said Patterson, after whom Brookfield Park was renamed in 2008. "But around me he was always a little subdued. Of course, I knew his mother and father. And when you have that kind of relationship, a guy is going to tend to not do anything to get in trouble. His mother had told him, 'Go over there with Bill; you can't get into trouble there.'"[9]

It might have been more than just a matter of staying out of trouble. The Oakland area was most progressive when it came to providing safe, structured havens for its minority youth — in fact, it was far ahead of its time. Patterson, a retired Oakland Parks and Recreation manager, saw firsthand at the Brookfield and deFremery Recreation Centers how an emphasis on leadership — rather than simply a roll the ball out and let 'em play approach — could pay huge dividends both at the time and for years to come. "We would try to get guys to see where they had weaknesses that they had to work on in terms of social development," Patterson said. "They were already talented athletes; you couldn't teach them much more in terms of sports. But our thing was to make men out of them."

Dorothy Seal Pitts, who would spend virtually her entire adult life working as an advocate for minority youth, served as deFremery's leadership director and was instrumental in stressing the fact that there was more to life than hitting a baseball square or putting a ball through a hoop. "We had leadership classes," Patterson recalled. "And Dorothy was the hero of the whole East Bay in terms of her impact on young people. She was the one who drove many people to UCLA and pushed them to get into the University of California, Berkeley. It was the training she gave."

Patterson said there was a time when the black high school athletes in Oakland were not getting the publicity that some of their white counterparts received, even though some of those athletes proved to be among the greatest in their respective sports. The list included Hall of Fame basketball player Bill Russell, who starred at Oakland's McClymonds High School before going on to stardom at the University of San Francisco and later with the NBA's Boston Celtics.

Patterson said he and others felt that publicity might be the key to getting those youngsters noticed by college recruiters and professional scouts. But it wasn't just a matter of harping to the press about providing more coverage — Patterson and others would work with the youngsters to prepare them in case the press came calling. "We provided them guidance and that helped in terms of their self-confidence," Patterson said. "We made them think about how they would respond to questions and how they could be able to articulate. We didn't just stay in the gym. When Bill Russell spoke at my retirement, he said the discussions that we had at deFremery prepared him for the world."

When Stargell arrived at Encinal High School, he wanted to make his mark not only on the baseball diamond, but on other fields of play. At one point, Stargell — at Harper's urging — tried out for football, ostensibly to haul in Harper's passes. But Stargell hurt his knee in practice before the regular season started and that ended his football career. He also played basketball, but at 5-foot-10 did not distinguish himself on the court.

Despite featuring three players who would eventually make a living in the major leagues, the Jets' baseball team did not even win its league title during the senior year of Stargell, Harper and Motton. First-year coach George Read had plenty of firepower in the lineup — in addition to the trio he also had Davis, whom he called the best third baseman he ever coached — but no pitching, and that's what kept the Jets from winning a league title. That, and an overall knowledge of the game. "It was a good group, but I would have given anything if they were juniors," he said. "They were very good athletes and could do a lot of things, but they really didn't know a lot about baseball. It takes a little time to get kids to understand the game and what you should do in different situations."[10]

Read remembered Stargell as a good-natured youngster who loved to hit. "He couldn't come out for the team right away because he was still playing basketball and they were going for the championship," Read said of Stargell, referring to his senior season. "But he would come out early before practice and want to hit. He was always eager to practice baseball—and especially hit." When Stargell eventually joined the team and took his position at first base, he was a force in more ways than one. "He was not what I would call a character, but he was fun to be around," Read said. "He'd talk it up—he was always in the ballgame. He would keep the team alive. If I would have had him for two years, I think he would have been on the mound also. He had a great arm from the outfield—he could really throw."

The idea that Stargell would sign a professional baseball contract immediately after leaving Encinal never entered Read's mind because he figured Stargell would accompany some of his teammates to Santa Rosa Junior College. But Read, who later was later asked by Stargell to present him at his induction into the Bay Area Sports Hall of Fame, said he wasn't exactly shocked that Stargell developed the way he did. "When you get to be that good, maybe it's always a surprise," he said. But Read said Stargell had decent size and the promise of growing much bigger and that helped him stand apart from some of his contemporaries. "Nowadays, my goodness, there are so many players who are big, strong guys," he said. "Back then, a lot of guys didn't have the power that he had. He had to have the good eyes, too, but I think the strong hands, the arms and the wrists were the big thing."

But Stargell had something else, something that couldn't be measured or taught—the passion to develop his baseball skills. "That was the difference between him and the others," Read said. "Harper was an outstanding athlete—he was athlete of the year in the North Coast and all-conference in three sports. He and the other guys were good, but they all needed a little more motivation than Willie. Willie was always the one who was eager to play. He was always, 'Let's get going.' And I'm sure that's the way he was on his pro teams. He enjoyed the game and he was always eager to play. That was just his personality.

"His desire to get out and practice played such a big part in his success. Lots of guys can be big and strong, but if they were natural athletes, they didn't always have to work that much. They don't think about it as much as the guy

Willie shows off his ability to stretch at first base in a game during his senior year at Encinal High School in Alameda, California (courtesy Sandrus Collier).

who really enjoys the game and has to work at it, although I don't think Stargell had to work at it more than anyone else. He just grew into it. He was tall and skinny in high school, but he certainly grew into a big man."

Stargell's growth and development as a man wasn't limited to his physical traits. A major change occurred during his junior year of high school, when his family left Alameda for a home that Gladys and Percy purchased on 82nd Avenue in East Oakland. Although relatively close geographically, the move was a big one for Stargell, since he and his Alameda friends had often left their mark on their East Oakland adversaries, whether it was during competition on the athletic field or vying for the favors of young women. Now he had to make his home essentially behind enemy lines.

Patterson recalls the move was not easy for Stargell. "Having grown up in Alameda, he was kind of a step out of place in Oakland," he said. "He had given Oakland guys a bad time, and of course anytime you come into someone else's territory, the girls always look more interesting. So you follow the girls.

But it was a little more than that with them at the time. Alameda had some outstanding athletes, as did Oakland. These guys were always in competition. They met not only in real games, but on the sandlot. At Brookfield, half the guys hanging out were from Alameda — they had gravitated there with Will and some of the others.

"Eventually, a lot of Alameda families moved into East Oakland. But in the beginning, it was not so easy for Will. He had never expected his parents to move to Oakland. But it wasn't easy for people of color to buy homes anywhere at that time, and East Oakland was one of the areas that began to open up."

The transition wasn't entirely smooth. But eventually, Davis's family also relocated to East Oakland, and Stargell had a natural ally. And over time, he became accepted by those in his neighborhood. Patterson was not surprised. "Will was different," he said. "He was always like a father figure, always helping other kids. He had a knack for the kind of leadership that you'd call indigenous. Willie would show up and then everyone else would come. He was kind of magic that way. He was kind, he was friendly and he was outgoing — and he didn't misuse people. He had the trust of his friends. He was the kind of guy you'd want to be around. He looked out for you. He was never worried in his group — he was always secure in his group and people wanted to be around him. He took that everywhere he went. He was a leader on all the teams he was on. His leadership wasn't the kind where you were out front screaming, but more of a quiet leadership. The kind when you're down, he'd want to know how you're feeling — he'd want to spend time helping you turn things around. If you had a problem, he could speak to that and help you change your course. He was smart that way."

Stargell's senior year at Encinal High School was marked by another significant event. It was then that he met and began cultivating a relationship with the woman who would turn out to be his first bride, Lois Beard. Beard and her family had moved to Alameda in 1950; the Beards lived on 78th Avenue, just a few blocks from the Russell home on 82nd Avenue. And it was in 1957, as a freshman at Encinal, that she remembered seeing Stargell for the first time. "I'm going to PE class and he's coming out," recalled Lois, who would divorce Stargell in 1966 and later marry a man named Leonard Booker. "As a freshman, you were just awed by the seniors. Back then, they had these '49er coats' — jackets with leather sleeves and cloth in the middle. That was the big thing back then. And you were hot stuff if you got a guy's jacket. I went to his prom and later, he went to mine."

Lois said what attracted her to Stargell was his outgoing, friendly nature. "He was kind of the class clown person," she said. "He was always positive and he was always playing jokes on people. His one thing with me was, whenever we'd meet, no matter where we were, he'd step on my toe. I'd hit him in the chest and he'd say, 'How does it feel to hit steel?' This is when he weighed about one-sixty." The two shared a love of music — and a love of dancing. "He was known as a dancer," Lois said. "And he dressed well. He was just very outgoing and he was popular with guys as well as girls." Even then, Lois said, Stargell was dedicated to his sport. "He breathed it, ate it, slept it," she said. "Baseball. You couldn't get him interested in anything else. He was focused. A lot of our dates we'd end up at the batting cages in San Leandro. I'd go out and sit in the fog while he hit the ball. He always wanted to be playing baseball. For him, it was breakfast, lunch and dinner."[11]

Although Stargell's Encinal Jets team failed to win a league title his senior year, it was hardly a lost season for him. Scouts looking to secure talent for their respective major league baseball organizations — all of which had deep minor league systems in those pre-amateur draft days — had found their way to the East Bay. One of those scouts — a young West Coast bird dog named Bob Zuk — came out to take a look at Harper and Motton and then, at the behest of Read, turned his attention to Stargell. After a couple of nonproductive appearances before Zuk — once at a tryout and once at an Encinal game — Stargell showed the scout some of his skills at a third and final attempt, and Zuk eventually called the Stargell family to arrange a meeting to talk contract.

Arnerich recalls that scouts were not beating down the doors to get to Stargell. "No scouts except one scout — and that was Bob Zuk," Arnerich said. "I knew Bob very well and he had a penchant for looking for something that somebody else didn't see. He took a flier on people and he took a flier on Willie. He was this untapped person — everything had not developed."

Arnerich believed Zuk saw one thing — raw power. "That's all he saw," he said. "Willie was a pretty big kid. He was an average player for high school. He wasn't much on finesse. He was a big, awkward kid. Sometimes it's just something you see in someone. It's in the eye of the beholder. Like when the scouts went to see Mickey Mantle — some of them didn't like him."

Arnerich said he wasn't surprised that Zuk went after Stargell and in fact encouraged him to do so. "I told Zuk, 'Give the kid 500 bucks or a thousand bucks and give him a chance,'" he recalled. Even if Stargell never developed into a star, Arnerich figured, major league organizations like the Pirates at that time had many more minor league clubs than they have now and someone had to fill those rosters. In the early 1950s, for example, more than 400 teams were active in some five dozen leagues. "When I played ball, there were 55 minor leagues," Arnerich said.

Cabral said that when Stargell was being courted by the Pirates and eventually signed with the club, no one in the neighborhood made too big of a deal about it. "It was kind of a quiet thing," he said. "It's not like it is today, with all the publicity. Baseball was still innocent. It wasn't corporate. You just went. Willie was going to play baseball. We never thought anything of it."

Cabral said the fact that major league baseball didn't arrive on the West Coast until the Giants and Dodgers moved to San Francisco and Los Angeles, respectively, from New York and Brooklyn prior to the 1958 season might have had something to do with the lack of fanfare that accompanied professional baseball signings. "We weren't a baseball area, really," he said. "Willie just went off the play baseball. He played quite a few years before it struck us what he was doing."

Davis didn't bat an eye when Stargell signed with the Pirates. "Nobody was surprised," he said. "He definitely had the ability, even then. He always had the potential."

Motton said Stargell flew under the radar in terms of notoriety, as he wasn't getting headlines in the local newspapers based on his performances at Encinal or in summer amateur ball. He didn't get the publicity of, say, Curt Flood, who made his mark at Oakland's McClymonds High School and the local American Legion circuit a few years earlier and went on to a successful major league career before ultimately challenging the game's very foundation — its reserve clause — in a case that went all the way to the U.S. Supreme Court.

"If I knew an American Legion game was being played that afternoon, I'd always get the *Oakland Tribune* the next day just to see what Flood did," Motton said. "He'd go 5-for-6, 6-for-6 with two home runs. Did he always do that? I'm not sure. But I'm thinking, 'That Curt Flood must have hit .950.' So, to put Stargell in that context, no, he didn't come out of the area with expectations of stardom."

Looking back on it, Motton — who coached and later did some scouting with the Baltimore Orioles after he retired as an active player following the 1974 season — said he understood what Zuk saw in Stargell. "If I had been scouting in our area at the time Willie was in high school, I would have seen him as a better prospect than a lot of guys, for the simple reason that when he hit the ball, he always hit it good," he said. "It always had good life on it. I've always felt that the key to being successful as a hitter is not how much you miss the ball, but what happens when you hit it. Do you hit it on the label, on the end of the bat or on the sweet spot? When Willie hit the ball, he pretty much hit it on the sweet spot. The ball had good life and good carry. With him, it was always a matter of how much contact he'd make. If he hit the ball, he always made good contact.... A lot of guys can hit the ball but when you put a defense out there, they're going to take away a lot of hits from guys if they hit it softly. If Stargell hit a ground ball, it would be a one- or two-hopper into the outfield. I'd hit a nine-hopper — and if it didn't go through, there's a good chance I'd beat it out. Willie always had the potential to be the hitter he became because of the power — the life in his bat."

Motton also said Zuk likely saw something in Stargell's physical build that led him to believe he had plenty of growing to do. "Willie was taller than the rest of us and he was lanky — he was on the thin side," Motton said. "If someone would have told me then that Stargell would be playing at 225 or 230 pounds in the big leagues, I wouldn't have believed it. I would have said maybe 195 or 200, but not that big. But now, having scouted myself, maybe this is what (Zuk) saw: yes, he was lanky, but his shoulders were broad. And his arms were long. That's all part of projecting — how much is this 16- or 17-year-old kid going to fill out? If he naturally puts on another 35 or 40 pounds, he's going to be a good-sized man. Maybe that's what Bob Zuk saw. Put 30 pounds on him and let him keep hitting like that, and those long singles are going to be long home runs."

Zuk, who died in 2005, remembered the 17-year-old Stargell as a "boneyard." "He had a real good swing, but he didn't make good contact," Zuk would say years later, following Stargell's election to the Hall of Fame in 1988. "He couldn't throw worth a lick. He showed me no physical ability at all." But Zuk said Stargell did possess something special. "All the kids liked him," Zuk said. "Everybody would help him. He had this tremendous charisma."[12]

Willie's senior class picture at Encinal High School — Class of 1958 (courtesy Sandrus Collier).

The Pirates weren't the only ballclub interested in Stargell. Both the New York Yankees and the Philadelphia

Phillies liked what they saw, but they dragged their feet in trying to sign him. The Yankees reportedly wanted to give Stargell a $20,000 bonus to sign. "If they had told me that before I agreed to the Pirates' terms, I would have waited," Stargell told *Pittsburgh Post-Gazette* sports editor Al Abrams in 1973. "But they told me after it was too late."[13]

The Pirates offered Stargell a $1,000 bonus to sign, but Percy Russell countered with $1,500 and after some deliberation Zuk agreed. Stargell took the money and spent $288 on a 1951 Mercury, put $700 in the bank and "had a little fun" with the rest.[14] Although he signed his contract and received his bonus, Stargell did not report immediately and instead spent the summer following his high school graduation playing American Legion and Connie Mack baseball in the East Bay area with former high school teammates and other local standouts.

Zuk said he didn't want Stargell to start playing immediately after his signing because he was so raw that he feared he might be released quickly without getting a true opportunity to show what he could do. During the days following his signing, Stargell toiled in a local Chevrolet plant and played baseball when he could. All was going well until Stargell decided to practice his sliding technique at nearby Santa Rosa Junior College. During one attempt, his cleats caught and Stargell crumpled to a heap, the victim of a broken pelvis. Doctors inserted a four-inch pin to aid with the healing process, and one doctor told Stargell his athletic career was history.[15] Undaunted, Stargell had no interest in giving up his dream and he never complained about the pain he felt, even though it lingered for the next three years.

Stargell remained in the Bay Area for the next several months, even enrolling at Santa Rosa, where he hoped to be reunited on the field with his former Encinal teammates Motton and Harper. But Zuk got wind of that and told the Santa Rosa baseball coach, who quietly dropped Stargell — a professional who was ineligible to play at the amateur level — from the team. Finally, shortly after 1958 gave way to 1959, Stargell packed up and headed off to Jacksonville Beach, Florida, for his first professional big-league spring training camp. It would be an eye-opening experience in more ways than one.

CHAPTER 2

Life in the Bushes

STARGELL HAD EXPERIENCED his share of hardships during his early years —
being abandoned by his father before he was even born and then being
shuttled off to Florida to live with an aunt for the better part of six years were
events that no doubt affected his development as a man and impacted the way
he related to people. But nothing compared to his experiences in baseball's
on-the-job training ground — the minor leagues. It was there, over the next
three years in particular, that Stargell would run smack into his most formidable adversary. It was far tougher to solve than the nastiest Steve Carlton
slider.

Racial discrimination.

He got his first taste of it during his initial spring training with the Pirates
organization in 1959 in Jacksonville Beach, Florida. There, white players stayed
and ate separately from black and Latin players — an arrangement that Stargell
would have to accept for his first three years in the minor leagues. It was a
life-changing experience for some young players who had never been exposed
to such treatment. Ron Brand, a white catching prospect from North Holly-
wood, California, spent his first spring training — as did Stargell — at Jacksonville Beach. There, the white players would receive meal tickets and be taken
by bus to a local restaurant. "The first time I went in there, I didn't see any
black or Latin players," Brand recalled. "I said, 'Geez, we don't have any.' And
then someone told me they were around back. I went out there and they were
in a tin shed — it must have been 100 degrees in there. They were sweating.
Most of them were sitting outside on the ground eating their food."[1]

The conditions were appalling to all the players, but especially to the
handful of minority players in camp. One of them was Preston Bruce Jr., a
black pitching prospect who had signed with the Pirates in 1958 after grad-
uating from Lyndon State Teachers College in Lyndon, Vermont. Bruce, who

grew up in Washington, D.C., where his father worked as a doorman at the White House for several presidents, including Dwight D. Eisenhower, called the living quarters at Jacksonville Beach "ridiculous." Although Bruce had experienced segregation in Washington — he could not attend school in his own neighborhood, for example, and also wasn't allowed to play at the local playground — nothing had prepared him for the experience at his first stop in the Pirates' system at Salem, Virginia, or his first spring training in Jacksonville Beach.

"We slept over top of ... it wasn't even a nightclub," he said of the living quarters in spring training in 1959. "You couldn't even call it that. But underneath us was a bar and that's where we stayed. And until midnight or 1 o'clock in the morning every night, you had juke box noise and everything else. Many times you'd go out on the field the next day with hardly any sleep. And the white guys were living in a very different atmosphere. But you didn't have a choice — you had to go out there every day and compete. The coaches were always there to tell you, 'Look, every kid growing up wants your job.' And not only that, but every person you were there with in camp, you had to compete with."

The noise wasn't the only issue with the living arrangements. Bruce remembers them being roach-infested. "And the place where we ate — most of the guys would tell you it was almost like a chicken coop," he said. "And the food was.... But you did it because you loved the game."[2]

The hellish conditions didn't seem to embitter Stargell, at least outwardly. Gene Alley, a young white infield prospect, recalled getting to know Stargell in the clubhouse, largely by making small talk. It was a new experience for Alley — as a native of Richmond, Virginia, he had never played with or against black players before. But he found it easy to befriend Stargell. "Every day we'd sit there and talk — 'Man, another day of this' and things like that," he said. "He was big and I was a little runt — I weighed 145 pounds. We kind of hit it off, just like that. He was such a nice guy — to me, he was like a big ol' teddy bear."[3]

Alley may have treated Stargell with respect, but he was in the minority. The treatment that Stargell and all the black and Latin players received did not improve when teams broke camp and headed off to play in their respective leagues. Stargell, tutored at first base in camp by minor-league veteran Tony Bartirome — who later became the big league club's trainer and a close friend of Stargell's — was assigned to San Angelo, Texas, Pittsburgh's affiliate in the Class D Sophomore League. The eight-team circuit featured three teams in New Mexico (Carlsbad, Hobbs and Artesia) and five in Texas (Alpine, Plainview, Midland, Odessa and San Angelo). The Pirates' club, which moved to

Roswell, New Mexico, midway through the season due to fan disinterest in San Angelo, struggled to a last-place finish with a 48–77 record, 41½ games behind league champion Alpine. Just three of Stargell's teammates would go on to reach the major leagues — Brand, catcher Vic Roznovsky and pitcher Bob Priddy.

The left-handed hitting Stargell compiled solid offensive numbers playing for manager Al Kubski's club, hitting .274 and driving in 87 runs. But the long-ball power that would make him one of the game's most feared sluggers mostly lay dormant amid the dusty, dirty, southwest towns, as he finished with just seven home runs. "And I think he only hit two of those to right field," Roznovsky said. "He couldn't pull the ball."[4]

While his bat showed promise, Stargell had his share of challenges at the plate. "It seems to me he struck out at least half the time," said Dick Doepker, a teammate at San Angelo/Roswell that season. "But he had a swing that you could tell — once he became more disciplined, there was definite potential."[5]

Priddy also recalled the swings and misses, which came in great frequency that season. "I remember talking to Kubski one time about Stargell and I asked him, 'What is it you see in him?' He said, 'Look, every once in a while he'll hit a ball and it's what you call major league power.' He only hit seven home runs, but, boy, when he hit one, he hit it. The ball went a long way down there, but when he hit one, you just knew from the sound of the bat. It was just like an explosion."[6]

Brand recalled that Stargell "struck out a ton that first year. I'm one of the few guys who played with him a full season and hit more home runs than he did — I hit 11 and he hit seven. I think he led every team he played for after that. But that first year, three or four of us hit more home runs than he did. But that was because he wasn't fully developed."

Brand said when he first saw Stargell in spring training that year, he was hardly bowled over, as Stargell couldn't have weighed more than 160 pounds. "He was really skinny and really awkward," Brand said. "I remember thinking that everyone was talking about what a prospect he was, but, man, I didn't think that guy could play."

While Stargell held his own at the plate — save for the strikeouts — he had plenty of adventures in the field. His primary problem? He couldn't solve the mystery of the pop-up. Stargell and John Mason, a utility infielder, simply couldn't catch them, so Kubski told Brand — then a shortstop — and another infielder, Sandy Johnson, to essentially catch any ball in the air that came down in the infield. "It wasn't like, 'Teach 'em how to do it,'" Brand said. "It was more like, 'Get 'em out of the way.' So anything we could get to, we'd run

Willie off. The problem was, he'd get too far underneath the ball, then go back, then he'd have too much weight going back and fall down."

"We used to kiddingly tell him to wear a helmet out there," Doepker said.

Stargell did possess one defensive weapon that later would serve him well: his left arm. Some who played in the Pirate system at the time say Stargell's arm strength rivaled that of fellow Bucco Roberto Clemente — considered the owner of perhaps the greatest throwing arm in major league history. Brand said Stargell's arm was even better. "You could hear it go by — it was like a rope," he said. "He would throw the ball so hard that it would go 70 or 80 feet off one bounce. He would bounce it off the grass close to third base and it would bounce all the way in on one hop."

And, despite still feeling the lingering effects of the broken pelvis he suffered the previous year, Stargell had more than adequate speed. "He could run like crazy," Roznovsky said. "But he had a lope to it — it was like a limp. I don't know if he was still favoring his injury or what."

While Stargell was able to pass most of the on-field tests he faced, it was the off-field challenges that proved tougher than an inning full of mile-high pop-ups. Specifically, the communities of the Sophomore League did not accept minority players and, in fact, Bruce said the league did not allow more than four minority players on any team, in part to keep attendance from dropping and also to keep a lid on any potential racial unrest.

The prejudice manifested itself in numerous ways — and all of them were particularly galling for the black players, including Stargell, whose childhood neighborhood was a melting pot and not a monocultural ghetto. He had never experienced racial prejudice and he got it in megadoses in places like Roswell, Midland and Odessa.

On the outside, Stargell tried not to let the hurt show — and he was rather convincing, a couple of his teammates recalled. Brand remembered Stargell as a happy guy who laughed readily and enjoyed dancing. "He was a big California junkie — he had this felt-tip pen drawing of the state of California on his sweatshirts," Brand said. "He was always having fun. I never saw him upset. He used to laugh at me because I was a high-energy player — I used to bust a helmet or punch a wall every now and then."

Roznovsky had the same view. "He was always a very joyful guy. He didn't seem like he ever had a bad day." Doepker couldn't understand how Stargell managed to keep his spirits up, given the treatment he received on a daily basis in the Sophomore League. "You have to remember that in 1959, there was still overt discrimination in Texas and the Deep South. When I look back, I say, 'My Lord.' But we've made some strides. We're talking 50 years now. We've made some real good strides. But we're not there yet."

They were nowhere near it in 1959. San Angelo/Roswell's four minority players — Emiliano Terreria, Julio Imbert, Mason and Stargell — lived and ate separately from the white players, both at home and on the road. Bruce, Stargell's spring training mate, had been had been released before the club moved from San Angelo to Roswell; he had been unable to recover from a serious auto accident that occurred the previous off-season while he was teaching school in Vermont. But before Bruce left, he was subjected to the most horrific kinds of prejudicial treatment, not only from fans but also instructors in the Pirates' system.

"I had come from an environment in Vermont where I was the only black and moved into an incredibly oppressive one," Bruce said of life in the Sophomore League. "They'd call you the n-word. They'd call you 'watermelon boy.' They'd call you '8-ball.' And you had no recourse. You would put yourself in danger and your teammates in danger if you said anything. And no one else was going to step up and do anything about it."

Bruce said the prejudicial treatment was as common as "breathing." And it wasn't just on the road. Bruce said the black players heard it from the home crowd as well. "It was simply pervasive — you were 'boy.' You were 'nigger.' Anything that they wanted to call you, they called you — you just looked up and kept moving."

White players certainly were aware of the verbal abuse. Brand said he can remember having to defend the black players to the white fans. "I would get in people's faces," he said. "People would be there in the stands with their kids, calling them those names, just because they were black. Jiminy Christmas — what kind of example were they setting? I would hear, 'There are a lot of good niggers, but they're still niggers.' Several people said that to me. And these are well-dressed people with their families, sitting in box seats."

While Bruce said most of the minor-league coaches, instructors and managers in the Pirates' system were fair, he recalls one pitching instructor who had racial issues and also seemed to resent Bruce because of his background, having grown up in Washington, D.C., and graduated from college before signing with the Pirates — at Eisenhower's recommendation. "He was from the old school," Bruce said. "He had some major issues. There was a distinct difference in the way he would deal with you, just in terms of how he talked with you, the kind of instruction he gave you. He was very condescending."

It was 1959, five years after the landmark legal case, *Brown vs. Board of Education*, in which the Supreme Court ruled that segregation in public schools was unconstitutional. But change did not occur overnight — indeed, substantive change was years away. So even though the law said school segregation was illegal, it took time for many schools to implement the new law.

Congress passed the Civil Rights Act of 1964, which prohibited discrimination based on race, color, religion or national origin in public establishments that had a connection to interstate commerce or were supported by the state.[7] That act and others that followed also struck blows against discrimination in public schools and higher education — but that was years after Stargell, Bruce and a handful of other black Pirate farmhands were trying to negotiate the sharp turns of life in the dusty Texas and New Mexico towns of the Sophomore League.

In the meantime, the minority players got on the best they could. "Did it affect you? Obviously it did," Bruce said. "But guys just did what they had to do in order to move on. Some did better than others. And not only were you talking about the conditions there — you also had [white] teammates you had the sense weren't that happy about it either. They were coming from conditions where they hadn't played with black ballplayers that much."

On the field, black and white ballplayers generally got along well. Bruce said teammates worked together and pulled for one another but didn't socialize much. The black players typically would find a room in a black neighborhood — somebody with a home would take a player in. "And that's where you stayed," Bruce said. "Very few places had restaurants where you could go. If you didn't get food from the family you were living with, there were a limited number of black establishments and those were pretty much the only places you could eat."

Bruce said the black players talked about their situations from time to time but didn't dwell on it. "It didn't matter — that was the condition under which you had to play and that was the condition you had to deal with. Pure and simple. It wasn't going to change. Nothing there by law or anything else could change it. This was the climate of that time. You were dealing with segregation."

Bruce said he could not remember a single black player complaining about the racial discrimination, whether during the regular season or during spring training. And neither could he recall a coach or manager coming to a black player to console him about what was going on. "You would take virtually anything," he said of the abuse. "You wanted to play. That was your dream. The dream was to play the game.

"There were just certain things you understood. We all came from different places, but we all understood the game. Not the game of baseball. We all understood the *game*. The white guys didn't have to deal with that. They came out to play ball. But we were dealing with a host of things you knew you were going to deal with. You knew you would deal with a limited number of spots on the team; you knew you would deal with a limited number of places you could break in. It didn't matter how hard you could throw. You knew that not only were you competing for a roster spot, but you were also competing with your black ballplayers because only a few of you could be on that same team. We were dealing with a whole lot of mess. And also trying to be competitive and learn the game and do all the other things you had to deal with that the other guys didn't. You wanted to make it to The Show. And you were willing to do that and more."

Among the things black players had to contend with was the unofficial Sophomore League "quota" that Bruce claims existed and to which Stargell referred in his autobiography. "Looking back, even in the major leagues at that time, you did not typically find three or four black ballplayers playing at any one time during that period on the field," Bruce said. "You understood that. And you did not find them up the middle — pitcher, catcher, shortstop, second base, centerfield. That was the brain trust. That was the game. And you understood that. And you knew that's what you had to work with, so that's what you worked with. You would battle it any way you had to make it. You would walk through crap to be there. And you did."

Stargell boarded with a black family in Roswell and the accommodations were acceptable, but the same couldn't be said for his living quarters on the road. For example, on one road trip to Artesia, New Mexico, the four minority players were scheduled to stay with a woman who used her home as a base for her fishing bait business. The conditions were deplorable. It was a lonely existence for Stargell, who missed his friends and the freedom that came with living in the Bay Area. In particular, the road trips were most difficult; that's when he felt most isolated, as half of the minority players on the team did not speak English. "The only time I saw the rest of the team," he said, "was at the ballpark."[8]

Brand recalled the team bus leaving the black players off in a different part of town from where the white players stayed. "I can't even describe some of the places we dropped them off," he said. "They were just dumps. It was sickening. They never made a big stink about it, though; that was the way it was. But it makes me sick to think about it. I didn't think much about it then, but I knew it was wrong."

Roznovsky, who hailed from Shiner, Texas, didn't think much about it either. "Anyone who grew up in the South, they thought that was the natural thing," he said. "But guys like Willie grew up in Oakland, and it wasn't that way there. He was a pretty verbal guy, but he didn't complain." Roznovsky said Stargell and the rest of the minority players went along with the program but they didn't like it. "It was degrading," he said. "Looking back, I didn't realize how much the guys hurt. They just weren't used to that."

Meals, particularly on the road, also were a challenge, since the minority players could not join their white teammates in restaurants. Again, they had to either eat in the kitchens or stay on the bus and rely on teammates to bring them food. Priddy doesn't remember the minority players ever openly complaining about it. "But you could see it in their faces," he said.

Roznovsky recalled Bruce "had it bad" over the treatment he received. "He couldn't take it — he didn't think that type of thing should happen in the United States. He complained to the manager about it," Roznovsky said of Bruce, who doesn't remember that happening.

Bruce also doesn't recall the racial discrimination ever getting to Stargell, nor does he remember specifically talking about it with his one-time roommate. "If you sat around to discuss it or go through all of it, you probably wouldn't have stayed," Bruce said. "You were focused on wanting to get to the Big Show. That was your goal. Your dream. That's all Willie talked about — getting to The Show. In the apartment, he always had a bat in his hand. He would wake up swinging the bat. That swing — that same swing that you saw later — that was not something he concocted at some later date. That was him, period. He was a lot of fun. He was very serious about the game, but he was a lot of fun. He was not rebellious. You would not have made it if you were rebellious. That's how it worked."

Stargell might not have displayed much of a rebellious attitude, but one incident sticks out in Doepker's mind. On one of the many long road trips, this one from Hobbs, New Mexico, to Midland, Texas, the Roswell team bus stopped at a restaurant outside the Texas town and, in customary fashion, the black and Latin players were led around the back to the kitchen. Stargell, though, would not go. Instead, he sat on the bus, crying. "Willie had his pride," Doepker said. "He just would not go along with being ushered back into the kitchen. So he sat on the bus and we brought him back his food. Generally speaking, you did not see any overt reaction on his part. But that one time showed me, well, he does hurt inside — but he doesn't show it on the outside. He never became angry and he had every reason to, for heaven's sake. That's the way things were then. It's unbelievable that he didn't have more resentment or more overt anger. That's one of the things I admired the most about him. He was always such an 'up' person. He never became bitter."

Lois Beard Booker, Stargell's first wife, said the racism definitely bothered Stargell. "But he was a person who was definitely focused — he was not going to let outside situations affect what his goal was. And his goal was to play in the major leagues."[9]

To that end, Stargell chose to focus his energy on improving his game. It's no wonder; there was little else to do in San Angelo, Roswell and the other

Sophomore League towns. "What I remember most is a lot of dust," Priddy said. "And, boy, when it hailed ... I never saw hail like that. It was the size of baseballs. And they had these tarantulas — they'd come right out on the field."

The schedule featured mostly night games, so daylight hours were filled with killing time until the players could head to the ballpark. It was on one of his walks to the ballpark in Plainview, Texas, that Stargell's life was forever changed — and not surprisingly, race was at the center of it. Walking across town, Stargell saw two men wearing trench coats and standing at the gate, near the clubhouse. As Stargell approached, he began to feel uneasy, but tried to remain calm. As soon as he reached them, one of the men opened his trench coat, pulled out a rifle and put the barrel to the middle of his forehead. "And his exact words were, 'Nigger, if you play tonight I'm gonna blow your brains out,'" Stargell said in a *New York Times* interview in 1988. The man then walked away. Stargell gathered himself and continued into the clubhouse. He faced a major decision — give in to the demands of an armed bigot and save himself, or put his life on the line by playing the game he loved — the game for which he lived. "My kidneys were weak and I was frightened, real scared," he said. "But by the time the rest of the team got there, I decided that if I was gonna die, I was gonna die doing exactly what I wanted to do. I had to play ball."[10]

Although shaken for hours, he didn't say anything to anyone at the time and ultimately he did play. And rather than let the incident serve as a distraction, Stargell said it helped sharpen his competitive urge and essentially served as a touchstone of sorts for the rest of his life — no situation would ever be tougher. Nothing could be insurmountable. "When your life is threatened ... it forces you to take a stand," Stargell said years later. "I had only one alternative — to keep playing."[11]

Stargell concluded his first professional season with a .274 batting average to go with seven home runs, 28 doubles, six triples and 87 RBIs. He totaled 118 hits — an average of exactly one hit per game — and finished with a .415 slugging percentage. When the season ended, Stargell — some 20 pounds lighter — returned to his family home in East Oakland. He resumed his job at the auto assembly line and — starving for social contact — reconnected with friends on the local dance circuit. He also resumed seeing Lois. But after a few weeks, he began itching to play baseball again, and he found several outlets, including one at his old stomping grounds at Encinal High School, where his old coach, George Read, was sending his latest Jets' club through some winter workouts.

With a steady diet of Gladys's home-cooked meals, Stargell regained some of his lost weight. And by the time he showed up at Encinal one day early in

1960, he looked like a new man. "He wasn't the same person," Read said. "He had hit his growth and his weight. We were out there practicing one day and he wanted to hit. Naturally, I wasn't going to say no, but our running track at Encinal was right by the baseball field. And if they were running in a race, they'd be facing home plate — and there was no fence. I prayed that Stargell would not pull the ball because I could just see him ripping one and some track guy trotting along would get beaned — and that would be it. I was so glad when he was through hitting that day."[12]

Plenty of changes were in store for Stargell when he returned to Jacksonville Beach for his second spring training early in 1960. The Pirates' front office, enamored with Stargell's throwing arm and knowing that another solid first-base prospect already was in the fold in Donn Clendenon, decided to convert the erstwhile first baseman into an outfielder. The news came as a shock to some, including Priddy, the pitcher who played with Stargell at San Angelo/Roswell.

"When they said Willie Stargell was now a center fielder, I could not believe it," he said. "They made this guy a center fielder? This guy could not catch a pop-up." Rex Johnston, a Pirates farmhand who had excelled in football and baseball at the University of Southern California, had worked with Stargell in spring training and also recalled him having difficulty with pop flies. "The first thing I did was hit him a pop-up and the damn thing hit him on the head," he said, "I asked him, 'Are you OK?' He said, 'Yeah, I have a hard head.' He just could not catch them."[13]

But in other ways athletically, Stargell was blessed; even Johnston could see it at first glance. "He was a big, gangly kid but he had a helluva gifted body," Johnston said. "He had all the talent — it was just raw talent. You knew he was gonna be great and he had everything he needed to make it."

Stargell had one other key attribute for an outfielder. "He could throw the damn baseball," Johnston said. Priddy agreed. "They always talked about Clemente, but Willie Stargell had an unbelievable arm," he said. "He had the greatest arm I ever saw." Johnston said Stargell took a while to unload the ball, which might have been one reason the Pirates moved him to the outfield. "He had to wind up and throw, and as an infielder, you have to get rid of the ball quickly. But when he threw from the outfield, the ball actually *rose*. You could just see the darn thing take off. He'd throw a line drive and if you watched it, it would take off and go an extra 20 or 30 yards. He and Clemente could have had a helluva throwing contest."

It didn't take long before Stargell made himself into a more than respectable outfielder. Priddy saw others hit their stride in their second year as professionals, and it made sense to him that Stargell would come into his own then, too. "Something happened," he said. "But it happens to a lot of guys at that point. You start growing up; you start figuring things out. You get rid of the homesickness and you figure, 'This is what I'm going to do the rest of my life.'"

Stargell was assigned to Grand Forks, North Dakota, in the Class C Northern League — a step up from the Sophomore League, but two more minor-league stops remained before the big leagues. The Northern League featured teams in cities such as St. Cloud and Duluth, Minnesota; Minot, North Dakota; Aberdeen, South Dakota; and even across the border in Winnipeg, Manitoba. The racial prejudice that Stargell experienced the previous season had dissipated to a degree; in some of the towns, for example, the black players were permitted to stay with their white teammates. Johnston said from his vantage point, Stargell and the other minority players were treated well, particularly in Winnipeg. "When we'd go to Canada, they loved him," he said.

In Grand Forks, Stargell was reunited with his old spring-training pal Alley, who had spent the previous year in the Midwest League, in Dubuque, Iowa. Also assigned to Grand Forks was Stargell's spring training tutor, Johnston. Life in Grand Forks was rather uneventful, to hear Alley tell it. "You'd wake up, eat breakfast, wait around and then go to the ballpark," he said. "That's life in the minor leagues." Grand Forks did not exactly have a plethora of options to tempt the young players, as Alley recalled it. "The city was like four blocks square and not a whole lot there. Most of the black guys were staying at the YMCA, and that's where I ended up staying for a while. Willie and I used to eat at the same little restaurant together — Don's Café. And we used to make jokes about it. Then when we got to the majors, and we'd be eating someplace, Willie would say to me, 'Hey, this is just like Don's Café.'"[14]

Road trips meant long rides on buses — nearly 300 miles to Aberdeen and more than 400 miles to Eau Claire. Stargell earned $200 a month playing in the Northern League and aside from the Chinese cuisine at Don's, Grand Forks didn't have much in the way of memorable diversions. However, the town's lack of nightlife had a positive impact on Stargell's development as a player — essentially, there was nothing to do *but* work on his game. Statistically, Stargell showed more power — he banged out 11 home runs in 396 at-bats compared with seven in 431 at-bats the previous year and showed a greater propensity to pull the ball — despite the fact that the first few months of the season were played in what would not be considered quintessential baseball weather. Springtime in Winnipeg is a bit different than April in San Angelo, Texas, and it took some players a while to heat up — figuratively and literally.

As a team, the Pirates' club did nothing to distinguish itself, finishing

61–62 under Bob Clear despite the presence of seven players who would reach the big leagues, including Alley, Johnston, Stargell, Gene Michael and Ramon Hernandez, who would later team with Stargell on the 1971 world champion Pittsburgh Pirates. Michael, meanwhile, would go on to achieve some level of fame as manager/general manager/sparring partner of New York Yankees owner George Steinbrenner.

Although the team underperformed, Stargell individually showed enough to remain a prominent fixture on the Pirates' radar, and he went home to the Bay Area following the 1960 season—a campaign in which he batted .260 with 19 doubles to go with his 11 homers and 61 RBIs in 107 games—in a positive frame of mind. Things only got better for Stargell after his return to East Oakland. He resumed his off-season job at the Chevy plant, and it was that winter that he made acquaintance with a young player who would become a very close friend, a fierce rival and one of Stargell's biggest supporters—fellow Hall of Famer Joe Morgan. And it was also that winter that Stargell connected with a man whose last name he bore, but whom he had never met—his estranged father, William Stargell.

Willie Stargell met Morgan playing in a semipro winter league in the East Bay that was home to a number of outstanding amateur players as well as several area products who had signed pro contracts but needed a place to stay sharp during the off-season. Stargell also was introduced to another young player coming through the Bay Area amateur ranks—left-handed pitcher Rudy May, who would go to have a solid career in the major leagues. May, who was four years younger, recalled Stargell working out at several places around Oakland, including Washington Park and McConnell Field. "I knew he could hit the ball a long way," said May, who threw batting practice to Stargell and some of the others—and who later would witness one of Stargell's longest-ever home runs, a tape-measure job that would go down as the biggest big fly ever hit at Montreal's Olympic Stadium.[15]

Morgan, who went unsigned out of Oakland's Castlemont High School, said Stargell pushed him to keep his spirits up when it looked like no one would ever offer him a professional contract. "I remember talking to him about what possibilities I had," he said. "He kept telling me I could make it, that I was as good as the other guys and I just needed to keep working hard. He wanted the Pirates to sign me and that never happened, they never offered. But he said it really didn't matter who it was—the key was to get into professional baseball and prove you can play. He understood that even though I was small, that meant nothing. He recognized I was a good player. Sometimes scouts were looking for bigger players, especially in that era. But because Willie had worked out with me and seen me do things, he knew I could play. I don't know if he knew I could make it to the major leagues at that point, but he knew I was a good player."[16]

Although other players from the Oakland area had gone on to make major marks in the big leagues — Frank Robinson and Vada Pinson were just two of them — their presence was not as prominent during the off-season. "Willie was kind of ... I don't know if 'godfather' is the right word, but he was always *the* guy," Morgan said. "Not just for me, but other guys realized he was the guy to follow and listen to. He always made sense — a lot of sense — about whatever we were talking about. And it was not just about baseball. He talked to us about how to conduct ourselves and how not to."

Although Stargell pushed for the Pirates to sign his young friend, Morgan ended up going on to Merritt College in Oakland before signing with the Houston Colt .45s in November 1962. He needed just two seasons in the minor leagues before reaching the big leagues, where he won Rookie of the Year honors in 1965. But it wasn't until his trade to Cincinnati following the 1971 season that Morgan reached the upper echelon of major league players. His speed, power and leadership helped guide the Cincinnati Reds to a major run of success and in the process he pocketed back-to-back Most Valuable Player awards in 1975-76 en route to his enshrinement in the Baseball Hall of Fame.

Like Morgan, May said the winter of 1960-61 and subsequent winter workouts with Stargell and other professional players who came back to the Bay Area had a major impact on his life and his decision to pursue baseball as a career. "Just the fact that I had a chance to play or work out with players like Stargell — players who had Major League ability and were in fact in the big leagues — influenced me," he said. "I remember seeing Jesse Gonder, the Pointer brothers, Stargell, Motton, Harper — all those guys from Alameda. And Ernie Fazio. I didn't always have the opportunity to play on those ballclubs when I was younger. But when I got in the 11th grade, I finally got my chance to play. At that time, Willie had a reputation in the Bay Area like you wouldn't believe. And to watch him swing the bat and run and throw, it was awesome."

Following Stargell's third spring training in Florida — a third straight spring in which he and the Pirates' other black players were required to live separately from their white teammates — he was assigned to the Asheville Tourists of the South Atlantic League. At the time, the Sally League affiliate was just a rung below the Pirates' top farm club in Columbus, Ohio. It was there, in Asheville, North Carolina, that Stargell truly began to elbow his way into the Pirates' major-league plans.

"He began hitting with a lot more power," said Priddy, one of his Tourist teammates during that 1961 season. "You could see something special then."

Alley recalls that season as "the year that Willie made his move. You could see the change. He made a lot of improvements — he started pulling the ball and hitting with power."

Doepker, a teammate of Stargell's at San Angelo/Roswell and then again in Asheville, said he noticed a difference in Stargell the hitter. And the difference had less to do with the actual swing than Stargell's approach to hitting. "As far as the mechanics of the swing, I don't know that they changed much at all," he said. "By that time, he was playing the outfield and I don't know if that took a little pressure off him. Maybe it was just having seen so many different kinds of pitches and pitchers, he became more selective. He always struck out a lot, but you could tell there was an increment of improvement. He didn't lose his free-wheeling swing, but he made more contact because he became more selective and disciplined."

Johnston, another Asheville teammate, said Stargell was evolving into a truly dangerous weapon by that time. "You made a mistake with Willie, man, and it was gone. He just had a beautiful swing."

The power, combined with the unique orientation of Asheville's home ballpark, made for a rather memorable connection between Stargell and the local fans — despite the fact that the club's home was in the heart of the South at a time when racial tensions were on the rise. Black players still had to stay in separate quarters, but racial epithets hurled from those in the stands were not an everyday occurrence, as they had been in the Sophomore League two years earlier. "The people in Asheville pretty much accepted everybody," Johnston said. "Asheville seemed like it was more of a tourist town, where you had a lot of outside influence. The black players were pretty well accepted there. And the fans loved Willie there."

Still, it wasn't outright enlightenment. In most of the ballparks, black fans sat segregated from white fans. Doepker remembers making two trips to Savannah, Georgia, home of the Chicago White Sox affiliate, and for the first trip in, the club drew a solid crowd. "The next road trip," Doepker recalled, "there wasn't anybody in the stands." It seems that the wife of Deacon Jones, a black White Sox farmhand from San Diego, "had the audacity to sit near the dugout with the other white spouses and so the word got out and the fans boycotted it," Doepker said. "We're talking 1961 now. There was an entrenched culture. It was just historical and part of their upbringing — and part of their existence."

Asheville fans displayed no such animosity toward Stargell. In fact, they had taken to calling Stargell "On the Hill Will" because a major hill rose beyond the right-field fence of Asheville's McCormick Field. And many of Stargell's 22 home runs that year landed on the side of that hill.

It was in Asheville that Pirates general manager Joe L. Brown got his first in-depth look at Stargell in game competition. Although ultimately Stargell is remembered as a large man with plenty of muscle and girth, he grew up reed-thin and did not begin gaining weight until well after he signed with the Pirates. Brown remembered Stargell as a big man, but not nearly as big as he became. "He came from the projects," Brown said in a 2010 interview, "and I don't think he ate very well. But he could run and he was a fine out-fielder — and he had a great arm. And in Asheville, he hit so many home runs onto that hill — when he hit them, there wasn't any doubt. He didn't hit any cheap home runs."[17]

Stargell's individual success — he batted .289 and drove in 89 runs to go along with 21 doubles, eight triples and the 22 home runs in 130 games — was mirrored by the Tourists, as they rolled to an 87–50 record and left the nearest contender 13 games behind in the chase for the Sally League title. The performance in Asheville prompted the Pirates to send Stargell to their fall Instructional League camp in Chandler, Arizona. Stargell was among a bevy of high-end prospects in that camp. Among them was a young pitcher out of Canaan, Connecticut, named Steve Blass. Two things struck Blass immediately about Stargell: he could hit the ball out of sight and he could throw it like few others could.

"In terms of arm strength, he had a purely stronger arm than Clemente," Blass said. "Later on when he played left at Forbes Field, where it was 365, he'd go down into the corner and make it very interesting at second base. He just had a rocket. Clemente was more accurate and more visible and had the reputation. But a lot of people don't remember that when Willie came up, he had an absolute gun." Stargell also made an impression with his bat. That fall in Chandler, the Pirates' Instructional League team played in what amounted to a community park. It had a baseball configuration, but no fences. "Willie would hit the ball eight miles and because there wasn't any fence, he'd have to run it out," Blass recalled.[18]

The Instructional League gave way to another winter home with Gladys, Percy and Sandrus in East Oakland. Stargell continued to date Lois, whom he would marry early the next season, and — determined to make the big-league club in the spring of 1962 — he stepped up his workout regimen, fueled by regular communication from Pirates GM Brown. He was invited to the major league spring training camp in Fort Myers, Florida, and — despite the segregated living conditions — he remained focused on his goal. While many players complained, Stargell did not, and in fact he enjoyed staying in the black section of Fort Myers because the players did not get the scrutiny that the white players received after hours in town. In addition, the system was more of a family-type atmosphere, where players were served home-cooked meals by the host families.

Bob Veale, the strapping left-handed flamethrower who would spend the 1962 season in Columbus, Ohio, with Stargell and then make the jump to the Pirates with him later that season, recalled his stay at the Evans household. "Boy, you had some of the finest cooks you'd ever want to meet," he said. "We ate way better than the white ballplayers at the Bradford Hotel. We'd get breakfast and we'd get dinner. And twice a week, we'd have big ol' sirloin T-bone steaks. We'd have fried chicken smothered in kale, tomato and cucumber. We'd have squash casserole. For breakfast, you'd have whatever you wanted. I couldn't wait to leave the ballpark and get home and eat dinner."[19]

Like Stargell, Veale — who was born and raised in Alabama, where segregation was a way of life — didn't complain about the separate living conditions. And he said the racist comments that he heard while coming up through the Pirates' system never got to him either. "You'd hear lots of things," said Veale, who made minor-league stops at San Jose, California; Las Vegas; and Wilson, North Carolina, before finishing his minor-league climb at Columbus. He recalled playing at Raleigh when he was with the Wilson Tobs (short for Tobacconists) and they had a devout fan who would sit in the same seat for every game and say the same thing every time Veale's club would arrive — "Here come the Tobs with all that black magic."

Veale said a few minority players were offended by some of the remarks but none of them bothered him. "To me it was just funny," Veale said. "I grew up in Alabama and I got used to hearing stuff like that. It was just another stepping stone to success, I guess. All of the black players then had to have thick skin. Sometimes a player on your own team would have something to say about you. Or maybe there would be some joking — some black joke or something would come up. If you didn't know the individual saying it, you might get hurt. But things like that were easy for me to turn into a positive stroke. I would just turn a frown into a smile. Once you smile, the joke is all over." Still, Veale said it was sometimes difficult to brush aside the remarks. "A man is the worst animal of all that God created. But whatever it took to stay there, that's what you did. Those remarks just made you work harder to achieve the goals that you had in sight."

The racist remarks might not have bothered Veale, but they certainly couldn't be ignored. Even some of the white players were painfully aware of the conditions that prevailed in the South and what was transpiring in American society while they spent their hot summer evenings playing a child's game. Brand, the catching prospect who broke in with Stargell in 1959 and who wound up being reunited with Stargell in Columbus in 1962, said he can remember in one ballpark, someone put up a poster of a monkey in a cage. "They had written something on it like 'Richie Allen's mother is here,'" Brand said, referring to the Phillies' powerful black slugging prospect. "It was awful." That summer, Brand said, he watched the Ku Klux Klan flood Peachtree Street in Atlanta, its members covered with sheets. "We were playing there at the time and we were staying at the old Peachtree Hotel," Brand said. "Here they came, marching right down the street. All our black players were in some motel in shanty town."

Stargell had a standout spring in 1962 — he showed the second-best arm in the entire organization behind only Clemente, and he was hitting .357 late in camp. But some apparently weren't impressed. "His hits are either infield bounders, bloops or misjudged fly balls," wrote Les Biederman of the *Pittsburgh Press*.[20] Stargell was given an opportunity to show what he could do along with three other young outfielders — Howie Goss, Larry Elliott and Johnston — but none of them won over Pirates manager Danny Murtaugh or the front office. Late in camp, Stargell received word that he would not be going north with the big club, but instead would be assigned to the Columbus Jets, Pittsburgh's top farm club in the International League. Although disappointed, he brightened after arriving in the Ohio city, as he no longer had to battle the outright racism that was prevalent in much of the South at the time. That burden lifted, he was able to relax and put together an outstanding season for the Jets, hitting a solid .276 with 27 home runs and 82 RBIs in 138 games.

Brand, who hadn't seen Stargell since their time together in the Sophomore League, said he hardly recognized Stargell in Columbus. "I'd been hearing about how great he was and when I saw him, he looked like a whole different player. He got better every single year. I peaked. I got a little better but physically I was as good as I was gonna get at 19 or 20. But he got a little bigger and stronger. He'd hit the ball and, geez, they're still going."

While in Columbus, Stargell began to forge a relationship with Veale, who became one of the major leagues' top strikeout pitchers in the 1960s and in fact set an International League record that still stands when he struck out 22 batters in a nine-inning game on August 10, 1962. The two would exchange silly nicknames and spend time away from the ballpark together. Stargell had a few mishaps along the way. "One time we wanted to go skinny dipping in a swimming pool that a friend of ours owned," Veale said. "It was at night, and Willie wanted to show me how to dive — and he dove right into the concrete. The front of his head looked like a unicorn. I had to pull him out of there. I don't think we ever went swimming again."

While Stargell's numbers at Columbus were impressive, they came up a

bit short in comparison to bonus baby Bob Bailey, who had struggled the previous year at Asheville but rebounded with the Jets to hit .299 with 28 home
runs and 108 RBIs en route to winning the International League's Most Valuable Player award. Still, something about Stargell stuck with his teammates.
"When I came home that off-season, someone asked me, 'Who did you like
at Columbus?'" Priddy recalled. "They were thinking it'd be Bailey. But I said
Willie Stargell will be the star. It was just ... you could just see the power."
Johnston, who also played at Columbus with Stargell, had an almost identical
story. "I was asked a few times, 'Who's the best player at Columbus?' I said,
'Right now, this guy is, but Willie's going to be better than all of them.'"

Stargell's standout season at Columbus came to an end late in the year
when he got the word from Jets manager Larry Shepard while in the clubhouse
following a game in mid–September. The Pirates wanted Stargell in Pittsburgh — and they wanted Veale, too. Earlier that season, Veale had scraped
together enough money to buy a used Studebaker — "I used to fill it up with
oil and check the gas," he joked — and the two piled into the old car and set
out for Pittsburgh. "Columbus wasn't too far from Pittsburgh," Veale said.
"But I burned a case of oil before we got there."

The Studebaker eventually reached the greater Pittsburgh area, and the
two wide-eyed rookies approached the city from the west through one of the
city's best-known landmarks, the Fort Pitt Tunnel. Stargell recalled emerging
from the tunnel and getting his first look at what would become his professional home for the next 20 years:

> Last night, coming in from the airport, we came through the tunnel and the
> city opened up its arms and I felt at home.

This quote would be preserved forever at the base of a statue that would be
built nearly 40 years later to honor Stargell at the Pirates' new home: PNC
Park.

CHAPTER 3

The Show

U NLIKE TWO YEARS EARLIER, when the Pirates were in the midst of a pennant run that would culminate with the most unlikely of World Series championships, the 1962 version that Stargell joined was on its way to a fourth-place finish in the 10-team National League, albeit with a sparkling 93–68 record. It was a mostly veteran club filled with holdovers from the '60 Series champs—fixtures such as second-baseman Bill Mazeroski, shortstop Dick Groat, pitchers Vernon Law and Bob Friend, catcher Smoky Burgess and outfielders Bob Skinner, Bill Virdon and Roberto Clemente.

Virdon, who later worked with Stargell as a hitting instructor and also managed Stargell and the Pirates in 1972-73, said that when he first saw Stargell as a minor-leaguer in spring training, Willie had as much natural talent as anyone he'd ever seen. "He could run, throw, hit and hit with power," Virdon said. "As he grew older, he matured and got bigger and put on weight, and he didn't have the speed he had earlier. He wasn't necessarily out of shape—he was just a big person. And he had as good an arm as anybody until he got a little older and hurt it a little bit. When he was young, he could throw with Clemente. And that's saying something."[1] At the plate, Virdon said, Stargell's approach could be summed up in one word: aggressive. "He swung the bat—he had good power and he didn't just pull it, he hit the ball all over. And he loved to hit." Virdon said Stargell had virtually no weaknesses as a hitter. "The only problem he had was with real slow stuff. Because he had a tendency to be aggressive, they could fool him on some of the off-speed pitches, but I think he learned how to deal with that. I don't know whether he needed to go up there looking for the curve ball or if he got to where he just recognized it. But he got to the point where he could hit just about everything."

Skinner wasn't surprised the Pirates summoned Stargell as the '62 season wound down. He recalled seeing Stargell in spring training the previous couple

44

of years "and you could see the type of player he was going to be. He had everything. But the best thing he had was the person he was. I've been around a lot of ballplayers in my life and he has to be right at the top as far as his attitude and being a gentleman."[2] On the field, though, the writing was on the wall for Skinner — both he and Stargell were left-handed hitters who played left field. No one was going to supplant the superstar Clemente in right field, and Virdon won a Gold Glove for his defense in center. "I was getting down near the end and he was just coming along," said Skinner, who would be moved to Cincinnati for Jerry Lynch the following season to make room for Stargell in left. "It was very apparent."

Skinner, who later became a successful hitting coach and in fact coached with Stargell under Chuck Tanner in Atlanta in the mid–1980s, said the thing that struck him about Stargell in the early days was his ability to hit with power to all fields — particularly his non-pull fields. "He would hit balls to left-center like nobody else could," he said. Stargell utilized what became his calling card — a looping or windmilling of his bat while awaiting a pitcher in the batters box — to help him get ready. "That was his timing device," Skinner said. "He'd get that bat going in a circle. But when the pitcher was ready to turn his back to him and throw, his bat was very still, in the cocked position. And his record shows what happened after that."

Part of the record shows a whopping 1,936 strikeouts, which ranks him sixth on the all-time major-league list. But the strikeouts never seemed to faze Stargell, said Skinner, who was Stargell's batting coach with the Pirates later in his career. "It was like if he struck out, the next time somebody's going to pay. That was his attitude. Striking out was part of the game. For him to do the things he did, he had to strike out."

Stargell would later say that he never considered striking out to be a failure because those experiences yielded crucial knowledge that essentially fueled his successes. The first of his 1,936 learning experiences came in Stargell's very first big-league at bat, on September 16, 1962, at Pittsburgh's Forbes Field, in a game against the San Francisco Giants. Wearing No. 8, Stargell was called upon to pinch-hit for Virdon with Bill Mazeroski on second base and one out in the bottom of the 10th inning of a 4–4 game. A wild pitch put Maze-roski at third, the winning run a mere 90 feet away. But Stu Miller, a diminutive relief pitcher who specialized in off-speed stuff, set Stargell down on strikes. The next hitter, the veteran catcher Burgess, sent the Pirates home a winner when he took Miller deep for a two-run homer.

Stargell's debut didn't do much to rouse the interest of Biederman, the veteran *Pittsburgh Press* reporter. "During Miller's strikeout of Willie Stargell, a pitch went a little wild and Maz ran to third. Burgess didn't give Miller time to think of putting him on first base. He went after the first pitch and sent it on a line into the right field seats."[3] Two days later, against Cincinnati, Stargell made another plate appearance and was intentionally walked while pinch-hitting for starting left-fielder Howie Goss in the bottom of the ninth inning of a 4–4 game. In addition, Stargell appeared for the first time in the field, relieving Goss in left, where he registered one putout. The next night, again at Forbes, Stargell earned his first start — this one coming against the Reds' fireballing right-hander Jim Maloney. Stargell, playing right field in place of Clemente, went hitless in four plate appearances, walking once and striking out once as the Pirates squeaked out a 1–0 victory behind Friend's six-hit pitching.

Like his teammates Skinner and Virdon, Friend knew the Pirates had a major keeper in Stargell, even at the age of 22. "He stood out," Friend said. "He just seemed very comfortable in his own skin — where he came from and what he wanted to do. He was a very confident individual — he had a lot of talent and he was a good guy with it. The others players respected him and knew he was going to be a big help."[4]

Stargell's first big-league hit finally came in the series finale against Cincinnati, on September 20, against Reds' right-hander Bob Purkey — a Pittsburgh native who originally signed with the Pirates. With the Pirates trailing 1–0 in the fourth, Skinner doubled and Stargell sent a blast to Forbes' spacious center field, scoring Skinner with the tying run. Stargell had third base made, but Pirates' third-base coach Frank Oceak went for the kill and sent Stargell to try for an inside-the-park home run. He was cut down at the plate and the game remained tied until the sixth, when the Reds scored a pair of runs to go on top 3–1. With one out in the bottom of the eighth, Stargell was lifted for pinch-hitter Jim Marshall, who grounded out, and the Reds remained in front 3–1. But the Buccos rallied in the bottom of the ninth, scoring three times to take a 4–3 triumph, making a first-time winner out of Stargell's former minor-league teammate Priddy, a local boy from nearby McKees Rocks who had come on to work the ninth in his major league debut.

Stargell played in six more games that season, making 24 plate appearances. The young left-handed hitting slugger compiled a .290 batting average, going 9-for-31 with three doubles, a triple and four RBIs to go with 10 strike-outs and four walks. After the season ended, Stargell was sent to the Pirates' Arizona Instructional League team for the second straight year with the rest of the club's top prospects. After his stay there, he returned to the East Bay, where the young Stargell family — which now included his wife, Lois, and their daughter, Wendy — set up shop in an apartment in East Oakland, near Gladys, Percy and Sandrus as well as Lois's family. Being a family man brought on new responsibilities for Stargell, and his usual off-season activities — pickup basket-ball games and dancing with his friends — gave way to more family time with Lois and Wendy.

Stargell's first winter as a true family man led to some major physical changes, as Lois's home cooking went directly to Stargell's waistline. And by the time he reported to spring training in Florida in February 1963, he had gained considerable weight. Brown, the Pirates' general manager, was not pleased and let Stargell know about it. Despite his unhappiness over Stargell's weight, Brown felt he had a good relationship with the budding slugger. "Early in his career we became close," he said. In fact, Stargell did not hesitate, for example, to go to Brown when he was short on money during his first few seasons as a professional. Brown said that Stargell came to him at one point and told him he was in over his head with bills, and Brown showed him how to make a budget for the very first time. Brown said he never brought up Stargell's money issues later on when it came to talking contract. "He was my friend and I was his friend," Brown said. "And he knew it."

Despite Brown's genuine interest in Stargell, the young slugger resented Brown's inference during the winter of 1962-63 that the additional weight Stargell had gained resulted from his laziness and said that no matter how much he had exercised or dieted, he had difficulty keeping off excess weight. While Stargell was enjoying his bride's home cooking, Brown was busy remak-ing the Pirates, peddling key pieces from their '60 world title team in shortstop Groat — traded to the St. Louis Cardinals for fellow shortstop Dick Scho-field — and third baseman Don Hoak — dealt to the Philadelphia Phillies for Pancho Herrera and Ted Savage. Also sent packing was slugging first baseman Dick Stuart, traded along with pitcher Jack Lamabe to Boston for pitcher Don Schwall and catcher Jim Pagliaroni.

Those moves freed a spot in the lineup for young Clendenon at first, while Schofield was tabbed to fill Groat's position at short and Pagliaroni split time behind the plate with the veteran Burgess, still a force with the bat at the advanced age of 36. Stargell reported to Florida with an eye on a starting outfield spot, but when Opening Day arrived in 1963, the Pirates' outfield featured the same three starters as it did the previous year — Clemente in right, Virdon in center and Skinner in left. Still, it was clear that the Pirates had a significant role in mind for Stargell at some point. "I never get enough of looking at that youngster," Murtaugh said of the budding slugger a few weeks into the season.[5]

Stargell, relegated to part-time play and pinch-hitting, did not make a plate appearance in the season's first nine games and it wasn't until game No. 11 that he earned a start — this one coming against Glenn Hobbie and the

Chicago Cubs at Forbes Field. And it took him until May 8, in the Pirates' 24th game of the season — and Stargell's 21st career contest — to strike the first of his 475 major-league home runs. With Skinner and Schofield aboard in the eighth inning of a game the Pirates were trailing 5–1, Stargell took reliever Lindy McDaniel deep with two outs to pull Pittsburgh within a run in what proved to be a 9–5 loss. McDaniel, a 27-year-old right-hander out of Hollis, Oklahoma, would be joined by 243 other pitchers who were touched up for home runs by Stargell before his retirement in 1982. It would be the first of two occasions that Stargell deposited a McDaniel pitch in the seats, and although nearly a half-century later McDaniel didn't remember what Stargell hit or where he hit it that May day in 1963, he clearly remembered the other time the left-handed slugger would homer off him. It was five years later, in his first relief appearance of the 1968 season for the San Francisco Giants. McDaniel came on in the sixth inning and gave up singles on the first two pitches he made to Gene Alley and Matty Alou. Clemente then lined a shot to center that bounced over Willie Mays' head for an inside-the-park home run. McDaniel then tried to slip a curve, low and away, past Stargell, but the young slugger hit it over the scoreboard to the opposite field for a home run. "I'd thrown five pitches and given up four runs," McDaniel said. "My earned run average was infinity because it could not be figured. The next game, I did get somebody out, so the next day in the newspaper, my ERA was 168."[6]

Homer number 2 for Stargell did not come until the Pirates' 39th game of the season, on May 24 — a day after the Pirates dealt starting left fielder Skinner to the Cincinnati Reds for fellow outfielder Lynch. It was a Friday night game in Milwaukee's County Stadium against the Braves, and with Pittsburgh leading 4–2 in the sixth, Murtaugh sent Stargell up to pinch-hit for Savage. He promptly launched a three-run homer off Tony Cloninger to give Friend all the cushion he needed in a 7–2 victory.

Roughly a quarter of the way through his rookie season, Stargell was hitting a robust .321 with a .371 on-base percentage and .482 slugging percentage. But during the next month, Stargell would see his average drop nearly a hundred points, enduring a 4-for-39 slide in the process. A few bright spots surfaced, with perhaps the brightest coming against the Braves in Milwaukee on June 17, when he had his first two-homer game and drove in six runs in a 9–3 Pirates win. The two bombs gave Stargell five on the season — three of which came against the Braves, much to the consternation of Milwaukee manager Bobby Bragan. Stargell, meanwhile, tried to explain what happened afterward. "I took my troubles to Hank Aaron before the game and he told me to relax and take it easy," Stargell told Biederman of the *Pittsburgh Press*, referring to the man who in 1974 would surpass Babe Ruth as the game's all-time home run leader. "He kept saying, 'Easy does it' and I guess that's the way."[7]

Aside from the occasional highlight, though, Stargell's slump would continue through the rest of June, all of July and into the final week of August, when his batting average slid below the .200 mark to .195. But from that point on, Stargell got hot, finishing the season on a 31-for-84 tear with five home runs and 18 RBIs. The late-season surge left him with a final batting average of .243, an on-base percentage of .290 and a .428 slugging percentage. He finished with 11 home runs, 11 doubles, six triples and 47 RBIs in 304 at-bats. He also struck out 85 times for the Pirates, who finished in eighth place, 25 games behind the World Champion Los Angeles Dodgers. The Bucs' 74–88 record was only better than the league's two second-year franchises, the Houston Colt .45s and the New York Mets.

Stargell did not set the baseball world on fire, but he became a known commodity in the game and began endearing himself to Pirates fans. Although his family and close friends back home in Alameda called him by his given name, Stargell became universally known in the baseball world as "Willie." Bob Prince, the Pirates' venerable play-by-play man during much of Stargell's career in Pittsburgh, would occasionally call Stargell "Wilver," and Vin Scully, the Dodgers' Hall of Fame broadcaster, made it a point to use "Wilver" throughout his career. Scully said Stargell once told him that his mother, Gladys Russell, considered Scully her favorite of all baseball broadcasters because he used Stargell's given name.

Stargell's rookie numbers were good enough to convince a team in the Dominican Winter League — the Aguilas Cibaenas of Santiago — to offer him a contract following the conclusion of the Pirates regular season. There, he was reunited with his former Arizona Instructional League teammate Blass, who had spent the 1963 season with Class AAA Columbus in the International League, where he went 11–8 with a 4.44 ERA as a 21-year-old.

At the time, the Dominican Winter League featured some established Latin stars from the major leagues, but it also was a place where U.S. prospects would go to work on parts of their games that needed development. Blass said it was also a chance to make a few extra bucks. "That's the reason I went down there," he said. "I was making about $800 a month in Triple-A and they said they'd give me $1,350 a month for two months, with no taxes. I said, 'I'm getting married, but I could use the cash.' So I got married and then went down there." When he arrived, he and his new bride, Karen, were in for a rude awakening. "I got married on October 5 and two days later I walked into a country under siege," he said. "My first day there, my wife and I walked down the street in Santiago and everyone started whistling at her and calling her the Spanish name for 'prostitute' because she was wearing Bermuda shorts."[8]

Blass recalled that Stargell had rented a room above a brothel and it was during that winter that he got to know Stargell. "We weren't soul mates," he said. "I didn't know him intimately — just as a teammate who was a good guy, friendly. He liked to drink rum and coke. And he could play. We were both full of piss and vinegar. He was free and easy and it looked like he was having the time of his life. He was doing what he wanted to do. He had gotten out of the projects and made it to the big leagues. Even at that young age, in 1963, he had felt like he had beaten the system."

The Aguilas team had a bushelful of standout players. All three Alou brothers — Jesus, Matty and Felipe — suited up, as did Rico Carty and Juan Marichal — the latter of whom was among the top five pitchers in major league baseball throughout the 1960s and earned his induction to the Baseball Hall of Fame five years prior to Stargell. Stargell made the most of his opportunity, slugging eight home runs to lead the winter league. "Willie had a monster year," Blass said. "He just killed it. And we dominated our league."

Aguilas reached the best-of-seven championship playoffs, where the club promptly won the first three games — and then somehow lost the last four in a row. The rowdy hometown fans, upset with the collapse, tipped the team bus over on its return. That wasn't the only scary moment for Blass. In fact, the entire winter was a bit stressful, as the country was still reeling from the assassination of former dictator Rafael Trujillo two years earlier and the world was knocked wobbly by the killing of U.S. President John F. Kennedy in November 1963. Blass recalled that Dominican military police, armed with machine guns, stood watch at each end of the dugouts during winter league games. "One night we were playing and the lights went out," he said. "We had to crawl back to the dugouts on our hands and knees, like we were out on maneuvers at Parris Island."

Stargell's productivity carried over into spring training in 1964 and he was ready to take on a larger role in the Pirates' outfield, now that Skinner was gone and Lynch was nearing the end of his line. Murtaugh said in the spring he planned to spot Stargell against right-handed pitching. "I think he has the potential to hit 25 or 30 home runs," Murtaugh said. "He has a great arm. I thought he was a little lax in '63, but he has to improve with all that talent."[9]

Stargell rewarded the franchise's faith in him by getting out of the blocks quickly and remaining hot throughout the season's first half. Through the month of June, Stargell batted an even .300, with 11 homers and 46 RBIs in 203 at-bats over 49 starts. Dodgers' manager Walter Alston, who headed the National

Willie taking it easy during one of his early spring training trips with the Pittsburgh Pirates to Fort Myers, Florida (courtesy Sandrus Collier).

League All-Star team by virtue of his team's title the previous season, took notice and named Stargell to the mid-season classic roster, where he joined fellow Bucs Clemente, Burgess and Mazeroski. Al Abrams, the *Post-Gazette* sports editor, called Stargell "a future star of great promise" and wrote there were "stars" in Stargell's eyes when he took the field for batting practice prior to the All-Star Game. "I'm excited," the husky Pirate youngster admitted. "I don't think I've ever been as excited about anything as I am today."[10] Although he did not start, Stargell did appear in the game, pinch-hitting in the bottom of the third for starting NL pitcher Don Drysdale of the Dodgers. Facing AL starter Dean Chance, a standout with the Minnesota Twins, with the Mets' Ron Hunt at first, Stargell hit a ground ball back to Chance, who threw him out at first.

The Pirates maintained their solid first-half start into the dog days of

August, as they were 10 games over .500 at 63–53 on August 17, trailing the first-place Cardinals by only 1½ games. But they tailed off badly down the stretch, winning just 17 of their last 46 — including only four of the final 16 — to finish 80–82, good for a tie for sixth with the defending champion Dodgers, 13 games behind new champion St. Louis. With the end of the season came the resignation of manager Murtaugh, who cited health reasons for stepping down. Murtaugh's decision came as a blow to Stargell, who regarded his first big-league manager with the utmost respect and admiration and appreciated the way Murtaugh brought him along at the start of his career.

In addition to having a losing record on the field, the Pirates brought up the rear at the gate, drawing only 759,496 people, good enough for just 15th among the major leagues' 20 teams. It was the Pirates lowest home total since 1955, when they attracted only 572,957 fans to Forbes Field, and paled in comparison to the title season of 1960, when the club drew 1,705,828.

Individually, Stargell continued to make strides. Despite missing time with several injuries, he clubbed 21 home runs, 19 doubles and seven triples in 421 at-bats over 117 games. He also drove in 78 runs, second on the team only to Clemente, who had 87 RBIs but played in 38 more games than Stargell. Stargell's production tailed off as the season went along, however. On August 6, after going 1-for-4 against the Dodgers, he was batting .300. But over his final 40 games, Stargell hit just .216 with 5 home runs and 14 RBIs in 134 at-bats and finished with a .273 batting average.

Still, the rising slugger had several stellar moments during the 1964 season. On April 17, he collected four hits and unloaded a rather memorable drive — the first home run struck in the New York Mets' new home ballpark, Shea Stadium. The line drive, which landed in the lower right-field stands, just to the left of the 341-foot sign at the foul pole, came off Jack Fisher in the top of the second inning. Then, on May 11, he showed off his prodigious strength by clubbing a line drive toward Forbes Field's right-field roof off Cincinnati's Sammy Ellis. The ball hit a girder under the roof and at least one long-ball expert estimated the drive would have gone about 505 feet had it not struck the girder.[11] Later that season, on July 22 against the Cardinals in St. Louis, Stargell would hit for the cycle — collecting a single, double, triple and home run — becoming only the 14th Pirate to do so. Abrams, the *Post-Gazette* sports editor, observed a day later that Stargell, when healthy, can "take his place alongside the top power hitters in the majors. The big boy, whom I dubbed the 'colored Babe Ruth' the first time I saw him in Ft. Myers last year, can't miss making it big with the Bucs."[12]

Stargell opted not to play winter league ball following the 1964 season, electing instead to undergo surgery to repair the same knee he had damaged

Willie kicks up dust as he slides safely into third base (courtesy Pittsburgh Pirates).

while trying out for football at Encinal High School. The Pirates off-season, meanwhile, was marked by upheaval and change. With Murtaugh moving from the manager's office to a role that would include a mix of scouting and instructing, the team was in the market for a new field manager and hired Harry Walker, son of a major leaguer and younger brother of another big leaguer, Dixie Walker, a former National League batting champion. Known as "The Hat," Harry was considered a hitting guru of sorts, and while he was able to work his magic with a couple of the Pirates — most notably outfielders Manny Mota and Matty Alou, the latter of whom would go on to the win the National League batting title in 1966 with a .342 average — he did not draw rave reviews from Stargell largely because he decided to platoon the Bucs' big bopper. That meant Stargell would play largely against right-handed pitching and see fewer plate appearances against left-handers — an approach that Stargell did not support, given his selection to the NL All-Star team a year earlier in his first season as a fulltime starter.

The Pirates got off to a sluggish start in Walker's initial season, but won 62 of their last 108 games to finish 90–72, good enough for third place behind the eventual World Series champion Los Angeles Dodgers and the runner-up San Francisco Giants. The free-swinging Buccos also recaptured the hearts of Pirates fans, who streamed into Forbes Field at a much more robust clip than they had the previous season. The club drew 909,279 fans, an increase of 20 percent.

Despite Walker's platoon strategy, Stargell was chosen to his second straight All-Star team and finished with numbers good enough to place him 14th in the league's Most Valuable Player voting. In 533 at-bats, Stargell collected 145 hits, mashed 27 home runs to go with 25 doubles and eight triples and drove in 107 runs while finishing with a .272 batting average and a .501 slugging percentage. He also walked 39 times — more than double the previous year's total of 17. Also on the rise, though, was his strikeout total, as his 127 whiffs were fourth in the league. It was in 1965 that he also began to show more signs of his prodigious power. In the month of May, Stargell clubbed 10 home runs and drove in 20 while batting .320, and he topped himself the following month when he struck 10 more home runs and drove in 35 runs in just 106 at-bats. There were also several memorable individual clouts. On June 8, leading off the bottom of the second inning of a scoreless game against Houston's Dick "Turk" Farrell, Stargell became one of a select group of left-handed batters that included Willie McCovey of the Giants to hit a ball over Forbes Field's massive left-field scoreboard. Just 16 days later, his monstrous power surfaced once again, this time before a crowd of 28,867 at Dodger Stadium in Los Angeles, when he twice took Hall of Fame right-hander Don Drysdale deep and added a three-run homer off John Purdin. Then in the eighth off left-hander Mike Kekich, Stargell hit a long drive down the left-field line, barely missing a fourth homer when it struck a railing in front of the stands near the bullpen. He would settle for a double in what would prove to be a 13–3 Pirates victory punctuated by five home runs in all. "Six inches higher — even four inches higher — it's his fourth home run of the game," said GM Brown, who accompanied the club on that road trip.[13]

Frank Finch, reporting for the *Los Angeles Times*, called Stargell and the Pirates' long-ball effort "the most violent display of slugging power in Dodger Stadium's four-year history." "I don't want to hear any more complaints from our players that this park is too big," Dodgers general manager Buzzie Bavasi said afterward. "The Pirates proved it isn't."[14] Stargell, meanwhile, was understandably ecstatic. "Those three homers were the thrill of my life," he said.[15] The outburst boosted his home run and RBI totals to 20 and 54, respectively, and it appeared he had a legitimate shot at reaching his spring training goals of 40 home runs and 130 RBIs.

Stargell capped his break-
out first half with a show at
the All-Star Game at Metro-
politan Stadium in Bloomington, Minnesota, going 2-for-3
with a base hit off starter Milt
Pappas and then a two-run
bomb off hometown hero Jim
"Mudcat" Grant, who would
later cross paths with Stargell
both as a teammate on the
Pirates and on a memorable
off-season journey to the bat-
tlefields of Vietnam. After the
home run, he sped around the
bases rather than go into a slow
home run trot. "I took my
time running the bases on the
very first home run I ever hit,
and my high school coach gave
me a dressing down for show-
boating," Stargell laughed after
the game. "And I haven't trotted since."[16]

Hot hitter: Willie's bat was on fire — literally —
in this promotional photograph taken before a
game at Pittsburgh's Forbes Field in 1965 (courtesy National Baseball Hall of Fame Library,
Cooperstown, New York).

The good times that came with the 1965 season only got better the following year in what would prove to be Walker's second and final full season
with the Bucs. A quick start helped the Pirates rise to the top of the National
League standings by the beginning of May and they remained on top until
the final month of the season, when a flat final 45 games turned what could
have been a season to remember into a second straight third-place finish
behind the league champion Dodgers and bridesmaid Giants. Pittsburgh, led
by Stargell and eventual Most Valuable Player Clemente, owned a 70–47
record at one point but slogged to a 22–23 mark down the stretch and wound
up three games in back of Los Angeles.

On the whole, Stargell had another outstanding campaign, as the powerful cleanup hitter established career highs in home runs (33), batting average
(.315) and RBIs (102). Stargell was selected to the All-Star Game for the third
straight season after slugging 22 home runs and driving in 63 while hitting
.337 in 75 games before the break. Included in that stretch was one remarkable
two-game burst where he collected nine consecutive hits against the Houston

Astros in Pittsburgh. Afterward, he brushed aside the back-to-back performances and swore he wasn't concerned about trying to tie — or break — the National League record for consecutive hits, which stood at 10 and was held by eight players. "Honest, I'm not interested in records. I can't be an individual. The name of this game is team." Interjected teammate Andre Rodgers, "He means it. Willie's that kind of guy." Stargell acknowledged that it was great to be close to the record "because a lot of great people have played in this game" but said he didn't want to establish unreal expectations — something he believed happened the previous year when he hit 10 home runs in a month. "I began to get the idea the public expected me to hit a home run every time I swung. I learned a lesson — just swing and the home runs will come."[17] Stargell had a premonition his streak would end before the next game when he broke his bat in pre-game batting practice. He had used the same bat to rap out nine straight hits and 13 in the previous four games. He was correct, as the streak ended in the first inning when he grounded out to short against the Cardinals' future Hall of Fame right-hander Bob Gibson. But he wound up going 2-for-5 that night and helping the Bucs to a 9–1 victory.

In assessing the club's 1966 shortcomings and trying to address them for 1967, the Pirates brain trust decided that hitting wasn't the problem. Indeed, Clemente — one of five Pirates to finish in the top 23 of the MVP balloting — put up numbers of 29 homers, 119 RBIs and a .317 batting average in 1966. Alou, Walker's pet hitting student, won the batting title with a .342 mark. Stargell made his presence known once again and shortstop Gene Alley, who shared a few meals with Stargell back at Don's Café in Grand Forks of the Northern League, wound up 11th in the balloting after hitting .299 with seven home runs and 43 RBIs. Ol' reliable Mazeroski, meanwhile, chipped in with 16 home runs and 82 RBIs while batting .262. And first baseman Clendenon broke through in the power department, slugging 28 home runs and driving in 98 runs while matching Alley in the batting average department. Although the starting pitching performed reasonably well — all five starters finished with records above .500 — management turned its attention to the mound corps in the off-season, sending knuckleballer Wilbur Wood to the Chicago White Sox for veteran Juan Pizzaro and bringing in Dennis Ribant from the New York Mets in exchange for Don Cardwell.

The club did make one major deal that did not involve pitching, sending former bonus baby Bailey and future Yankees GM Michael to the Dodgers for veteran infielder and base-stealer supreme Maury Wills. A shortstop for the Dodgers, Wills was tabbed as the Bucs' starting third baseman, and his steady presence was expected to pay huge dividends for a team that had legitimate aspirations as a title contender, given its previous two seasons. Many oddsmakers agreed, favoring Pittsburgh to win the 1967 National League pennant. Pirate players liked their own chances, and why not? As Blass — who had won 11 games in his first full season in 1966 — said, the team had future Hall of Famers in right field (Clemente), at second base (Mazeroski) and in left field (Stargell). "Hit the ball to them — I'm going to get a sandwich," he cracked, referring to his gifted teammates. "It was rather reassuring. And as Virdon always said, it's nice to drive to the ballpark when you know you're going to get six or seven runs every night."

Although Stargell was still young — he was starting just his fifth full season in the big leagues — Blass said the gifted outfielder was beginning to show signs of the leadership that he ultimately would display in huge quantities later in his career. "Willie started becoming somewhat quotable," Blass said. "He was always accommodating and always kind of a steady figure, so the press liked him. And the fans loved him — he hit home runs and had a gun for an arm."

He was also beginning to make his presence felt off the field, showing teammates and opponents alike how much fun baseball could be. During a particularly rough stretch at the plate, Stargell took a bat and buried it in the ground near one of the Forbes Field dugouts. He pounded it in such a way that only a few inches of the barrel stuck out of the ground; a longtime Pittsburgh journalist named Roy McHugh said the bat "remained as immovable as the legendary sword of Kumasi, in Ghana, planted two centuries ago by an Ashanti sorcerer, who said the nation would endure as long as the sword remained in place." Even heavyweight boxing champ Cassius Clay — later and better known as Muhammad Ali — couldn't extract it, and neither could Joey Diven, described by McHugh as a "celebrated Pittsburgh strong man."[18] Then one day, Chicago Cubs third-baseman Ron Santo happened by and — voila — he extracted the bat. While Santo was a slugger of some repute, he was no physical brute at 6-feet and 190 pounds. Even Santo didn't know what to make of his heroics. "He had this bat and it was known that if anyone could pull it out of the ground, you'd get a beer," Santo recalled in a 2010 interview. "Willie was a funny guy and a great guy, too, and one day I was walking down the tunnel and he says, 'Ron, come here — nobody's been able to pull this bat out.' I'm looking at it in the ground and the barrel was sticking up. I don't know how he got it in there, but I had a feeling it would be pretty tough to do. So I said, 'Well, OK.' But I knew this must have been impossible knowing Stargell. So I gave it a try and I pulled the barrel out. And he was amazed."[19]

Little did Stargell know that teammate Clendenon had taken a crowbar to the bat and loosened it up before Santo's attempt.

Stargell's fun-loving nature soon became well known, and influenced multiple generations of Pirates. He often would point out that the umpires don't yell "Work ball!" at the start of a game, but rather "Play ball!" Still, once the game started, he was a focused professional, intent on winning games and terrorizing pitchers. He had several in particular whose lives he made miserable — Ted Abernathy, for one. A right-handed reliever who threw sidearm and submarine, Abernathy had virtually no chance against Stargell. In 10 career at-bats against Abernathy, Stargell collected six hits, including a home run and two doubles, and he walked eight other times for an on-base percentage of .778. "Poor Ted Abernathy — he's probably in a psycho ward," Blass said. "Willie just pummeled him. It was just cruel. We'd turn our heads so we wouldn't have to see the carnage. It was like a white-gloved butler serving you a chest-high hanging slider — 'Here, sir, I believe this is yours.'" But others had the young slugger's number. Take Joe Hoerner, for example — over their careers Stargell would manage just four hits in 29 at-bats against Horner for a paltry .138 average — and he struck out nearly half of the time (14). "I remember Willie talking about trying to hit Hoerner," Blass said. "He said it's like 'eating soup with a fork.'" Stargell was quoted as saying the same thing about two other tough lefties with stronger pedigrees — Hall of Famers Sandy Koufax and Steve Carlton.

The Pirates were a loose club under Walker. Blass recalled that in one of the three years Walker managed the club, the team broke spring training and did a bit of barnstorming on its way north to open the season. One of the stops was in Birmingham, Alabama, and Blass said Walker stood up in the plane and announced that a picnic would be held near Leeds, Alabama, where Walker lived. "Willie got up and asked, 'Do you know where we are?' referring to the racial climate of the south at the time. 'Are us black boys invited?' And Harry said, 'Yes, Willie — we're going to use your ribs.' Then Willie comes walking up with a sheet over his head. We had quite a bunch."

People noticed the talent — and they also noticed the club's complexion. Literally. The *Pittsburgh Courier*, in February, noted that it was very possible that the Pirates could field eight "Negro" players in their starting lineup, with second-baseman Mazeroski being the only exception. As of 1966, the *Courier* reported, no major league team had ever sported more than seven minority players in a starting lineup. The *Courier* praised Pirates management for "making it almost mandatory for Negro fans to keep at least 3,500 of their kind seated in Forbes Field seats this summer."[20] Nothing much was said about that development during that particular summer, but much would be written about a day four years later when, with no fanfare, the Pirates rolled out the first all-minority starting lineup in big-league history.

While the players were feeling confident heading into the '67 season, both

GM Brown and field manager Walker were not pleased when Stargell arrived for spring training weighing 225 pounds —15 pounds heavier than the two had hoped. Once again, some home cooking had more than a little something to do with it, as Stargell — whose divorce from Lois became final early in 1966 — had remarried in the off-season. His new bride was the former Dolores Parker, a Pittsburgh native whom Stargell had met at a fashion show. The two began a serious relationship following Stargell's divorce and it culminated in marriage in November of 1966.

Stargell's winter full of good eating not only drew rebukes from Walker and Brown, but the GM hit Stargell where it truly hurt — in the pocketbook — as he fined him $1,500 for showing up in Florida overweight. The media wasted no time in pouncing on Stargell's weight issue; a headline in the *Pittsburgh Press* on March 1 blared, "Mrs. Stargell's cooking too good" and a smaller sub-head announced that Stargell had to shed 15 pounds. Said Stargell, "I just got married in November and my wife's a good cook." According to the local media, team doctor Joseph Finegold's diet was to include no potatoes, no desserts and very little liquids. "I want you to weigh 210 pounds when we leave here," Walker told Stargell. "And 210 hard pounds."[21]

Whether it was the weight issue, a lack of game preparation or something else, Stargell got off to an exceptionally slow start in 1967, carrying a .193 batting average with seven home runs and 17 RBIs into the month of June. The media zeroed in on Stargell's weight. The *Post-Gazette*'s Charley Feeney wrote that Stargell's weight was just as much a conversation piece as his "anemic average." Feeney also wrote that Stargell and Walker had a difference of opinion regarding Stargell's optimum playing weight. Walker wanted Stargell at 215, but Stargell said he had his best season the previous year when he played at 222. Stargell told Feeney that his attempts to shed weight in spring training may have cost him. "Losing all the weight made me weak when the season started," he said. "I wanted so much to get off to a good start, especially since there was so much talk about my weight." Despite his struggles, he said he would maintain a positive attitude. "When I get in there again, I will keep swinging. I will think of getting base hits — not of making an out."[22] Somehow, the rest of the bats in the Pirates lineup held steady and the team remained several games above the .500 mark through late June. But with the favored Bucs sporting a break-even 42–42 mark, the front office had seen enough and sent Walker packing on July 18. In the process, the club brought back former skipper Murtaugh to manage for the rest of the season.

The change didn't yield positive results, as the Pirates went on to finish a disappointing 81–81, good for sixth place in the 10-team National League. For Stargell, the year was equally disappointing in terms of his personal statistics.

He did rally from his slow start and, by mid–August, the *Post-Gazette*'s Feeney was singing a different tune. "His batting average is a rising .275 and those left-handers who were supposed to be death on murderous Willie are being clobbered by his big bat along with the right-handers," he wrote. "'Let Willie alone' is the new Buc theme. The people who wanted Willie to weigh about 215 pounds when the season opened are beginning to see their mistake. A 230-pound Stargell carries a lot of power and contentment. He's a growing 230 and he's no longer hurting. The only ones hurting now are rival pitchers who must challenge Big Willie and his big bat."[23]

Still, Stargell's .271 batting average, 20 home runs and 73 RBIs marked his lowest production in all three categories since he became a fulltime player in 1964. As far as Brown was concerned, there was no mystery to Stargell's drop in productivity. "I thought he got heavy — he got too heavy," he said. "He really wasn't playing well."

Following the 1967 season, Brown's approach to Stargell's conditioning changed to some degree. Instead of ordering a strict diet, Brown told Stargell about an athletic trainer he knew at the Pittsburgh Athletic Club by the name of Alex Martella. By this time, Stargell was a year-round resident of Pittsburgh, and he made a commitment to arrive at spring training in 1968 in the best shape possible. "Willie went over there every day except Sunday and went through a regime," Brown said. "This guy really worked him and Willie worked hard — he got himself in good physical condition. He had him doing aerobic things, working on his arms, his legs, the whole body routine, the big ball. I watched one whole workout one day and even I was tired when he got through. But Willie never complained. He thought it was a good idea. After doing it a couple of weeks he said, 'You know, I really feel good doing this — I feel better.' He certainly had some marvelous years after that. I think he realized how necessary it was to stay in shape."

While Stargell focused on his waistline, Brown had several holes to fill, most notably in the manager's office and on the mound. He filled his first vacancy by hiring veteran minor-league manager Larry Shepard, who knew a number of the Pirates players — including Stargell — by virtue of managing the organization's Columbus team in the Class AAA International League from 1961 to 1966. On the field, Brown shipped two of the club's top prospects — Don Money and Woody Fryman — to Philadelphia for veteran right-handed starter Jim Bunning.

Now that Stargell was once again a family man — he and Dolores had their first child together, a son named Wilver Jr. that winter — he was eager to put down roots in his adopted home town. He focused on a neighborhood just outside downtown Pittsburgh that reminded him of his boyhood neighborhood back in Alameda. Known as the Hill District, it had at one time been a fashionable place to live but had fallen on hard times after a sizable portion of it was gutted to make room for the new Civic Arena. Within a couple of years, Stargell would become involved in a business there that caught the fancy of Pirates fans everywhere and spawned one of the most memorable phrases in baseball broadcasting history.

But that was still two years down the road. Stargell and the Pirates were focusing on the upcoming 1968 season and making amends for their major flop the season before. In spring training, Stargell befriended Gene Clines, a young outfielder who had idolized him while growing up in the San Francisco Bay Area community of Richmond. Clines had met Stargell once before, while serving as a batboy at a March of Dimes benefit All-Star Game that involved Bay Area professional ballplayers including Stargell, Pinson, Robinson and others. "I used to go watch those guys come to the park to take batting practice," Clines recalled. "I met Willie then, but not in my wildest dreams did I ever think I'd be his teammate and play with him or play next to him." But in the spring of 1968, Clines found himself in Fort Myers, Florida, and had a chance to renew acquaintances with the now-established big league slugger. The two began talking and Clines told him some stories about the March of Dimes game back in Richmond. "From that day on," Clines said, "he called me 'Homes.'" Stargell became a mentor to Clines, who spent five seasons with the Pirates and played a key role in several division championship teams, and the two spent hours talking baseball. "He was the one who showed me how to play this game and play it the right way," Clines said. "How to respect it. He was the one who took me under his wing to show me what professional baseball was all about and how I should carry myself."[24]

He didn't do it in a loud way or call attention to himself, Clines said. "His demeanor was very low key. If you had something on your mind, if you had a question, you didn't hesitate to ask. If you had information for him, you didn't hesitate to give him that information. But one thing about Willie was, he would always say if you asked him a question, he was going to be up front. He'd say, 'I'm going to tell you exactly how it is.' So when I asked him a question, he shot right from the hip. He gave me the information I needed to know for what I inquired about, whether it was good news or bad. If I asked him a question, I knew I would get an honest answer."

All went well in spring training that year for the Pirates, but before the 1968 season could gain traction, the nation was rocked by one of its darkest deeds — the assassination of civil rights leader Martin Luther King Jr., on April 4 in Memphis, Tennessee. As they did in many urban centers across the nation, African Americans rioted in Pittsburgh's Hill District, triggering a duskto-dawn curfew that lasted for five days in the city. In the hours directly following King's shooting, the situation reached a boiling point. Sections of town hit by violence included Uptown, Herron Hill, lower Oakland and Lawrenceville, and firebombs were reported tossed on some streets. Dozens of windows were shattered, looting occurred in a number of stores and police cars were stoned.[25]

Even after Mayor Joseph M. Barr lifted the curfew on April 9, several other "safety measures" remained in place, including a ban against outdoor gatherings of more than 10 people, a ban against the sale of alcoholic beverages anywhere other than by beer distributors, and a ban on the sale of gasoline unless it was directly dispensed into a vehicle's tank.[26] In Pittsburgh, state and local police joined with the National Guard to keep watch over the city, even manning check points at various locations. A *Pittsburgh Press* reporter who went on a ride-along after curfew related an incident in which a guardsman pulled over a car occupied by four "Negroes," including a minister who was behind the wheel. As the guardsman checked the driver's papers, he noticed a passenger in the back seat unzip his jacket. "Then, when the man in the back seat began to reach slowly inside his unzipped jacket, the lieutenant quickly cocked his gun, held it to the minister's head and ordered everyone in the car to freeze or he would shoot. The man in the back seat stammered that he did not have a gun but was only reaching for identification papers. Nevertheless the four men were ordered out of the car and searched by the guardsman. Eventually they were sent on their way after the lieutenant "apologized profusely." The unrest upset even those in charge of keeping the peace. "This whole scene is wild," the guardsman said. "I mean like unreal and it scares the hell out of me," he added, waving his hand in the direction of the Hill.[27]

While blacks rioted in the Hill District and other urban centers across the land, black major-league baseball players wanted time to grieve in their own way. By April 6, two major-league openers scheduled for Monday, April 8, were postponed, but at that point, the Pirates' scheduled opener for that day in Houston remained on. However, the *Post-Gazette* reported that the Pirates' black players planned to boycott that game if it was not postponed — along with an exhibition game on April 7. The boycott never occurred, as the hometown Astros chose to postpone their opener with the Pirates until April 10, and the exhibition game was canceled.

Stargell felt a kinship with the slain King and years later would talk about those feelings in more detail while narrating some of King's writings as part of a symphonic piece performed by an orchestra in several of the nation's largest cities.

In 1968, though, Stargell was focused on hitting the curve ball and showing Pirates brass — and fans — that his down season of 1967 was an aberration
and not a portent of things to come. The media certainly expected big things.
In his preview of the season opener, the *Post-Gazette*'s Feeney wrote:

> HOUSTON, April 9 — It's the beginning of a new season for the Pirates tomor-
> row night in the Astrodome and it could be the year that Willie Stargell really
> makes it big.

Feeney wrote that Stargell "could be the difference from a fourth-place finish
and a pennant. He is capable of 40 home runs and 125 RBIs. He also has proven
he can slump miserably and drag the club down with him."[28]

But for the second straight season, things didn't go according to plan. It
took Stargell most of April to lug his batting average above the .200 mark,
and by May 19 the Bucs' cleanup hitter and primary power source had just
two home runs. He broke out of the doldrums in a major way on May 22 at
Wrigley Field, when he went 5-for-5 with three home runs and seven RBIs
and just about single-handedly propelled the Bucs to a 13–6 comeback win
over the Cubs. He added a double and a single, giving him 15 total bases, and
scored four times, helping the Pirates erase a 5–1 deficit.

Brown, the Bucs' general manager, was in Chicago that late spring day
and watched his slugger assault three different Cubs pitchers — starter Joe
Niekro and relievers Dave Wickersham and Chuck Hartenstein. "His double
hit off the wall in left and I mean way up there — off the very top of the wall
and bounced back in," Brown said. Richard Dozer of the *Chicago Tribune*
reported that Stargell missed "by a fraction of an inch" of getting his fourth
homer that day, noting that it hit a yellow rail atop the left-field fence.[29]
Stargell couldn't hide his elation afterward. "It's a funny thing," Stargell told
reporters later about his just-miss double. "I thought I hit that ball better than
the other three. But I guess it just wasn't my day to get four of them."[30]

Even the enemy fans at Wrigley appreciated the performance, as some
of those sitting near the Pirates dugout gave Stargell a standing ovation as he
rounded the bases following his third homer of the game. "What a warm feeling that gives a player, especially a visitor," Stargell remarked. "The home
runs make you feel good all over and the applause is welcome music. I just
wish I could do this someday at Forbes Field and reward the Pittsburgh fans.
I never had a better day."[31]

Stargell's surge continued for several weeks and he reached the .300 mark
on June 2. But that would be his high-water mark for the season, as his average
tumbled into the .260 neighborhood around the All-Star break and ultimately
settled at .237 by season's end — his lowest mark yet as a big-league hitter in

what would become known as The Year of the Pitcher. His other numbers were equally disappointing — he played in 128 games, managed just 15 doubles in 435 at-bats and finished with 24 home runs and only 67 RBIs while striking out 105 times. He did manage a few noteworthy performances, however. On August 24, with Cardinal Bob Gibson in the midst of one of the greatest pitching campaigns in history, Stargell did what he could to inflict a little damage on the menacing right-hander, who absolutely hated hitters. Gibson, who would go on to post a 1.12 earned run average and a 23–9 record that included 13 shutouts — third-most all-time — and 268 strikeouts in 304 innings, was working on a 15-game winning streak when the Pirates visited Busch Stadium. Number 16 looked like a lock when the Cardinals bolted to a 4–0 lead, but Stargell connected for a three-run homer that pulled the Pirates within a run and then, with the score tied at 4–4, he led off the ninth inning with a double. His pinch-runner would score the winning run that snapped Gibson's streak at 15 games.

Stargell's subpar year fit with most of the rest of the club, as the Pirates finished a disappointing 80–82 and wound up in sixth place, 17 games behind the league champion Cardinals. Stargell's injuries, which he said sparked a run of periodic headaches that neither glasses nor a neck brace could cure, prompted the slugger to announce that he no longer wanted to play the out-field. That meant a transition back to the position he played both at Encinal and in the low minor leagues — first base.

That wouldn't be the only change to greet the Pirates in 1969. In fact, the baseball world in general was in upheaval. Both major leagues added two new teams — San Diego and Montreal joined the National League, while the American League welcomed franchises in Seattle and Kansas City. Both leagues also split into two divisions, with six teams in each of the East and West divisions. Changes also took place on the field — literally — in an attempt to negate the upper hand that major league pitchers had seized. The 1968 season saw an abundance of dominating pitching performances, with Gibson's NL-leading 1.12 ERA and 13 shutouts being Exhibits A and 1-A. But Gibson was not alone; Denny McLain of the Detroit Tigers became the major leagues' first 30-game winner in 34 years. Both hurlers would claim their respective league's Cy Young *and* Most Valuable Player awards. Don Drysdale of the Los Angeles Dodgers tossed six straight shutouts, putting together 58⅔ consecutive scoreless innings. And two other pitchers — San Francisco's Gaylord Perry and St. Louis' Ray Washburn — threw no-hitters on consecutive days. The pitching was so dominant that only one American League hitter finished with a batting average higher than .290, and the batting title went to Boston's Carl Yastrzemski, who finished at just .301.

In response, the major leagues made two substantive changes, lowering the height of the mound from 15 inches to 10 inches and adjusting the strike zone, essentially making it more difficult for pitchers to get the high strike called. The changes, in conjunction with watered-down pitching that resulted from the addition of the four expansion teams, seemed to work, as the mean earned-run average climbed from 2.99 in 1968 to 3.60 in 1969 — a jump of 20 percent.

The Pirates also were in the midst of several key changes. First, the club moved its spring training operation from Fort Myers to Bradenton, Florida, where it had constructed a complex known as Pirate City. In addition, an influx of young players began making their way into the Pirate lineup, players who would lay the foundation for an unprecedented run of success in the following decade. Bartirome, the long-time Pirates minor-leaguer who helped show Stargell the first-base ropes way back in spring training in Jacksonville Beach in 1959, became a trainer with the big-league club in 1967 and could see the young talent coming of age. "I used to tell people about the Instructional League teams we had in 1968 and '69," Bartirome said. "More than 90 percent of the guys we had on those teams went to the big leagues. Now, if you have two or three players from Instructional League make it to the big leagues, you're doing something. That's the kind of farm system we had."[32]

The players — particularly the young ones — certainly were aware of it. Young outfielders like Clines, for example, looked out from the dugout only to see two future Hall of Famers — Clemente in right and Stargell in left — patrolling two of the three positions. Catching prospect Milt May slugged 20 homers for the Bucs top farm team in Columbus and he was only 19 when that season started. But with young Manny Sanguillen almost ready to make the jump to the big club in 1969, the future was clouded for May. At second base alone, the Pirates had a future Hall of Famer in Mazeroski but nipping at his heels in the farm system were Dave Cash, Rennie Stennett and Willie Randolph — all of them All-Star caliber.

"There were so many guys in our system," Clines said. "Such an abundance of talent and a lot of us played the same positions. Guys had to be traded or shipped out to make room. But I never got discouraged. My whole focus, even with all that talent there, was to play in the major leagues. I never thought I would play for another organization when I came up as a Pirate."

Indeed, in 1969, the Pirates elevated three key players as everyday starters — catcher Sanguillen, a free-swinging Panamanian with an ever-present smile and a gun for an arm; third-baseman Richie Hebner, a left-handed hitting New Englander who dug graves in the off-season; and Al Oliver, a sweet-swinging left-handed line-drive machine who played mostly at first base but got into 32 games as an outfielder as well. Oliver finished tied for second in the Rookie of the Year voting after batting .285 with 17 home runs and 70 RBIs. Sanguillen hit a robust .303 in 1969, driving in 57 runs, while Hebner checked in at .301 with eight homers and 47 RBIs.

The new talent helped the Pirates make an eight-game improvement over the previous season and kept the club in the pennant race for a while. Stargell also had more than a little something to do with it, as he rebounded from his two straight sub-par seasons to post an outstanding year. His batting average hovered in the uncharacteristic .340 range into the month of August before tailing off. Still, he finished with a line of .307 batting average, 29 home runs, 92 RBIs and 31 doubles in 522 at-bats. Stargell's standout season and another Hall-of-Fame caliber year from Clemente (.345 batting average, 19 home runs, 91 RBIs) couldn't save the Pirates or Shepard, who was fired with just five games remaining in the season and replaced by third-base coach Alex Grammas.

That season would be the last full campaign in Forbes; taking shape on Pittsburgh's north shore, just across the Ohio River from the city's Golden Triangle, was a new sports playground — one that would be home to numerous championship performances in both baseball and football for the next three decades. And one that ultimately became home to one of the most memorable collections of talent in Pittsburgh sports history — the Pirate Family.

CHAPTER 4

Becoming a Force

THE DECADE OF THE 1960s had brought forth a slew of unpredictable, shocking and spectacular events — and people — the likes of which man had never seen before. Assassins cut down three of America's top leaders — John F. Kennedy; his brother, Robert; and Martin Luther King Jr. Thousands of miles from America's shores, a conflict in the remote Southeast Asian nation of Vietnam escalated into a full-scale war, claiming the lives of thousands of young Americans, sparking massive demonstrations on college campuses and dividing scores of homes. The use of drugs such as marijuana and LSD and liberalized attitudes toward sex came out of the closet and occupied a front-and-center spot in America's consciousness. A landmark civil rights law took effect, aimed at ending racial and other types of discrimination once and for all. The Beatles burst upon the scene, revolutionized the world's musical land-scape forever, and disbanded, all in the course of a decade. In the final year of the decade, the formerly hopeless New York Mets did the unthinkable — they won a World Series championship — just three months after Neil Arm-strong took one step down from a tiny ladder and set foot on the surface of the moon. Both events showed the world that the impossible was, indeed, possible. And in the decade's final days, a St. Louis Cardinals outfielder named Curt Flood decided he would fight his team's decision to trade him to Philadel-phia, and in the process challenge one of the fundamental building blocks of Major League Baseball — the reserve clause.

But for all of those memorable and earth-shattering events, the 1960s — which had started with the highest of highs in an improbable World Series championship over the vaunted New York Yankees — ended with barely a whimper for the Pittsburgh Pirates. Larry Shepard's firing in the final week of the 1969 season created an opening in the dugout, and once again general manager Joe Brown turned to his trusted friend, Danny Murtaugh, to take over as manager. The two had gone back a ways, to the minor leagues when Brown was running a ballclub in New Orleans and Murtaugh was his field manager for three years. "We were poor together in New Orleans," Brown said of Murtaugh. "I came to know and love him there. He was a marvelous man with a marvelous family."[1]

The decade of the '70s would not enter with a whimper, but a bang. In May of 1970, campus unrest — fueled by rising dissatisfaction with the U.S. policies in Vietnam and continued racial tension — turned violent 10 days apart in two separate places, Kent State University in Ohio and Jackson State College in Mississippi. In both instances, protesters lost their lives, gunned down by those sent to quell the respective disturbances. In the case of Kent State, it was Ohio National Guardsmen, and at Jackson State, it was city police officers and Mississippi State Police. The President's Commission, chaired by former Pennsylvania Governor William W. Scranton, found that at Kent State, "The indiscriminate firing of rifles into a crowd of students and the deaths that followed were unnecessary, unwarranted and inexcusable." At Jackson State, nearly 400 bullets or pieces of buckshot struck one of the school dormitories, resulting in the death of two people, one of whom was a Jackson State student and the other a local high school student.[2]

Baseball, though, continued unabated — Flood's challenging of the reserve clause notwithstanding. The Pittsburgh club that awaited Murtaugh in 1970 was far different from the one that he left at the end of the 1967 season. The young players who had risen to the big club in 1969 — Hebner, Oliver, Sanguillen — had a full year of seasoning and, with plenty of help from holdover veterans Clemente, Mazeroski, Veale, Blass and Stargell, were about to lead the Pirates into a decade of unprecedented and unmatched success. And while they were at it, the Pirates shook baseball's stodgy foundation to its core, particularly with regard to racial makeup and clubhouse attitude — and even on-field fashion.

"It was an interesting group — the team that changed baseball," said Blass, who won 78 games for the Pirates from 1969 through 1972 before inexplicably losing the ability to throw a strike; he struggled through the '73 and '74 seasons before retiring. "It was a unique atmosphere. We didn't have cliques — we had three separate but equal entities. We had almost as many black, white and Latin guys. Think of the figureheads — Maz is white, Clemente Latin and Stargell black. Willie's leadership was not a lot of verbal, nor was any of the three. Clemente would scream about things, but it had nothing to do with leadership. He'd scream in a fun way. He'd holler at (Dave) Giusti and Giusti would holler back in Italian. It never meant anything. Maz never said anything. I never referred to them as leaders, but examples of how to go about your business." All of the club's leaders were available for encouragement, but none pushed himself on any of the younger players. "I'd see Clemente and Stargell in other people's lockers, talking," Blass said. "The unique thing about Willie was, it didn't matter if you were white, black or Latin, he'd be in your locker."[3]

While the Pirates of the early 1970s got along for the most part, they weren't all choirboys. Murtaugh appointed Veale — the strapping 6-foot-6, 215-pound left-handed strikeout artist whose thick glasses had a tendency to fog up and create even more trepidation on the part of faint-hearted hitters — as the sheriff. "Anytime anyone got in trouble, I had to go get 'em," Veale recalled. "Murtaugh would send me to go because he knew I would bring them back. They'd go out and get drunk and I'd come back walking with them or have them across my shoulders — it didn't matter to me. As long as they didn't bring any disrespect to the organization. I had a lot of guys the next day tell me, 'Bob, I appreciate what you did.' I might have saved the guy a couple thousand dollars in fines." One time, Veale had to retrieve a player off the street and bring him in for a Sunday afternoon game at Forbes Field. Veale stuck him in a cold shower for 10 minutes and then in the bottom of the ninth, Murtaugh called on the player to pinch-hit and he delivered a game-winning triple. "He hit one of the most hellacious line drives to left center you'd ever want to see," Veale said. "And he was highly inebriated."[4]

Murtaugh's quiet, patient manner worked well with the blend of old and young Pirates. And unlike previous managers who often felt a need to bench Stargell against some left-handed pitchers, Murtaugh wrote his slugger's name in the lineup on a regular basis. The confidence Murtaugh showed in Stargell certainly could have been questioned early in the 1970 campaign, as Stargell got off to a horrific start. He went hitless in his first 22 at-bats and wound up hitting just .093 through the month of April. Still, he managed to show off his Ruthian power on two occasions that month — on April 20, he sent a Jim Bouton offering over the right-field roof at Forbes Field, his sixth and penultimate rooftop blast. It was the 17th homer deposited over the roof at Forbes. "I like to think the hits will start coming now," Stargell said after the game. "There's no place to go but uphill. I looked at that Sunday paper and saw that I was last in the league." Stargell wasn't pressing; he recalled that in 1966, he ended the month of April hitting less than .100 and wound up the season with 33 homers and 102 RBIs.[5]

Five days later, he entered the Pirates game against visiting Atlanta just 3-for-43 on the season, and his .070 batting mark was the lowest average among National League regulars that day. In the clubhouse before the game, broadcaster Nellie King was showing Stargell a plaque he was having made — a plaque commemorating the balls that Stargell had launched onto the Forbes Field roof. "Maybe," King told Stargell, "it'd be a good idea to wait until Forbes Field closes before we send this thing to the engraver." It was a splendid idea. Stargell, despite feeling weak from an undisclosed illness, jumped on the first pitch he saw from knuckleballer Hoyt Wilhelm in the last of the seventh and launched one, closing the curtain on his epic roof demolition show at the old ballpark. It was only the second time he had ever faced the 46-year-old Wilhelm, who had struck Stargell out two days earlier. This time, though, Wilhelm's famous knuckler failed to dance. "The home run pitch didn't do anything," Wilhelm said afterward. "It didn't dip and was out over the plate."[6]

About the only other good news that came from Stargell's slow start was that he didn't have to worry about many payoffs at a new chicken restaurant to which he had lent his name. The venture, emblematic of Stargell's desire to invest in his adopted home city of Pittsburgh, involved a Hill District restaurant that was owned by a Pittsburgh Steelers defensive back named Brady Keys — an up-and-coming entrepreneur who, like Stargell, wanted to develop business ventures in Pittsburgh's inner-city area. In this case, Keys said he owned the restaurant but paid Stargell to use his name. But it was widely reported that Stargell was the restaurant's owner. Stargell said in a 1970 interview that he put money into the restaurant because "there weren't any decent places for the people there to eat. I went into it expecting to lose money because black people don't tend to support black businesses. But we went into it thinking we'd treat people who came in nice, treat them like they were somebody, and it's done real well."[7]

Keys, who eventually would own more than 100 All-Pro Chicken restaurants, called the one in Pittsburgh "Chicken on the Hill with Will," partly due to its Hill District location and partly in a tribute to the former slogan that fans in Asheville, North Carolina, took to using when Stargell was belting home runs onto the hillside behind McCormick Field during his 1961 season in the South Atlantic League.

Prior to the 1970 season, Stargell and Keys had talked about launching a promotion that would enable all patrons ordering a meal in the restaurant at the time Stargell hit a home run to receive their order for free. Bob Prince, the Pirates' iconic broadcaster and a character of gargantuan proportions, was told about the promotion but somehow managed to convey the idea that if Stargell hit a home run, anyone coming into the restaurant would receive free food. The promotion turned into a nightmare, at least for Keys. "When Willie hit a home run, I'm telling you, the whole damn community came out," he said in a 2011 interview. "From all over the Hill, 250 or 300 people would come. I'd have to rush over there and monitor the damn thing. We couldn't feed all

the people. We would feed until the food ran out, which was very difficult."
Keys said he couldn't do anything to stop the onslaught. "Bob Prince said it,"
he said, "so it was the law." Keys said he went and talked to Prince — on the
air, during a Pirate game — after the first incident in hopes of clearing up the
misunderstanding. "We wanted to make sure Bob understood this was only
for the people in the restaurant at the time Willie hit a home run," Keys said.
"But then Bob would get on the air the next game and mess it up again. This
happened about five times. And we never stopped — we had to just keep serving the food. Finally, the season ended. And we did that for only one year."[8]

Stargell's April funk brightened a bit in May, as he slammed six homers,
drove in 20 runs and finished the month with a .246 batting average. He held
steady in June, as did the Bucs, who received a major shot in the arm on
June 12 when Stargell's roommate, Dock Ellis, no-hit the San Diego Padres
in a 2–0 win in San Diego. It was hardly a masterpiece: Ellis walked eight and
hit a batter, and was bailed out by a superb defensive play from the veteran
Mazeroski, who from his second base position made a diving back-handed
stab on a ball hit by Ramon Webster in the seventh inning. "I thought it was
a base hit," Maz told Charley Feeney of the *Post-Gazette* after the game, "but
I dove and there it was in the glove."[9]

Stargell supplied all the firepower his roomie needed, belting a home run
that just made it into the first row of the left-field seats in the second inning
and then smashing one to right in the seventh. Bill Christine, covering the
game for the *Pittsburgh Press*, noted that Ellis was breathing heavily in the ninth
inning of his gem, but wrote that it wasn't because the eclectic right-hander
had never faced pressure before. Just five years earlier, Ellis's neighborhood was
ground zero for one of the nation's worst race riots — Watts, in Los Angeles.
There, Ellis's light-complected mother was nearly shot because rioters mistook
her for a white woman. "The tanks were parked right outside our house," Ellis
told Christine. "That was pressure." Ellis said if his neighborhood nickname —
Peanut — hadn't been stenciled to his car, his mother might not have made it
through Watts alive. "They thought she was white and they were going to
kill her," said Ellis, who at the time was the fifth pitcher in franchise history
to throw a no-hitter and the second in two years; Bob Moose turned the trick
against the Mets the previous September. "She got in my car and then they
knew. She was Peanut's mother."[10]

Ellis's pitching gem took on added significance more than a decade later,
when he claimed that he had taken LSD before pitching the no-no. Ellis, who
by that time was a drug counselor in Los Angeles, told Bob Smizik of the
Pittsburgh Press in April of 1984 that he didn't even know the Pirates were
scheduled to play that day until six hours before game time. Ellis told Smizik

he had taken the drug in Los Angeles because he thought it was an off-day. A woman he was with looked at the paper and told him he was pitching that day. The woman drove him to the airport and he arrived in San Diego at 4:30 P.M. for a 6:05 start. Ellis said he could remember only portions of the game but he did remember feeling "psyched. I had a feeling of euphoria. I was zeroed in on the glove but I didn't hit the glove too much."[11]

The Pirates' 1970 schedule was top-heavy with road games from mid–June until mid–July to accommodate last-minute construction on the Pirates' new home, Three Rivers Stadium. Pittsburgh's last home date at venerable Forbes Field came on June 28 in a doubleheader against the Chicago Cubs. For Stargell, the day was a forgettable one, as he said good riddance to the ballpark that he believed could have robbed him of 100 home runs or more by going 0-for-8 in the two games. However, the Pirates were none the worse for Stargell's woes, as they took a pair of games from the Cubs, 3–2 and 4–1, and found themselves 40–35 and in a first-place tie with the New York Mets. And heading into the All-Star break, which was to be followed by the long-awaited opener at Three Rivers Stadium on July 16 against the Cincinnati Reds, the Bucs owned a 50–39 record and a 1½-game lead over second-place New York in the National League East.

That July evening, some 48,846 fans made their way into the glistening new ballpark, which took its name from the nearby Allegheny, Ohio and Monongahela rivers. What the fans saw stunned them — an ultramodern, wide $1 million scoreboard, spotless eateries that carried names like Zum Zum and Wienerstop, a new type of ersatz grass known as Tartan Turf and, unlike the heavily girdered Forbes Field, an unobstructed view of the playing field. The sports palace, which would also become home to the soon-to-be resurgent Pittsburgh Steelers, cost more than $35 million but would provide priceless sports memories for several generations of Pittsburghers.

The stadium wasn't the only new thing on the agenda for the fans who turned out that night. Perhaps most stunning of all, their beloved Pirates were bedecked in dazzling new white uniforms that would revolutionize the baseball fashion world. Rather than sporting their traditional sleeveless button-up flannel tops and belted pants — a look they began using in 1957 — the Pirates took the field in short-sleeved pullover double-knit tops with no buttons and belt-less pants that relied on an elastic waistband and a drawstring to hold them up. "It's like taking off a girdle," one player was quoted as saying.[12] If that weren't enough, the traditional black cap was gone, replaced by a two-tone job that boasted a black bill and a dark mustard beanie. No major-league team had ever worn a button-free pullover jersey or pants with an elastic waistband.[13]

"They're outta sight, man, they're outta sight," exclaimed Ellis, the Pirates'

starting pitcher for the historic event. The media weren't as kind; local newspaper columnist Phil Musick wrote in the next day's *Pittsburgh Press* that it
looked like the uniform designer had "crossed a softball outfit with a pair of
Carol Burnett's old pajamas."[14] Neither was the enemy enthralled; Reds first
baseman Tony Perez, whose ballclub debuted in a similar stadium the same
year in Cincinnati, told members of the press that the Pirates looked like
"sissies" in their new duds.[15]

A huge portion of the 48,846 fans who witnessed the first game came
away impressed with the new stadium. "There's just one word for it," said
Pittsburgh native Al Udell, who made the trek from Youngstown, Ohio. "It's
class." Even the price tag didn't seem to bother some, at least on Opening
Night. "From what I can see, it was worth all the money they spent on it,"
Herb Soltman of Mount Lebanon told Robert Voelker of the *Post-Gazette*.[16]
Just about everything was perfect that night. Even the politicians kept their
remarks short. About the only thing that wasn't perfect was the outcome, as
the Reds edged the Pirates 3–2. Stargell crushed the first Pirates home run in
their new playground, a sixth-inning shot into the second-tier box seats that
earned him nearly $1,000 in a promotional giveaway from a local lumber yard.
The homer certainly caught the attention of the Reds' right fielder Ty Cline,
over whose head Stargell's drive sailed before landing in the new seats. "Did
anybody measure it?" Cline asked later. "It had to travel 450 feet, at least. It
was 200 feet over my head."[17]

It only took one game for people to realize that the Pirates were not playing at Forbes Field anymore. That moment of clarity materialized when Perez
launched one to center field with a man on base and two outs in the fifth
inning. At Forbes Field, Perez's drive would have been a long out. At Three
Rivers, the ball cleared the center-field wall for a two-run homer. "You had
better forget Forbes," wrote the *Post-Gazette*'s Feeney following the game,
"because it's just a ball yard with a history now."[18] Stargell certainly was looking forward to the move to Three Rivers Stadium, with its symmetrical outfield
and the friendlier-than-Forbes dimensions — 340 feet down both lines, 410
feet to straightaway center and 385 feet to the right- and left-center field
power alleys. He figured those numbers would enhance his own numbers; in
fact, Stargell claimed on several occasions that his wife Dolores had tracked
Stargell's at-bats in 1969 and concluded that he would have hit 22 more homers
that season if he had been playing in Three Rivers Stadium rather than Forbes
Field.

Stargell continued to flex his power muscles both in his new ballpark
and on the road, including a major display on August 1, when he rapped out
two home runs and three doubles and drove in six runs in a 20–10 victory

over the Braves in Atlanta. Stargell became only the third player at the time to manage five extra-base hits in a game, joining Lou Boudreau and Joe Adcock. "I know I'm one whipped man," Stargell said after the game. "I can't ever remember being this tired."[19] By August 9, Pittsburgh had surged in front of the NL East pack and an 8–3 win over New York that day that was punctuated by the first of what would be many tape-measure homers by Stargell at Three Rivers left the Pirates with a 3½-game lead over the Mets.

It was the first home run hit into the upper deck of the new park and it came off Ron Taylor, a Mets reliever who said after the game that, despite the distance, the blast was "still only one run." Christine of the *Press* wrote that Stargell hit the ball "so hard and so far so quick yesterday that there were at least 43,000 opinions regarding where it landed."[20] He noted that Pirate owners John and Dan Galbreath planned to visit the upper-deck section in right field to find anyone who might have witnessed Stargell's blast. Dan Galbreath said if the shot made it to the seats, he would paint the ultimate destination seat a different color and have the date placed on it. "If it hit the concrete façade in front of the upper deck, we might put an X there. We don't feel that there'll be a lot of balls hit that far in this stadium." He was right; only 13 balls reached Three Rivers' upper deck before it gave way to PNC Park for the start of the 2001 season. Stargell was responsible for the first three, and four in all. As was his custom, Stargell downplayed the 469-foot distance afterward. "At contract time, distance doesn't mean a thing," he said. "It's how many you hit out that does the talking for you." While Stargell was not impressed, teammate Oliver was. "If somebody had tried to catch that ball," Oliver said, "his hands would have come off."[21]

Although the outlook seemed bright in mid–August, a 1–9 skid to end the month had fans a little on edge. And when the Pirates lost three in a row the second week of September, the defending World Champion Mets grabbed a share of the NL East lead. But the Bucs rebounded to win seven out of the next 10 to right the ship and take command, and the club finally clinched the NL Eastern Division title with three games to play by beating the Mets 2–1 on September 27, capping a three-game sweep of their top rivals. Brown, the Bucs' general manager, was all smiles in the champagne-soaked clubhouse afterward. "You were a helluva man in 1960; you were five times as great this year," he told Murtaugh. Brown was alluding to the numerous replacements that the Pirates had called upon to spell injured players like Alley, Mazeroski, Stargell — who was dogged by a bruised heel most of the season — and Clemente at various times throughout the season. Brown saluted the role players — players like Clines, who was summoned twice from the minor leagues to fill in for injured players, and Jim "Mudcat" Grant, the veteran hurler who was acquired

September 14 and appeared in seven games down the stretch, pitching 11⅓ innings and allowing just one run while picking up a pair of wins. "He's another example of what I mean," Brown said of Grant. The win had Stargell — who pulled a leg muscle the previous game and could not play in the division-clinching victory — talking in terms of a new magic number. That would be seven. "Three from Cincinnati and four from somebody else and we're in," Stargell said amid the popping of more champagne corks.[22]

The Pirates, who drew more fans than any season since 1960 — 1,341,947, including 955,040 in 36 dates at Three Rivers — were a balanced bunch. Clemente hit a sparkling .352 but played in only 108 games while Stargell led the club with 31 homers and 85 RBIs and — displaying his powerful arm — also led all NL outfielders in assists with 16. Bob Robertson, the burly young first baseman, supplied right-handed power with 27 home runs and 82 RBIs to back the other productive youngsters — Sanguillen, Oliver and Hebner. On the mound, Blass, Ellis, Veale, Luke Walker and Moose each won at least 10 games. But perhaps the most valuable arm belonged to reliever Dave Giusti, who won nine of 12 decisions and closed out many a victory. Still, the Pirates went into the best-of-five National League Championship Series as underdogs to the Reds, who had beaten them eight out of 12 times during the regular season. Cincinnati won 102 games and boasted a lineup that included two future Hall of Famers in catcher Johnny Bench and first-baseman Tony Perez, not to mention the all-time hit king Pete Rose, and were skippered by another future Hall of Famer in George "Sparky" Anderson. Stargell had three hits in the opener, including a one-out double in the seventh that was followed by a walk to Oliver. But Reds starter Gary Nolan came back to strike out both Sanguillen and Hebner, and that ended the Pirates' biggest threat. Pittsburgh's offensive troubles continued in Game 2, as lefty Jim Merritt gave the Reds five-plus quality innings, and Cincinnati's 3–1 win put the visitors up two games to none heading home to Riverfront Stadium.

The Reds finished off the three-game sweep the following day, winning 3–2, although the Pirates had the tying run at third with two outs in the ninth before Oliver grounded out to end the game. Afterward, Murtaugh told reporters it wasn't that the Pirates played poorly in getting swept but that the Reds played exceptional baseball. He compared them to the Brooklyn Dodgers "Boys of Summer" teams in the '50s, a club that was fundamentally sound in all three phases of the game — pitching, defense and hitting. Pittsburgh held the high-powered Reds to just nine runs in three games but scored only three runs of its own, stranding 29 runners, including 12 in the deciding game. "If somebody had told me before this thing started that we'd hold the Reds to three runs a game and lose, I wouldn't have believed them," Murtaugh said.[23]

Though disappointed, the Pirates' fortunes were most definitely on the rise. While America continued to grapple with the myriad social issues that dominated the news, Stargell and his teammates were looking ahead to what would be an unprecedented run of success. But first, before the Pirates could mount a run at a second straight National League East crown and a longer run in postseason play in 1971, the big slugger had a little off-season business to take care of. He drove to the Hill District on a regular basis to work with youngsters and tell them the wrong way isn't the only way. "I find out who they respect the most, the bad man," he said in a 1970 interview. "He's usually the strongest one, the one who smokes the most pot and takes the most pills. I tell the kids that I did almost all the things they're doing, but somehow I always felt I wanted something more. I tell them they're not chained and bound. There's something they can do."[24] He had made similar remarks two years earlier when he first began working with youngsters in the Hill District. "They thought it was all uphill. I'd like to spend more time with them and show them how to get more out of life. I feel I owe it to them. If they learn I'm sincere, I know I can help them. This is the least I can do."[25]

Stargell's other summer project took him much farther than the Hill District. His destination? Vietnam. He didn't go alone. But Stargell was the unquestionably the biggest name among a group of major leaguers invited to tour the war-torn country in November 1970. He was joined by his Pirate teammate Grant, Braves knuckleballer Phil Niekro, two members of the new World Champion Baltimore Orioles — outfielder Merv Rettenmund and pitcher Eddie Watt — and the irascible Pirates broadcaster, Bob Prince. For 17 days, the group traveled around what was then called South Vietnam, looking to boost the spirits of U.S. servicemen and women who were hip-deep fighting in what had become a largely unpopular war that — along with deepening racial tensions — was polarizing the nation.

Rettenmund had responded in the affirmative to a questionnaire sent out by the commissioner's office months earlier, asking if he'd be willing to go on the tour. But he had forgotten about it until he received a phone call near the end of October inquiring if he would indeed give up nearly three weeks of his off-season. Roughly two weeks later, Rettenmund and the rest of the group met in the San Francisco Bay Area and took off from Travis Air Force Base. The first five-hour leg of the trip took them to Anchorage, Alaska, then another eight hours to Japan and five more hours to Saigon. "I'd never been on a plane for more than five hours," Rettenmund recalled. "But the trip to Vietnam was just one flight after another — and all of them were long. But there was no sense complaining. The soldiers were doing it. And they weren't going to be coming back in 17 days."[26]

The first night in Vietnam, the group was taken to an army hospital. They were told what types of things they could talk about — and what types of questions not to ask. You weren't, for example, supposed to ask an injured soldier how he was doing. "They were in the hospital," Rettenmund explained. "Obviously they were not doing well." Most of the talk with the injured soldiers focused on where they were from — and when they were going home. "But even most of the injured ones would say they were going to re-up," Rettenmund said. "Here they are, sitting there with a hole in their thigh and they want to re-up." Although Rettenmund made a living playing baseball, it wasn't hard for him or the others to put themselves in the place of those they were visiting. "I thought I'd be going over there [to serve] when it first started," Rettenmund said. "But for some reason, I never even got a letter from the military. When you get over there and see what we saw, you just feel so bad. These guys had it so tough. They go out on patrols at night and they might not come back. It wasn't like going 0-for-4."

Being in close quarters thousands of miles from home — and undergoing some stressful situations — brought the traveling contingent close in a relatively short period of time. Grant recalled flying through monsoons more than once — and one particular hairy occasion. "We were sweating that out pretty good," he said. "We were in one of the oldest airplanes in the war. And we had to land somewhere in Cambodia. This was serious stuff. Eddie Watt was with us and he had taken a few drinks. He got pretty upset — he turned all kinds of colors and started sweating. Eventually we knew we'd get through the monsoons but we didn't know if that plane would last."[27] Rettenmund said such incidents helped the visitors "learn about each other right away. Willie had that smile — he could make people talk and feel it ease. Being the big name player in our group made it easy on all the rest of us." Grant said the Vietnamese people were most excited to see Stargell "because he was the largest person they probably ever saw. They called him the 'beaucoup man' — much large man."

The group of ballplayers witnessed firepower — and devastation — beyond their comprehension. During their first night in Vietnam, they had to walk through a burn ward. Lying in a bed was a helicopter pilot. "You wouldn't eat a steak if it was burned that bad," Rettenmund recalled. "He was split up both sides so his skin could breathe. People told us not to spend too much time with him because he was going to die at any time. I felt so bad about that." Later, Grant encountered one particular soldier who had sustained major injuries. The rest of the group moved on, but Grant stayed behind to visit a little longer. "They had his purple heart on his pillow, so that meant you were not going to last very long," Grant said. "He had sat on a booby trap. I whispered in his ear that I was going to read some passages from a couple of books and I hoped that he would hear me." Amazingly, Grant learned after returning to the states that the man did indeed hear him. The man and his family attended a game while Grant was pitching for Oakland and the man asked a clubhouse attendant if he could have a word with Grant after the game. "I went outside the clubhouse and there he was with his family," Grant said. "He said, 'I just had to come and tell you that I heard you.' That was unbelievable."

Equally hard to believe, though, was the specter that was Vietnam. Rettenmund couldn't get over the sheer mountain of raw materials waiting to be put to use by the U.S. military forces. "It was beautiful country, but from the air all you could see was miles and miles of tanks and jeeps all parked," he said. "I think they had more equipment than soldiers to operate it. You could fly for miles and miles and see nothing but that equipment and bomb holes. Those bomb holes looked like swimming holes." While they never were directly attacked during their visit, Stargell, Rettenmund, Grant and the others weren't exactly on vacation in Vietnam. Up at the crack of dawn, the group would motor to the nearest military air base, hop on a helicopter, fly to their next destination — mostly hospitals and officers clubs — and hop off. "It was a tough 17 days," Rettenmund said, "simply because we were going somewhere every day at least twice a day. They'd wash our clothes on the run — we'd put our clothes outside our door at night and they'd be back in the morning. We didn't have much luggage."

One thing all of them packed was fear. "We were all kind of afraid," Grant said. "We were in the Cambodia area and there was fire there. But they had us protected pretty good. One thing we were really worried about was Agent Orange — everyone knew about that." It was the uncertainty about chemical warfare and other aspects of the fighting, Grant said, that weighed on the visitors' minds. "Wars are not easy — they're not easy to figure out," he said. "You don't know what's going to happen in the next minute."

Stargell said virtually the same thing a few months after his return. "We were in enemy territory, flying in choppers with machine guns at the ready, and yes, I was afraid, to be very honest," he told Jim O'Brien of the *New York Post*. "It was a different type of fear. At any given time, at any given moment, you could have your life taken from you." Stargell said he had some doubts about making the trip and that, in fact, he had put it off for two years. "My family was against me going," he said. "But I think we did some good and that made me feel good about the whole thing. It was some experience. I've been rewarded in many ways."[28]

The experience stayed with all of those who made the trip, and whenever any two of them would cross paths, they would reflect on their time together, far, far from home. "You talked about how fortunate you were not being in a war," Grant said. "You talked about the complexity of it all, the family members those soldiers had to leave behind, many of them never to return, many of them battered and bruised and maimed. When you go into a war zone, baseball is the last thing that you think about in terms of what it means in life. You might think about maybe the soldier that you see might not be coming home when you leave there. It's a whole different circumstance."

Stargell's experiences in Vietnam certainly left an impression on him. That, combined with some complications that his oldest daughter, Wendy, began experiencing during the 1970 season, prompted him to want to make a greater contribution to his fellow man. Yes, he was providing top-shelf entertainment to a city that was starved for a winner, and his entry into the business world with Keys' All-Pro Chicken restaurant showed that Stargell was serious about investing in the heart of an underprivileged — yet culturally rich — section of his adopted hometown. But when Wendy began having physical difficulties, a series of tests was completed and the verdict came down — Wendy was carrying sickle cell anemia, an inherited disorder that decreases the blood's ability to deliver oxygen to the body. "A doctor said she could lead a normal life, but if she married a man who also had the trait, her children would stand a chance of having it, too," Stargell told *People* magazine in December 1979. He knew nothing about sickle cell anemia in 1970 but began to research the disease in an effort to do something about it.[29]

According to the Sickle Cell Society, the disease changes the shape of a substance within red blood cells known as hemoglobin, and these altered cell shapes can form blockages in veins and arteries. The result is a low blood count, or anemia, and this can lead to a number of other issues, including strokes, seizures, severe joint pain and tissue destruction.[30] Research indicated that it's vital that at-risk people — mostly those of color — undergo a simple blood test to screen for the disease. That test can tell if a person carries the sickle cell trait or actually has the inherited disease. According to the society, while sickle cell is a unique and difficult medical condition, it can be managed with the proper care.

Little was known about the disease as the 1960s segued into the '70s, but Atlanta Braves slugger Henry Aaron was already involved, lending his name to a benefit bowling tournament staged to generate funding for the Atlanta Sickle Cell Foundation. Stargell followed suit and began holding a similar tournament in Pittsburgh — a tradition that would continue for 10 years. He also began working with a group known as the Black Athletes Foundation, a national organization leading the effort to bring more screening opportunities to test for sickle cell anemia. "I'm worried about what is being done on this sickle cell thing," he said in the fall of 1971, noting that some of his fellow athletes hadn't followed through with promises to help the cause. "If I have to do it myself, I'm going to do all I can to fight this disease because it's killing black folks the most." Stargell said his desire to help was all just a part of his desire to give back. "I think the black ballplayer should be responsible to the black community. The people, in many ways, have helped to put him where he is. He should be visible to the kids in the ghetto. Sometimes just a smile and a word of concern from him can help change the life of a young brother toward the better."[31]

Later, the Black Athletes Foundation would morph into the Willie Stargell Foundation and serve as the receptacle for donated funds used to fund sickle cell-related activities, including research. Eventually, tax issues prompted Stargell to shut down the foundation, but his work for sickle cell continued unabated, as he later was named to serve on the Washington D.C.-based National Advisory Board.

Although committed to pursuing what he envisioned as his heroic efforts outside the lines, Stargell — heading into spring training in 1971— remained focused on helping the Pirates finish what they started in 1970. In December, GM Brown pulled off the first of two key off-season deals, sending shortstop Freddie Patek, catcher Jerry May and pitcher Bruce Dal Canton to Kansas City for pitcher Bob Johnson, shortstop Jackie Hernandez and catcher Jim Campanis. Johnson made 27 starts and fashioned a 9–10 record with a 3.45 earned-run average while Hernandez did not hit much but played well in the field — particularly in the season's final weeks. Then, in late January, with players just a few weeks away from reporting to Bradenton, Florida, Brown dealt outfielder and former NL batting titlist Matty Alou and pitcher George Brunet to the St. Louis Cardinals for pitcher Nellie Briles and outfielder Vic Davalillo. The trade opened up a ready-made spot in center field for Oliver to slide into, and Briles became one of the club's most reliable pitchers that season, appearing in 37 games — including 14 as a starter — and winning eight of 12 decisions while posting a fine 3.04 earned run average. Davalillo, meanwhile, became a pinch hitter deluxe and a valuable spare outfielder.

Most of the players remained quiet about their pennant chances, but Stargell wanted to set a tone even in spring training and the Bucs stormed out of the Grapefruit League gate, winning nine of their first 12. "A lot of people say that it doesn't make any difference what you do in the games down here," Stargell said, "but I don't buy that. You go north losing more than you win in Florida, and you have to be thinking to yourself. This is the time and the place to create a winning aura."[32] The Bucs' top brass was not shy, either.

"Pirates Pennant Timber And Murtaugh Knows It" blared the top headline on the first page of the *Pittsburgh Press* sports section the day before the season opener. Writer Christine noted that the Bucs entered the opener as consensus favorites to win the Eastern Division "and Murtaugh, never a negative thinker, has said nothing in Florida to discourage the notion."[33] Stargell, quietly determined to have the best season of his career, put together an April of historic proportions, at least in terms of the long ball. Twice in an 11-game stretch he clubbed three home runs, both times against Atlanta. In both games, he struck out in his final bid for a fourth home run — the last time on three straight mighty swings-and-misses that *Press* columnist Musick wrote "probably altered atmospheric conditions in Charleroi."[34] The mighty cuts were no accident. "I know one thing," Stargell said after his first outburst against the Braves, "if I ever connect, I'm not going to miss No. 4 by inches." He no doubt was referring to his ultra-close calls against the Dodgers in Los Angeles and the Cubs at Chicago's Wrigley Field years earlier, when he had to settle for near-miss doubles to go with his three homers. Afterward, Stargell had no clue what led to his latest outburst. "It's just a funny game, I guess. I was out there trying to do my best and the balls went into the seats."[35] He was also making mental notations of how much money he might have lost in free chicken dispensed to customers at the All-Pro Chicken restaurant on The Hill. "I better go down and see what they've been doing," he said later, flashing back to the time he had homered and dished out $17 in free food to one customer. "Sometimes it's a snack pack, which cost a dollar; sometimes it's a superburger, which costs 59 cents. But this one guy, he had a cab waiting outside. He'd ordered six buckets."[36]

Stargell continued his long-distance onslaught; on April 22 he became the third major-leaguer in history to hit 10 homers in April, tying Baltimore's Frank Robinson (1969) and Cincinnati's Tony Perez (1970). Ridden by the flu, he was not in a mood to celebrate after the game. "I'm going to take some penicillin and go find a casket," he told reporters.[37] Then, on April 27, he carved out a spot for himself in the major league record book when he blasted his 11th home run of the month. The record-breaker was a 430-foot drive to center that came off Los Angeles Dodgers reliever Pete Mikkelsen in the ninth inning of a 7–5 loss before a sparse gathering at Three Rivers Stadium.

The game was played on the same day that another famous slugger reached a milestone of his own, as Henry Aaron — who would go on to become the career home run leader in 1974 — slugged his 600th homer. And on the same day, Curt Flood, who had challenged baseball authority by refusing to accept his trade to the Phillies and ultimately took baseball to the Supreme

Court, ended an ill-fated comeback with the Washington Senators by bolting
for Barcelona, Spain.

After Stargell blasted home run number 11, a fan came into the clubhouse
to give Stargell the historic ball, but he wanted no part of it. "What do I want
that ball for?" he asked. "I can put any ball in the trophy case. Let him have
it."[38] By hitting 11 home runs in 19 games, Stargell was on pace to hit more
than 90 home runs. Ruth didn't hit his 11th home run until the 34th game
and Roger Maris did not club his 11th until game number 40. But Stargell
had no interest in talking about either one of them. After he had hit his 10th
of the month, reporters brought up the immortal sluggers — Ruth, who set
the all-time single-season home run record of 60 in 154 games in 1927, and
Maris, who eclipsed it with 61 in 162 games in 1961. "Babe Ruth, I'm not concerned about," he said. "Or Roger Maris." When someone brought up Ruth's
career numbers 714, Stargell said, "If I hit a hundred a year for five years, we'll
talk about it."[39]

Despite Stargell's long-ball exploits, the Pirates did not get off to a similar
blazing start, going just 12–10 and holding onto third place in the NL East
heading into the month of May. Still, the Bucs maintained confidence, based
in large part on their performance the previous season and the various personalities that dotted the roster. The '71 clubhouse, Blass said, was a unique
atmosphere. "Nothing was sacred. In a clubhouse of athletes, you hear degrading, defaming and insulting. But we were like brothers. It was a way to get
rid of the tension and deal with pressure. It was really formed from a base of
affection. But if an outsider walked in, he'd think, 'My God, it's awful.' But
that's the inside of a clubhouse. We were pretty much aware of when the door
was closed and when it was open. We'd create rumors and leak them to the
ground crew, and then see how quickly it got to the *Post-Gazette*. 'Tonight it
went over the edge — Hebner attacked all of us with a tire chain.' It was a
great atmosphere. And it was all based on the fact that we knew we were
good. You don't have that type of atmosphere when you know you're horseshit.
Success breeds confidence and camaraderie."[40]

Soaking all of it in was Bruce Kison, a 21-year-old pitcher who opened
the '71 season at Charleston — then the Pirates' top farm club in the International
League — and won 10 of his first 11 Triple-A decisions as a starter. That earned
him a recall to the big-league club in July, and he had a front row center seat
to the craziness that was the Bucco clubhouse. Kison, whose boyish looks
made him look even younger than his age, said the bantering that went on
was partly entertainment value, but it also served a purpose in that it told the
players who was strong enough to survive in the white hot caldron of a pennant
race. "If you have thin skin, you can't handle it," he said of players getting

on one another. "If you can't handle it in the clubhouse, how are you going to handle it between the lines? We were a championship-caliber club and if you have that kind of a group and you add a player, you want a championship-caliber individual. You don't want a meek, non-championship caliber guy just passing through. You want the best you can get on the team. Willie orchestrated a lot of that on a daily basis."[41]

Nelson "Nellie" King, a one-time Pirate pitcher who began broadcasting his former team's games in 1967, said Stargell "ran the clubhouse in a way that nobody noticed it. Nobody was above anybody. Everybody was open for jokes and everything else. That team was as close as any team I'd seen there."[42]

Stargell told *Sports Illustrated* writer Roy Blount Jr. that he wasn't sure why the various cultures got on so well in the Pirates clubhouse when that wasn't always the case with other ballclubs. "It really doesn't make a difference what color you are, you're just a guy to me. I know some black so-called friends who are dogs."[43]

Clines, the young outfielder who would ascend to a key role on the '71 club, said the clubhouse atmosphere was special. "We could say anything about each other and get on one another," he said. "But we did everything together. Everyone talks about the '79 team being 'We Are Family.' For me, that started back in the early '70s — '71. There was no theme song or anything, but we treated each other like brothers. If someone's kid had a birthday, everyone showed up. If someone had a party, everyone showed up."[44] Stargell was known for his team parties — and for a special elixir that he would whip up for just about everyone. He called it Purple Passion, and while the ingredients were somewhat of a mystery, there was nothing mysterious about its impact. "He'd get this big bucket," Clines recalled, "and he'd put Welch's grape juice and these other things in there. It was like punch that had a punch." Blass recalls Stargell going to Sears and buying a big rubber garbage can. "He'd fill it halfway with ice and then put every conceivable type of alcohol in it, and then disguise the poison with five gallons of grape juice — and then stir it with one of his bats." Blass joked that Stargell "could have sold the stuff in Home Depot as paint thinner. But we couldn't get enough." Oliver did not drink, but he would partake in the Purple Passion anyway. "It was grape juice — and everybody loves grape juice," he said. "But Willie would put grain alcohol in there. I mean, it was good. You'd drink it like it was Kool Aid. But before you knew it, you were laid out. You were through."[45]

Oliver, who played the game aggressively and with great passion, said Stargell "really knew how to throw parties — and nobody on the team would be left out. He was a great host — he had a great demeanor about him. Nobody could say they didn't have a good time. We'd sit around and talk about everything. And laugh — we were a laughing team. We were serious on the field, but after a game, we were as loose as we could be. We were loose when we took the field. Most games can be won or lost in the clubhouse, and when we left the clubhouse, we knew our chances of winning were good. That's how much confidence we had as a team. We had as much confidence in our teammates as we had in ourselves. That's why those Pirate teams in the early '70s were so strong. Our '71 and '72 teams were probably the best teams the Pirates ever had, talent-wise."

For his part, Stargell did his best to keep the club on an even keel, as he had inherited — partly by the force of his personality and partly by the force of his prodigious hitting — a piece of the leadership mantle. Blass certainly could sense it. "You could see him emerging and being a presence," he said. "He was a big man, and he had a big physical presence. But he had that wonderful soft voice when he wanted to use it. He had a wonderful delivery. You could see him go over to a locker and spend time with guys who were struggling. And he was also part of the levity. We played clubhouse tricks on writers and clubhouse boys that were just obscene."

Sam Nover, a young Pittsburgh television sportscaster, was victimized in one such prank — the infamous "three-man lift." A few of the players were telling Nover for weeks that Bartirome — the team's trainer, who stood 5-foot-10 and weighed 155 pounds in his playing days — was so strong that he could lift three men at one time. Nover was skeptical and wanted to see proof. So the players had Nover lie on his back in the clubhouse, with coach Don Leppard on one side and pitcher Johnson prone on the other side. "I had my suit and tie on, so Jose Pagan tells me to take off my shirt and tie because I might get a little sweaty," Nover recalled. "All the players are sitting around watching. Stargell's laughing his ass off. I'm lying down and Johnson and Leppard intertwine their arms and legs with me — I couldn't move if my life depended on it. I had a photographer shooting the whole thing — I was going to see Bartirome lift three people weighing over 600 pounds. So Tony steps over me and puts a belt around my waist. This is how he's going to do it — by lifting that belt, he's going to lift everybody, since we're all bound together. I'm shouting instructions to the photographer — 'Ronnie, you got a good shot of Tony? Can you see me?' I'm directing this thing flat on my back. Tony says, 'When I count to three, clench your muscles.' He says, 'One, two, three.' I clench my muscles. Bartirome leans over and pulls my pants down. I jerked and tried to fight it, but I wasn't going anywhere. I'm completely naked from the waist down." What happened next wasn't pretty, as a mixture of analgesic balm and orange juice was dumped all over Nover's testicles and legs. "Clemente's standing there laughing, saying, 'You good sport, Sam, you good sport.' The clubhouse was howling. I was laughing my ass off. It was a classic setup — and that's the kind of relationship you could have with ballplayers in those days."[46]

Stargell wasn't above getting involved in such clubhouse hijinks but he was clearly taking on more of a leadership role, according to Bartirome. "He was blossoming and it was him and Clemente who were the leaders of that club," Bartirome said. "They did it in different ways — Stargell did it in a quiet way. Clemente was more vocal when he was in the clubhouse. He exerted his feelings more — he was more of a fiery leader. Then we had Maz, who was quieter than Stargell."[47]

Clines certainly viewed Stargell as a key leader on that team. "He was a leader by example. All you had to do was follow his lead. He wasn't a big rah-rah guy. You just watched the way he went about his job, how he played the game. He was not a big cheerleader. But for me, Stargell and Clemente were leaders by example." Oliver, then a young player trying to get comfortable in center field, said Stargell "knew when to approach a player when he wasn't going good. That's the type of leader he was. He always had great timing when going to a player." Oliver said one important thing he learned from Stargell was the idea of self-control. "Every now and then, especially when I first came up, I would throw a batting helmet," he said. "Ask anyone on that team and they'll tell you that Hebner and I were the president and vice president of the lumber company — we'd go down in the runway next to the dugout and tear up some bats if we didn't get a hit. But Willie always kept calm. Win or lose, 0-for-4 or 4-for-4, he was always the same. And as a young player, when you see someone like him carry himself that way, you start to follow suit."

The '71 club — packed with plenty of hitting, solid defense and sufficient if not exactly spectacular pitching — moved into first place in late May, right about the time Murtaugh had to be hospitalized. The veteran skipper remained out of commission until the second week of June, and although the club fell out of the top spot during his absence, it remained in the thick of the race, thanks in part to consecutive shutouts hurled by Moose, Blass and Ellis from May 30 through June 3, the last of which boosted the Bucs' record to 30–19. Less than a week after Murtaugh returned, the team regained first place and went on a 22–8 rampage to open up a nine-game lead at the All-Star break.

Stargell's hot home run pace in April did not cool off much, as he established another major-league record, this time for most home runs by the end of June — 28. He was also hitting for distance — he clubbed a 458-foot shot off the Cubs' Ken Holtzman that reached the upper deck of Three Rivers

Willie crosses home plate and is greeted by Pirates teammates Roberto Clemente (21), who scored ahead of him, and Al Oliver (16), who was hitting behind Stargell (courtesy Pittsburgh Pirates).

Stadium on May 30, and then on June 20, he again launched one into the top deck at his home park, this time a 472-foot blast off the Expos' Howie Reed.

Murtaugh attributed Stargell's record-breaking start to being in top shape; Stargell came into spring training having lost 18 pounds over the winter. "The time he used to spend running off fat, he spent at batting practice," Murtaugh told Dick Young of the *New York Daily News*. "He got off to a great start."[48]

Roy McHugh, a legendary Pittsburgh journalist, first encountered Stargell during the player's earliest days with the Pirates and he watched him evolve from a young colt to a thoroughbred who was mashing everything in sight in 1971. McHugh painted a word picture of Stargell's hitting stature that year. "Tall, weight shifting rhythmically from one foot to the other, his bat moving in circles like an airplane propeller, Stargell creates a feeling of menace as he waits for the pitch. He takes a full, free swing with his entire upper body committed and there is never anything hesitant about it. Once Stargell decides he will swing, the decision is not subject to change."[49]

By the time Stargell showed up for the All-Star Game in Detroit — his first trip to the Mid-Season Classic since 1966 — he had collected 30 home runs and 87 RBIs. So it was no surprise that the media wanted to talk to him about Ruth and Maris. But Stargell said he spent no time at all thinking about them or any home run records. He did allow that the move from spacious Forbes Field, whose 457-foot distance to center field was so cavernous the Pirates would store their batting cage there — in play, no less — to Three Rivers Stadium certainly was aiding his home run cause. He was able to hit the ball to all fields rather than concentrate on pulling the ball to right because the new park was symmetrical. Going to all fields made him a better hitter.

Stargell used the opportunity at the All-Star break to talk about his work on the sickle cell anemia front, telling the media about his work in the Pittsburgh area to raise funds for research and to raise awareness of the disease. He also used the forum to wonder aloud about the possibility of a black man becoming a major-league manager — speculation that was spawned when someone asked Stargell about Murtaugh. "I like to think that the owners will make it happen, that there will be a black manager soon," he said. "But the way they're going to have to do it is the way Branch Rickey did it with Jackie Robinson. The owners are going to have to give that manager full backing. They're going to have to say to that man, 'You're my man and you go out there and run things your way and I'll back you all the way.' The man will have an awful lot of pressure. He'll take an awful lot of things."[50] Later that year, Stargell would say that at least a half-dozen black or Latin players were qualified to manage in the big leagues — Frank Robinson, Maury Wills, Junior Gilliam, Roberto Clemente, Hank Aaron and Willie Mays.[51]

At the All-Star Game, Stargell also alluded to knee pain he was experiencing, telling reporters that some days it felt fine, but other days he was in great discomfort. He injured one knee before the break at the same time he had been experiencing pain in his other knee. The problems left him unable to properly pivot at the plate and that cut into his power production, as his home runs dropped off markedly in the season's second half. Murtaugh and others suggested he have surgery then, but Stargell declined, not wanting to miss a potential pennant drive. "I had a chance to be in a World Series," he would say after the season. "I told the doctor the only way I was coming out was in a wheelchair."[52]

Stargell also used his newfound notoriety to speak out — albeit somewhat quietly — about what he perceived as a lack of endorsement opportunities for the game's black stars, noting that Clemente had virtually no such opportunities despite his stature in the game. "It just irks me, but it shouldn't even have to be discussed," Stargell said. "Why doesn't Clemente have his own sports program here in Pittsburgh? I mean, baseball has gotten a lot off this man. Why do they feel he shouldn't reap something because of what he's done? He doesn't say these things, but I know how he feels. We get together and talk about them. Maybe they don't even want us to talk about them, but it's not fair to the guys coming up if we don't talk."[53]

The Pirates rolled to a 67–39 record by the end of July and at one time owned an 11½-game lead in the NL East. But they slumped badly in August, winning just seven of their first 22 games. By August 16, the resurgent Cardinals had pulled to within four games, but the Bucs rebounded with an 18–5 run and wrapped up the division title on September 22 by beating St. Louis 5–1.

Somewhat lost in the regular season's final month was a game in Philadelphia against the Phillies on September 1. It was that night that the Pirates made major-league history by fielding an all-minority starting lineup. It wasn't completely out of the blue; in a game at Connie Mack Stadium against the Phillies in 1967, the club started eight Latin or black players, with pitcher Dennis Ribant being the only white player. King wrote in his book *Happiness Is Like a Cur Dog* that Stargell got everyone's attention that night in the clubhouse before the game and said, "Fellows, they will not be playing the National Anthem today. They're gonna play 'Sweet Georgia Brown.'"[54] On September 1, 1971, though, there were no exceptions. Murtaugh's lineup card read:

Rennie Stennett, 2B	Dave Cash, 3B
Gene Clines, CF	Al Oliver, 1B
Roberto Clemente, RF	Jackie Hernandez, SS
Willie Stargell, LF	Dock Ellis, P
Manny Sanguillen, C	

It wasn't completely out of the ordinary, although it was unusual that the left-handed hitting Oliver — who had played mostly center field that year — would start at first base in place of Robertson against Phillies left-hander Woody Fryman. It didn't take long for reporters at the game to notice that Murtaugh had fielded a starting nine consisting of all minority players and researchers concluded it was the first time that had happened since Jackie Robinson integrated baseball 24 years earlier. Bruce Markusen, in his book *The Team That Changed Baseball: Roberto Clemente and the 1971 Pittsburgh Pirates*, wrote that several players certainly noticed the all-minority look to the lineup that night. "We had a loose group, [so] we were all laughing and hollering about it and teasing each other," Blass said. "I thought that was a great reaction." Oliver, though, was not even aware of the historic nature of the lineup until Cash mentioned it to him in the third or fourth inning. He said he didn't think Murtaugh had the racial makeup of that lineup in mind when he wrote the names on the card that night. "I think Danny was just putting the best team cn the field and he probably didn't notice [the all-black lineup] until later. I didn't know until the third or fourth inning."[55]

While the Pirate players seemed most comfortable with the roster's racial mix, the same could not be said for many of the hometown fans. Brown, the general manager, said he would hear about it during his public appearances. "There were bigots in Pittsburgh," he said. "I would hear people say that the reason we couldn't draw more people when we had all those good teams was that we had too many blacks. I remember going to a luncheon one day and the question/answer session was a major part of my talk. A guy in the back of the room stands up and says, 'I know why you're not drawing: you've got too many niggers.' I said, 'Let's put it this way. Do you want me to get rid of Clemente?' He said no. 'Bob Veale?' No. 'Stargell?' 'Sanguillen? Oliver?' No. I named all the blacks and he wanted me to keep them all. So I said, 'I guess we don't have too many.' I didn't see them as blacks. I saw them as black people who were good guys and could play baseball."[56]

The Pirates' win over the Cardinals on September 22 sparked the customary championship-clinching clubhouse scene, highlighted by the agitated Ellis dumping a small washtub filled with champagne and water on the head of the stately Clemente. "The old man got it, the old man got it," Ellis kept repeating. Stargell, who had scored his 100th run of the season — the first time in his career he had ever reached that milestone — also went after Clemente with a bottle of the bubbly.[57]

Up next for the Pirates was a second straight trip to the National League Championship Series, this time against the San Francisco Giants. Pittsburgh, installed as a 6-to-5 favorite despite winning only three of 12 regular-season meetings with San Francisco, tabbed Blass to start the series opener but the Giants won 5–4. But in Game 2, Robertson — the young first baseman whom broadcaster Prince would occasionally refer to as "The Maryland Strongboy" — bludgeoned three home runs to go with one by Clines, enabling the Bucs to win 9–4 and earn a split in San Francisco. Meanwhile, over in the American League playoffs, Stargell's boyhood friend from the Alameda projects and his former Encinal High School teammate Curt Motton drove home the tying run with a pinch-hit single that keyed a four-run seventh-inning rally and lifted Baltimore to a playoff series-opening win over the Oakland A's. A 5–1 victory in Game 2 put the defending champion Orioles on track for their third straight World Series appearance.

The ever-unpredictable — and often volatile — Ellis made things interesting before Game 3, ripping Pirates management for what he viewed as substandard travel accommodations, both on the air and on the ground, during the trip to San Francisco. But Game 3 was even more riveting on the field, as Hebner — the young off-season grave-digger — put a nail in the Giants coffin by depositing a Juan Marichal screwball just over Three Rivers Stadium's right-field fence, snapping a 1–1 tie in the eighth inning and giving the Pirates a pivotal 2–1 win. Right-fielder Bobby Bonds, who made a leaping attempt to flag down Hebner's drive, told reporters afterward he missed it by five inches. Bonds and his teammates did not take the loss lightly. "Get the (bleep) out of here, you (bleep)," one Giant player told *Press* reporter Musick, who wrote that he "promptly got the (bleep) over to a small office where Giants manager Charlie Fox froze a used-car salesman's smile on his wide Irisher's face and allowed the words to leak from his mouth one at a time. Fox was more quotable than his players, at least for a family publication."[58]

The Bucs wrapped things up the next day in a 9–5 win, getting key contributions at the plate from Hebner and Oliver — each of whom homered — and on the mound from Kison. The young right-hander allowed only two hits in 4⅔ innings after relieving a battered Blass, who surrendered eight hits and five runs in two innings. By the end of Kison's stint, the Bucs had gained the upper hand and booked their tickets to the World Series for the first time since the magical 1960 season. "He's ice water out there," Murtaugh said of Kison. Oliver, meanwhile, who often played with a sizable chip on his shoulder, felt slighted because Fox ordered an intentional walk to Stargell — despite being 0-for-14 in the playoffs — in the sixth inning just after the Pirates had taken a 6–5 lead on Clemente's RBI single. The walk put runners at first and second, and Oliver promptly lashed a three-run homer to put the game away. "I hate it when they walk someone to get to me," Oliver said later. "I think I can hit, see."[59]

The Pirates now turned their attention to Baltimore's Birds, they of the four 20-game winners, the clutch-hitting Frank Robinson, slugging first-baseman Boog Powell and peerless third-baseman Brooks Robinson. The series opened in Baltimore, where the oddsmakers had installed the Orioles as 9–5 favorites and where hometown fans were justifiably confident that their club would polish off the Bucs for a second straight world title. Dave McNally, one of Baltimore's four 20-game winners, would start for the home club against Ellis. Getting home runs from Don Buford, Frank Robinson and Rettenmund — Stargell's traveling companion to Vietnam less than a year earlier — and a solid if not perfect pitching performance from McNally, the Orioles came from 3–1 down to post a 5–3 win in the opener. Baltimore collected 10 hits to just three for the Pirates, chasing Ellis in the third inning. After a rainstorm delayed things for a day, the misery continued in Game 2, as Baltimore parlayed 14 singles, seven walks and a Pirate error into an 11–3 beating, knocking out Pittsburgh starter Bob Johnson with one out in the fourth inning. If there was a silver lining, it was that Stargell's long post-season hitting drought finally ended at 18 at-bats with a single in the seventh inning, but by then the Orioles were roosting on an 11–0 lead. Only Hebner's three-run homer in the eighth stood between Baltimore starter Jim Palmer and a shutout.

The first two games seemed to substantiate what most of the experts predicted before the series — Baltimore clearly had the better ballclub. Jim Murray, the noted *Los Angeles Times* sports columnist, wrote after Game 2: "This World Series is no longer a contest. It's an atrocity. It's the Germans marching through Belgium. It's the interrogation room of the Gestapo. It's as one-sided as a Russian trial."[60]

The Pirates finally made a series of it in Game 3, returning to Three Rivers Stadium, where they posted a 5–1 victory behind Blass's complete-game three-hit gem. Pittsburgh was aided by — of all things — a missed sign that led to the game's key hit. With the Bucs nursing a tenuous 2–1 lead in the seventh and Clemente and Stargell aboard, third-base coach Frank Oceak flashed the bunt sign to the slugging Robertson. But the big first baseman, not often called upon to lay one down, missed the sign and instead touched Orioles' starter Mike Cuellar for a three-run homer that put the game away. Robertson learned of his missed sign as he crossed home plate and Stargell — there awaiting him — told him, "Attaway to bunt that ball."[61] Both Clemente and Stargell had seen the bunt sign, but Clemente wasn't completely positive, given that Robertson hadn't been given the sign all year, and he attempted to ask for time. But umpire Jim Odom rejected his request — thankfully for Robertson, his teammates and Pirate fans everywhere.

Game 4, played on October 13, had a historic tone to it, as it was the first night game in World Series history. It did not start out in promising fashion for the Pirates, as the Orioles mugged Bucs' starter Luke Walker before he could work up a sweat, scoring three times in the top of the first inning. But the young Kison again turned in a masterful long relief appearance, holding Baltimore to only one hit while working 6⅓ innings. That enabled the Pirate batters to regroup and hammer out a 4–3 victory, squaring the series at two games apiece. Stargell, who claimed he'd been booed by Pirate fans in Game 3, had his best offensive game of the series, going 2-for-5 with a double and an RBI and he also scored once. Milt May, the young backup catcher, delivered the key blow — a pinch-hit single in the seventh inning that, he told Bing Crosby — one of the nation's most beloved entertainers and also a member of the Pirate ownership group — "just fell in." Crosby, who was on hand for the win, wasn't buying it. "Fell in, nothing," Crosby replied. "That ball was barkin', bitin' and screamin' by the time it got out there."[62]

That left the two teams to battle it out in a best-of-three for the title. For Game 5, Baltimore tabbed Game 1 winner McNally while the Pirates called on the versatile Briles, who delivered only the game of his life — a two-hit shutout as the Bucs took a 3–2 series edge with a 4–0 blanking of the O's. The scene shifted back to Memorial Stadium in Baltimore, with the Pirates needing only one win to wrap things up. They wouldn't get it in Game 6, though, despite holding a 2–1 lead in the seventh inning, as Davey Johnson singled home the tying run off Giusti and Baltimore won it in the bottom of the 10th on a walk to Frank Robinson, Rettenmund's single and Brooks Robinson's sacrifice fly off reliever Bob Miller.

So it came down to Game 7, just as it did 11 years earlier, when the Pirates — again heavy underdogs — knocked off the vaunted Yankees on Maz's once-in-a-lifetime, bottom-of-the-ninth game-winning homer. This time there would be no bottom-of-the-ninth heroics, only a classic pitchers duel between the clever Blass and the no-nonsense Cuellar. Earl Weaver, the Orioles' crafty manager, tried to throw Blass off his game by complaining early on that the right-hander was violating a rule that required pitchers to maintain contact with the pitching rubber on the mound while delivering the ball to the plate. Blass said later that Weaver's decision to come on the field and complain actually settled him down and helped him focus because had been a little out of sorts at the game's outset.

The game was scoreless through three, and then in the fourth, Clemente — who had made the series his personal showcase, displaying for all the nation to see his splendid hitting, all-star fielding and other-worldly throwing arm — smacked a two-out homer on the first pitch he saw to give Pittsburgh a 1–0 lead. It remained that way through seven, with Blass limiting the Birds to just two hits. In the eighth, Stargell — dropped from the cleanup spot in the batting order for the first time all year due to his post-season slump — led off with a single. With Jose Pagan at the plate, Murtaugh called for the hit-and-run and Stargell took off with the pitch. Pagan lined a double to deep center and Stargell rumbled all the way around to score to boost the Bucs' lead to 2–0. That play loomed most large in the bottom of the inning, as the Orioles finally broke through with a run against Blass and moved the tying run to third. But Johnson grounded out to end the threat and the O's went down in order in the ninth, giving the Pirates a 2–1 win and the series championship, touching off a wild celebration that started on the field in Memorial Stadium and spread quickly to every corner of the greater Pittsburgh area.

The Bucs had gone all the way — again — and this time the hometown folks got carried away. What started as a celebration morphed into a small-scale riot as storefronts were smashed and stores were looted, at least three taxicabs were overturned and police reported a dozen rapes and more than 50 injuries. One estimate put the crowd that had made its way downtown at 100,000.[63] The team plane arrived back in Pittsburgh about 8:30 P.M. and it took the team caravan 30 minutes to travel a mile from the freight depot — where the plane had landed — to the main portion of the old Greater Pittsburgh Airport, as well-wishers jammed the route. It wasn't until 10:30 P.M. that the caravan traveled the 14 or so miles to reach downtown, as cars had jammed the Parkway West, parking in every direction as adoring fans fought to get a glimpse of their conquering heroes.

Stargell had a somewhat forgettable series, going 5-for-24 with just one extra-base hit — a double — and one RBI. And that came on the heels of his 0-for-14 performance in the NLCS. But he did walk seven times and scored three runs against Baltimore, including what proved to be the series' winning run. Brown, the club's GM, would say years later that Stargell's performance in the clubhouse after those World Series games was among the classiest he'd ever seen in all his years in baseball. "He did nothing in that World Series," he said. "But after every game, his locker was surrounded by the media. And Willie never retreated. He didn't hide. He stayed and answered every question, until the last dog had died. He never alibied. He never gave excuses. He answered them all in the most gentlemanly fashion." Brown said there was almost a sense of poetic justice that Stargell would score what proved to be the winning run on Pagan's double. "I thought it was payback for him being such a class guy," he said.

For Clemente, the '71 Series was vindication of sorts, as he finally received the accolades he felt he had been unjustly denied for well over a decade. He hit a blistering .414 with two doubles, a triple, two home runs and four RBIs and walked away with the Series' Most Valuable Player award. He showed his skills off the field as well. King, the Pirates' broadcaster, recalled being in a Baltimore hotel elevator with his wife the night before the series opener and seeing Stargell and Clemente together in the same elevator. "Roberto says, 'Willie, when we get off here, you go to your room if you have to, but come over to my room — I want to talk to you.'" A year or so later, King asked Stargell about that incident and he said Clemente told him that his first time in the World Series, in 1960, he was young and the flurry of excitement and all the publicity made the pressure seem more extreme to the point where it wasn't same sort of a game. Clemente told Stargell he had trouble handling that, and although he got a hit in every game, he didn't think he performed particularly well. He told Stargell not to try to do too much and that because he'd been through it before, he would carry the load. "Well, Willie didn't have a good World Series that year because he was hurt," King said. "But Stargell really appreciated that a guy like Clemente would take the time to discuss that with him. And he got that big hit and scored the winning run in Game 7."

Although Stargell fared poorly in the postseason, he had figured he was in a good position to take home an award of his own — the National League's Most Valuable Player award. He had carried the club through the first half of the season with power numbers of record proportions, and finished his first full year at Three Rivers Stadium with an eye-popping line of 48 home runs, 125 RBIs, 104 runs scored and a .295 batting average. But when the ballots were counted, the Cardinals' Joe Torre was voted the league's top player and Stargell was the runner-up. Torre, who received 21 first-place votes to just three for Stargell, certainly had MVP-worthy numbers, as he smacked 24 home runs and led the league in three offensive categories — hits (230), average (.363) and RBIs (137). But Stargell's Bucs finished ahead of the Cardinals in the NL East and the Pirates slugger was surprised he didn't win it. "I feel I deserved it," he told a reporter after the voting. "I'm basing my thoughts on the fact that I did everything I set out to do and we won the World Series." Stargell harkened back to the previous season when Billy Williams, Tony Perez and Johnny Bench all enjoyed standout seasons, but Bench earned the MVP award because many believed he played the key role in leading the Reds to the NL West title. "Now everybody says if the player does well day in and day out, he deserves it," Stargell said. "I was under the impression that if a fellow had a big year and his team got into the division playoffs, he would win the MVP. I thought I had the credentials."[64]

Stargell said he believed that if hadn't hurt his knee that season he could have eclipsed Ruth and Maris and hit more than 61 home runs, given that he already had 30 — and 87 RBIs — in the season's first 76 games. "I was seeing the ball very well," he said later. "But my knee got to the point where I couldn't stand all the way up on it. I couldn't put any pressure on it at all. I probably struck out a hundred times in the second half of the season."[65]

Stargell believed his poor post-season play cost him the MVP, but traditionally votes are submitted before such play begins. In any event, he didn't let the snub darken his mood, for he had done what he'd always wanted to do — play for a World Series winner. And the way the Pirates were built, many believed it might not be their last.

CHAPTER 5

Changing of the Guard

GIVEN THE CLUB'S SUCCESS IN 1971, few moves of any significance were made prior to the 1972 season. One major change did occur, however, as Murtaugh chose to step down as the team's manager. Speculation that Murtaugh would retire had surfaced periodically during the '71 campaign, particularly when he had to miss a stretch of 16 games due to health problems, and similar talk could be heard during the World Series against Baltimore. Pirates superscout Howie Haak told the media he had a hunch that Murtaugh would quit if the Bucs won the series. "Murtaugh's a guy who likes to win and he wants to go out while he's on top," Haak said while the Pirates held a 3–2 series edge. "What better time would there be than this year?"[1] Murtaugh at the time remained noncommittal, saying only that his family would sit down and discuss his future after the season was over. But on November 23, Murtaugh did indeed retire and Bill Virdon, who had patrolled center field for the 1960 World Series champion Pirates and had served as a coach under Murtaugh, was named to take over as manager. Virdon felt he was ready — in fact, he felt he was ready years earlier, even before he did a two-year minor league managerial stint in the New York Mets' system. "I think I can manage," he told the media at a press conference announcing his hiring and Murtaugh's retiring. "Time may prove otherwise."[2] Virdon did not lack confidence in his team, either. "We have a good ballclub," he said. "There's no reason why we shouldn't keep on winning."[3]

And win they did in '72, despite injuries that slowed both Clemente and Stargell, who had undergone off-season knee surgery. The Pirates started slowly and found themselves in sixth place in May. But the club latched onto first place for good on June 18 and posted an overall mark of 96–59, good for an 11-game margin over second-place Chicago. The regular season was highlighted by a piece of history that occurred on September 30, when Clemente became the 11th player in major league history to collect 3,000 career hits with a double off the Mets' Jon Matlack in the Great One's final regular-season at-bat. No one knew at the time, but it also would prove to be his last at-bat in the big leagues.

Stargell enjoyed another outstanding season — not as robust as the previous year but still worthy of MVP consideration, as he finished third in the balloting behind winner Johnny Bench and runner-up Billy Williams of the Cubs. Playing mostly first base — in part to rest his sore knees and in part to bail out the slumping Robertson, who hit only .193 — Stargell batted .293 with 33 home runs and 112 RBIs, scored 75 runs and banged out 28 doubles in 495 at-bats over 138 games. He posed no problems for his new manager, even though he was one of Murtaugh's biggest boosters. "If you wanted him to do something, he'd do it," Virdon said of Stargell. "He loved to hit. He played mostly first base that year and I might have had to push him a little bit defensively to make him work, but he didn't mind it. He didn't resent it. He did what you wanted him to do. He wasn't a militant. He always had a good frame of mind — he was always smiling and keeping everybody loose, encouraging people. He was a good person and he knew how to operate in the clubhouse. He just loved it."[4]

Virdon's first year at the helm was like a dream, at least in the regular season. "It was the easiest team to manage," he said of the '72 club. "When I went to the ballpark, I knew we were going to get six runs — and I had pretty good pitching, too." Stargell had plenty of help at the plate. Clemente had somewhat of an off-season but still hit .312 with 10 homers and 60 RBIs in 102 games. Oliver continued to excel, batting .312 with 12 homers and 89 RBIs, while Hebner batted an even .300 with 19 homers and 72 RBIs. And that wasn't all — catcher Sanguillen drove in 71 runs and hit .298, while Clines excelled as a fourth outfielder, hitting at a .334 clip in 107 games. Stennett, the young second baseman, also contributed, hitting .286 in 109 games. On the mound, Blass enjoyed perhaps his finest season, going 19–8 with a 2.49 ERA, while Ellis won 15 games; Briles, 14; and Moose, 13. Giusti continued to loom large as the closer in the bullpen with a 1.93 ERA and 22 saves in 74⅔ innings, and Ramon Hernandez — Stargell's former Grand Forks teammate from the 1960 Northern League campaign — was nearly as effective as Giusti, posting a 1.67 ERA and 14 saves in 70 innings.

For the second time in three seasons, the Pirates matched up with Bench, Perez, Rose and the rest of Cincinnati's Big Red Machine in the National League Championship Series. But unlike 1970, the '72 Reds featured a dynamic Hall-of-Famer in the making — Stargell's old friend from the East Bay, Joe Morgan. Now in the prime of his career, Morgan scored a whopping

122 runs, smacked 16 homers, drove in 73 runs and stole 58 bases to go along with a .292 batting average. Gary Nolan anchored the pitching staff, winning 15 of 20 decisions with a 1.99 ERA.

The teams split the first four games in the NLCS, with each team winning once at the other's home park. Blass and Hernandez combined to stifle the Reds in a 5–1 Game 1 win at home, but Cincinnati produced a four-spot in the first inning of Game 2 and went on to post a 5–3 win. Briles, Kison and Giusti limited the Reds to eight hits and two runs in a 3–2 Game 3 win at Cincinnati, but Morgan and Company evened things with a 7–1 pummeling of Ellis in Game 4, as the Pirates managed just two hits off Ross Grimsley. It all came down to a decisive Game 5 at Cincinnati's Riverfront Stadium, and the Pirates scratched out a pair of runs off Don Gullett in the second to take a 2–0 lead. Hebner doubled in one run and Cash singled in another. The Reds scored once in the third off Blass on Rose's RBI double, but the Pirates answered in the fourth on consecutive singles by Sanguillen, Hebner and Cash. The Reds managed another run off Blass in the fifth, but the Pirates maintained their 3–2 lead into the bottom of the ninth. Giusti came on in relief of Hernandez, who had gotten the final two batters in the eighth after taking over for Blass. But Giusti could not make the lead stand up, as Bench deposited a palm ball into the right-field seats, and Perez and Denis Menke followed with consecutive singles. When Giusti went 2–0 on Cesar Geronimo, Virdon called on Moose to come on in relief and the right-hander retired the next two Reds to leave runners at first and third. But with Hal McRae at the plate, Moose uncorked a wild pitch in the dirt on a 1–1 delivery, allowing pinch-runner George Foster to score the game- and series-winning run.

Virdon, asked if he regretted calling on Giusti to start the ninth, would have none of that. "I thought Giusti had good stuff," Virdon said. "Bench got a pitch that was up and hit it out. That upset him. Then he tried to rush and he was a little wild. I had to get a strike-thrower in there. But Dave Giusti doesn't have anything to apologize for."[5]

Momentarily lost in the gloom was yet another subpar NLCS performance by Stargell, who went 1-for-16 in the five-game set with the Reds. When coupled with his performance in the previous year's playoffs against the San Francisco Giants, Stargell was in a 1-for-30 funk in NLCS play. The Pittsburgh media did not jump on him, however, after his most recent tailspin. "Willie Stargell asks no pity for his 1-for-16 playoff bat," the *Post-Gazette*'s Feeney wrote on October 12. "Willie Stargell hurts inside today. He hurts because he wanted desperately to help carry the Bucs all the way. It wasn't to be. Maybe next year.... Willie's long ball was missing, but it was not a one-man loss to the Reds. Pittsburgh, as a team, won a world championship last year. This year, the team didn't make it."[6]

Indeed, Stargell wasn't the only one who failed to deliver at the plate. Oliver started strong but had only one hit in his last 13 NLCS at-bats. Hebner was 1-for-12 before getting two hits in his last game, and Alley did not have a hit in 16 plate appearances. The team had a .190 batting average for the five games.

Stargell, not surprisingly, didn't have much to say afterward. "It's tough right now," he said softly to reporters. "Six months of planning and preparation and everything and it comes to this. Just like that, it's over." Clemente — who unbeknownst to him or anyone else had just played his final game in a Pirate uniform — tried to pick up the mood in the clubhouse. "Giusti! Damn you, Giusti," he screamed at the veteran right-hander, who was sitting on the floor, his chin slumped against his chest. "Look straight ahead. Pick up your head. We don't quit now. We go home and come back in February."[7]

But Clemente would not come back in February. On New Year's Eve, a four-engine DC-7 piston-powered plane that was carrying the 38-year-old outfielder and relief supplies from his native Puerto Rico to earthquake-stricken Nicaragua crashed shortly after takeoff from San Juan International Airport at 9:22 P.M. The plane, carrying a crew of three and one additional passenger, came down in the sea about a mile and a half from shore, and Clemente's body never was found. Clemente, who was leading his nation's efforts to aid the Nicaraguan quake victims, made the trip personally because he was concerned that supplies were falling into the wrong people's hands in Nicaragua. Clemente's efforts were not unnoticed, even before his fatal crash. A letter to the editor that appeared in the *Post-Gazette* on New Year's Day — the day before the crash was reported — praised his efforts. "[A]mid this world of bombings, murders and overall destruction, it seems an anachronism to find a person such as Roberto Clemente, filled with pride, strength, determination and love. But Sr. Clemente could never be more right for his time. His is an example it would do us all good to follow," wrote Trudy Labovitz of Pittsburgh.[8]

Clemente's death stunned everyone connected with the Pirates. "He died caring," GM Brown said. "I'm sorry about baseball last. The big thing is losing Roberto Clemente, the man." Giusti couldn't grasp the reality of the situation two days after the fact. "I've been around other superstars. I never saw any of them have as much compassion for his teammates like Clemente did. He would treat a rookie like he was Willie Stargell." It wasn't just his leadership that would be missed, though, as Virdon well knew. "When you think of baseball in Pittsburgh, you think of Clemente," he said. "There's no way to replace him. We will just fill the spot. He was the best I ever saw in my era."[9]

When the Pirates reassembled the following February, Clemente's loss became all too apparent. For his part, Stargell tried to step into the breach, accepting the offer to become team captain — an offer made by Murtaugh, who while no longer managing the club still remained involved as the team's director of player acquisition and development. Stargell, concerned over the losses of Clemente and Mazeroski, tried to convey his own personal philosophy of remaining on an even keel — never getting too high or too low. It was the same approach he had learned from his stepfather, Percy Russell, while coming of age back in the projects of Alameda. "Roberto meant so much to the Pirates and made players like me feel so welcome," Stargell would say years later. "He taught me what an important influence you can have on a team and in the clubhouse. It was a lesson I never forgot and tried to relate to young players on the team."[10]

Kison, who missed much of the 1973 season while nursing a shoulder injury, said he appreciated Stargell's efforts in the wake of Clemente's death. "It was a sudden shock to the team and Willie took over in effect as the leader and stabilized the group. He had a calming influence on one and all. With his sense of humor and with his leadership characteristics, which included being a father influence to some and a brother influence to others, he just stabilized the situation. He had an uncanny way of verbalizing things, whether it was soothing someone or firing someone up. It was a gift. The man had huge shoulders and he took on the responsibility of a lot of things. He was a very stabilizing force both on and off the field."[11]

Stargell never proclaimed himself as the club's leader. He didn't have to, said Bob Smizik, a longtime Pittsburgh journalist who had the Pirates beat at the *Pittsburgh Press* from 1972 through 1977 and remains active today on the city's sports scene, having crossed into the blogosphere several years ago. Smizik characterized the Pirates' effort in 1973 as "heroic" and said Stargell did what he had to do. "He had to pick up the mantle for Clemente and he did," he said. "I remember after Clemente died, Al Oliver saying he needed to step up and be a leader on the team. But Willie never said that; he never changed."[12]

On the field, the Pirates sported a different look, with Sanguillen moving out from behind the plate to take over for his best friend Clemente in right field, backup Milt May stepping in for Sanguillen as catcher and Robertson reclaiming first base, a move that allowed Stargell — no longer worried about his knee — to return to left field. The moves did not pay off at the outset, as the club got off to a dreadful start, even falling into the NL East cellar for several days in late June. The team continued to scuffle but somehow remained in the thick of things into September despite Clemente's absence and the bewildering loss of form by Blass, who went from a Cy Young-caliber starter to a 3–9 record and a mind-boggling 9.85 ERA in 23 appearances. He worked only 88⅔ innings and yielded 84 walks, hit 12 batters and threw nine wild pitches. It was then, with the Pirates 68–70 and trailing first-place St. Louis by three games in the NL East, that Brown lowered the boom on Virdon, firing him on September 6 and replacing him once again with his longtime friend and collaborator, Murtaugh. Brown wouldn't elaborate on his reasons for the firing. "It's enough of a blow to be relieved," Brown said. "I don't want to be specific. I don't want to get into chapter and verse. It's unfair and unreasonable. My criticisms are kept within me." Virdon took his dismissal with his usual stoicism. "I did what I thought I had to do," he said later. "It didn't work out. But it's only natural to be hurt."[13] Some players were not pleased with the change; others were not unhappy. "I have no feeling," Stargell said. "The shock hasn't subsided yet."[14]

The change energized the club, at least for a while, as it won seven of nine and reclaimed first place by mid–September. But the Bucs faltered down the stretch and finished 80–82, in third place behind the division champion Mets and runner-up St. Louis. The lackluster mark, particularly coming off a championship-caliber performance the year before, was not a surprise, given the void left from Clemente's death. "It was an emotional year, trying to get over the shock of losing one of your leaders, one of your teammates," Kison said. "It was certainly not something you could prepare for."[15]

Stargell certainly was not to blame for the Bucs' downturn, as he had one of his best seasons, crushing 44 home runs and driving in 119 runs while batting .299. He appeared in 148 games — the most in his 21-year career — and posted career highs in runs (106), doubles (43), slugging percentage (.646) and on-base-plus-slugging (1.038). His herculean homers also came, including a 468-foot upper-deck bolt off Gary Gentry on May 31 at Three Rivers Stadium and a shot on May 8 that cleared the right-field pavilion at Dodger Stadium, the second time he had hit one out of that particular park.

Stargell was a master at work, and all who watched recognized it as such. "He was one of the smartest hitters I've ever been around," Bartirome said. "He would set pitchers up. I used to call him on it. He'd swing and miss in the first inning if nobody was on. The pitcher would throw a curve or a slider, or whatever pitch was the best that pitcher had. He'd swing and miss by a foot. He'd turn and ask the catcher, 'What was that pitch?' I'd never seen anything like it. Then in the eighth, if we were behind with a couple of guys on, he'd know that pitch was gonna come."[16]

Oliver related nearly an identical observation. "He was one of the few hitters I knew who could go to the plate and on occasion look for certain pitches in key situations. It might be a pitch you got him out with in the first inning, but in the eighth or ninth inning, you couldn't get him out. He looked for it, and if he got it, he didn't miss it. Lots of guys look for pitches and get them and then not capitalize on them. He could do it. He just knew how guys were going to pitch him in certain situations. Most of the time in key situations, he outsmarted them."[17]

Stargell was miles removed from the days of being platooned against left-handed pitching, as all the hard work he had put in over the years had finally paid off. The left-handed Veale recalled the hours of time Stargell spent in batting practice, asking Veale to throw to him so he could get comfortable hitting against southpaws. "I would

Willie unleashes his mighty swing, the one that propelled 475 balls beyond outfield walls throughout the major leagues and made him one of the game's all-time great sluggers (courtesy Pittsburgh Pirates).

pitch him off-speed stuff just so he would get used to it," Veale said. "We'd come out early and he'd hit a couple of bags of balls. I would tell him, 'If I hit you, just chalk it up to on-the-job training.' He got to the point where he wasn't afraid to hang in there against left-handers. At that time, I could throw just about every day. So I'd throw to him for five or 10 minutes. I'd tell him that I was coming inside or going away or high and tight, just to let him get an idea what a fastball looked like coming out of my hand. Then I'd show him a few breaking balls, and move them around from one side of the plate to the other. I would try to explain to him that all he needed to do was keep his eyes on the ball from the time it leaves my hand to the destination of where he wanted to hit it. All he had to do was make solid contact. And if it got into his power zone, he would smash it. And it was gone."[18]

Stargell's home run, double and RBI totals led the National League that season. But once again, he came up short in a close vote for the Most Valuable Player award, this time finishing second to the Reds' Rose, who hit .338 with 230 hits, 64 RBIs and 115 runs scored. Rose finished with 274 total points and 12 first-place votes to Stargell's 250 points and 10 first-place votes. One voter — Bill Conlin of the Philadelphia Daily News — ranked Stargell eighth although he said later he had done so mistakenly and had meant to vote Stargell second behind Rose.[19]

Willie shows his appreciation to the crowd as he jogs out onto the Three Rivers Stadium turf to take his defensive position (courtesy Pittsburgh Pirates).

Stargell said he felt like the '73 season was his best, but he added, "I knew when the season was over that I wasn't gonna win it. There's a lot of things that can be said, but it's nothing but talk, nothing ever comes out of it. Awards are fine, but if it's done on a political basis, I don't want any part of it. I don't know what goes into it. They should let the fans know just how does one player qualify as most valuable player?[20]

Despite his MVP-worthy numbers, Stargell might have done some of his best work off the field that year, filling the leadership void created by Clemente's death and helping Blass to maintain some semblance of order in a life that had spun out of control — literally. "When I was going through all my crap, all of the players stood tall for me," Blass said. "But I don't know if anyone stood taller than Willie."[21]

The Pirates' sub-par season prompted a number of changes for 1974. Brown dealt catcher May to Houston for pitcher Jerry Reuss — who would go on to win a team-leading 16 games and complete 14 of his 35 starts — shuttled second-baseman Cash to Philadelphia for pitcher Ken Brett and swapped Briles to Kansas City for utilitymen Kurt Bevacqua and Ed Kirkpatrick. Stennett, who broke out with 10 homers and 55 RBIs the previous season, was tabbed as Cash's replacement at second. Alley retired, opening the door for a pair of young shortstops — Frank Taveras and Mario Mendoza. Blass somehow made the club even though in one spring training appearance against the Cardinals he walked or hit seven straight batters of the 11 he faced in the first inning and he walked 25 in his first 14 Grapefruit League innings. But he would not be around for long.

The myriad changes didn't seem to do much good, at least in the early going. Two months into the season, the Pirates were 14 games under .500 at 18–32 and in last place in the NL East. And things didn't improve all that quickly; by July 15, the club was still struggling at 39–49. But an eight-game win streak got things moving in the right direction, and in the waning days of August, the club won eight of nine to head into September with a 70–62 mark before winning 18 of its final 29 to finish 88–74 and claim the franchise's fourth division title in five years. Stargell more then held up his end of the offensive attack, collecting 153 hits in 140 games, scoring 90 runs, bashing 25 homers and driving in 96 runs while hitting .301. He got a major hand from young outfielder Richie Zisk, who ripped 17 homers and drove in 100 runs to go with a .313 batting average. But it was another young outfielder who served notice that he was the one to watch. His numbers were hardly spectacular — he hit .282 in 220 at-bats with four home runs and 29 RBIs, which came on the heels of a .288 effort in 139 at-bats in 1973 — but it wouldn't be long before Dave Parker would become a major force with the Pirates and one of the major leagues' most talented players.

While Parker was getting comfortable with life in the big leagues, Stargell and his Pirate teammates said goodbye to a onetime mainstay whose sudden and inexplicable slide confounded teammates, fans and virtually everyone connected to baseball. Blass — who won 78 games over a five-year stretch that culminated in a 19–8 mark and a glittering 2.49 ERA in 1972 — made his final regular-season appearance in a big-league uniform in 1974. It came on April 17 against the Cubs in Chicago. The loquacious right-hander, whose wit and humor delighted teammates, fans and media members alike, came on to start the fourth inning of a game in which the Pirates trailed 10–4, and he proceeded to give up five runs in the fourth, two in the sixth and one more in the eighth. In addition to the eight runs, five of which were earned, Blass surrendered five hits — two of which left the park — and walked seven while striking out two in five innings of work. Blass wouldn't quit, though, taking an assignment with the Pirates' Triple-A franchise in Charleston, West Virginia. But things didn't get much better there; in 17 starts he fashioned a 2–8 record with a 9.74 ERA, walking 103 batters in 61 innings and nearly hitting as many men (16) as he struck out (26).

Blass's struggles were not the only odd development of the '74 season. In August, word leaked about the pending release of a book ostensibly about Stargell titled *Out of Left Field*, which was written by Bob Adelman and Susan Hall and was scheduled for publication by Little, Brown and Co. later that month. In a letter written in March, 1973, to David Litman — Stargell's agent — Hall said she and Adelman were interested in Stargell "as a successful black man who has worked to earn distinction, and who, in turn, contributes to the success of his team and to aid those people who've helped him on the way up — he pays his dues."[22]

But the book — researched during the challenging 1973 season — was reputed to contain intimate conversations and details of activities that did not put Stargell or some of his teammates in a favorable light. "This book is not the kind I expected," he said. Jerry McCauley, a New York literary agent who represented Adelman and Hall at the time they were writing the book, called it "a gossip tale, an outrageous breach of confidence, a lousy way to sell a book." Adelman defended the work, saying he was surprised at Stargell's reaction. "I thought Willie would love the book. It was understood that the book would be candid, spontaneous and controversial. It was to be an unvarnished account. But I don't think it hurts Willie at all. We tried to be fair and sensitive."[23] The Pirates did not want the book published. Hall's attorney, David Blasband, sent a telegram to the Pirate offices that said the club had "intentionally and maliciously interfered with Susan Hall's contractual relations with her publisher and have caused substantial damage to her and her reputation."[24] Blasband threatened legal action unless arrangements were made to correct the situation. Ultimately, at the end of August, Hall did file a federal lawsuit. In the wake of the controversy, Little, Brown and Co. canceled the book's publication. But it did not go away — it would resurface two years later with a different publisher.

The Bucs, who clinched the '74 NL East crown on the same day that the Cleveland Indians made history by naming Frank Robinson as the major leagues' first black manager, edged the second-place Cardinals by a game and a half. That put the Pirates on a collision course with the Los Angeles Dodgers in the NLCS. The Dodgers put together a 102–60 mark, besting the second-place Reds by four games. And they kept rolling in the playoffs, polishing off the Pirates in four games. Right-hander Don Sutton did the bulk of the damage, shutting out the Pirates on four hits in the opener and then limiting the

Bucs to three hits in a 12–1 series clincher in Game 4. Pittsburgh's only win came on a solid outing from Kison in a 7–0 victory in Game 3. Unlike his previous two playoff series, Stargell performed well, collecting at least one hit in each game and going 6-for-15 overall. He also ended a streak of 73 at-bats in the playoffs without a home run, crushing a three-run shot in Game 3 that gave him and his teammates hope, at least for a while. "Willie can inspire a team without opening his mouth," Zisk said after the game. "When he hit that home run it showed me what a little aggressiveness can do. If we're going to go down, let's go down swinging."[25] The hope was short-lived, however; while Stargell homered again off Sutton in Game 4, that was the only run the Pirates could muster.

Stargell returned for yet another go in 1975 and most of his teammates did likewise as the Pirates made few changes prior to the season. One note of finality sounded, as in late March the club requested waivers on Blass, who had spent most of the previous year in the minors trying to regain the form that had made him one of baseball's top right-handed starters earlier in the decade. One other transaction — the acquisition of outfielder Bill Robinson from the Phillies — certainly helped the club but would pay even bigger dividends a few years down the road. But perhaps the most noteworthy development that occurred in 1975 was the full-scale arrival of Parker, who surpassed Stargell in both batting average and power numbers as the Pirates rolled to their fifth NL East title in six seasons, putting together a 92–69 record to outdistance the second-place Phillies by 6½ games. Off the field and inside the clubhouse, things remained pretty much the same as they had been throughout the '70s — a rollicking conglomeration of all-inclusive, equal-opportunity cut-ups. With Clemente gone three years now, Stargell — now entrenched at first base, where he had played for the second half of 1972 before being moved back to left field at the start of the '73 season — was the undeniable team leader. Not because he chose to be, but because the role simply came to him. "Leadership is something that just evolves when you get a group of players together in a clubhouse," said Reuss, who in his second year with the Pirates in '75 again led the team with 18 wins and had a stellar 2.54 ERA. "Willie didn't try to hide any problems — instead what he did was accent them. When I was there, all the white players were on one side of the clubhouse and then there was the door. And then there was what Willie called the Ghetto, and then Spanish Harlem. He had fun with it. If you'd come over to talk to him, he'd say, 'What are you doing over here — you know better than to come over here.' Or if he came over, he'd say, 'I just want to smell the air there. It's so much cleaner than in the Ghetto.' He knew it was this way in society. So rather than try to hide it, he'd call it what it was and try to have some fun with it. In some cases, for the guys who were uptight, it loosened them up. You could pretty much say whatever you wanted. If you said those things today, it would be on YouTube and you'd sound as if you were the most incredible racist or bigot. But in the clubhouse, in those days, it was OK — it was accepted. And guys just laughed about it. What it did was allow guys from different cultures and ages and parts of the country a chance to come together and say, 'This is common ground — bring these things up and talk about them; whether you want to be serious or laugh about it, we'll get past it. Willie was the one who invited everyone to be that way. It allowed everyone to go out and play the kind of game they were capable of playing. I was there for five years and every year I was there, we were in the hunt. And Willie played a big part in that."[26]

Reuss played for eight clubs during a 22-year career and said it wasn't that way in every clubhouse. "Each club has its own distinctive personality and is driven by the strongest personality in the clubhouse," Reuss said. "Murtaugh refused to be bigger than the players. He had certain players and he'd say, 'I want you to take care of it. And you do it your own way.' And Willie did. Those clubs I played on had Willie's stamp. He made the clubhouse his own and not because of his ego, but to bring people together first, to allow people to be comfortable in a situation where you have 25 different people of different ages, different backgrounds and different places. As a person, rather than a player, he wanted everyone to be comfortable. This was everyone's home to share and he wanted everyone to be as comfortable as if it *was* someone's home. And he knew that would help them be comfortable and produce. That's one reason why the Pirates had so much success. I don't think it was a coincidence at all. That's how he made the Pirates his own, just like Clemente made the Pirates his while he was there."

Reuss remembers the prankster side of Stargell as well. In 1977, when Reuss notched his 1,000th career strikeout in a game against the Cubs, the victim was Clines, the former Pirate who grew up watching Stargell in the Bay Area. The next day, Clines received a baseball with a note that read, "Gene, this was my 1,000th strikeout. Would you please sign it?" A little while later, Reuss received a baseball that was signed, "____ you, Gene Clines." Reuss had no idea what was going on, so he went over to find Clines and ask him about it. "You didn't send me the ball?" Clines asked Reuss, who told him he had done no such thing. "Then the same thought came to both of us simultaneously — Stargell," Reuss told Mike Littwin of the *Los Angeles Times*.[27]

In 1975, Stargell remained a formidable offensive force, pounding out 22 home runs, driving in 90 and hitting .295 despite missing 18 games with a broken rib. He said later that although he felt he should have been considered for the MVP award, he knew he wasn't the favorite — that tag belonged to Stargell's old East Bay buddy Morgan, who hit .327 with 17 home runs, 67 stolen bases and 94 RBIs. Before the MVP voting that year, Stargell — disgruntled over failing to win the award in 1971 and 1973 — said he would not accept it even if the voters chose him.

Even on his own team, Stargell was surpassed — at least statistically — by the brash young Parker, who belted 25 homers, collected 101 RBIs and batted .308, second on the team only to Sanguillen, who finished at .328. Parker and Stargell had crossed paths years before, in '71, when Parker had made his first visit to spring training with the Pittsburgh organization, just a year removed from high school. "He was impressed with my ability — he told me that," Parker recalled. "My first year in the majors was '73, but I should have been in the big leagues in '71. But look at what I had in front of me — Clemente, Oliver, Stargell and then you had Dave Arrington, Zisk, Gene Clines."[28] Stargell told Parker about the importance of keeping an even keel, and he didn't just talk the talk. He lived it. "I'd watch him go to the plate and strike out nine out of 10 at-bats and he'd never change his demeanor," Parker said. "He never threw his helmet, never threw a bat."

But Stargell's even-keeled philosophy didn't resonate so much with the huge left-handed hitter, who had picked up the nickname "Cobra" from Bartirome, the Pirates' trainer. "He wouldn't get too high or too low and that worked for him," Parker said. "But I needed to verbalize. I was a hard-nosed, very physical player and I would express my feelings right away. Willie was one who held his in. What worked for me was putting myself on the line. I would tell people before the season started that I would win the batting title. I'd say, 'When the leaves turn brown, I'll be wearing the batting crown.' By putting myself on the line, I had to live up to it. Being aggressive and carrying that aggression out onto the field helped me as a player. It's whatever works for you."

Parker's aggression helped the Bucs enjoy a solid regular season, particularly in the first half when they put together a 55–33 mark. The club took possession of first place for good on June 7, but went just 37–36 after the All-Star break and by mid–August the Phillies had clawed their way into a tie for first base. But by September 8, the Bucs had rebuilt their lead to 6½ games and they were never truly challenged down the stretch. However, the same couldn't be said for the post-season, as the NLCS proved a rocky road once again. This time, the Pirates met their old nemesis, Cincinnati, and the results were eerily similar to their first NLCS battle, back in 1970. Again, the Reds swept the series in three games, winning 8–3, 6–1 and 5–3. Stargell reverted back to his earlier form, going just 2-for-11 and failing to drive in a single run.

He was not alone; the club hit just .194 in the three games, going a collective 25-for-129. "We knew about their hitting and speed and defense," Murtaugh said of the Reds after the clincher. "But we didn't think their pitching would be strong enough to hold us. They just stopped our bats." Stargell remained dignified in defeat, despite yet another post-season cold spell. "I'll tell you one thing," he told the media later. "I'll take my chances with these 25 guys again next year."[29]

But a few of those 25 would be somewhere other than Bradenton, Florida, when the Pirates gathered for spring training in 1976. During the off-season, Brown sent Brett, Ellis and highly regarded minor-league second baseman Willie Randoph to the Yankees for pitcher George "Doc" Medich, who was expected to become the ace of the staff. He also shipped reserve infielder Art Howe — like Randolph, a future major league manager — to Houston for infielder Tommy Helms. Even those calling the action on the Pirates flagship radio station KDKA would be different, as the venerable Prince and his sidekick King were fired. Prince's outrageous wardrobe and colorful use of the language had endeared him to generations of Pirate fans since his arrival in Pittsburgh in 1948. Hundreds of distraught callers supported Prince, who had offered to step down voluntarily if given the chance to work one more season. "It's the first time I ever begged for anything," he said later.[30] Stargell was taken aback by the firings of Prince and King, even participating in a parade in their honor. "That was an example of Willie's caring attitude," King said. "It didn't surprise me, coming from him, and I certainly appreciated it."[31] The outpouring of support from players and fans had no bearing on KDKA's decision to dismiss the two broadcasters. Prince moved on to a network position and then the Houston Astros and King landed a sports information position at Duquesne University. Meanwhile, new broadcasters came on board.

And on the field, the '76 Bucs — sporting new black pillbox-type caps with gold stripes, in honor of the nation's bicentennial celebration — continued to do what they had done most of the '70s: hit and win. Parker's power numbers dipped a bit, as he managed just 10 home runs, but he still knocked in 90 and hit a robust .313. Oliver hit for an even higher average — .323 — while finishing with 12 homers and 61 RBIs, and Zisk tied Robinson for the club lead in homers with 21 while driving home 89 with a .289 average. Robinson, who managed to pile up 416 at-bats despite not having a regular starting position, also contributed 64 RBIs to go with his .303 average. On the mound, four of the five starters enjoyed outstanding seasons — young John Candelaria led the staff with 16 wins while fellow lefty Jim Rooker chalked up 15 and Kison and Reuss each won 14. None lost more than nine, and Reuss' 3.53 ERA was the highest among the quartet. Only the newcomer Medich, who came from New York with great expectations, failed to deliver, as he went just 8–11.

Also failing to deliver, at least in the manner in which Pirate fans and team management had become accustomed, was Stargell. The big bopper did hit 20 home runs but drove in only 65 — his lowest RBI total since his rookie year in 1963 — while batting a subpar .257. But the slugger had good reason to struggle. On the night of May 26, Stargell's wife, Dolores, began experiencing a pounding headache, and a short time later, the couple went to a nearby hospital, where Dolores suffered a stroke and a brain aneurism. She underwent surgery but was left partially paralyzed on her left side and was required to undergo extensive rehabilitation. The experience devastated both husband and wife; Dolores later said she believed it triggered the ultimate demise of their marriage. Stargell missed a number of games during Dolores's illness, and after he returned to the lineup, he never found his customary groove. "The '76 season was hell, capital H-E-L-L," Stargell told *Sports Illustrated* writer Anthony Cotton three years later. "I couldn't concentrate. I could only see Dolores with all this equipment strapped on her, and my mind drifted quite a bit."[32]

If Dolores's medical issues were not enough of a weight to bear, *Out of Left Field*— the controversial book that raised eyebrows all over the baseball world before being pulled in 1974 — was back and ready for distribution by Two Continents Publishing Group. The 223-page book consisted largely of transcribed conversations with Stargell, general manager Brown, Murtaugh, Virdon and several teammates, including Blass, Briles, Zisk and Ellis. It even featured Dolores Stargell and a self-proclaimed baseball groupie named "Gayle." The book featured discussions about baseball — including an account of Stargell's contract negotiations — but it was the sexual escapades and tales of drug usage that had the baseball world buzzing. A Two Continents Publishing Group press release characterized it as a "searing, startling, brutally honest book ... baseball as the powers would rather you didn't know it, baseball as the fans couldn't know it, baseball in its real glory, warts and all."[33] Ellis, by this time, had moved on to the New York Yankees but his Pittsburgh-based attorney, Tom Reich, called the book "disgusting. The bottom line is that it makes me sick. It's one of the most offensive things ever. Willie Stargell is one of the finest men and athletes in this town and he's being victimized by this stuff."[34]

Dolores — known as Dee in the book — revealed that her famous husband would bring cards home from women who missed him "very much. Just funny little cards signed by women. Willie denies everything. As long as he denies it, that's fine with me. It can never hurt me if I don't know about it specifically."[35]

Despite the distractions Dolores's illness posed, the publication of the controversial book and Stargell's subpar individual effort, the Pirates went 92–70. But when post-season play began, they were on the outside looking in, as the Phillies claimed their first-ever NL East title. It didn't come easy, though. After trailing by 15½ games on August 24, the Bucs made a late run and cut the margin to just three games on September 17. But they proceeded to lose their next three in a row and saw their deficit grow to 4½ games. It never got smaller and they wound up second, nine games back. The '76 season would signal a major changing of the guard in the Pirate organization, as Brown stepped down as general manager on September 29 and Murtaugh retired just three days later, citing his health as a major factor. Brown, who was 58 and had been with the Pirates for 21 years, said he thought his departure might actually help the organization in some ways. "The nature of my position is that you leave a stamp on the team," he told the media. "The people in Pittsburgh feel a certain way about the team, and it's not all good. A change could be good. We've been doing it Brown's way for 21 years. Maybe it's time for new ideas, new thoughts."[36]

Harding "Pete" Peterson was named to replace Brown as general manager, and his first order of business was finding someone to succeed Murtaugh. Among the names that surfaced early was none other than Stargell; after all, he was universally respected, and another black player-manager had been hired recently in the Indians' Frank Robinson. But Stargell dismissed such talk before it gained any momentum. "All I want to do is play," he told the media on the same day he was named the recipient of the Catholic Youth Association's second annual Art Rooney Award. "I have a few years left before I think about that."[37] On November 5 — the day before Stargell was to receive yet another award, this time the Brian Piccolo Award from the national YMCA in Seattle for "unselfish contributions to the betterment of man and community"— Peterson ended the speculation about who would manage the Bucs by "acquiring" Chuck Tanner from Oakland. Peterson had to send catcher Sanguillen and cash to the Oakland A's for the rights to employ Tanner, a native of nearby New Castle who was coming home for his dream job. Tanner joked at his press conference that he had agreed to take the job only after Murtaugh took "an oath that he really retired."[38] Sadly, a little more than three weeks later, Murtaugh suffered a stroke at the age of 59 and died two days later on December 2. That wasn't the only death in the Pirate family that off-season, as the right-handed Moose died in a car accident on October 9 — his 29th birthday — while headed to a dinner party that followed a golf outing near St. Clairsville, Ohio. "Here's a young man in the prime of his life, alive and healthy one minute and not with us anymore the next," a distraught Murtaugh said after hearing the news. "I can't tell you how depressing that is."[39]

Peterson wasted no time in putting his stamp on the ballclub. In addition to bringing in a new manager, he dealt away a couple of backup infielders for reliever Grant Jackson, then shipped Zisk and pitcher Silvio Martinez to the White Sox for pitchers Rich Gossage and Terry Forster — both of whom Tanner had managed before. Then, in the middle of spring training in March 1977, Peterson sent Giusti, Medich and five prospects to the A's for Phil Garner. The scrappy Garner had been playing second base in Oakland but was expected to take over at third for Hebner, who had played out his option and signed with Philadelphia.

The changes, coupled with Tanner's natural and infectious enthusiasm, had players and fans alike keyed up for the '77 campaign. The Bucs caught fire early, winning 16 of 17 before the season was a month old. By May 24, the team was 26–12 and in first place by 2½ games. But within a week, the Pirates had yielded the top spot to the defending division champion Phillies and, despite coming close during the dog days of August, never quite caught up to their cross-state rivals, finishing second, five games back. Still, the club put together an outstanding 96–66 record — the most wins since the '71 championship team collected 97.

Perhaps the pivotal — and most memorable — game of that season occurred on July 8, when the Pirates roared back from a 7–3 deficit and a bench-clearing brawl to pull out an 8–7 win over the Phillies. With the Pirates leading 3–2, the Phillies' Garry Maddox hit a two-run homer in the seventh to put his team ahead 4–3. Kison then hit Mike Schmidt with a pitch, prompting Schmidt to bark at Kison, who then challenged the Phillies' slugger to back it up with some action. Schmidt obliged and headed to the mound, and a wild melee ensued, emptying both benches in the process. But the fireworks weren't over. The Phillies scored three more runs off Kison and reliever Kent Tekulve in the eighth and led 7–3. But after Oliver led off the bottom of the inning with a double, Phillies reliever Tug McGraw hit Stargell in the back with a pitch, and that sent Stargell slowly toward the mound — with a bat in his hand. Again, both benches emptied and this time McGraw and Phillies manager Danny Ozark — both of whom had been warned after Kison had hit Schmidt — were tossed.

"It hurt," Stargell said, when asked why he headed toward the mound. "Out of instinct I started out there. Then I realized I had a bat in my hand and I wasn't going to start swinging a bat." The Pirates, though, started swinging, rallying for four runs in the eighth to tie the game and then pushing home the deciding run in the bottom of the ninth on a four-pitch bases-loaded walk in one of the year's most satisfying wins. "If the adrenalin on our bench were water," said Oliver, "everybody in Pittsburgh would have drowned."[40]

Even after the win, the Bucs sat in third place, 8½ games out of the lead. But it sparked a run that saw them trim their deficit to a single game by August 6. That was as close as they got, though, as the Phillies held on, eventually finishing with a five-game margin over the Pirates. The Bucs made their run with virtually no help from their slugging first baseman, as an injured elbow incurred while trying to pull the Phillies' Greg Luzinski out of a pile during the Kison–Schmidt brawl left Stargell unable to generate any power. So, after playing for another week, he was taken out of the lineup and relegated to a seat in the dugout, where his teammates ribbed him, calling him "Judge" for spending so much time on the bench. "I want to get back in there real bad," said Stargell, by then the club's all-time leading home-run hitter with 401, "but there's nothing I can do until the numbness goes away."[41] The club placed him on the disabled list August 5 and he underwent surgery in September, his season cut short after just 63 games. Despite missing two weeks in mid–April and another week in early July, Stargell finished with 13 homers and 35 RBIs in 186 at-bats — roughly the equivalent of 40 homers and 105 RBIs over a full season — and a .274 batting average.

Some began to wonder if it was the beginning of the end of Stargell's career. After all, he had come off his worst season in years in 1976 and followed it up with just a 63-game effort that was punctuated by a season-ending injury. And he was 37 years old — not exactly the age when ballplayers figured to resurrect their careers. Some even called for the gentle giant to step aside and make way for one of the younger prospects. But Tanner stood by his first baseman. "Nobody's going to tell Willie Stargell when to quit!" Tanner said. "He'll have a job as long as he wants one."[42]

While Stargell worked to rehab his surgically repaired elbow, Peterson was busy operating on his roster, trading the veteran Oliver to Texas as part of a four-team deal that brought pitcher Bert Blyleven — a future Hall of Famer — and outfielder John Milner to Pittsburgh, signing free-agent pitcher Jim Bibby and then reacquiring Sanguillen from Oakland.

The 1978 Pirates were counting on those new faces, along with a return to form from Stargell and second baseman Stennett — who suffered a broken leg the previous August — and more of the same from Parker, who had a monster year in 1977, leading the league with 215 hits and 44 doubles, pounding out 21 homers and driving in 88 runs while hitting .338. But Parker's big bat and the new faces didn't help the club get off on the right foot, as it was scuffling in mid–June with a 27–31 mark in fourth place, 6½ games back. By that time, Stargell had registered seven homers and 34 RBIs. Included during that run was a two-homer night on May 20 off Wayne Twitchell in Montreal, with one of them traveling 535 feet — among the longest Stargell ever hit and *the* longest ever hit in Olympic Stadium. "How can anybody hit a ball that far?" Tanner marveled afterward. Stargell was unfazed, noting that a couple of the balls he had hit into Three Rivers Stadium's upper deck had traveled farther than the shot he hit off Twitchell.[43]

Willie bundles up on a chilly day in Pittsburgh (courtesy Pittsburgh Pirates).

The club sustained a major loss at the end of June when Parker — trying to tag up and score the tying run in the bottom of the ninth inning against the visiting Mets — dived head-first into catcher John Stearns. The result: a fractured left cheekbone and a three-stitch cut about his left eye that kept him out of the lineup for 11 games. By the time he returned on July 16, the Pirates were 43–43, in third place, six games back. Some members of the local media gave the Bucs up for dead. The *Post-Gazette*'s Feeney wrote on August 7: "The Pirates yesterday were placed in the funeral parlor, reserved for teams due to be eliminated from the pennant race in September. The burial date is anybody's guess." The headline read, "Bucs Dead, Funeral Date Pending.[44] It got worse; by August 12, the club sat in fourth place, 11½ games back, with a 51–61 record. But from that point on, the team went on a tear, winning 37 of its last 49 games to make a late — but ultimately unsuccessful — charge. It all came down to the last series of the year, a four-game set with the first-place Phillies, who held a 3½-game lead. The Pirates won the first two — the second one coming on a balk that brought home the game-winning run in the bottom of the ninth inning — but the dream died the following night. The Phillies took a 10–4 lead into the bottom of the ninth, but the Pirates rallied to cut it to 10–8 and had the tying run at the plate in the person of Stargell. But the big slugger did not come through, striking out instead, and when Garner grounded out to end the game, it also ended the Pirates pennant hopes.

For Stargell, though, the season represented a major achievement, as he showed he was far was finished. Thanks to some judicious use by Tanner, who gave the veteran a day off now and then, Stargell slugged 28 homers and drove in 97 runs in only 390 at-bats and batted .295. His performance did not escape notice; he was named the league's Comeback Player of the Year. Although clearly in the twilight of one of the game's best-ever careers, he also clearly had a little gas left in his tank — and he would show the baseball world just how explosive that fuel could be in 1979.

CHAPTER 6

We Are Family

T HE CLUB THAT ASSEMBLED in Bradenton in early 1979 looked very much like the one that made a late — albeit ultimately unsuccessful — run the previous season, although Peterson did acquire reliever Enrique Romo from the Seattle Mariners in what proved to be a key addition. The rest of the regular lineup, led by Parker — who became the game's first million-dollar-a-year man when he signed an off-season deal for $5 million over five years — and the rejuvenated Stargell remained intact. However, a major shakeup occurred on April 19 when Peterson swapped shortstops with the Mets, sending Taveras to New York for Tim Foli, who had developed a reputation as a hothead but whose energy and defensive talents would make him a perfect fit in the Pirates infield.

An early six-game losing streak put the team in a 4–10 hole in late April, and it wasn't until May 29 that it again reached the .500 mark at 21–21. Nothing much changed by late June, as the Pirates remained around the break-even point. But fortunes turned on June 28 when Peterson pulled the trigger on a five-player deal with the San Francisco Giants, acquiring two-time league batting champion Bill Madlock and pitcher Dave Roberts in exchange for three pitchers — Ed Whitson, Al Holland and Fred Breining. In Madlock, the Pirates obtained the quintessential professional hitter who gave the club much-needed punch from the right side and carried the league's highest active career batting average at .325.

Stargell was elated with the acquisition and said it would help all involved. "It was good for Madlock because it's a change of atmosphere for him, just what Bill needs. I feel sure Bill is happy to be coming over here." Not everyone was as thrilled with the deal, though. Garner, who figured to be the odd man out at third base with Madlock's arrival, said, "It looks like a good trade but I'll think it's a horsefeathers trade if I wind up watching the games from the bullpen."[1]

115

On July 8, the Pirates found themselves 40–38 and in fourth place, seven games out of first, but they then reeled off 13 wins in their next 14 starts to improve to 53–39 and climbed to second place, just a game behind Montreal. A week into August, the Bucs had moved into first place and by mid–August had opened up a four-game lead. But a three-game skid in mid–September dropped the Pirates out of the top spot, a game behind Montreal. After splitting the first two games of a four-game showdown with the Expos on September 24, the Pirates were in second place, a half-game back. But convincing wins each of the next two nights — 10–4 and 10–1— put Pittsburgh in first place by a game and a half with four to play. A 13-inning, 7–6 loss to the Cubs — made possible in part by a Stargell throwing error — on the season's next-to-last day cut the Bucs' lead to a single game with one to play, but a 5–3 win over Chicago in the regular-season finale clinched the division and left the Pirates with a sparkling 98–64 record.

Dan Donovan, a Pirates beat writer with the *Pittsburgh Press* in the late 1970s and early '80s, recalled the next-to-last game loss to the Cubs. "He butchered a play at first base and basically cost them the game," Donovan said of Stargell. "He hardly ever made really bad plays at first base, but he did on that one. He walked into the locker room later talking about it to everyone. 'I looked like a monkey fucking a football,' he said. I had no clue what that would look like. So I wrote, 'A monkey playing with a football.' That was his way to keep the team loose and to take responsibility for things. They laughed and joked and kidded him and they realized it wasn't the end of the world. That's the kind of thing he would do."[2]

Stargell didn't hit for much average down the stretch — just .222 for the month of September — but he slammed eight home runs, including one in the season-finale, and drove in 18 runs that month to lead the charge. His final two RBIs came in the division-clinching win and gave him 1,476 for his career — enough to move him past Honus Wagner and into the top spot among all Pirate players. "This is the most warm-feeling thing I've ever been associated with," he said afterward as champagne flowed in the victorious clubhouse. "We don't have many .300 hitters and we don't have any 20-game winners; what we have is 25 guys who play hard. What we have is a lot of junkyard dogs."[3]

Junkyard dogs with pedigrees; statistically, the Pirates had their share of heavy hitters and standout pitchers. Stargell put together his second straight outstanding season, hitting .281 with 32 homers and 82 RBIs in 126 games. Parker belted 25 home runs, drove in 94 and hit .310, and was a major force down the stretch as he ripped 15 hits in his final 24 regular-season at-bats, Madlock did just what the Pirates had hoped when they brought him in from

San Francisco, hitting .328 while Robinson — who played 125 games in the outfield and another 28 at first base — offered solid power numbers with 24 homers and 75 RBIs. Garner, inserted at second base after the Madlock trade, hit 11 homers, drove in 59 runs and batted .293 in 150 games. On the mound, no one pitcher dominated but six Pirate hurlers — Blyleven, Candelaria, Kison, Romo, Jim Bibby and Kent Tekulve — reached double figures in wins. Tekulve, the tall, thin right-handed reliever who threw from down under, saved 31 games to go with his 10 wins in a mind-boggling 94 appearances.

But it wasn't the numbers that were the sum of the Pirate parts. Rather, it was the atmosphere and the spirit that separated the Bucs from their division rivals. Reminiscent of the Pirate teams from the early '70s, with players getting on one another with abandon night after night, the '79 squad had its own brand of no-holds-barred clubhouse camaraderie that was a sight — and a sound — to behold. Bartirome, the longtime trainer, had been present for both eras and said that while the teams of the early '70s were close, they couldn't compare to the '79 club in that respect. "I have a World Series ring from 1979 and on one side of it, it says, 'We Are Family.' And that's just exactly the way it happened. There was no dissension. The '79 team was like they were put together in heaven because they got along so well. The early '70s teams got along well, but there wasn't the cohesion that the '79 team had."[4]

And the ringmaster of it all was Stargell. "Anything that happened in the clubhouse that was funny, he was in the middle of it," Bartirome said. "But he gave more than he received. That whole club was crazy. I was the trainer but I really wasn't the trainer — I was the psychiatrist. I was the zookeeper. They were all crazy — the craziest bunch of guys I ever met in my life. Ed Ott, Candelaria, Jim Rooker, Enrique Romo — every one of them was nuts. But they'd all go along. And it's tough to have 25 guys live together all summer and work together and not have a fight. But there was nothing. Everything that happened was some kind of a joke." Bartirome believed that attitude definitely showed up in the standings. "They never thought they were gonna lose. It didn't matter who was hurt — when they walked out on the field, they knew they were going to win that game. Lots of people don't remember this, but when Foli was hurt the last month of the year, Dale Berra had to play and he played the hell out of the game. He really stepped up because we didn't have anybody else to play shortstop and we needed him. And he did it. Omar Moreno had the best year of his life. Bill Robinson had the year of his life. Mike Easler, John Milner — those guys were crazy, but all they thought about was winning."

The outstanding talent, mixed with the fun-loving and confident nature, made the Bucs fan favorites. But when one other ingredient — an iconic disco-based anthem — was added to the recipe, the '79 Pirates became an unforgettable creation. Greg Brown, now a Pirates broadcaster and then an intern in the team's promotions department while studying at what was then Point Park College in Pittsburgh, was responsible for running any number of errands in the clubhouse as well as taking care of in-game entertainment and the sound system at Three Rivers Stadium. In between organist Vince Lascheid's offerings, Brown would spin records designed to go along with a particular development. For example, when the reed-thin and rubber-armed Tekulve would come on in relief, Brown would play "Rubber Band Man" by the Spinners. When the Pirates beat the Cubs, he would put on "The Night Chicago Died" by Paper Lace. A win over the Braves? "The Night the Lights Went Out in Georgia" by Vicki Lawrence. "It was kind of scripted," Brown said. Occasionally, Brown's duties would take him inside the Pirates' clubhouse and he noticed one song in particular would often be playing there — a song by the group Sister Sledge titled "We Are Family." Brown mentioned to his boss that perhaps he should play the song during one of the in-game breaks, but his boss, Steve Schanwald, said it wouldn't be a good idea. "He said, 'It sounds like a disco song and we're not into disco here,'" Brown recalled of Schanwald, who went on to become a front-office executive with the Chicago Bulls of the National Basketball Association. But Brown's instincts said otherwise. One day, he asked his older brother, who was going shopping, to pick up a copy of the Sister Sledge album. And then one night, following a dramatic comeback victory, Brown threw caution to the wind and cranked it up over the stadium sound system. The place went crazy. Virtually overnight, the fans adopted the song. And it became the soundtrack to the '79 championship season.

"It was Willie (Stargell) who made it the theme song in the clubhouse, but it never went public until we started playing it in the stadium," Brown recalled. "And from that point on, about mid-summer, we just blared it on the sound system. We'd put that record on and blast it. Almost everyone would stay in the stadium to dance to the sounds of it. It all happened at once — it was playing in the clubhouse, it was playing in the stadium."[5] Lanny Frattare, the longtime Pirates broadcaster who was in his fourth season with the team that year, said the family atmosphere that Stargell cultivated certainly helped in the clubhouse, and that might have aided several key platoon situations on the field as well — most notably with Milner and Robinson in left field and Ott and Nicosia behind the plate. Frattare heard plenty of ribbing that went on in the clubhouse "and there's probably a lot of stories about that clubhouse that we don't know about," he said. "They were smart enough to know what they wanted to show to the media and not show to the media. Even the 'We

Are Family'—I think some players were disappointed that what had become the clubhouse song found its way out into the stadium. It was their clubhouse song. But there was no doubt in anybody's mind that because that was shared with the public, it gave the public a chance to share a lot of the atmosphere about what went on with 'The Family.'"[6]

Like Frattare, Brown had plenty of opportunities to see the '79 Pirates in action — not just on the field, but in the clubhouse before games. With a roster that included players from Panama, the Dominican Republic, Mexico and the Netherlands in addition to the United States, the club featured a veritable racial potpourri that — in the wrong hands, under the wrong leaders — could have been explosive in all the wrong ways. Instead, the pre-game gatherings might have been even more impressive than what took place between the white lines — and that was mighty memorable in its own right. It was an act that played nowhere else in baseball, according to those who were lucky enough to be a part of it. Not only were there verbal hijinks, but Stargell had taken to awarding what he called "Stargell Stars" — small gold stars that players could affix to their black pillbox caps. Essentially, the stars were handed out in appreciation for a positive contribution of any kind. The players did not take them lightly. "We fought for those stars," Bill Robinson said. "Those were precious. If he forgot to give you one, we'd be at his locker saying, 'Willie, I did this' or 'Willie, I did that.' To get those stars from your leader and captain, that was special."[7]

The stars also caught the public's imagination — who couldn't relate to getting a gold star for a job well done?— and along with "We Are Family" only added to the club's growing mystique. Stargell said the idea for the "Stargell Stars" germinated after he had dinner with a friend and his wife who had taken to giving out stickers that looked like roses whenever someone did something that impressed him. Stargell liked the idea and mentioned that he might like to do something like that for his teammates. The friend had a catalog with numerous stickers, and when they came upon the page with a "star" sticker on it, all three of them said, "'That's it!'" Stargell recalled nearly 20 years later. "With my name being Stargell, the star was a natural fit." Stargell said he didn't want to decide who would receive the stars, so — after getting Tanner's permission — he chose to have a different player decide who should get the stars each week. "That way, it wouldn't be that people were getting them just because they were close to me," Stargell said. "The idea just kind of took off, especially when we made it to the World Series."[8]

It wasn't just the fans who got caught up with it; the players were having just as good a time with the '79 club. "Ask anyone who went through the Pirate clubhouse and then played on another club — you never had the fun that you had in the Pirate clubhouse," Kison said. "The clubhouse presence was a form of entertainment in itself." Ott, who started 103 games behind the plate that year, spent seven of his eight big-league seasons in the Pirate clubhouse and said he didn't realize what he had until he finished his career in Anaheim with the California Angels. That was a strong club — in fact, with players like Rod Carew, Freddie Lynn, Don Baylor, Brian Downing, Rick Burleson and Butch Hobson, the Angels might have had more raw ability than the '79 Pirates. "But we went nowhere," Ott said of the '81 Angels, who finished fourth in the first half and sixth in the second half of that strike-truncated season. "Why? We didn't have the unity of saying this is a team effort and we're gonna do things we have to do in order to be successful. That's the difference between the '79 Pirates and the '81 Angels. In '79, we knew what we had to do in order to perform for the best of the team. The California Angels, they wanted to perform the best they could for themselves.

"In '79, the chemistry we had was the most important element. Did we have a good ballclub? Yes. Did we have the best? No. If you matched our starting rotation against Baltimore's, we shouldn't have won a game. And we ended up winning the World Series. And we did it because everyone stayed within himself. Me hitting seventh, I knew what I had to do. Garner at number 8 knew what he had to do. And Stargell at number 4, and so on. We all stayed within ourselves. That came from the camaraderie of the ballclub. I never played with any club that was so close-knit. We respected each other, monitored each other, took care of each other. If Parker made a mistake, someone would go to him at the end of the game and say, 'You gotta do better.' If I had a passed ball that cost us a game, someone would come to me and say, 'You gotta do better.' Today, no one wants to monitor themselves. If one player goes up and says something to someone else, the other guy will want to fight. That's not what it's all about."[9]

Ott said the '79 Pirates had the best of two leadership worlds in Stargell and Parker. "Willie led by example," Ott said. "He very rarely raised his voice or got into confrontations. The other was Parker and they had two very different styles of leading. Willie was a very confident individual. David, in my opinion, was a very insecure person, so he had to be boastful in order for him to perform at the highest level. We had two leaders. When we got into brawls, we took on Parker's attitude. When we really got serious about winning and trying to get the little things done, we took on Willie's personality." Parker certainly appreciated Stargell's example. "He only spoke out when he had to," Parker said. "He was a practical joker — he made the clubhouse fun. I led in a different manner. I was more of a guy who would get 'em up. I was the sergeant at arms. That was my role. I got 'em up by verbalizing, yelling, screaming. Willie held on his own accord. He was a silent leader and when he said something, everybody listened. But we both got the job done."[10]

The two different leadership styles didn't run counter to one another, but rather they seemed to mesh nicely in the clubhouse, particularly in the latter part of the '70s. "People have different personalities and sometimes those personalities fit together," Parker said. "One thing we had jointly — we cared about each other as teammates and people. The '79 team was just that — a family. I don't think you could ever duplicate that feeling, that camaraderie, again. Garner was the clubhouse lawyer — that was his role. He tried to keep stuff going, playing one player off against another. He tried to verbalize — he was one who would challenge me, but I would chop him up every day. And he liked it. He was a masochist. He couldn't verbalize. That was something everyone looked forward to."

The verbal brawling that took place in the clubhouse before games is the stuff of legend. Perhaps the two biggest players, at least in terms of the club-house shenanigans, were Parker and Garner. The two men couldn't have been more different. Parker was a giant, a heavily muscled African American man generously listed at 6-foot-5, 230 pounds, who played high school baseball in Cincinnati. The 5-foot-10, 175-pound Garner, who referred to himself as "a poor white boy," was born in Jefferson City, Tennessee. But when the two verbally squared off in the clubhouse before games, it was sheer magic. Their verbal sparring actually began within minutes of Garner's arrival in spring training in 1977, just after the Pirates acquired him from Oakland in exchange for Giusti, Medich and several prospects. "When I walked into the clubhouse in Bradenton, the first guy I see is Jim Bibby. Then Stargell walks in a little later. Bibby's 6–6, 250 and Stargell's 6–3, 250. Then Parker comes walking in at 6–5. These guys were massive. Parker looks at me and his comment was, 'How could we trade four black guys for one little itty bitty gray boy?' That was the first thing he ever said to me." It wasn't the last time he said it, either. Parker kept harping on Garner about the trade until finally Garner had enough. "I finally turned around and said, 'There's a good reason why they needed a white boy here — we have to have someone to tell you what to do.' Stargell started laughing at that one."

As it turned out, Parker and Garner became good friends, and their needling became part of the routine on the way to a championship two years later. Garner would insist on verbally sparring with Parker, even though he knew he was no match. "Not only was he bigger and stronger physically, but he's very smart and very articulate and you couldn't get the best of him in a verbal battle either," Garner said. "He's just quicker." Parker would often bring up what he believed to be mistreatment that he felt he and other black players were receiving. Garner and others knew that Stargell and other black players of his generation had suffered just as much if not more abuse and racial discrimination, but many of them — Stargell included — opted to internalize those difficulties. "They had to sit in the back of the bus and couldn't go in the same restaurants," Garner said. "Willie couldn't stay in the same hotels or eat in the same restaurants in the minor leagues. He grew up in baseball with that, but he suppressed it. Guys like Stargell and Bibby internalized some of the ugly things that happened."

Parker did not, but the back-and-forth agitation in the clubhouse didn't seem to bother Stargell, and in fact Garner said Stargell encouraged that type of banter. "But he had a way of not letting it escalate into hatred or fighting," Garner said. "That was the real key. That's what happened with that team and why we ended up being so good. The majority of the credit goes to Stargell, and Tanner deserves some, too. It became like group therapy. In any other situation without a guy like Stargell, there would have been a racial tension deal. Black vs. white. That's where it would have gone. Black vs. white. It couldn't have been anything other than that. But Stargell was somehow able to monitor everything. If it went one way or the other too much, he had a great way of bringing it back to the center and putting a little levity in it. He had a great way of diffusing potentially difficult situations with a bit of sly humor. And he included everyone in the deal. He allowed the black guys to get off their chest the anger for the wrongful treatment they had received. But it was also an environment where a white guy could say, 'You've gone too far — I understand, but you've gone too far.' Stargell monitored that group therapy and he was brilliant with it. That's why we called him 'Pops.'"[11]

While Stargell was a presence, not many players targeted him for ribbing. "The only guys who ever said anything to Willie were Parker or Sanguillen," said Don Robinson, a young right-handed pitcher. "Nobody ever got on Willie. And it was never Willie giving it to someone. He'd do it in a different way. He would not yell and scream. He would talk to you in a low manner and make you feel good. Even if you were going bad, he'd try to make you feel good."[12] Garner said Parker would throw a jab or two in Willie's direction. "And now and then we'd try to do it," he said. "But he was held in such high esteem, people didn't go after him very often."

Garner said he considered Stargell a renaissance man; his love of fine wine was just one way that manifested itself. "He was really marvelous. For a young guy like me, relatively new to the big leagues, he had what I would call great elegance. He knew fine restaurants. He had figured out how to live. He put a lot of the ugliness from earlier in his life behind him; he chose to go forward and not look back. If you wanted to talk about ugly things, he could. But he wouldn't do it out of anger — he'd do it in a way that people didn't know any better. It elevated him in my eyes and I think other people might have looked at it that way, too." Garner said that rather than "fire" on the people who mistreated him, Stargell chalked it up to his persecutors not knowing any better. "That elevated him to a higher status," Garner said. "At a time when civil rights was in its infancy and you had the Black Panthers and other groups in the early '70s, with all the anger coming out, Stargell was one of the cooler heads on the planet."

If Stargell had chosen to go the other way and let his anger guide him, Garner said, he could have been just as influential in a negative fashion. Instead, he sang a different tune, one to which Garner could relate despite their obvious racial differences. The reason? Garner felt he, too, had been discriminated against while growing up poor in rural Tennessee — and he claimed that discrimination didn't end, even after he made it to the big leagues. "I couldn't get into some of the more prestigious academic schools because I was a poor white boy from east Tennessee," he said. "Plenty of doors were not open to me, either." Garner also claimed he was "blackballed" from a Pittsburgh country club because of his background. "Who do I blame? It can't be because I'm black. I was a poor white baseball player. I wasn't a doctor or a lawyer."

One of Stargell's great qualities was his desire to include everyone in the act. For example, Garner said Stargell would go out of his way to softly needle Omar Moreno, the ultra-quiet Panamanian centerfielder. "We'd get on the bus going to the ballpark and Willie always had a little something to say to Omar. 'Omar, is your room OK? I don't know if they treat Panamanians well here.' When we'd go into Montreal, we used to drive along the river going out to Olympic Stadium. At one point along the way, there was a pole that stuck out of the river about five feet. It looked like a periscope if you just glanced at it quickly. One day, Willie said, 'Hey Omar, that's a Panamanian submarine over there, trying to attack the United States. Those dirty sons of guns, they're lost.' So every time we'd go to Montreal, we couldn't wait to go on the bus and hear Willie make a comment about the Panamanian submarine that got lost trying to blow up the United States. That's how Willie was."

Stargell didn't just help the regulars; he made sure that the little-used players were a part of the action, even though several Pirates said Tanner had an unwritten rule that young players should only be seen and not heard — unless they were spoken to. "He took the rookies on like they were his own kids," Blyleven said. "I remember one time on a bus, Willie asked Dale Berra if he'd ever eaten a fish called carp and Dale said no. So Willie says, 'Let me tell you how to cook it up. Go down to the lumber store and get this good piece of redwood, two inches high. This carp you're gonna catch is two feet long. Set the oven at 400, then take the carp, clean it up, gut it and everything.' Then he describes all the spices and herbs that Dale is going to put on this piece of redwood with the carp on top. He's going on and on and Dale's sitting there with his mouth open, listening to how he's going to eat this carp. Willie says, 'After you cook it for 20 minutes, you broil it and get it all good and crispy. And then when it's all said and done, Dale, you take it out of the oven, you throw the carp away and eat the redwood.' He had us rolling. It was unbelievable. It was Willie. And his love of life."[13]

Nicosia, who platooned with Ott behind the plate in his first full season in the big leagues in '79, said he had been around Stargell for several years during spring training before he made the big club, and initially he wasn't sure if what he was seeing was real. "When he talked to you, he made you feel special, and it didn't matter if you were the guy emptying the trash or cleaning out the bathrooms or the president of the United States. He greeted you with a smile and treated you with respect. At first, it made you wonder. But the longer you got to know him, the more you realized this was not a façade. This is the real deal. That's how he treated everybody. That's how he became so revered. People just loved the guy."[14]

Stargell's influence was well known throughout the game; former Pirate players who had shared a clubhouse with Stargell told their new teammates and it became common knowledge. Rudy May, who grew up near Stargell's boyhood home in Alameda and worked out with Stargell during the off-seasons before Stargell relocated permanently to Pittsburgh, said he imagined the influence Stargell had on the Pirates was similar to the influence Thurman Munson wielded over the New York Yankees clubhouse. "When I was first traded to the Yankees, it was really weird how Thurman and I bonded," May said. "I was older than Thurman but it wasn't very long before I looked up to him as a leader on the field. So then you start to talk to people in the game — players and coaches — and it starts to get around what a great influence Stargell was in all of his teammates' lives, simply because he took a personal interest in all the guys on the ballclub. The manager has to have a leader in uniform on the field that he can go to to get things done with certain players. And Stargell was that guy. And everyone on every team knew that."[15] Although Stargell certainly was an understanding and sensitive man, Nicosia said the big slugger was not all smiles, handshakes and pats on the back. "A lot of people have asked me about Chuck Tanner and while he was our guy, he didn't have to do a lot of discipline or say much to anybody. If you didn't run a ball out, or if you were out late or not getting the job done on the field, you had to go through Stargell. He didn't say a whole lot, but all he had to do was look at you from his end of the bench and you knew it was time to straighten up. That's the kind of presence he had, both on the field and in the clubhouse. I'll never forget this one day, I was in my second or third year and feeling kind of cocky; I was a big-league veteran. I hit a lazy fly ball and jogged around first base, and then turned and headed back toward the dugout at Three Rivers. And Pops is standing there. All he did was give me that look of his, like he was scolding one of his children. He never said a word. But I knew. That was the last time I ever did it. He would be standing at the dugout waiting for you."

But Stargell would also stand up for the young players if they needed a boost. Nicosia recalled one incident early in spring training during his rookie season when he was catching Dock Ellis during batting practice. Ellis, like all pitchers at that stage of spring training, was throwing nothing but fastballs and after Stargell had touched him for four or five straight homers, Ellis surprised Stargell — and Nicosia — by unleashing a big breaking curve ball, which bounced in the dirt in front of home plate and caught Nicosia in the throat. "Stargell stopped and walked out to the mound, whispered something to Dock and turned around and walked back," Nicosia said. "I didn't know what was going on; I was so embarrassed that I didn't catch the ball and I had this lump in my throat. About an hour after the workout was over, Dock came up to me and apologized — and he didn't apologize to anyone. He said, 'Hey, catch' — he didn't even know my name — 'Sorry — Pop told me what I did out there wasn't cool, so I apologize.' That was the kind of stuff Stargell did. He didn't make a big deal out of it, but here he is, telling a 10-year vet to apologize to a rookie. You had to be around him every day to realize what he meant to everybody."

Stargell's influence wasn't confined to the clubhouse, bus rides to and from ballparks, offering needed direction to young players momentarily losing their focus or arranging for apologies from veteran players to rookies. On the field, he delivered — and did so in a big way in 1979. Even at an advanced age, he continued to be a force at the plate. "He was a tremendous hitter," Parker said of Stargell. "He would have hit .300 every year if he hadn't tried to hit for power. He was maximizing his swing just about every time a run was needed or we were behind. He knew hitting inside and out. His bat speed was tremendous. You could hear his bat go through the air like a broomstick from the on-deck circle." Nicosia said it was most evident from behind the plate. "Nobody else had that swoosh sound coming through the zone. The sound the bat made from his shoulder to meeting the baseball was something else. You could hear the bat go through the zone." Garner said if you walked into a ballpark during batting practice, you'd know when Stargell was hitting in the cage. "There was just a different sound coming from his bat," he said. "A different bat speed. You'd get a louder, better crack of the bat when he hit the ball."

Parker maintains that when he was negotiating his contract before the 1978 season, Pirates management indicated that Stargell — coming off two straight sub-par seasons — might not be part of the plan. "I told them me and Willie had a dream of being in a World Series together. If Willie's not there, I didn't want to be there. We had that kind of relationship. I ended up signing, and he stayed. It was poetic justice. And then in '79 he won the MVP."

It was more than his power and bat speed that continued to make Stargell a dangerous hitter, even at 39. It was his cerebral approach that played a major role in his success. Garner recalled an incident when the Pirates were playing in St. Louis against the Cardinals and Stargell was facing Darold Knowles, who relied more on guile in the form of a changeup and slider than velocity to get hitters out. "They bring Knowles in to face Stargell in the seventh inning with a couple guys on base and Darold strikes him out with a changeup in the dirt. I'm standing there and Willie walks back and calmly puts his helmet in the rack. He says, 'I'll hit that changeup next time. I'll hit it a long way.' Well, it's the ninth inning and Knowles is still in there and Stargell comes up. He throws a slider for strike one, then a fastball, and maybe a ball or two. Then here comes the changeup, six inches off the ground and Stargell hits it through an exit in the upper deck. It was one of the longest ones I've seen. Absolutely mammoth. Sure enough, it was that little changeup and Stargell hit it a mile."

Nicosia remembered a similar episode in '79 when the Pirates were facing the Mets and catcher John Stearns was calling pitches for right-hander Craig Swan. "The first pitch, Swan throws a fastball 88 miles an hour right down the middle and Stargell takes it for strike one," Nicosia said. "Stearns asks him, 'Will, what were you looking for?' and Stargell looks at him and says, 'It was not in my zone.' Next pitch — fastball again, middle of the plate, he takes it for strike two. Stearns asks him, 'Were you looking for something else again?' and Willie says, 'Not in my zone.' He throws a ball, then throws a curve about ready to bounce — a 59-footer. But he's a dead low-ball hitter, down and in. And he golfs it into the upper deck at Shea Stadium. He's rounding the bases and comes down the third base line and says to Stearns, 'Now that one was in my zone.' That's what Stargell would do — he'd look for a certain pitch in a certain zone and that was it."

While the Pirates were fashioning a reputation as a rollicking, rabble-rousing group that knew how to cut up and have a good time, behind it all they were a seriously competitive bunch. Peterson, the general manager, said every player on that team was a fierce competitor. "They hated to lose. But when they did lose, it was still a happy-go-lucky type atmosphere. I think Willie played a part in that. He would say, 'OK, we got beat today but we'll win tomorrow.' It wasn't, 'We got beat today and that'll carry over to tomorrow.' It was, 'This loss was forgotten about and we'll win tomorrow.' It showed in the World Series when we were down three games to one. Baltimore had a good ballclub but the atmosphere around the clubhouse was, 'We're still gonna win this thing.'"[16]

It was a lesson that many Pirate players carried with them after they left the ballclub and went elsewhere. Ott, who stayed in the game and eventually wound up managing a team in the independent Can-Am League in New Jersey, said he attempted to pass that philosophy — the one he learned from Stargell — on to his players. "I tried to get them to understand that at the end of the game, it's over. Once the last out is made, it's history. And you can't do anything about history. You have to look to the future. Put your heads in your lockers for five minutes, go over the things you did right and the things you did wrong. For the things you did wrong, you think about how you can correct them. For the things you did right, you try to remember them. But once you bring your heads out of your lockers, the game is over. If you bring yesterday's game to today, an 0-for-4 can turn into an 0-for-8. Forget it — it's history. It's over and done. That's basically what Willie taught me."

Don Robinson, who won 14 games as a 21-year-old rookie in 1978 and played a key role on the '79 club, said soon after his arrival in Pittsburgh, Stargell sat him down and offered some friendly advice. "He told me if I wanted to stay in the big leagues a long time, I had to be able to accept the failure part of the game. The success part, he said, was easy to accept. But things were gonna happen — you were gonna get whacked and beat up some time. It's how you come back from those failures that determines how long you're going to stay in the big leagues. I spent 15 years in the big leagues. I guess I took what he said to heart because I had never really thought of it that way. Never in my whole career up to that point had I gotten hit very hard. Maybe once or twice. But he was telling me it was gonna happen."[17]

Pirate players to a man say that one of Stargell's greatest attributes was his ability to somehow release pressure that his teammates might be feeling. In Game 1 of the 1979 National League Championship Series against the Reds, Tanner summoned the young Robinson from the bullpen in the bottom of the 11th with runners at first and second and two outs. The Pirates were holding a 5–2 lead that Stargell provided with a three-run homer in the top half of the inning, but Robinson was a bit amped and walked the first batter he faced to load the bases. "I was throwing hard," he said. "Willie came over and said a few words and put a grin on my face and took all the pressure off. After that, I kind of relaxed. This was the most important game of my career and he made me start laughing. I'm sure I'm not the only one." After the game, Stargell was asked what he told Robinson on his visit to the mound. "I asked him if he wanted to play first base and let me pitch," he told the media. "He laughed. He knew I was only kidding him."[18]

While Robinson came up through the Pirate system, Rooker was obtained in a trade in 1972 and recalled that Stargell was one of the first Pirates he met after joining the club. "It didn't take long for Willie to make you feel comfortable, to make you feel like you were part of the team," he said. "You didn't really have to earn your way even though you wanted to prove you belonged there. He wasn't the type of person who made you prove yourself."[19]

When people reflect on the '79 club and the success that it enjoyed and the way it endeared itself to Pirate fans — and baseball fans in general — perhaps the two most enduring figures are Stargell and the club's manager, Tanner. A native of nearby New Castle, Tanner signed as an 18-year-old with the Boston Braves in 1946 and spent nearly a decade in the minor leagues before making his major-league debut in 1955 at the age of 26 with Milwaukee. In that game, he homered in his very first big-league at-bat, against the Cincinnati Reds' Gerry Staley, pinch-hitting for future Hall of Famer Warren Spahn. Tanner's homer tied the game, which the Braves eventually won 4–3. He wound up spending parts of eight seasons in the big leagues and finished with a .261 career batting average. But it was in the dugout where Tanner earned his reputation, managing four clubs over 19 years, including his hometown Pirates for nine of them. Being a Pittsburgh area guy, Tanner was well aware of Stargell when Tanner came over from Oakland to manage the Pirates for the 1977 season. "He was a star," Tanner said of the slugger. "He was a quiet leader. He just went about his job. He was getting older, so I kind of babied him that first year. I didn't want to kill him. I'd just give him days off here, days off there. He had bad knees and I wouldn't overuse him. He never complained. He knew he couldn't be in there every day. His legs wouldn't let him. He was 37 years old."[20]

Stargell had played sparingly in '77 — just 63 games — but Tanner liked what he saw. "I thought he did a good job that year. I was pleased. He made the other players better. They had a chance to watch him play and at the same time they got their rest. Against certain pitchers, I'd play guys they had good luck against. Some of the guys they had problems with, I'd play Stargell. I'd try to pick my spots, not just for Willie, but for Bill Robinson and others. I tried to use their pluses — and I used everybody." And if Stargell wasn't in the regular lineup, he always posed a major threat off the bench as a pinch hitter. Tanner would look for strategic spots to use him; he'd never insert him with first base open, for example, because the opposing pitcher would simply walk Stargell. "I put him in when people had to pitch to him," Tanner said. "But people were afraid of him. They'd even want to walk him with runners at first and second."

While Stargell's playing time was somewhat limited in '77, Tanner found a way to get his bat into 122 games in 1978, and Stargell responded with 28 homers and 97 RBIs. Tanner used a similar approach in '79, as Stargell played in 126 games and produced similar numbers (32 home runs, 82 RBIs). "Down the stretch, I played him every game," Tanner said of Stargell. "He said, 'I feel good.' I said, 'That's all I want to hear — you're in there every day.' And he said, 'I'm ready.' When I played him, he felt strong — he acted like he was 29. He appreciated the way I used him. I really believe that using him the way I did kept him feeling like he was 29, not 39. That's what made him so effective." The two talked often; Tanner wanted to keep his finger on Stargell's playing pulse. "I'd ask him, 'How do you feel today, Willie?' Sometimes he'd say, 'I feel great.' Sometimes he'd say his knee or his back or his shoulder was bothering him and I'd say, 'All right — be ready in case I need you coming off the bench.' We communicated a lot." Tanner obviously appreciated Stargell's leadership qualities, but said it was his ability to produce that was the key. "When the other players see that, it gives them more incentive to do well," he said. "They realize he's busting his tail. Here's a guy 39 years old and he's going out there and winning games for us. Parker was just as important in his own way, though. He was a leader, too — he led us with 95 RBIs and had 25 homers."

It sounds like the hokiest of clichés, but the Pirates truly were a team that season, as Tanner had a wealth of players who could perform at multiple positions — and perform well. Players like Milner and Bill Robinson could play both first base and the outfield; the young Berra provided some middle infield depth, and even Garner saw action at shortstop in addition to second base and third base. Matt Alexander, an outfielder by trade, was used almost exclusively as a pinch runner; he scored more runs (16) and stole as many bases (13) as he had at-bats that year, but he appeared in 44 games. "It was just a well-rounded group," Tanner said of his team. "You know that 'We Are Family' song? That's what we really were. They all fed off one another. But Stargell was the quiet man on top." Tanner did not discourage the "We Are Family" talk. "I loved it. That's what you want — a family. They argued all day in the clubhouse and then went out there like a family and they played to win. That's what we were like."

Tanner was often shown smiling and acting as a benevolent leader when it came to guiding his group, but he said he was hardly a softy. "They'd ask

Parker about me always smiling and Parker would say, 'Don't go in a room with him by yourself because he's the only one who'll come out.' Don't give me that smile shit. Maybe for the news media and the TV reporters. But in my clubhouse, that was my team. And Willie knew. He had a way to get his point across, a way to get to people."

It wasn't so much that Stargell had one way to reach people — he somehow found what made each person tick and could make the connection when needed, Tanner said. "That's what you have to do because everyone's different," Tanner said. "There were a couple of guys I could hammer, some I'd pat on the back and some I wouldn't. Some guys you kick, some guys you hug. He knew stuff about each individual. And to me, that's the key to how you communicate. Take Ed Ott — I could scream at him and get in his face. But Omar Moreno, you could never yell at. It'd break his heart — he'd be afraid to do anything. So I'd hug him."

Tanner said his '79 team had a once-in-a-lifetime personality and it was the club's resilience that separated it from other teams he managed. "We'd be losing by two runs in the sixth inning and Stargell would say, 'They don't even know — they think they're ahead but they're really behind.' We came back 25 times to win that year. We just had that kind of attitude." One of the most amazing comebacks occurred on August 11 against the Phillies at Veterans Stadium. The Pirates trailed 8–0, and Madlock — still relatively new to the club — wondered aloud why Tanner wasn't pulling some of his regulars to give them some much-needed rest. "And Tony Bartirome said, 'The game isn't over yet,'" Tanner recalled. "Stargell's sitting on the top step of the dugout and he says, 'Let's go, men, let's show them what the Buccos are made of.'" The Pirates rallied for five runs in the fifth to make it 8–5, then pushed across four in the seventh to take a 9–8 lead. They nursed that lead for another inning before Ott smashed a grand slam off the Phillies' ace reliever, Tug McGraw, and the Pirates held on for a 14–11 win. Afterward, a bemused Tanner was entertaining questions from disbelieving Philadelphia writers. "How did that happen?" one writer asked. "They just don't give up," Tanner said. "They believe they can win. That's the way they've been since I've been here. I know that people laugh at me. They make fun of me in the papers, and on radio and TV. They laugh. I know that. But that's the way it is."[21]

And when they wrapped up the division title on the season's final day on September 30, the players all celebrated and more than a few tipped their hat to their elder statesman — number 8 — who helped carry them down the stretch. Milner, who played for the '73 Mets team that won the NL title, saw Stargell shed a few tears in the clubhouse after the regular-season finale and was touched. "I watched Willie Mays cry in 1973 and we dedicated the playoffs to him," Milner said amid pouring champagne that followed the regular-season finale, "and I watched Willie Stargell cry today, and we're dedicating these playoffs to him."[22]

The playoffs brought a foe familiar to Stargell and a couple of other Pirate holdovers from the early- to mid-70s teams: the Cincinnati Reds. But unlike 1970, 1972 and 1975, the Pirates had Cincinnati's number — sweeping the Reds out of the playoffs in three games just as Cincinnati had swept the Bucs in 1970 and 1975. In the opener at Cincinnati's Riverfront Stadium, the two teams battled to a 2–2 standoff through 10 innings as Candelaria and Tom Seaver matched wits, but in the 11th, Foli and Parker opened with singles off the Reds' Tom Hume, and Stargell — who lugged a career .220 playoff batting average into the game — followed by hitting the first pitch over the right-center wall for what proved to be the game-winning three-run homer. Tanner was not surprised Stargell came through in the clutch. "This is what he's done for me ever since I've been here," he said later. "Willie's come up with the big hit, time and time again, for us. In my opinion, he's the Most Valuable Player in the National League."[23]

Nine innings weren't enough to settle Game 2, either. Thanks to a couple of timely hits and a strong seven-inning performance from Bibby, the Pirates took a 2–1 lead into the bottom of the ninth behind their ace reliever Tekulve. But with one out, Hector Cruz and Dave Collins smacked back-to-back doubles to tie the game and send it into extra innings. Then, in the 10th, Moreno led off with a single, moved to second on Foli's sacrifice bunt and scored on Parker's base hit, and Don Robinson retired the side in order in the bottom of the inning to send the Pirates back to Pittsburgh with a 2–0 series lead.

No such drama ensued two days later in Pittsburgh in Game 3, thanks in part to Blyleven, who tamed the Reds on eight hits, and Stargell, who hit a solo homer in the third and then cracked a two-run double in the fourth that turned a 4–0 lead into a 6–0 edge that ultimately finished in a 7–1 series-clinching win. However, there were some theatrics, as a group of Pirate wives leaped onto a cement wall behind home plate during the seventh inning stretch and began boogying to "We Are Family." "I thought it was something they deserved," said Stargell, who was named the playoffs Most Valuable Player after hitting a pair of home runs, driving in six runs and posting an NLCS-record 1.182 slugging percentage. "When you've got high-strung athletes around, coming in at all times, they're mother and father most of the time. They deserve as many stars as we get. To look up there and see them letting it go, I was very happy." He was also elated for the win and a ticket to his second World Series — another matchup with the Baltimore Orioles. "If they took a picture of my body," he said, "it would show goosebumps everywhere. The good Lord lets us shed tears at touching moments, and that's what transpired with me. I wish there was a way to thank every fan individually."[24] It took an hour before Stargell was finished with media interviews and then he finally made it into the Pirate clubhouse, where he talked about how proud he was of his teammates — his Fam-A-Lee members. "These guys," he said. "They made it happen."[25]

Stargell told reporters it was the loose clubhouse atmosphere that played a key role in the club's success up to that point. "We feel we can have fun in the clubhouse, and that way there's no way we can wrap ourselves up so tight that we'll go onto the field and do things unnaturally. The Series will be like this. We'll be out there playing good country baseball. Nothing fancy. If we keep that up, we'll give Baltimore a good Series."[26]

But after Game 4 of the Series had ended, it looked like the Pirates had done exactly the opposite. In Game 1, Kison — traditionally a big-game pitcher — surrendered five runs in the first inning and the Orioles held on to win 5–4. The Pirates outhit the O's 11–6, and Baltimore managed just one hit after the second inning. Stargell did his part, driving in a run with an infield out and then hitting a solo homer in the eighth that trimmed the margin to one run, but he also popped out to short left field with Parker on third base and two outs in the top of the ninth inning to end the game. While Kison did not pitch well, he was also betrayed somewhat by his defense. Garner, for example, fielded a potential double-play ground ball with the bases loaded, and threw it — as he said — "like a bar of soap" beyond shortstop Foli and into left field, allowing two runs to score. "The ball was wet and my fingers were numb with cold," Garner told reporters later, referring to the 40-degree game-time temperature, which followed intermittent rain and snow earlier in the day — a continuation of the type of weather that forced Game 1 to be pushed back a day. "I couldn't feel the stitches and get a grip on the ball."[27]

Garner was disconsolate after the game — and it was just the type of situation where Stargell was known to work his attitude adjustment magic. Although he didn't preach to his teammates, he seemed to have a knack for knowing when one of them needed a pick-me-up. Garner needed just that following Game 1. Even 30 years later he believed his throwing error "cost Kison three runs and probably cost us the game. If I make the play, they don't score. So I'm feeling pretty crappy. I sit down on the bus after the game and Willie sits down beside me. I'm looking out the window. He coughs. I turn around and look at him. Now, take your index finger and bend it toward the palm of your hand and stick your knuckle in your nose hole. That's what he was doing. And he says, 'You know, in the '71 World Series, I made an error and I cut my finger off.' He said it with such a deadpan delivery. I started laughing. That's all he did. That's leadership. That wasn't a rah-rah speech. I think there's a subtle way that leaders head off problems. We had players who could be volatile. You didn't know what Parker would say and you didn't know what I would say. But Willie had a way of guiding it into a fun sort of thing. That's how he led. That was his style and how he did it. He did it because he was in close communication with everyone as individuals. He didn't have to stand up and deliver a group thing, although he could speak brilliantly."[28]

Stargell spoke about his approach to Mike Littwin of the *Los Angeles Times* years later. "The game is 85 percent mental. The parts that are physical, everyone has when he comes to the big leagues. But if you're going to make it, you have to be able to live under a microscope. You have to learn to deal with pressure. Maybe that's part of what I do. If I see someone who isn't dealing with the pressure, I try to loosen him up."[29]

Blyleven bounced back to pitch well in Game 2, limiting the Birds to five hits in six innings, and relievers Robinson and Tekulve combined to allow just one hit in the final two frames. The Pirates took a 2–0 lead off Baltimore starter Jim Palmer in the second inning on consecutive singles by Stargell, Milner and Madlock, and Ott's sacrifice fly. Eddie Murray's home run in the bottom of the second cut the margin in half, and his RBI double in the sixth tied the score. Then in the ninth, with two outs and nobody on, Ott singled, moved to second on Garner's walk and scored when the veteran Sanguillen — a key cog in the '71 club that vanquished the Orioles in the Series but now relegated to spot duty — served a soft line drive to right field for a pinch-hit single. Tekulve set the Orioles down in order in the bottom of the inning and the Pirates had evened the series at one game apiece.

The Series shifted to Pittsburgh for Game 3, and after two innings it looked as though the Pirates were off and running, scoring once in the first and twice in the second off Orioles starter Scott McGregor. But the Orioles narrowed the margin to 3–2 in the third off Candelaria and then erupted for five runs in the fourth to take a 7–3 lead on the way to an 8–4 win. The inning was punctuated by an error, a wild pitch, a hit batsman and — as in Game 1— the Pirates' inability to convert a double play. "We're going to have to start playing better baseball," Garner said afterward, "or we're not going to make it back to Baltimore."[30] The frustration continued for Pittsburgh in Game 4. After scoring four runs in the second — one coming on Stargell's solo homer — and then adding single runs in the fifth and sixth, the Pirates appeared on course to even the Series, taking a 6–3 lead into the top of the eighth inning. But a pair of singles and a walk off reliever Robinson loaded the bases and prompted Tanner to call on Tekulve with one out. The submarine-style closer was not up to the task, though, yielding two-run doubles to John Lowenstein and Terry Crowley and then surrendering a base hit to Tim Stoddard and a run-scoring groundout to Al Bumbry, giving the Orioles a 9–6 advantage. The Pirates put a pair of runners on base in the ninth to bring Ott up as the potential tying run, but Stoddard struck him out to end the game and give the Orioles what appeared to be a commanding 3–1 lead.

Afterward, Tanner stood behind his battered closer Tekulve, saying if the same situation presented itself in Game 5, he'd make the same move and bring the reliever — known as Teke — into the game. "Kent saved our life," Tanner said. "He took us to the World Series. But today, he threw a couple of balls that didn't sink. It was as simple as that. But I still think he's the best reliever in baseball." Tekulve, a standup guy, offered no excuses. "I threw the right pitches for the situation but I didn't get the location," he said. "The ball doesn't always do what you want it to do."[31]

Facing elimination at home in Game 5, the Pirates sent the veteran lefty Rooker to the mound to start — this despite the fact that he was just 4–7 with a 4.59 ERA during the regular season. "He's the only guy I can start," Tanner said, noting that Kison — the Game 1 starter — was unable to go because of a tender forearm. Rooker certainly had respect for his opponent. "They've put on a baseball clinic," he said, referring to the Orioles' performance in the Series' first four games, "and we've watched it."[32] Through the first half of Game 5, things did not look good for Pittsburgh, but it was no fault of Rooker's. The 37-year-old started strong, retiring 12 of the first 13 hitters he faced and, heading into the fifth inning, the game was scoreless. But in the fifth, Rooker yielded a double to Gary Roenicke and a single to Doug DeCinces, and when Rich Dauer bounced into a double play, the Orioles took a 1–0 lead. Just as Rooker was sharp early, so was Orioles starter Mike Flanagan, who allowed just two hits through the first four. Then in the sixth, the slumbering Bucco bats finally awakened. A walk to Foli, Parker's single and Bill Robinson's sacrifice left runners at second and third, and Stargell plated the tying run with a sacrifice fly that also moved Parker to third. Madlock then followed with a base hit to drive home the go-ahead run. Pittsburgh added two more runs in the seventh on Foli's triple and a double by Parker and then put the game away with three in the eighth to seal a 7–1 victory. Blyleven, who came on in relief of Rooker in the sixth, was even more effective, limiting the Birds to three hits and no runs in pitching the final four innings. Rooker, who came through with a clutch performance, said the club finally played its game. "The *real* Pirates played today," he said later. "The first four games, we had some no-shows. Today, we rose to the occasion."[33]

Game 6 started out just the way Game 5 did, with neither team able to muster much of an attack, as starters Candelaria and Palmer had their way with the opposing hitters. With the game scoreless through six, the Pirates finally broke through against Palmer with two runs in the seventh. Singles by Moreno and Foli set the stage, and Parker followed with an RBI single. Stargell then contributed a sacrifice fly, and that proved to be all the offense Pittsburgh would need in what ultimately proved to be a 4–0 series-evening victory. Candelaria rebounded from a sub-par Game 3 effort, yielding just six hits and no walks through six innings, and the resilient Tekulve allowed only one base runner in his three-inning save.

The Bucs' second straight win set up a Game 7 showdown between Bibby and Scott McGregor, and brought with it all the drama that usually accompanies a winner-take-all meeting. If that wasn't enough, hanging over Tanner's head was the death of his mother, which occurred the same day Game 5 was played. Baltimore struck first on Dauer's solo homer in the second and the Orioles got into the Pirate bullpen early, as Tanner called on young Don Robinson to start the fifth. He recorded two outs but also allowed a single and a walk, and Tanner then summoned Grant Jackson from the pen, and the veteran lefty escaped with no further damage. Then in the sixth, the tide turned for Pittsburgh. With one out, Bill Robinson singled to left and on the first pitch, Stargell took McGregor deep and beyond the right-field wall for a two-run homer for what proved to be the deciding runs. Stargell said later that McGregor threw him a breaking ball. "I didn't want to commit myself on the pitch too soon. I was out in front of it, but I got the bat speed I wanted. At first, I didn't think it would travel that far. When it did, I was just thrilled."[34] McGregor tipped his hat to the Pirates' slugger afterward. "Mr. Stargell is an amazing man," he said. "He must be 50 years old, but God bless him, he's just a fantastic hitter."[35]

Jackson worked into the eighth before yielding a pair of walks and giving way to Tekulve with one out. Stargell came in from first base to offer a few words of encouragement. "I said, 'Teke, show how you are the best reliever there is,'" Stargell said after the game. "'And if you can't, you play first base and I'll pitch.'"[36] Tekulve induced Terry Crowley to ground out, then intentionally walked Ken Singleton to load the bases before retiring Murray on a deep fly ball to right field, preserving the 2–1 lead. In the top of the ninth, the Pirates added some insurance as Garner—who doubled to lead off the inning—scored on Moreno's base hit, and Moreno came around to score when Bill Robinson was hit by a pitch with the bases loaded. Then in the bottom of the ninth, Tekulve mowed the Orioles down, striking out Roenicke and DeCinces swinging on seven pitches combined and then getting pinch-hitter Pat Kelly to fly out to Moreno in center on the first pitch.

On the day that Mother Teresa of Calcutta won the Nobel Peace Prize for her tireless work with the poorest of the poor, the Pirates were champions again — becoming only the fourth team in World Series history to erase a 3–1 deficit and win a title. Stargell was brought to an interview room between the two clubhouses, where he answered questions from the media. While he was talking on a wooden platform, his sister, Sandrus Collier, made her way into the room, and Stargell spotted her sitting there. "There will be a short pause," he said and then brother and sister embraced, and all the memories of Willie's childhood came roaring back. He could not control his emotions and as he continued to embrace his sister, the tears came pouring out. He reached for the towel around his neck to wipe away the tears. "We've been together a long time and it's been hell, but...."[37] The embrace earned applause from the reporters who remained in the room. Later in the clubhouse, Sandrus answered a few questions as well. "Ever since I was a little girl, I always loved my brother," she said. "Our whole family loves him — whether he ever hits another home run or not."[38]

For Collier, the moment was a dream come true. She had moved to Pittsburgh the year before to help Stargell with his sickle cell anemia foundation and so she was on hand for the entire "We Are Family" magic that culminated with that moment in the clubhouse following the seventh game. Collier, like other family members, was ushered into a room while the clubhouse celebration commenced, but she went looking for Willie. She found a room and a man at the door told her she could not enter. "I said, 'I don't care,'" she recalled 31 years later. 'How many people have a brother who just became the MVP of the World Series?' He said, 'OK.'"[39] So Collier made her way into the interview room and embraced her big brother. "I was very proud of him," she said. "He had come a long way to reach that point where he was in his life and I was really happy that he had finally gotten some recognition. I always felt he was such a good baseball player. People used to talk about his strikeouts, that he was such a strikeout king. But it was nice to hear people in the stadium cheering for him. And when we got back to Pittsburgh, the people in his hometown went literally crazy."

Before Stargell left the interview room on that victorious night in Baltimore, a reporter asked him if he ever had a moment in baseball that was more satisfying than his triumphant effort in Game 7. "One other time," he said. "When the Pirates signed me in 1959, they gave me a $1,500 bonus and $175 a month. I was elated then. But then and now ... it's hard to find the words to say how I feel."[40]

Stargell was named the series Most Valuable Player after hitting .400 with three home runs and seven RBIs in the seven games. He also set a series record for most extra-base hits with seven — three homers and four doubles — and finished with 25 total bases, which tied Reggie Jackson's mark set in 1977. In the seventh game alone, he had four hits — two doubles and a single to go with his game- and series-deciding home run. None of his teammates were surprised. "He is," Garner said, "a thoroughbred junkyard dog."[41] In addition to celebrating with real family members, Stargell defended the importance of the family-like atmosphere that the ballclub had cultivated all season long — something that several Baltimore media members had questioned earlier in the series. "Someone asked me if The Family was overrated," Stargell said afterward. "That bothered me, because this person didn't live with us and didn't see how much we depended on each other. There's really no words to put into the way I feel. We had to scratch, we had to crawl and we did it together because we are family. We didn't mean to be sassy or fancy, but we felt the song typified our ballclub."[42]

Although beat writers have a tendency to be somewhat cynical at times, Donovan said the "We Are Family" theme was legitimate and Stargell took the song's lyrics to heart. "That was all him," he said. "The words reflected how people from different backgrounds all came together with the Pirates — and they worked together. That team made a lot of moves and had lots of people playing roles, but they all seemed to get along. It wasn't fake or anything." The close-knit attitude paid off when the team was staring at a three-games-to-one deficit; no finger pointing ensued but rather a determination to start playing Pirate baseball and chip away at that deficit, one game at a time. "When we were down and had to win the last three, Joe Safety, our PR guy, walks past Garner and Garner says, 'What the hell's wrong with you?'" Tanner recalled 31 years later. "And Joe says, 'Well, you know...' Garner says, 'Don't worry — we got 'em right where we want 'em.' So we beat 'em that day and then went down there and won the last two and we're world champs." Donovan recalled seeing Stargell exude the same attitude with the Pirates facing elimination. "He acted as if it was just a game," he said. "He'd be asking, 'Who's tight back there?' and then they'd end up joking with one another. That was his way of saying, 'There's nothing to be nervous about. Just go out and play the game and things will work out the way they work out,'" Donovan said.

Amid the pandemonium of the clubhouse, Stargell recalled a former teammate, one who had set the tone for a previous Pirate championship team eight years earlier. "I thought 1971 was Roberto Clemente's moment of glory," he said. "He had started something with his winning, driving attitude. Whatever contribution I've made has been merely an extension of what he started."[43]

The next day, some 25,000 fans packed Market Square in downtown

Pittsburgh to pay tribute to the new champions. Stargell had to wipe tears away from his eyes before he addressed the crowd. "The greatest thing we can do, is this winter when we're all traveling, to say, 'We are from a city that has nothing but champions.' You people are just as responsible for our winning as we are. We really are a big family. I can't think of another place I want to bring my kids up in."[44]

CHAPTER 7

Twilight Time

STARGELL'S PERFORMANCE IN the '79 World Series vaulted him into national prominence, just as Clemente's did eight years earlier and it didn't take long for the networks and other major media to pounce. Although Stargell talked shortly after Game 7 ended about wanting to get away for a bit, he appeared on two network morning television shows in the days following the series, set up a visit to Merv Griffin's talk show and lined up a 13-city tour sponsored by Gordon's Dry Gin Company to increase awareness about sickle cell anemia. The tour was due to start November 4 and conclude December 7 and take Stargell to Boston, Portland, Los Angeles, Atlanta, Miami and Washington, D.C. In addition to paying for the tour, Gordon's donated $10,000 to the Willie Stargell Foundation — the successor to the Black Athletes Foundation.

He also made it to New York in late October to collect the World Series Most Valuable Player award — a silver Corvette, courtesy of *Sport* magazine. There, he signed scores of autographs, picked up a gold record album that a Sister Sledge representative provided him — commemorating the million-records-sold mark of "We Are Family"— and met with the media, using the opportunity to get a jump on his sickle cell awareness campaign. "Sickle cell hasn't received the attention other diseases have," he said. "People are being crippled, others are dying. We're trying to get a message out here." He spoke on a variety of other topics while in New York, including his adopted home town. "I complain about the potholes and shoveling the snow, too," he said, "but when I come through that Fort Pitt Tunnel, especially after being away for a long time, it means a whole lot to me." He spoke about the future, saying he'd like to work with younger players, "being able to help them over some hurdles I've seen." And he shared his personal philosophy. "Blacks and whites came together on our club and we sacrificed. I can't see why men can't work together like that everywhere in the world."[1]

139

Two days after the *Sport* magazine appearance, he was introduced as a new executive with the Sperry-Remington Company, promoting a new electric shaver. In fact, as he stood at the microphone at the "21" Club, he pulled an electric razor from his pocket and shaved off a three-day growth of beard, triggering a chorus of laughs and applause from the packed house. Stargell talked about his long wait to be discovered by Madison Avenue, saying that he wasn't bitter about the fact that businesses were reluctant to provide blacks the same opportunities as whites. "I would never tell anyone how to spend their money," he said. "But at the same time, I'm extremely happy to be one of the first blacks who will participate in the growth of a company." Howard Cosell — perhaps the top sportscaster in the nation at the time and never one to mince words — told the audience that it was a crime black athletes hadn't had the same commercial opportunities as white athletes. "This chance has come Willie's way because he now is a superstar — the World Series made him a star for the whole country to see," Cosell said. "And it's a crime black people have had to wait so long. To me, Willie Stargell is transcendental to the role of merely an excellent athlete and has brought dignity to the sport he represents."[2]

From New York, it was on to Buffalo for another business meeting and dinner speech. Then to Chicago for more of the same, followed by a trip to Las Vegas to take care of still more dinner and business engagements. And that was followed by a visit to Los Angeles and then a stop in San Diego to volunteer some time at Bob Skinner's baseball camp. The camp visit was completely in character; in addition to his work for the sickle cell anemia cause, he was active in a program in Pittsburgh aimed at helping juvenile criminals and drug abusers and served on boards for the local United Way, Boy Scouts of America and a Public Broadcasting Service television station.

His volunteer work did not begin after his coming-out party in the 1979 World Series; he had been involved in the sickle cell anemia fight for years and had worked during the off-season with various programs aimed at helping underprivileged youth in Pittsburgh. His work did not go unrecognized; he was given the Brian Piccolo YMCA Award for Humanitarian Services in Los Angeles in January 1977. Three years earlier, he received Phi Delta Theta's Lou Gehrig Award, and that same year he was named recipient of the Roberto Clemente Award, presented to the major league baseball player who best exemplifies the game of baseball on and off the field. In 1978, he was voted the Hutch Award winner, named in honor of former Cincinnati Reds manager Fred Hutchinson, who died of cancer.

In addition to taking home the World Series MVP award, Stargell finally earned a piece of the National League's Most Valuable Player award in 1979, as he shared the prize with fellow first baseman Keith Hernandez of the St. Louis Cardinals. He had finished second twice before — to Joe Torre in 1971 and Pete Rose in 1973. The tie was the first in the 49-year history of the MVP award. Hernandez, who was named on every ballot, batted .344 with 11 home runs and 105 RBIs for the third-place Cardinals, who finished 12 games behind the Pirates in the NL East. Stargell, who hit .281 with 32 homers and 82 RBIs for the world champion Pirates, received 10 first-place votes to four for Hernandez. But four writers left Stargell completely off their ballots. All four of them — Mike Littwin of the *Los Angeles Times*, Kenny Hand of the *Houston Post*, Tim Tucker of the *Atlanta Journal* and Harry Shattuck of the *Houston Chronicle*— defended their action, saying others were more deserving of the award, and that included some of Stargell's Pirates teammates. "I thought Kent Tekulve was the most valuable player on the Pirates because they came around when he came around," Littwin said. He also said he voted for who he thought were the 10 best players in the league and he didn't think Stargell was one of them. Hand said Stargell had a good year "but there were other guys more valuable to their teams than Stargell over the whole season." In fact, Hand said, Parker — who finished 10th in the voting — was the Pirates' MVP. Tucker, meanwhile, felt the speedy Moreno — the catalyst at the top of the lineup — was the Bucs' MVP, "and if you think Moreno is the most valuable player, then you can't vote for Stargell as Most Valuable Player. Without Moreno, the Pirates never would have won their division."[3] Stargell said he did not want to get into any negative discussion when asked about the four writers who left him off their ballots.[4] Instead, he reacted to the voting in his typical classy manner. "A taste of honey is better than none," he said before defending the four writers who chose to leave him off their ballots. He said he figured the award would go to someone who played every day or nearly every day, pointing out that he and Tanner had judiciously picked his spots and as a result he played in just 126 games. Since he had finished second twice before when he figured he might win, he said he wasn't getting his hopes up for this particular season but he certainly appreciated it. "I'm pleased with the award, don't get me wrong," he said, "but I wasn't revved up about it."[5]

It wouldn't be Stargell's last award that off-season. *Sports Illustrated* selected Stargell and another of Pittsburgh's star athletes — Steelers quarterback Terry Bradshaw — as co–Sportsman of the Year. It was a choice that made all Pittsburghers proud, including one of Bradshaw's high-profile teammates. "That was so exciting," former Steeler running back Franco Harris said in an interview in 2011. "Talk about the City of Champions — that really solidified that. The championships that we won during the 1970s really started a whole new era in Pittsburgh sports that still continues today. And there's no doubt that Willie's spirit is a big part of that. He definitely had an impact on our city, on the culture and the personality of our city. And he will always be remembered." Harris, who joined the Steelers in 1972 as a highly touted running back from Penn State, said he spoke with Stargell from time to time during his stay in Pittsburgh, which ended after the 1983 season. "I didn't have the opportunity to spend a lot of time with Willie, but I always enjoyed the time that we were together. He was a very insightful person about so many things. And it was always interesting to talk with him. When I first came into the city, I would tell people I really had some great role models to look up to that really helped set the stage for myself. And Willie was definitely one of the people that had a great influence on me and my community involvement. It was what he did and also in what he said. One of the things he told me was, 'You know what, Franco? Wherever you go, in whatever your actions are, always picture your little brother by your side. And do the things that you would do with your little brother by your side. I think that's a very good principle and I use that in talking with athletes today.'"⁶

Stargell also was named the Dapper Dan Man of the Year for 1979 — the award is considered the city of Pittsburgh's most prestigious sports award. "I'm going to need another house to keep all these awards in," Stargell said — and that was before he collected the *Sports Illustrated* and Dapper Dan honors.⁷ In addition to the awards and the travel to spread the word about sickle cell anemia, Stargell also squeezed in a trip to Hawaii with his teammates, members of the Baltimore Orioles and the NFL's top two teams — the Steelers and the Los Angeles Rams — to film an ABC television show known as "Superteams." Players competed against one another in a series of athletic competitions; the show was a spinoff from the original "Superstars" series, which pitted individual athletes from various sports against one another.

The winter eventually gave way to spring, and Stargell joined his defending world champion teammates in Bradenton to prepare for another season. While Stargell found his off-season exploits "exhilarating," he also conceded that the constant activity left him worn down — and that was before the season even started. The interview requests in spring training became so numerous that he took to writing stock answers to questions that he knew he'd be asked — and posted the answers at his locker. Still, he managed to get off to a fine start. After his first 34 games of the season, through June 13, the reigning league co–MVP was batting .310, with nine home runs and 31 RBIs in 113 at-bats. But he did not homer again that month and drove in just three runs during that stretch, while his average plummeted to .255. A pulled hamstring on June 19 was the main culprit, and the injury restricted him to mostly pinch-hitting for nearly a month. Ultimately, he wound up on the disabled list and

Willie receives congratulations from an adoring Three Rivers Stadium crowd during the first of two days honoring him — this one on July 20, 1980 (courtesy Pittsburgh Pirates).

did not appear in a game from July 7 through the end of the month. In the midst of that stretch, he was saluted in the first of two Willie Stargell Days — this one on July 20 at Three Rivers Stadium against the Los Angeles Dodgers. He was showered with gifts and well-wishes in an emotional ceremony. He cried when his teammates came out in a group to honor him and when the Dodgers players lined up to shake his hand. The ceremony was punctuated by an unforgettable scene — Stargell's father, William, being brought out onto the field in a wheelchair, and father and son exchanging a long, tearful hug. Stargell broke down while trying to speak and sobbed, "I'm doing the best I can."[8]

Stargell used the opportunity to publicize his foundation's fundraising efforts in the area of sickle cell anemia. A committee of the slugger's friends established a goal of raising $500,000 for the foundation, and the group commissioned artist Leroy Neiman to do an oil painting of Stargell and produce 300 serigraph prints, each of which would be sold for $2,500. Stargell had high hopes for the project and planned to use the proceeds to buy an existing

Pittsburgh Pirates broadcaster Lanny Frattare addresses a packed Three Rivers Stadium crowd that turned out to honor Willie on July 20, 1980. On hand to share in the moment were members of Willie's family and several Pittsburgh luminaries, including Steelers' great Franco Harris (third from left) (courtesy Pittsburgh Pirates).

building that would serve as the foundation's home. "I think we need a permanent place with the right amount of footage," he said.[9]

Ironically, on the day that Pirates fans saluted Stargell, one of them used the occasion to fire a two-inch, nine-volt radio battery in the direction of his teammate, Parker. The battery missed Parker and bounced some 200 feet off the Three Rivers Stadium artificial turf. This was not an isolated incident; during the home opener in April, someone threw a bag of tightly wrapped nuts and bolts at Parker, who was earning a reported $1 million annual salary. "I could hear it go by me," Parker said later of the battery. "It was too close for comfort." Parker was removed from the game and GM Peterson warned the fans that if a similar event occurred again, he'd take his team off the field and forfeit the game. "The Pirate management is sick and tired of these acts, admittedly performed by a handful of our spectators," Peterson said in a statement.[10]

The day honoring Stargell prompted him to look ahead just slightly, although as he put it, "I don't like to plan my destiny. There's so much that can happen. I don't want to hope that I can go out hitting a home run to win a ballgame, because when you plan something like that, all you do is disappoint yourself."[11] But, he said, when his playing days ended he wanted to stay in the game. Specifically, he said he wanted to work as a special front-office assistant, with an emphasis on tutoring the younger talent in an organization. He envisioned spending time as a traveling instructor in the minor leagues, working in both the fall instructional and winter leagues and also spending 40 to 50 days a year with the major league team. But he still had a ways to go as a player. He appeared in 17 games in the month of August, but he injured his left knee while diving to stop a line drive off the bat of the Mets' Steve Henderson on August 12, an injury that forced him back on the disabled list later in the month and ultimately resulted in arthroscopic knee surgery that put him out for the year. The Pirates, meanwhile, finished the 1980 season a disappointing 83–79 and in third place in the NL East — a far cry from the glorious '79 campaign.

The injury issues, combined with Stargell's advancing age, prompted questions about how much longer the veteran first baseman would continue playing. He insisted he was coming back in 1981, although he admitted he had thought about retirement. "It would be a grave injustice for me to go out there for selfish reasons, knowing there are certain things I couldn't do," he said in September. "But I'm just going to let it lie. When the time comes, I'll know it. The worst thing in the world is to have someone else tell you."[12] Tanner thought Stargell had something left in the tank because even at age 40, he managed to hit 11 home runs and drive in 38 in 202 at-bats. "That's what I wanted," Tanner said. "I got everything out of him I could. I played Bill Robinson and John Milner more, but Willie was just as valuable then as anytime he was with us, because of the way I used him. And the way he talked to players, communicated with younger guys that we brought along. He was not only a team leader, but he was a force because he could do one thing. You put him up there, baby, and he produced. That's what good leaders do. You can't have a guy hitting .180 and saying, 'I'm your leader.' Show me you're my leader — go out there and do something. Guys talk about being a leader but they don't produce. They don't show you."[13]

Members of the local media, who had an opportunity to watch Stargell on a daily basis — some of them for years, said there was no denying his leadership attributes. Sam Nover, who came to Pittsburgh in 1970, left in 1980 for a couple of years but returned in 1983 and stayed until 2001, said a lot of Stargell's success as a leader stemmed simply from his love for the game and placing it in the proper perspective. "Knowing its importance, and knowing the value of winning," he said. "Leadership qualities are so hard to identify.

They're a compilation of everything you do. He was a great player. He always had good common sense, so he was a guy that other guys could go to if they had a problem. And he had that infectious personality, that laugh that was infectious. He was always smiling. You want to be around those kinds of people."[14] As Pirates reliever Grant (Buck) Jackson put it, "If people love you, they seem to follow you. If they don't love you, they go the other way. That's what leadership is all about."[15]

Smizik, another Pittsburgh media member, said Stargell simply was a natural leader, just as Clemente was — and neither sought the role. Clemente, Smizik said, didn't reach for the reins of leadership and if anything, he pushed them away. "But they naturally fell to him. He was around a long time before he became a leader. Willie didn't push it away, but he didn't reach for it. It just sort of fell to him by his welcoming behavior and his kindness to people. And he just seemed to absorb it."[16] His kindness even extended to players on the opposing teams, said Dan Donovan, a former beat writer with the *Pittsburgh Press*. "It was very communal, and players would talk to him before and after games," Donovan said. "He'd be giving fatherly advice to other players." But it was in Stargell's own clubhouse where the respect was most evident. Greg Brown, the intern-turned-broadcaster, said the respect that Stargell received from his teammates "certainly was palpable without a doubt. You could see it in everything that the players did. He was the leader. I chuckle when people talk about guys in the clubhouse today who are so-called leaders. No one compared to Stargell. They truly loved him and respected him, and he worked hard on the field and did all the right things. But he couldn't have been a leader if he hadn't succeeded on the field. You can talk all you want, but you have to back it up. He came through in the clutch time and time again. He put that team on his shoulders and carried them."[17]

But his carrying days were dwindling. When the club gathered in Bradenton in late February 1981, Stargell was there. But it didn't take long for his aging body to suffer another setback, as he injured his left knee when he stepped in a hole while jogging on the beach. The injury came on the first day of the team's full-squad practice and forced him to miss several days of workouts. But Dr. Thomas Sprenger put Stargell's mind at ease when he told him the injury was not related to the surgery that Stargell had the previous season. Still, those close to the ballclub began to wonder just how much Stargell had left. "Last season he had arthritis in his ankle, a bruised thumb, a bad hamstring pull and his knee injury," Donovan wrote in the *Pittsburgh Press*. "Willie Stargell doesn't look fragile, but he is. And with him, so are the Pirates."[18]

Stargell's problems were not limited to physical ones. In early April, the *Post-Gazette* reported that the slugger and his second wife, Dolores, had separated — and in fact had separated late in the 1980 season. According to the story, Dolores was living in the couple's Point Breeze home with their two children while Stargell moved into another home nearby. "I try to protect my family as much as I can," Stargell said on April 10 in explaining why he was reluctant to comment on the separation. Dolores Stargell would not say whether the couple planned to be divorced. "We don't discuss our personal life with anyone," she said.[19]

Stargell wasn't 100 percent healthy when the season started, which meant the newly acquired Jason Thompson would start at first base. The Bucs had two other new starters in catcher Tony Pena and second baseman Berra, with the latter filling in for the injured Garner, who was coming off shoulder surgery. Stargell had just one at-bat in each of his first seven appearances through May 3, netting just one hit. Then, on May 7, he finally played nine innings in his eighth game — the team's 20th — and went 1-for-4. He had only 13 more at-bats the rest of the month, but made four straight starts at the beginning of June, only to see his season — and everyone else's — shut down on June 12 with a player strike. The work stoppage resulted in the loss of more than 700 games — or more than one-third of the season — and play did not resume until August 10. The layoff did not improve Stargell's health; he was bothered by a sore shoulder in early August, after the strike was settled but before the season continued. Then, after going 0-for-3 against Montreal in the first game after the strike, he was out of the lineup the following night with a bruised heel, which he hurt when he broke from the batter's box in his second post-strike at-bat. Stargell said that while his surgically repaired knee was not bothering him, it essentially was to blame for his other two injuries because he believed he altered his throwing motion and stretching regimen to compensate for the fact that the knee was not 100 percent. Stargell was convinced his season was not over, though. "I feel good," he said, although he acknowledged the heel bruise was painful. "I'm going to think that way until proven otherwise."[20]

He returned to the active roster on August 26, but did not start another game and appeared in only 15 games the rest of the season. He managed just 13 at-bats during that stretch and collected only four hits for the Pirates, who finished 46–56 overall — fourth in the first half and sixth in the second half of the strike-shortened season. Overall on the year, Stargell managed just 60 at-bats and batted .283 with nine RBIs. Also, he failed to homer for the first time since he was called up to the big leagues at the end of the 1962 season. Late in the season, speculation grew as to whether Stargell would retire, and that speculation reached its high point in the final week of September, with published reports that indicated he likely would not be back. According to a wire service report published in the *Pittsburgh Post-Gazette* on September 23, Stargell was asked in an ESPN interview if he expected to retire and he responded, "I'd have to say so, yeah, without being pessimistic or unrealistic. There's no question I will be 41, and it's highly unlikely that the ligaments in my knees will take away the bone-on-bone situation. I have a knee that is literally rubbing bone on bone. Right now, it would be very hard for me to play."[21] But the next day, he told reporters the report was premature and that it was based on an interview that was done in May, when his knees were in much worse shape. "It's a shame that something like this can happen," he said of the retirement report. "There was no mention that the tape was made in May, when my knees were aching. Since then, there has been a turn of events. I still might play next year. I'd still like to hit 500 home runs." Tanner was all in favor, saying that while Stargell no longer could play every day, he still had a quick bat and could be effective if he stayed healthy.[22]

He made it official in December, saying he wanted to play one more season without any interruptions. "I'm healthy and I'm looking forward to another spring training and a better year all the way around," he said. Peterson, the club's executive vice president, said he welcomed Stargell's decision. "He still swings the bat as well as ever," Peterson said, "and he contributes so many ways to the team that he is still a very valuable player."[23]

Stargell reported to spring training and proceeded to hit as if he were 15 years younger. He batted nearly .400 in Grapefruit League play but had accepted the fact that he would be backing up Thompson, the Bucs' everyday first baseman, and serve primarily as a pinch-hitter deluxe — a major power threat off the bench. That's exactly the role that he would play during the 1982 campaign, as he appeared in less than half of the Pirates' games — 74 — and had just 85 plate appearances. He hit .233 for his final season in the big leagues, with three home runs and 17 RBIs. He started only four games and had more than one plate appearance just four times in a game all season. Stargell admitted that adapting to the pinch-hitting role was a difficult and sometimes frustrating experience — largely because of his tendency to use earlier at-bats in a game to set up a pitcher for a third or fourth at-bat. "I had to get used to the fact that I was only batting once," he said. "I said I wanted to be a ballplayer this year, and I had to accept what that meant."[24]

The 475th and final big fly of Stargell's career came on July 21, and Tom Hume was the victim. This time, Stargell delivered while pinch-hitting for Larry McWilliams in the top of the eighth inning in what would be the slugger's last appearance at Cincinnati's Riverfront Stadium. Many in the crowd of 16,543 had stood and applauded as Stargell got ready to hit, showing their respect to a longtime visiting adversary who was making his final appearance in their home park. The shot, which tied Stargell with Stan Musial for 14th place on the all-time home run list — came with the score tied at 2–2 and proved to be the margin of victory in a 3–2 triumph. "Musial? I never thought I'd ever be in his company," Stargell said after the game, noting that the former Cardinals great was one of his idols. As Stargell remained on the field conducting an interview with Cincinnati media members, one fan shouted, "Thanks for a great 21 years, Willie." "It's heartwarming hearing something like that," Stargell said.[25]

The home run also tied Stargell for the most pinch-hit blasts in a season with three. "Willie did it in half a season," Skinner, the Pirates' hitting coach, noted. "He has more in his bag."[26] But there would be no more homers for the man who hit more than anyone in the history of the Pirates franchise. From that point on, Stargell would come to the plate 30 times and collect seven hits while driving in six runs. The Pirates honored him on September 6 in an hour-long pre-game ceremony that included an on-field phone call from President Ronald Reagan, who was in Santa Barbara, California. "You are one of the heroes who has made baseball great," Reagan told Stargell. "God bless you. Now get out there and play ball, you're not retired yet." On the field, Stargell thanked virtually everyone and called the day "without a doubt, my finest hour." Wiping away tears with a towel draped around his neck, he gave a special shout-out to those sitting in the highest reaches of the stadium. "If there's anybody from the projects sitting up there, here's living proof ... with hard work, determination and dedication, you can make a great indentation on the world." In a pre-ceremony press conference, he told the media he wouldn't have any trouble retiring. "It's getting harder and harder just to get up to the field," he said.[27]

The Pirates released a letter that Stargell had written to the fans — whom he addressed as "dear friend"— and in it he thanked the fans for their support, particularly when his now estranged wife, Dolores, was being treated for her stroke. "There was never any pressure placed upon me to hit a lot of home runs or drive in hundreds of runs," he wrote. "People were very supportive, and this is something which I will always remember. Over the course of my career, I probably could have hit more home runs or collected more RBIs, but from a humanistic standpoint, I could never feel better about my association with the people here in this city." He talked about what it was like to play in Pittsburgh. "I am sure that I am not the only athlete or person to come to this city trying to do their best who was made to feel like he really belonged. There is no greater thrill than to come through the Fort Pitt Tunnel, especially at night, and see the beauty of this city. It's a tremendous thrill, almost like a pair of arms embracing you. That is the way I have been made to feel in Pittsburgh."[28]

Willie's stepfather, Percy Russell, and his mother, Gladys, enjoy a light moment at a family function (courtesy Sandrus Collier).

Stan Savran, who has been involved in Pittsburgh sports journalism since the mid–1970s, said Stargell's legacy as one of Pittsburgh's greatest sports figures was "well-earned. And I got that from talking to other members of that team — guys I really respected, like Phil Garner and Jim Rooker and Kent Tekulve. They would know a whole lot better than I would. They absolutely said that he led that team." Savran said what separated Stargell from many Pittsburgh sports figures is that he understood the city and its people — black and white — so well. "Willie had a great understanding of the human condition," he said. "I think he understood race relations and what kind of town Pittsburgh was. And I do think he had a genuine understanding of the fact that this is a unique town. It's different. People might think they understand it but Willie definitely had a full understanding. And that's why he was larger than life here in Pittsburgh. Pittsburghers understand when you're one of them. They understand when you get it. If you don't get it, you're never gonna get it. They might like you, but they will never embrace you. My best take on Willie is that he got it — he understood Pittsburgh and therefore the people of Pittsburgh embraced him. Not every star gets that kind of treatment here."[29]

Willie and his mother, Gladys Russell, enjoy a moment together (courtesy Sandrus Collier).

On the field before that game on September 6, he shook hands with members of the Pirates and the visiting New York Mets, and then with two outs in the eighth inning, Tanner pulled Tony Pena from the on-deck circle and sent Stargell out to pinch hit. He took a pair of pitches, then stroked a single to right-center and was replaced by pinch-runner Rafael Belliard after reaching first base. Afterward, he was too emotionally drained to talk to some reporters. "Please wait until tomorrow," he said. "I'm just...."[30] During the last two months of his final season, Stargell made just two starts, one coming in the Pirates' final game of the season on October 3 against Montreal in Three Rivers Stadium. On that day — Stargell's last as a big-leaguer — Tanner penciled the slugger in to bat leadoff against the Expos' Steve Rogers. Stargell reached on an infield single — the last of his 2,232 career hits — in the bottom of the first when his comebacker eluded Rogers and neither middle infielder could make a play on it. With Moreno batting, Stargell took off for second and continued to third when Moreno singled. He then was replaced by pinch-runner Doug Frobel. The crowd of 14,948 roared and coaxed Stargell out of the dugout for a curtain call while organist Vince Lascheid played "Pomp and Circumstance." He blew two kisses to the crowd, and in a matter of a few hours,

Stargell's playing career was history. Twenty-one seasons, 2,360 games, 475 home runs, 1,540 RBIs. At the time of his retirement, he held several Pirate career records, including most home runs, most RBIs, most extra-base hits (953) and most strikeouts — his 1,936 were second only to Reggie Jackson at the time — and a handful of single-season records, including most extra-base hits with 90. He finished his career with a solid .282 batting average to go along with his eye-popping power numbers.

His manager, Tanner, had a difficult time acknowledging that the slugger was finished. "I was thinking about Willie ... it's his last game ... it's hard," he said later. "There were a few tears on the bench when he came out of the game." Teammates, coaches and opponents alike had nothing but good things to say. Team president Dan Galbreath remarked, "It's the end of an era. What he has accomplished, what he has meant to the team, is hard to put into words."[31]

Where Stargell would go from here and what he would do wasn't exactly clear. The player known affectionately as Pops was old in baseball terms, but at 41, he figured to have many more years ahead of him. He had talked about staying in Pittsburgh and not making a sudden and complete break from baseball, but rather gradually weaning himself away from it. But on his final day, he wasn't saying. Stargell, clearly spent in terms of answering questions from the media, summed it all up in a pregame press conference: "What can be said that hasn't been said?"[32]

Although Stargell certainly was a megastar within the Pirates organization, he never forgot those in less glamorous positions. Following his retirement as an active player, he made it a point to have his picture taken individually with everyone in the organization — clubhouse folks, secretaries, accountants, broadcasters — and then had individual plaques made for each employee. Each one came with a personalized message. "That said volumes about the kind of person he was," said Lanny Frattare, who broadcast Pirate games from 1976 through 2008. Greg Brown also received one of the plaques and considers it a prized possession. "My message reads, 'Greg, every time I see you, you're doing something for someone. That tells me therein lies a peace for giving.' I remember that like it was yesterday. You could walk into anyone's office or home today who was working for the Pirates then and they'll have that photo prominently displayed. That's how much it means to people."

CHAPTER 8

The Bombs and the Victims

S TARGELL WASN'T EXACTLY SURE where he was heading in retirement, but one thing was certain — wherever he went and whatever he did, he would no longer provide nightmare content for legions of major league pitchers. While a number of hitters compiled gaudier totals in terms of hits, home runs and RBIs, virtually no one instilled the fear in pitchers that Stargell did. "He didn't just hit pitchers," Hall of Fame pitcher Don Sutton once remarked, "he took away their dignity."[1]

He started that process long before he reached the major leagues. From the earliest days of Stargell's lifelong love affair with baseball, he began gaining notoriety not so much for the frequency of his home run blasts, but for the sheer power and the distance he hit them. Although not physically imposing as an amateur, Stargell served notice of what would come by launching several titanic shots at Washington Park, near the Encinal housing project in Alameda, where he spent his formative years. That power potential didn't immediately translate into home runs in the professional ranks though, in part because he was still growing. Bob Zuk, the scout who signed Stargell, said years later that Stargell weighed only 152 pounds when he first saw him. The future slugger didn't top 170 pounds during his first year with the Pirates organization, in 1959 at San Angelo, Texas, and Roswell, New Mexico, in the Class D Sophomore League, when he hit all of seven home runs. His second season, at Grand Forks, North Dakota, in Class C ball, he connected for 11 home runs. Still, Joe L. Brown — the Bucs general manager at the time — liked Stargell's chances down the road. "Willie had this sheer raw potential," Brown told the *Post-Gazette*'s Paul Meyer in 1988 after Stargell's election to the Hall of Fame was announced. "He always looked like he was going to hit more home runs than he did — until he did."[2]

By the time Stargell had advanced to Asheville, North Carolina — his third of four minor-league stops in the Pirates system — in 1961, "He didn't have to grow anymore," as Brown put it. "He was big enough." Stargell turned that 6-foot-2, 200-pound package of power and strength into 22 home runs in Asheville, where fans took to calling him "On the Hill Will" because of his propensity to hit home runs onto a hillside that loomed beyond the right-field fence at McCormick Field.

Stargell's reputation as a tape-measure slugger grew with age and experience, and after arriving in the big leagues, he began to turn heads — toward the highest reaches of NL stadiums and beyond — with regularity. His long-ball propensity made him a fan favorite in Pittsburgh and he remains a conversation piece among power aficionados to this day. No discussion about the ultimate slugger can take place without Stargell's name and his tape-measure home runs surfacing. He tried to downplay his penchant for going deep throughout his career, often saying he would trade a titanic shot for a victory and that organizations didn't pay for distance — only frequency. He was even somewhat embarrassed by some of his longer homers and said the shots only made pitchers bear down even harder against him. Even long after he had finished playing, he shrugged off talk of his ability to hit balls in places that few others could reach. "If you stick around 20 years and have that God-given ability to hit them, sooner or later you're going to tie into a few," he told Jerry Crasnick of the *Denver Post* in June of 1997. But he also told Crasnick it was gratifying and tried to describe — as Crasnick put it — what it was like to "hit a baseball a football field and a half long."

"It's like a cross between two locomotives on a collision course and your first sensuous encounter," Stargell explained. "On the one side, it's very destructive. On the other, it's mostly enjoyable."[3] In June of '97, he talked about what it felt like to have "the perfect swing. When you hit the ball just on the sweet part of the bat, it's such a great feeling. It's almost like the bat bends. There's no recoil. Two forces are meeting, the force of the bat and the force of the ball, and when they meet perfectly, you don't feel a thing."[4]

Stargell's first career big-league homer came off the Cubs' Lindy McDaniel on May 8, 1963, in his second game at Wrigley Field. According to the website Retrosheet.org, Stargell was an equal-opportunity slugger in that he hit plenty of home runs on the road — 254 of his 475 career taters were hit in visiting ballparks — as well as in his two home parks, Forbes Field (74) and Three Rivers Stadium (147). His home and road splits were remarkably similar; he played 1,178 games at home, for example, and 1,182 on the road. And he banged out 1,115 hits at either Forbes or Three Rivers, compared with 1,117 away from home. In the RBI department, Stargell amassed 781 at home and 759 on the road.

There's no telling how many career homers Stargell would have hit had he spent less time playing in old, cavernous Forbes, a nine-year stretch that he once claimed cost him as many as 150 home runs. But the gargantuan dimensions of old Forbes couldn't hold the longest of Willie's bombs, and his left-handed pull hitting stroke enabled him to zero in on the roof that covered the right-field grandstand. The first batter to clear the 86-foot-high roof was none other than George Herman Ruth, who did so on May 25, 1935, while playing for the Boston Braves. It was the last of the Babe's 714 career home runs. But Stargell one-upped the Babe — or rather he seven-upped him, as he clubbed seven of the 18 balls that sailed over the grandstand before Pirates moved to Three Rivers Stadium midway through the 1970 season.

The first of those seven came on July 9, 1967, when he snapped a 1–1 tie in the bottom of the ninth inning against Cincinnati by sending a Jim Maloney pitch through the pouring rain and over the right-field roof. "It didn't even feel good when I hit it," Stargell said after the game. "I thought it was going foul, afraid it would curve before it got to the roof." The *Post-Gazette*'s Charley Feeney described it like this: "Maloney went 2–1 on Stargell. Willie swung with the rain in his eyes and then everything seemed to be bright and clear to the Buccos as the ball cleared the roof."[5] Stargell would do it a second time on August 18, victimizing the Mets' Jack Fisher — who had served up the first-ever home run in Shea Stadium to Stargell in 1964 — as he went over the roof with no one on in the fourth inning of what would be a 7–2 Pirates win.

Stargell seemed to have a fondness for Fisher; on June 7 that year, Willie slammed a Fisher pitch over Forbes' 436-foot marker in right center for his 100th career home run. A *Pittsburgh Press* reporter the next day wrote that a local man named Phil Dorsey "paced off" the distance and found that the ball landed 40 paces beyond the outfield wall.[6] But that was a mere warm-up to a bomb he hit off the Los Angeles Dodgers' Don Drysdale on July 3 at Forbes. Witnesses saw the ball clear Forbes' 457-foot sign in center field and the ball reportedly landed in a Little League Field in nearby Schenley Park. According to the *Pittsburgh Courier* newspaper, a caretaker at the Frick Fine Arts building, beyond Forbes' 12-foot wall, told the media that Stargell's shot landed at third base on the Little League diamond, and the blast was measured at 542 feet.[7]

Although Stargell sprinkled long balls liberally throughout his 21-year career — he hit 20 or more home runs in a season 15 times — 1969 was a particularly memorable one in terms of Stargell's power display. On April 13 of that year, he enjoyed a two-homer game, with one of them again clearing the 436-foot marker at Forbes. He also deposited a shot over the wall in left, to the right of the scoreboard, in a win over the Phillies. When told it was the third ball he hit over the center-field wall, Stargell was not impressed. "I don't remember those other two I hit in centerfield very well," he said. "I can't even remember who I hit them off of. And I'll tell you another thing. A year from now, I won't remember this one."[8]

Stargell also continued his assault on Forbes right-field roof that year. He belted three balls that cleared the structure that season, including one on July 4 off New York Mets ace Tom Seaver. Of Stargell's August 19 shot, which came off fireballing Don Wilson of the Houston Astros, Pirates pitching coach Vernon Law, who was in the bullpen, noted, "I think that ball went over everything. I don't even think it hit the top of the roof." After the game, though, Stargell only wanted to talk about Wilson. "Wilson's going to be one of this league's great pitchers," he told the media. "Take what he was throwing tonight: a great fastball, a great slider and that fastball was overpowering." He tried to explain how he managed to hit Wilson that night. "To tell you the truth, I was fooled by that pitch. I wasn't expecting a breaking ball. But when it came up there, I figured I better swing at it because, man, I didn't want to have to try to handle that fastball of his again."[9] It only took another week for Stargell to belt his third roof shot of the season, as he took Atlanta's Ron Reed for a long ride in a 6–4 Braves' win.

Perhaps Stargell's most memorable clouts came away from home that season — one north of the border against the expansion Montreal Expos, in their cozy single-deck playyard known as Jarry Park, and the second in Los Angeles's pristine Dodger Stadium. On July 16 — the same day that Apollo 11 began its historic voyage that would culminate four days later with Neil Armstrong becoming the first human to set foot on the surface of the moon — Stargell launched a moon shot of his own. In Montreal, against a pitcher named Dan McGinn, Stargell hit a drive to right field that left Jarry Park and landed in a nearby municipal swimming pool. To this day, locals refer to the pool as "La Piscine de Willie."[10] Brown, the Pirates' general manager, stepped off the distance and came up with 495 feet from home plate to the edge of the pool — and the ball landed somewhere in the middle of the pool. It was the longest home run struck in the short history of Jarry Park.[11]

A blast in Dodger Stadium, struck off Alan Foster on August 5, had a bit more impact, as it was the first ball ever hit completely out of the ballpark — which opened in 1962 — and stood as one of just four balls to clear the stadium in its first 50 years of existence. Stargell claimed the first two while Mike Piazza (1997) and Mark McGwire (1999) launched the other two. The day after Stargell struck the first one, Melvin Durslag of the *Los Angeles Herald Examiner* wrote that the Dodgers' publicity man, Arthur "Red" Patterson, after huddling with a club engineer, adjusted the distance to 506 feet, 6 inches, in allowing for the height of the pavilion roof. Phil Musick, covering the game for the *Pittsburgh Press*, wrote the following lead that appeared in the August 6 edition:

> LOS ANGELES — Willie Stargell's muscles have now joined Jack Benny's violin, Bob Hope's nose and Raquel Welch's anatomy as all-time great conversation stimulators here in the neon capital of the western world.[12]

Ross Newhan of the *Los Angeles Times* opened his story like this: "It appeared to be Apollo 12."[13]

Foster couldn't bear to watch — and he didn't. "When it makes that kind of sound," he said years later, "you don't even want to turn around and look."[14]

Stargell, as always was the case, was not taken with the mammoth blast. "They don't pay you any more for distance," he told reporters later. Stargell said he had no idea the ball was headed on that type of a trip. "I wasn't trying to hit one," he said. "Every time I try, I can't do it."[15] Stargell would leave the Chavez Ravine yard entirely again four years later, on May 8, 1973, taking Andy Messersmith over the same right-field pavilion, although this one bounced on top of the pavilion roof before caroming into a parking lot.

Fred Claire, then the Dodgers' publicity director and later the club's general manager, wrote in a memo that he sent to the Pirates that 6-year-old Todd Shubin of Fountain Valley, California, retrieved Stargell's blast as he and his family were walking to the parking lot in the seventh inning and brought the ball to a security guard. The Shubins were leaving the game early because Todd's father, Dennis Shubin, had to be at work at 3:30 A.M. The Dodgers invited the family to attend the next night's game, and young Todd, obviously nervous as he was being interviewed by two Los Angeles television stations, worked up enough nerve to ask Stargell for his hat and an autograph. The gentle giant obliged. "I still have the newspaper article and the autograph," Todd Shubin said in a 2010 interview. He also still has the ball, though much to his surprise. "I thought someone would have asked for it by now — maybe the Hall of Fame," he said. "But they never did." So, the ball resides in the Shubin home, locked up in a case, although he is not shy about showing it off upon request — not a rare occasion since he remained close to the sport as a youth league baseball coach in Southern California for more than a decade. "Everyone knows the story — it comes up all the time," he said of Stargell's mammoth blast. "People will ask, and I'll bring it out and show it to them. It's a rare thing. We've gone to a million baseball games and we know how lucky it is just to get a foul ball, let alone the second ball hit out of Dodger Stadium."[16]

Ron Cey, then a young Dodger infielder, told Bob Hunter of the *Los*

Angeles Herald Examiner, "I honestly can say I never saw a ball hit that far, and I never want to see it again, unless it's someone from our dugout."[17] Cey's teammate, relief pitcher Jim Brewer, had a prime viewing position in the bullpen as Stargell's drive hit the pavilion roof and bounced into the parking lot. "Of course I saw it all the way," he told Allan Malamud of the *Herald Examiner*. "I could have seen it if I were in New York."[18] Stargell hit two homers that night off Messersmith, who had just come over from the American League that season and was amazed as he watched Stargell's blast leave the yard. "I said to myself, 'Oh, man, that's going a long way.'" Messersmith said it looked like the National League would be a tough go. "You toss one up over here and they really hit it. I couldn't believe it when Stargell started to run. I figured he'd stand there and watch it."[19]

But Stargell immediately began his home run trot and did not stop to admire the flight. "I really didn't think it was going that far," he said of the second-longest home run in the stadium's 12-year history. "It must have got caught in some wind." When asked how the blast compared to the first one, he said he didn't "keep up with these things," referring to his tape-measure drives. "But I know that ball a few years ago went further."[20] Stargell's exploits amused the Los Angeles media, including famed columnist Jim Murray of the *Los Angeles Times*, who wrote that Stargell was simply born to hit home runs. "Anything else looks silly for his 6-foot-3, 225-pound frame. The bat looks like something he might bite on. The massive chest, bulging arms and enormous hands dwarf it. He looks as if he should carry a tree to the

Willie adjusts the cap of 6-year-old Todd Shubin, who tracked down one of two home runs that Stargell hit completely out of Dodger Stadium (courtesy National Baseball Hall of Fame Library, Cooperstown, New York).

plate." Murray asked Stargell what it would take to hit 62 home runs in a season and break what was then Roger Maris' single-season mark of 61. Stargell told Murray he could do it, but that it wasn't one of his goals. "I'm more interested in breaking Hack Wilson's record than Roger Maris,'" he said, referring to Wilson's major league single-season RBI mark of 190.[21]

Stargell never hit four home runs in a game, but he did connect for three round-trippers on four different occasions. Those who'd been in the game a while were not surprised at anything Stargell did with respect to the long ball. Brown, the Pirates' GM, later said that in his time in the National League, Stargell was one of the two most respected power hitters, with the Giants' Willie McCovey being the other. "They could hit the ball so far," Brown said. "And pitchers knew that if they made a mistake, they could hit it out in any direction."[22] Stargell's former manager Harry Walker, considered a hitting guru of sorts, said he had never seen a hitter anywhere who hit the ball any harder. "For sheer crash of bat meeting ball," Walker once told a reporter, "Stargell was simply the best."[23]

Former Cubs third baseman Ron Santo, who died in December 2010, was around for Stargell's three-homer game in 1968 and saw more than he wanted of the Pirate slugger over the years. Stargell slugged more homers against the Mets — 60 — than any other team, but the Cubs were number three on Stargell's hit list with 50. Santo had an up-close-and-personal look at far too many of them to suit him, including one shot in particular that went a long way toward sinking the Cubs' pennant hopes down the stretch of their unforgettable 1969 collapse — one that paved the way for the Amazin' New York Mets to win their first National League pennant. "It was in September in Wrigley Field," Santo recalled. "It was about 50 degrees out, and the wind was blowing in. We were ahead 2–1 and nobody was going to hit a home run that day. Nobody. That's the way I felt. Phil Regan came on in relief to face Stargell. Had two strikes — a 1–2 count. It looked like [Stargell] hit a ball around his ankles and not only did he hit it ... he hit it over the bleachers and onto Sheffield Avenue. Oh, it was terrible. It ended up tying the game in the top of the ninth inning. Then we went extra innings and Matty Alou got a base hit to win the game for the Pirates."[24]

Santo also was on hand at Three Rivers Stadium on May 30, 1971, the day Stargell turned around a Ken Holtzman delivery and knocked it 458 feet into the upper deck in right field — the second of Stargell's four upper-deck shots at the park. Holtzman didn't have much to say after that game — only that he had made a bad pitch. "Heck," Holtzman said, "I supplied half the power myself."[25] Santo, though, was impressed — even nearly 40 years later. "The home run off Kenny Holtzman — I've never seen a ball hit that far," he said. "And Kenny Holtzman was a left-handed pitcher! I was on third and I watched it. When it left the bat, I couldn't believe it. They marked that seat at Three Rivers. But you know what? I was not surprised a guy like him could do that. The power he had. He was a big man, but I mean, he had a very quick bat." Santo said Holtzman's teammates gave him the business after that game. "Everybody was on him," Santo said. "We were asking, 'Did you hold it across the seams or with the seams?' Kenny was a very competitive pitcher, but a great guy."

Stargell's longest home run — the July 3, 1967, shot off Drysdale at Forbes Field — ranked as the 32nd longest home run ever hit in a major league game, according to Bill Jenkinson's *Baseball's Ultimate Power*. According to Jenkinson, Stargell authored four more of Major League Baseball's 100 longest home runs. Number 48, struck on May 20, 1978, in Montreal's Olympic Stadium, went 515 feet. He is credited with three homers that traveled 510 feet — tied for number 73 on the Longest 100 list. The first came August 19, 1969, at Forbes Field; the second on August 9, 1970, at Pittsburgh's Three Rivers Stadium; and the last on July 4, 1979, at St. Louis' old Busch Stadium. Jenkinson also credits Stargell with the eighth-longest opposite-field home run in the game's history — a 460-foot blast to left-center field on July 8, 1966, at Forbes Field. Batting right-handed, Mickey Mantle also hit a 460-foot opposite field homer in Detroit on September 17, 1952.[26] And Jenkinson claims Stargell's 475-foot shot onto the right-field grandstand roof at Forbes Field on July 9, 1967, was the sixth-longest walkoff home run ever, tied with Jimmy Foxx's blast in 1939 against Boston. In terms of power rankings by position, Jenkinson pegged Stargell as number two among all left fielders who ever played the game, behind Frank Howard. Of Jenkinson's top 100 "Tape Measure Sluggers," Stargell ranks number seven behind Ruth, Foxx, Mantle, Howard, Dick Allen and Mark McGwire.[27]

Stargell also owns some of the longest drives in the history of six stadiums — the Astrodome in Houston, Dodger Stadium, Montreal's Olympic Stadium, Veterans Stadium in Philadelphia and the two Pittsburgh parks, Forbes Field and Three Rivers Stadium, according to *Baseball's Ultimate Power*. At the Astrodome, Stargell's 490-foot bomb on May 28, 1966, was the longest to right-center. Stargell's Dodger Stadium shot off Foster on August 5, 1969, topped all homers hit to right field at that ballpark at 506 feet. His 515-foot bolt to right off Wayne Twitchell on May 20, 1978, was the longest hit at Montreal's Olympic Stadium, and his 505-foot shot to right on June 25, 1971, set the pace for all homers hit to right field in Philadelphia's Veterans Stadium.

The drive Stargell hit in Philadelphia — a blast off Jim Bunning that landed in Section 601—came on an off-speed pitch called by catcher Tim McCarver. Bunning told MLB.com in June of 2003 that he threw a "high slider that I used to get Stargell out on, only I didn't throw it hard enough and didn't get it in. It got over the fat part of the plate. He couldn't hit it any further."[28] Larry Bowa, the Phillies' shortstop that night who was stationed to the right of second base due to an infield shift, said it sounded like a golf ball coming off a metal driver. "I'd never seen anything like that," he said. Richie Hebner, the Pirates' third baseman at the time, said he went up to the spot where the ball landed two days later. "I couldn't believe it," Hebner said. "That's a $25 cab ride." Stargell said he knew it had distance. "But I had no idea it would carry that far."[29] Bowa said the ball was still rising when it reached the stands. "As an infielder, when a guy hits one that you know is a home run, you give it a casual look. When he swung, you didn't take your eyes off it because you wanted to see where it was going. It was majestic. I couldn't believe how far that ball went. It would take me three swings to get one up there—from second base."[30] Phillies third-baseman John Vukovich remembered saying, "'Wow, look at that son of a bitch.' It just kept going. It didn't come down. At the time, you knew it was a monster. And as time has gone on, you really realize how long it was." Among those who witnessed the blow in the stands that night was Joe Kerrigan, a student at Father Judge High School in Philadelphia at the time who later played in the big leagues and became a respected pitching coach as well—even doing one stint with the Pirates. Kerrigan was sitting in the upper deck—the same altitude as Stargell's moon shot—but behind home plate rather than in right field. "My most profound memory is that, for two or three innings, people were still buzzing about it," he said. "My reaction was that nobody could hit a ball that far. Especially in those days. We were talking about that home run on the playground for the next few days."[31]

Stargell's blast off Bunning was the longest hit at the Vet. When Stargell made his final appearance as a player in September, 1982, the Phillies unveiled a star to hold the spot where the home run came to rest. Over the years, the star disappeared a couple of times and finally the Phillies painted the star directly on the cement above an exit runway. When Stargell died on April 9, 2001, the club repainted the background from gold to black. McCarver said in 2003 that he never was so proud to call a home run as he was the shot that Stargell hit 32 years earlier. "It was a slider that didn't slide," McCarver said. "We were trying to go inside and didn't get there. Half the team was trying to figure out where it went instead of shaking his hand. There's a seat in Sky-Dome that's a different color because that's where Jose Canseco's landed. They do that in many parks. But the star isn't where the ball landed. It was where it was last seen."[32]

Stargell's 515-foot shot in Montreal's Olympic Stadium, also recorded as 534 feet by some historians, landed in Section 351, Row C, seat No. 3 — a seat that eventually made its way to the Canadian Baseball Hall of Fame. On the night of Stargell's death, the Expos held a moment of silence in his honor and then shone a spotlight on the seat, where a flower had been placed. Chuck Tanner couldn't believe Stargell's shot. "How can anyone hit a ball that far?" he marveled after the game that day.[33] Rudy May, who grew up idolizing Stargell in the East Bay, was pitching for the Expos at the time and called it "the longest ball I've ever seen hit in my entire life. It left the ballpark so fast and went so far. It was one of the most awesome things I have ever seen in my life. I will never forget it. It was almost like we weren't playing the same league — Willie should have been in a league or two higher than us to hit a ball like that. I was watching Andre Dawson, who was playing center field, and Ellis Valentine, who was playing right field. When he hit it, Andre didn't move. I remember asking him if he had ever seen ball hit like that before. He said no. I said, 'You didn't even move.' He said, 'There was no reason to.'"[34]

Jerry Reuss, a Pirate pitcher at the time, was sitting on the bench when Stargell unloaded. "It was kind of hard to see in there — there was a bank of lights at Olympic Stadium and when the ball got up in that bank, you'd lose it momentarily. But with Willie's, it got well above the lights and I was able to track it — and then it never came down. I said, 'Where in the hell did that go?' Then I looked at the reactions of the outfielders and they were doing the same thing — where did it go? And it was the same reaction on the bench. It was a monster of a home run." It was only one of several impressive homers that Reuss saw Stargell hit. "He hit one many years before that against Ken Forsch when I was with Houston. It was like a golf ball. You expect balls to have a downward arc as they leave the ballpark. This one just kept going straight — it was in right-center field at Three Rivers Stadium. It went into the lower deck and it was the damndest thing. God, that got out of there fast."[35]

Twitchell, a 6-foot-7, 230-pound left-hander, had faced Stargell on many occasions prior to May 20, 1978, and had what he called "fairly decent luck" against him. He felt he could get a read on Stargell's approach by studying his timing mechanism — the rhythmic windmilling of the bat while he awaited a pitch. "He'd loop the bat forward through the strike zone, to distract the pitcher and keep him from seeing the strike zone," said Twitchell. "I always thought hitters had bad intentions. It was probably more of a timing mechanism. But one thing you could count on. When he did a double loop, he was going to swing — it didn't matter where the ball was, he was going to be swinging at it. This was one of those situations. I thought first, 'Good — he's going to swing.'" But that was because Twitchell thought the ball would arrive belt high, in tight. It did not — it sunk low. "He made perfect contact with the ball," Twitchell said of Stargell. "The last I heard at the time, the best they could do measuring to where the seat was in the upper deck was 534 feet. And it hadn't even started to come down yet. I had fabulous eyesight. But by the time I could snap my head around, our right fielder Ellis Valentine was looking behind him. I can't tell you how fast it got there — this ball made it to the upper deck in a heartbeat. It was like trying to watch a tracer bullet. And to add insult to injury, you could hear it when it hit. Bang! It hadn't slowed down much."[36]

Twitchell said pitchers are conditioned to avoid thinking in the past tense when it comes to giving up home runs. "There's nothing you can do about it so you move forward. It's rare when pitchers show much emotion. We're just machines out there — you get the ball and throw it. But in that case, I was kind of in shock. I had never seen anything like that before. I'd given up some home runs, but nothing like that. I had no idea a baseball could be hit that far." None of Twitchell's teammates said anything to him the day Stargell took him 534 feet deep. But the next day, when he arrived at the ballpark, a present awaited him in the clubhouse. "There was a baseball lying in my chair," Twitchell recalled. "On it, someone had inscribed, 'Some French Canadian guy found this in Quebec City. He thinks Stargell hit it.'" Quebec City is about 160 miles east of Montreal.

Twitchell, who died in September 2010, showed no bitterness about being taken so deep and in fact almost seemed to appreciate his place in local home run lore. "For a pitcher, it's hard to say you take pride throwing a ball hit that far," he said. "But Willie couldn't have hit the ball that far off Jamie Moyer. It took someone throwing a 90 mph fastball. I played my part, I guess." Twitchell called the Olympic Stadium bomb the "product of the perfect storm — a 90-some mph fastball hitting a 38-ounce bat swung by a very strong man. As a team, they used fabulously large bats, the Pirates did. Willie gave me one of his bats and it was unbelievable how big it was. When I was playing baseball, I was 6–6, 230 and no way I could have swung that bat in batting practice and hit a ball to the left side of second base."

Twitchell had his successes against Stargell. One time in particular, while pitching for the Phillies, Twitchell struck Stargell out three times in a game. "The next day I'm out there playing catch and all of a sudden a baseball hits me gently in the back. Here [Stargell] is 50 feet away with big smile on his face. I can't tell you what the first word was that he said to me. But the second word was 'you.'"

While Stargell was capable of putting on a road show of the first order, he left more than a few of his marks at home, including four balls that he sent into the upper deck at Three Rivers Stadium. No one else hit more than one. The first of Stargell's upper-deck shots at Three Rivers came off Mets right-hander Ron Taylor — a mammoth blast estimated at 469 feet — on August 9, 1970.

The two were no strangers; Taylor and Stargell had battled one another over a period of more than 13 years, dating back to when Stargell played for Columbus and Taylor pitched for Jacksonville in the International League in 1962. The right-handed Taylor would try to keep his sinker off the plate and jam the powerful left-handed hitter with his slider. "Unfortunately, I didn't always have that much success," Taylor said. "But a lot of guys didn't. He just had this raw power. I observed him from a very dangerous position — the pitching mound." Taylor called Stargell's upper-deck shot off him at Three Rivers "majestic." "What I remember is that I thought I was throwing pretty hard that day," he said. "So I thought I'd try to throw one by him. It was just amazing. The crowd cheered as the ball left his bat, then it became silent."[37]

The previous year, Stargell connected for a Forbes Field roof shot off Taylor's teammate, Hall of Famer Tom Seaver, who surrendered eight career home runs to Stargell — tied for the most among any opposing pitcher. Phil Niekro — like Seaver, a Hall of Famer — also yielded eight round-trippers to Stargell. Although it had been decades since Niekro tried to flutter his knuckleball past Stargell, he had no trouble in 2010 recalling what it was like to face the powerful left-handed slugger. "As a hitter, the thing I remember most was his stance and that unusual way of getting that bat going before he got ready to hit the ball," said Niekro, who was among the group of players that Stargell traveled with to Vietnam in 1970. "What I was always wanting to see — not when I was pitching — was how far a human being could hit a baseball. And I always thought he was the one guy I was going to see it from. He could have been the guy. He had the physique, the strength, the quickness of the bat — he had everything going for him. And also — and I never thought about this until after a game was over or before it started — I would hope to God that he would never hit one back at me." Niekro said his approach to Stargell was no mystery. "I was a knuckleballer," he said. "He knew it was coming. No one was fooling anyone. If I had a good knuckler, I'd get him out. If I made a mistake, he'd hit it in the upper deck."[38]

Niekro said whenever the Braves would get ready to take on the Pirates, the first thing that came to mind was Stargell. "You'd just hope he had a bad four-game series and a bad game against me," he said. Niekro got the best of Stargell more often than not, holding him to a .225 batting average in 111 career at-bats. But there were those eight round-trippers. "I remember pitching in the old ballpark, Three Rivers Stadium, one time when Eddie Mathews was the Braves manager," Niekro recalled. "We were going into the bottom of the ninth and I was winning by two runs with two outs. Willie came up to the plate and I got two balls and no strikes. Eddie came out and said, 'I don't know if you realize it, but Bob Robertson is on deck and he hits home runs. If you put Stargell on and Robertson hits a home run, you've got a tie ballgame.'

"Eddie says, 'Just throw it right down the middle of the plate. Do you think he'll hit it into the center-field bleachers? Do you think he's God or something?' I don't think Eddie even got to the bench before I threw a fastball and Willie hit it into the center-field bleachers for a home run. And then I got Bob Robertson out and we won the game 3–2. I went into the dugout and walked up to Eddie and said, 'I know he's not God, but he might be a real close relative.'"

Stargell's other two upper-deck shots at Three Rivers Stadium came off the Expos' Howie Reed on June 20, 1971—a 472-foot drive—and off the Braves' Gary Gentry on May 31, 1973, a blast that traveled 468 feet. Gentry was no stranger to Stargell's feats of strength; he was on hand when the slugger took his Mets teammate Taylor into the stratosphere in August 1970—the first ball to reach the upper deck at the new waterfront park. "I tried to muscle him—I threw it too hard," said Gentry, who was working on a shutout in the eighth inning before Stargell's three-run bomb. "I didn't get the location I wanted on the pitch. I threw it as hard as I could and he hit it as hard as he could. I guess that's why it went so far."[39] Pirates starter Nellie Briles, who benefited from the blow, was stunned by its sheer distance. "I didn't think it was humanly possible for someone to hit the ball that far," he said.[40] Stargell, though, said he would have been happier if the ball had just cleared the fence. "When you hit balls like that, those pitchers don't forget," he said. "They bear down on you that much harder the next time. I'd rather hit 50 of them that just barely make it."[41]

He got his wish, at least when it came to his home park, as his blow off Gentry would be the last ball he would hit into Three Rivers Stadium's upper deck. But he wasn't done dialing long distance. And he didn't save his prodigious blasts for the big-league competition. On June 18, 1979, during the Pirates' visit to Portland, Oregon, for an exhibition game with their Class AAA affiliate, Portland general manager David Hersh was offering $100 to any player who went deep during a pre-game home run derby contest at Multnomah Stadium. Hersh offered Stargell $1,000 if he could reach the balcony of the adjacent Multnomah Athletic Club during the derby. The balcony sat

Willie lets loose with one of his patented home-run swings during the Hall of
Fame Game in Cooperstown, New York, in July 1980 (courtesy Pittsburgh
Pirates).

more than 55 feet high and some 403 feet from home plate, behind the right-
field wall. "Make it $2,000," Stargell reportedly told Hersh, who agreed. The
Pirates slugger then sent the next batting practice pitch onto the balcony and
into the middle of a crowd of spectators. "The ball that he hit is something
... you can call it once in a lifetime," Hersh said. "The fact that he called his
own shot made it more incredible."[42] The shot remains a legend of sorts in
the Portland area. Dwight Jaynes, a longtime Portland sports journalist, said

that at the time Stargell unloaded during the home run derby, no one had ever reached that part of the ballpark in batting practice or a game. The park had been used as a baseball field since 1956 before being reconfigured in 2010 to accommodate only soccer and football. "It was an incredible feat and it had to carry more than 500 feet," Jaynes said. "I think we estimated it around 527 at the time." Stargell hit more than one home run during the derby and Jaynes called them "startling in their majesty and made for special memories for those who were there. Even now, that first one is probably the most famous home run ever hit in that ballpark. And it wasn't even hit in a game!"[43]

Stargell worked his exhibition magic the following summer, this time in the picturesque hamlet of Cooperstown, New York, home of the Baseball Hall of Fame. While in town with the Pirates to play in the annual exhibition game on August 4, 1980, Stargell gave the visitors a thrill and a memory to cherish one day after they had watched outfielders Al Kaline and Duke Snider take their place in the hallowed hall. Stargell was not in the starting lineup that afternoon against the Chicago White Sox but as the game progressed, some of the 9,000 fans who had packed Doubleday Field to see the reigning World Champions — and the reigning co–MVP — began chanting, "We Want Willie." Their pleas went on for two innings before Tanner summoned Stargell to the plate in the sixth inning. It didn't take long for Stargell to deliver, as he pounced on Francisco Barrios's first pitch and rocketed it more than 400 feet for a two-run homer. "With one shrug of his broad shoulders and a snap of his bat, Stargell made the crowd momentarily imagine Al Kaline or Duke Snider knocking a ball out of sight," wrote Mike Brown of the Oneonta, New York, *Daily Star*. "Before Stargell's monstrous home run, everyone in Doubleday knew what he'd be trying for. So did Chicago White Sox pitcher Francisco Barrios. Willie did it, an awesome blast over the bleachers in rightfield and onto a barn roof."[44]

Stargell's feats of long-ball strength were renowned around baseball, and stories of his prodigious blasts were passed down from one generation of players to the next. Bob Walk, who pitched for three teams in the big leagues — including Pittsburgh — before going on to work as a color analyst on Pirate broadcasts, said that when he first came up to the big leagues with Philadelphia in 1980, he would notice seats of different colors in some of the ballparks the Phillies visited. When he'd ask his teammates why those seats were different colors, they'd tell him that Stargell hit balls in those seats. "You needed a telescope to see them," Walk said of Stargell's tape-measure blasts. "Everyone used to talk about them. He didn't hit home runs. He hit conversation pieces."[45]

CHAPTER 9

A Whole New Ballgame

CONVERSATIONS ABOUT STARGELL'S prodigious home run blasts didn't end when he slid his 35½-inch, 34-ounce Louisville Slugger into the bat rack for the final time. But the next time he'd be seen performing in front of a packed house, someone else would be swinging the lumber. And it wouldn't be a bat — it would be a conductor's baton. Just a couple of months removed from his retirement, he would embark on a limited tour with a group of elite musicians, echoing the words of one of his heroes — Dr. Martin Luther King Jr.

Although the tour took place in January 1983, the seed for Stargell's unique opportunity was planted more than three years earlier in the mind of a professional musician living in upstate New York. Robert Freeman, who spent much of his adult life leading some of the nation's most prestigious music schools, was at the helm of the University of Rochester's Eastman School of Music during the fall of 1979 when — like millions of baseball fans across the country — he became intrigued by the Pittsburgh Pirates' "Family" and the team's charismatic leader. Freeman watched as Stargell virtually willed the Pirates back from a three-games-to-one World Series deficit against Baltimore and helped them defeat the Orioles in the seventh game, hitting a home run to fuel the win. During the post-game interviews, Freeman fell under Stargell's spell — the earnest appreciation, the heartfelt gratification to be a part of such a wonderful team playing in a sports-crazy community, one that truly cherished its heroes and could see through a phony a mile away. Freeman remembered seeing the media "in Willie's face" — and was most impressed by the fact that rather than saying how great he felt personally, Stargell emphasized that he was just one player on a team of 25. "He talked about the fact that you can't play baseball by yourself— that it takes a team and a great owner and a great manager," Freeman recalled. "It all came forth in the most articulate, heartfelt and meaningful fashion, all representing Pirate baseball. I thought all of that was golden."[1]

Stargell's selfless display made Freeman think of another African American man who had the gift of galvanizing groups with the force of his personality and his ability to speak so eloquently — the late Rev. Dr. Martin Luther King Jr. This was 11 years after King's death, and the idea hit Freeman like bolt from Stargell's Louisville Slugger — find a musical piece that would feature text culled from the great writings of King and persuade the Pirate slugger to narrate it. He wanted the piece to be "accessible" — it wouldn't take a classical music aficionado to appreciate it, but rather it would appeal to the virtually anyone. "I remember lying on the floor with my wife and watching the Pirates celebrate — that's how this all came together," he said. "That's what I do — I put together the mustard, the peanut butter and the chocolate syrup and see what happens. I'm always looking for connections between things."

Freeman called Joseph Schwantner, an Eastman professor who had won the Pulitzer Prize in 1979 for his composition *Aftertones of Infinity*, and shared his idea over the telephone. Schwantner was not a baseball fan and had never heard of Stargell. But his son, Christopher, who was about 11 at the time and was a big baseball fan, overheard his father mentioning Stargell's name in connection with Freeman's idea. "My son said, 'That's Mr. Pittsburgh.' And I said, 'Mr. Pittsburgh who?' The name didn't ring a bell with me. But Freeman said he had heard Stargell on TV and was impressed with how articulate and thoughtful he was and his brainstorm was that Stargell might be the person to narrate this possible work. I said, 'Maybe — I don't know.'" Schwantner had good reason to be skeptical; he had no connection with Stargell and although the now-retired slugger enjoyed music and had been an avid dancer since his teenage years back in Alameda, he had never worked with an orchestra. "I thought it was rather bizarre initially because I didn't know anything about him," Schwantner said. "But Willie worked hard and did all the required background. In the end, I got to write the work I wanted to write. As a child of the '60s, King was such an important figure, and this was a way for me to give back."[2]

Giving back was what Stargell had in mind as well. Freeman arranged a meeting with Stargell's representative, attorney David Litman, and pitched the idea over lunch. Litman was intrigued but wasn't sure Stargell would be up for it, given that he had no formal musical training. Then Freeman had lunch with Stargell. "He told me, 'Anything that would help the memory of Dr. King, I'm very much in favor of,'" Freeman recalled. Later, during rehearsal prior to his stage debut, Stargell told the *Pittsburgh Post-Gazette*, "It's probably the finest thing I've ever done in my entire life. Something to commemorate such a great man — what he's done compared to what I've done. [I've been] playing baseball, a game, having fun — it's what kids do."[3] Stargell told Freeman when he first pitched the idea that his only connection with classical music came as a junior high school student back in Alameda and he could recall only "this guy standing on a box waving his hands around," Freeman said. "He was afraid he wouldn't be able to follow somebody doing that. But we told him we'd give him lessons and that the conductor would tell him when to start. And once you start, it's his job to follow you. But it's your job not to race. One day he said to me, 'I can't be Dr. King.' I said, 'Of course not, but you're a black leader of great charisma — people know who you are. All I want you to do is be you. Read Dr. King's words in your style.'"

Schwantner spent the summer of 1980 researching King, and his text drew from more than a decade of King's life. The result, titled *New Morning for the World— Daybreak of Freedom,* would not debut until January 15, 1983 — the day that King would have turned 54 — at the John F. Kennedy Center for the Performing Arts in Washington, D.C. It would be performed more than 200 times and recorded several others. Schwantner said Stargell "brought a kind of dignity and force of will to his performance that was quite captivating." He said only one narrator had surpassed Stargell in all the times he's heard it performed — and that was Coretta Scott King, Martin Luther King's widow, who performed it with the Indianapolis Symphony. Schwantner attended that performance and during a break, he said Coretta King asked him to stand with her while she finished. "My heart was just pounding," Schwantner said. "After the performance, I thought to myself, 'I am never going to be closer to the source than I am today.' But in terms of a musical, force-driven personality, Stargell's performance was one of the best of that piece I had."

Schwantner said after he agreed to write the piece and prior to its opening performance, he had a chance to meet with Stargell, just to see what he would be working with. "He had this naturally wonderful kind of booming voice — I could tell if we could train him to deliver on cue, the voice certainly was going to be a commanding one," Schwantner said. "No question he pushed that voice across the floodlights in a most convincing way. He was a man of substantial stature. And being in front of a microphone, he was kind of an imposing figure. And he was used to dealing with the public. He could look you right in the eye and you paid attention to him. He must have been incredibly intimidating on the ballfield." A Hall of Famer on the field, Stargell delivered in the symphony hall as well, at least the way Schwantner heard it. "Looking back, some of the best performances of that piece were his early performances, including the one at the Kennedy Center. As one who lives in the concert hall, that was an extraordinary event. A lot of those people there that night had never been to a symphony hall or a symphony concert. During parts of the text that can be very dramatic, people started to clap and holler and verbally respond to Stargell's narration. It was really neat."

It didn't come easily, however. Stargell received voice "coaching" lessons from Ben Shaktman, founder of the Pittsburgh Public Theater. Stargell praised Shaktman's work, saying that the text director brought out a new side of him. "I surprised myself," Stargell said. "This big lug can not only swing a bat but can stand up and chime in with beautiful music and say something with a direct meaning."[4]

David Effron, the conductor, certainly played a major role in helping Stargell

After retiring as a player, Willie became involved in a number of endeavors, including one in which he performed a composition titled "New Morning for the World: Daybreak of Freedom" with the Eastman Philharmonia early in 1983 (photograph by Jim Judkis, courtesy Eastman School of Music, University of Rochester).

perform. Effron, who left Rochester in 1997 for Indiana University, said he met Stargell for the first time prior to the start of rehearsal and he recalled the former slugger as being quite nervous. "He had no background in classical music—he didn't read music and didn't know what to expect out of this," Effron said. "You could see the fear in his eyes, actually. We told him he didn't have to worry about a thing because I was very reliable and I would just give him a cue with my left hand when it was time for him to say something, and when he finished that segment, he would stop and wait for the next cue. That went very well.

Willie visits with Joseph Schwantner, who composed "New Morning for the World: Daybreak of Freedom" (courtesy Eastman School of Music, University of Rochester).

What I remember was when he came onto the stage and I introduced him to the orchestra, the first thing we played was a very loud note where the whole orchestra was playing. He wasn't expecting it — he'd certainly never been that close to a classical orchestra. He was standing right in front and when they played this chord, the guy almost jumped out of his skin. From my viewpoint, it was very funny, but I felt empathy because he was completely out of his element."[5]

But just as he did on the field, Stargell worked at his new game, a fact that was apparent to everyone around him. "He was so into it and so believable — you'd have thought he was a trained actor," Effron said. "He did it with such passion and feeling. After a few rehearsals, he became very comfortable." Shaktman told the *Pittsburgh Press* in a January 1983 interview that Stargell worked diligently and that he reacted to direction as well as any actor he'd ever worked with. "The challenge cannot be understated," Shaktman said. "After all, this is a concerto written for the spoken voice. Stargell is really the solo instrument. This is a task which would really challenge an experienced actor."[6]

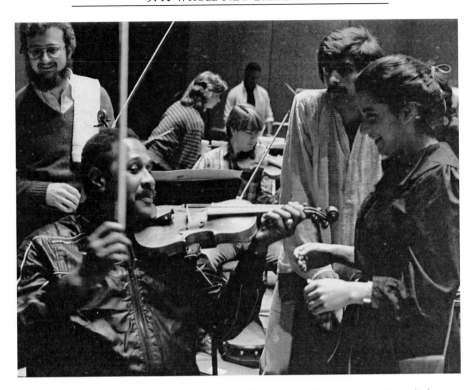

Students at the Eastman School of Music, University of Rochester, enjoy a light moment with Stargell during rehearsal for "New Morning for the World: Daybreak of Freedom." Students are (left to right) James Pember Lyon, Kristine Rebecca Fink, Nathan Norman, Christopher Allen Chappell (rear), Bryan James Dumm and Julie Ann Gigante (photograph by Louis Ouzer, courtesy Sibley Music Library, Eastman School of Music, University of Rochester).

Just like he enjoyed the camaraderie of the clubhouse, Stargell enjoyed the feeling of community that evolved during his work with the 110-member orchestra musicians, most of whom were students at the University of Rochester's Eastman School of Music. "He opened up to them very easily and they really loved him," Effron said. "You know how the Pirates called him 'Pops' because he was a leader and like a father figure? You could see that with the musicians. He was even like a father figure to me, although I was older. I was in my glory being around him." Schwantner and Freeman remembered the student musicians taking to Stargell once they realized he was in it for the right reasons. "I think a lot of our kids began with the idea that this was some sort of a PR hustle," Freeman said. "But David Effron did a marvelous job of making the kids take it very seriously. And it turned out to be a very moving experience for us all." Schwantner said some of the students were baseball fans and they all knew who Stargell was. "And those who didn't were made aware of who he was," he said. "I remember him going on the tour with us — we took the train from Kennedy Center to Philadelphia to Pittsburgh to Rochester and he went on that whole trip. The students had just the greatest time. He was handing out 'Stargell stars' all over the place. It was really quite something."

Although Stargell worked hard to improve his part of the performance, Freeman believed it was the fact that Stargell *was* an amateur that helped attract the crowds that the Eastman Philharmonia pulled in during the five-city tour that also featured stops at New York's Carnegie Hall, the Academy of Music in Philadelphia, Heinz Hall in Pittsburgh and the Eastman Theatre in Rochester. "Willie was completely unanticipatable, which was the charm of the whole thing," Freeman said. "Why do people go to NASCAR races? They seem deeply boring to me, but the reason 200,000 people go to watch cars speed around a track is they hope there'll be a crash. Part of the problem with classical music is that people do it so well. You don't go expecting to hear Itzhak Perlman play a wrong note. But here you had a major league baseball player — let's see if he's going to crash. But not only did he not crash, he performed magnificently. People were moved — there was so much cheering and applause. And he was really pleased by all of this, too. You can imagine, you have a retired baseball player coming into a whole new era of his life, where he's honoring Dr. King's memory through music. He enjoyed the whole thing."

Effron would not argue that point. "I think he felt so much for this subject," he said, referring to Stargell's feelings for King. "He didn't talk about it, but obviously he had a special connection with it because he could really reach the audience. He was a huge hit — and not just because he was Willie Stargell, but because he delivered his words with such great expression and sensitivity."

Schwantner said he puts *New Morning for the World* very close to the top of his accomplishments. The piece has now entered the standard repertoire; it's a well-known work and is performed numerous times during the year, particularly during the month of January to commemorate King's birthday. "Sometimes orchestra pieces take time to catch fire," Schwantner said. "Some are performed once and never again. This one is extraordinarily successful. I have to thank Stargell and his luminous career and this quirky connection between baseball and music that led to the initial interest in the piece. If Freeman had selected a prominent black minister from Rochester to narrate it, that would not have done it. It was Freeman's extraordinary genius at promoting the school, which he was extremely good at ... this was maybe his greatest stroke of media madness. And in the end, good things came out of this for many, including Stargell."

Stargell would go on to perform Schwantner's tribute to King a number of other times over the next several years, including once in 1990 in Syracuse. There, he told a local reporter that he was in awe at his first rehearsal seven years earlier. He felt he was in over his head and nearly gave up. "I'd look over and see how the students at the Eastman School were playing their hearts out," he said. "I'd make a mistake and look out of the corner of my eye and I'd see them cringe."[7] Stargell even tried his hand at other pieces, narrating Copland's "Lincoln Portrait" with several symphonies, including the Pittsburgh Symphony Orchestra in late September of 2000—less than five months before his death. Although by that time suffering from serious health issues, Stargell delivered a game performance at Heinz Hall that night, periodically staring "out into the audience with the same intense eyes that once terrorized countless pitchers."[8]

Freeman and the others weren't surprised that Stargell could adapt to other works of music. Years earlier, after the initial tour of the King tribute, Freeman envisioned Stargell fashioning a second career built around performing on stage — and doing the necessary work to promote those performances. That's how easy the big man was to work with. "Gracious and hard-working and honest and undemanding — that's how I would describe him," Freeman said. "Willie was superb, not only on the stage but also in all of the public relations activities that surrounded the event." When Schwantner's tribute to King opened in Washington in 1983, the Reagan White House held a reception that included the most elite power brokers in Washington — including the President himself. "He never said anything but the most appropriate things in a social situation," Freeman said of Stargell. "He was like a gold mine."

When he saw what Stargell was capable of doing, Freeman came up with yet another idea — this one involved sending Stargell to tour around the country with the New York Philharmonic, serving as an ambassador of classic music. He would perform in the morning for inner-city teenagers with major orchestras of National League cities, then accompany his audience to a ballgame in that city's National League park. Freeman had been moved to think about this project by something inspiring Stargell had said over dinner to Freeman's then 18-year-old son, John, a catcher who had been invited to attend Major League tryouts. When John demurred, saying he was not a fast enough runner, Stargell told him that the only National League record he held was for striking out. "Stargell told him, 'You see, John, you can't hit home runs if you can't learn how to strike out. And what is true in sports is also true in politics, in business and in the arts,'" Freeman recalled. Freeman said

Stargell's remarks immediately made him think how powerful that kind of a message would be for inner-city youth in a program that included elements of baseball and music, and he developed a proposal for the Ford Motor Company. But the financing fell through and Stargell got interested in other projects.

Those who collaborated on *New Morning for the World* would cross paths periodically later on. Effron, who grew up in Cincinnati, once attended a Reds game there when Stargell was coaching first base for the Pirates. "I was with some people and they didn't know that I knew him," he said. "I told them I was going to walk down between innings and talk to Stargell. They told me he wasn't going to talk to me. But he came running over and gave me a big hug. They all said, 'God, he knows Stargell.' It was the highlight of my life."

Although Stargell had no fulltime "next career" lined up yet, he strode into retirement confidently following his foray into the world of symphony music, "ready for tomorrow," as he wrote in an article that appeared in *Parade* magazine in April 1983. He was no longer driven to play the game that had brought him fame and a healthy paycheck. He talked about his work with the Willie Stargell Foundation and its focus on sickle cell anemia. "For each dollar I raise to aid in the cure of this disease, I think of a kid lying in a hospital bed who will never be able to live his or her dream," he said.[9] He'd first gotten involved in the fight against sickle cell more than a decade earlier, when he learned his oldest daughter, Wendy, was diagnosed as a carrier of sickle cell anemia, an inherited disorder that decreases the blood's ability to deliver oxygen to the body. Several noteworthy professional athletes, including Stargell and Atlanta Braves slugger Henry Aaron, got involved, lending their names to various fundraising efforts. But Stargell did more than generate money. Even during his playing days — first with the Black Athletes Foundation, which organized in 1963 before morphing into the Willie Stargell Foundation in 1979 — he sought out those in positions of power, hoping to open the nation's eyes to the little-known disease. In the winter of 1971, for example, he met with Pennsylvania Senator Richard S. Schweiker to discuss a pilot program designed to open the door to more screening opportunities. Schweiker even co-authored a senate bill that would authorize federal grants for voluntary screening and counseling, educational materials and research for the prevention, treatment and cure of the disease.[10]

Over the years, the Willie Stargell Foundation raised thousands of dollars, much of it used to buy laboratory equipment designed to diagnose the disease, although funding was spent in other areas. One of them was a 1980 seminar geared toward the world of academia and aimed at bringing sickle cell anemia into the classroom as a discussion topic.[11] Neddie Hollis, executive director of the Sickle Cell Society, Inc.—one of the nation's first community-funded sickle cell disease centers—said the Willie Stargell Foundation was not tied structurally to the society. "We were separate entities and had totally separate goals," Hollis said. "But Willie was very supportive of the society's efforts and accomplishments." Hollis's predecessor, Ruth White, was the society's executive director from the early 1970s until 1989, and during that time, Hollis said, Stargell was a major helper with fundraising activities, including bowling and golf tournaments. Hollis said, that Stargell "seemed to have had the presence to command respect among the most powerful people in the city." Hollis said Stargell and White had an excellent relationship. "To hear her tell it, Willie was genuinely concerned about the disease. He was sincere about helping in any way he could."[12]

Stargell's foundation had its share of success in terms of generating money for the sickle cell cause. In 1980-81 alone, the year after the Pirates' feel-good world championship of 1979, the foundation raised $159,805. But the next year, that number dropped to $50,000—and much of that was used to run the organization. As a result, less than $10,000 was made available in direct grants to those suffering from sickle cell anemia, Stargell told the *Greensburg Tribune Review* in June of 1982. "We haven't been able to give anybody the funds that we have in the past," Stargell said. "It doesn't make us feel very good."[13]

That's the year when the Pennsylvania Commission on Charitable Organizations ordered the organization to undergo an independent audit. According to a published report that cited state officials, the foundation started the 1980-81 fiscal year with $23,286. But by April of 1982, the commission ordered the organization to cease operations, claiming it had failed to submit to the audit and had spent too much on administrative costs.[14]

A key financial failing was linked to the foundation's 1980 decision to sell the 300 Neiman prints that Stargell discussed during the first of his "days" honoring him at Three Rivers Stadium. The goal was to raise $600,000 but over a two-year period, only 20 of the prints were sold. In the meantime, the foundation moved into new offices and hired several employees, figuring that the Neiman prints would bring in sufficient funding to operate at that level. Without revenue from the print sales, the foundation was unable to pay its bills.[15] Even though the foundation that bore Stargell's name had its problems, Stargell remained committed to the cause. In April 1983, a malt liquor company known as Champale initiated its second annual fundraising campaign to help the National Association for Sickle Cell Disease and named Stargell as its national spokesman. The firm also launched a major public service publicity effort to call attention to the NASCD programs.

The Commission on Charitable Organizations later reinstated Stargell's foundation fundraising rights, but by that time the damage had been done and in the first few days of 1984, the foundation was on its last legs. In January, the foundation's office equipment and sports memorabilia were put up for auction at its East Liberty headquarters after the foundation was unable to attract sufficient donors to keep its operation afloat. The storefront building was sold for $22,000 and the proceeds were to be distributed to several charities.[16] Stargell told the *Pittsburgh Press* that his foundation had "suffered from the economics of the times" and could not operate the way he wanted it to operate. "The corporations were unable to help us as they had before," he added.[17] Stargell's foundation was just one of the areas into which he had delved following his retirement from the game. By the middle of 1983, he had been promoting such disparate products as poetry, fur coats, sandwiches and politicians, and the local media speculated that his endorsements were earning him at least twice as much as the estimated $700,000 he had made during his final season as a player.[18] Stargell was broadcasting Pirate games for Home Sports Entertainment, a regional cable sports channel; earning $2,500 to $5,000 for motivational speaking engagements; operating a Pittsburgh-based construction firm; and endorsing various food products. He was even contacted about a possible role in a television show to be created by the producers of *Hill Street Blues*, a popular police drama at the time. Steven Bochco, creator and executive producer of the show, to be called *Bay City Blues*, said, "We're all big Willie Stargell fans here and we're in the process of casting and Willie's name just came up. We thought it would be an interesting avenue to explore." Stargell, though, couldn't find time to do a screen test. "I'm locked in with a lot of other things right now," he said. "As it is, I have about 30 seconds left for myself." Stargell said the multiple offers did not result from any sort of marketing strategy on his or his attorney's part. His lawyer, Litman, said Stargell's attractiveness stemmed from the way he comported himself. "He has the closest thing to a perfect personality," Litman said. "He's a beautiful man and it emanates from him." William Stankey, an agent at Greater Talent Network — the New York–based management firm that handled Stargell's lecture schedule — called Stargell a "bona fide national hero. Because of that, people see him in a different light. He cares about people, and it shows."[19]

Just as Stargell was able to bring all races and creeds together in a clubhouse to create a family atmosphere, he seemed able to transcend boundaries in the area of product promotion and endorsements — lending his name to everything from low-income natural gas grants to plush coats for a downtown furrier. Stargell said the key was to reach people on the most basic level. "You take away a title or a position and the person underneath is still important," he said. "It doesn't matter who or what he is." It wasn't as if Stargell was accepting every deal pitched his way, though. He told the *Pittsburgh Press* he rejected a $225,000 annual fee to serve as spokesman for the American Pork Association because he had concerns about potential links between the product and high blood pressure.[20]

Stargell kept busy in other ways. He was nominated to serve on the Pennsylvania Council of the Arts in early 1984 — the agency responsible for encouraging and developing the arts in Pennsylvania through a grant program. A few years later, he would become involved in something of a different nature — serving as honorary chairman of the "Share the Joy" program, designed to educate new parents about the dangers of child abuse.[21]

Although retired as a player, Stargell maintained an affiliation with the Pirates as Peterson's special assistant. The club's official news release, sent out on March 18, 1983, stated that Stargell would focus much of his part-time work with the organization's minor league players and would also handle various duties at the major-league level. He would also devote some time in working with the John W. Galbreath Company, a real estate development corporation owned by Pirates chairman John Galbreath and his son, Dan, the Pirates' president. "I can't say how pleased we are to have Willie working with the organization," Peterson said. "I can envision him doing so many outstanding things for the Pirates. He is a class individual who will be a great addition to the staff." Stargell said in the club's press release that the one thing he desired more than anything else was to remain with the Pirates in some capacity. "I wanted the opportunity to give back some of the many things this organization gave me," he said. "This is an ideal situation for me ... it is very refreshing to know that I'm still going to be around and involved with this group of people." Stargell told reporters he envisioned helping youngsters who hadn't yet found their way to Three Rivers Stadium, focusing on the psychological aspects of the game. "I am more interested in the kids in the minor leagues," Stargell said. "With so many players, it's not so much the talent, it's the mental part that allows you to sustain the time you have in baseball.... I want to be the friend of the kids in the minor leagues."[22] Stargell served his first two post-retirement seasons as a minor league adviser for the Pirates, and in October of 1984 the club named him minor league hitting instructor. "Willie has been an integral part of our organization and has had a great influence on our minor leaguers over the last two seasons," Peterson said. "We are quite pleased that Willie will continue to work in our minor league system."[23]

Early in his playing days, Stargell downplayed the idea of sitting in the manager's seat someday, although he had waffled a bit as he neared the end of his playing career. Indeed, teammates and even opposing managers had speculated about Stargell's interest and aptitude for managing while he still had some gas in his playing tank. During spring training in 1980, Sparky Anderson, who was then managing the Detroit Tigers but had faced Stargell from the opposite dugout numerous times as skipper of the Cincinnati Reds, said he believed anyone could be a good manager if he could communicate well with his players. "And Willie has never been a two-faced guy," Anderson said. "All he'd have to do the first few years he manages is go in with four excellent coaches — not friends, coaches — who can help teach fundamentals. Willie has always been able to produce and maintain dignity. If he could take over the Pirates someday, it would be perfect."[24]

By spring training in 1985, Stargell had grown comfortable with the idea of managing. "When I retired I did not want to manage," he said. "I didn't want to be on the other side of the fence. But now, after being around a while, my mind is changing. I need another year or two, time to observe. But I think I want to manage." He was getting a taste of it in Florida's Grapefruit League, managing in "B" games and picking Tanner's brain. "It is starting to intrigue me," Stargell said. Tanner said he thought Stargell would be a good manager but that he needed to go down to the minor leagues and manage a while — perhaps as long as four years. Stargell said he would not be averse to managing in the minor leagues but would not make it a lifetime job. He also said he would not have a problem working for another organization — even an expansion club — provided he would have some say in player acquisition. "I would not go into an expansion team with a two-year contract," he said. "I would have to grow with the organization." Stargell said he would keep his rules to a minimum if he were to lead a ballclub. "Be on time and play like hell on the field," he said. "You just have to try to make men be men and athletes be athletes."[25] Less than three months later, it appeared as though he was taking a significant step toward that end when the Pirates named him to serve as first-base coach under Tanner. Joe Brown, brought back as interim GM, said he didn't expect Stargell to work any miracles with the club, which was in last place in the NL East with an 18–37 mark at the time and averaging a paltry 10,100 fans per game, but was simply trying to make the team more attractive. "Chuck and I are enthusiastic about Willie's acceptance of our invitation to become a member of our field staff," Brown said. "He's a winner and always has been a winner." Tanner was all for the move. "Without question, he's a future Hall of Famer and one of the greatest players in Pirates history," Tanner said. "He always maintained the right attitude even when he was slowed by injuries. Willie has always stressed the mental side of the game and his mental approach was just as great as his physical abilities." Stargell, who would replace Steve Demeter in the first base coaching box, said he hoped to inject a spark into the moribund club. "It's just a case of having fun again, and that's what the game is all about," Stargell said. "I just want to get down there and see the guys have some fun. I'm glad to have a chance to be part of the atmosphere of the stadium again. I'm willing to help in any capacity. I just hope I don't miss any signs down at first base."[26]

He also reiterated his desire to sit where Tanner was sitting. "The more I'm connected with it, the more I sense the urge to manage," he said. "To be honest, I'm not ready yet because I haven't been around it. But this time next year...." Prior to his first game, Stargell told his old Pirate teammate Skinner—now the club's third-base coach—that he "didn't know a darn thing about coaching first base." And no one was about to argue a few hours later when, in the first inning, Pirate base runner Joe Orsulak was picked off first. "I thought to myself, 'What the heck is going on here?'" Stargell said later with a laugh. "Get me out of here and back to the minor leagues so I can teach these kids how not to get picked off." Pirate players were happy to see Stargell back on the field, pickoff or no pickoff. "I think a lot of us found ourselves saying, 'I wish Willie was here,'" outfielder Doug Frobel said. "He was always such a guiding force. He's still the biggest guiding force for this team." Added Madlock, who played a key role on the Bucs '79 title team: "It's important to have a guy who is familiar with the modern-day ballplayers. The players feel like they can relate to Willie."[27]

Perhaps, but Stargell's presence did little to cure the Pirates' woes, as the club finished the 1985 season 57–104, a whopping 43½ games behind the division champion Cardinals. That was hardly the worst of it, though. That summer, word surfaced regarding a federal drug probe that focused on activities involving cocaine sales to major league baseball players. At least a dozen players were questioned by a federal grand jury—three of them Pirates: pitchers Rod Scurry and Al Holland and outfielder Lee Mazzilli, and two former Pirates in outfielder Lee Lacy and infielder Dale Berra. Seven men were indicted, six of them from Pittsburgh. It seemed like a million years—and a million miles—from 1979 and "We Are Family," as Stargell would admit. "We had a feeling in this city back then that we could do anything," he said. "You know, the city of champions."[28] In September, the federal cocaine trafficking trial of a Philadelphia caterer named Curtis Strong began in Pittsburgh, and on September 10—the fourth day of testimony—Berra dropped a bombshell, testifying that Stargell and Madlock gave him amphetamines, a stimulant that was not uncommon among players before being banned starting in the 2006 season. Berra testified that amphetamines—referred to as "greenies" by many in the game—made players more alert and alleviated aches and pains.

"It just makes your body feel stronger," Berra testified. Berra, under questioning from Strong's attorney, Adam Renfroe Jr., said he used greenies in Pittsburgh as well as Portland, Oregon, a minor-league affiliate of the Pirates at the time. When asked who had given him amphetamines in Pittsburgh, he told Renfroe it was Madlock and Stargell.

"Willie Stargell gave you amphetamines?" Renfroe asked.

"Yes, when he played for us," Berra responded.

Stargell told the *Washington Post*, "It's not true. That's about all I can say about it." Madlock refused to respond, saying, "I don't have anything to say about anything like that." But he added, "A lot of those guys up there are trying to get some people mentioned to take the monkey off their back."[29] Two days later, Dave Parker — Stargell's former long-ball protégé— also testified that Stargell and Madlock provided him with amphetamines. Stargell referred to the allegations as a "dead issue."[30]

On September 20, the jury of nine women and three men found Strong guilty of selling cocaine three times each to three players — including Parker, who was then with the Cincinnati Reds — and twice to former Pirate John Milner. The jury acquitted Strong on one count each of selling to three players, and two other counts were dropped at the request of U.S. Attorney J. Alan Johnson. In October, another defendant, Shelby Greer, pleaded guilty to seven drug trafficking charges. All told, seven men either were convicted of or pleaded guilty to selling cocaine to players.

The hits kept coming that fall for Stargell. On October 2, a public-private partnership assembled by then–Mayor Richard Caliguiri announced it had reached a deal with the Galbreath family and Warner Communications to buy the Pirates for $22 million, assuring that the club would remain in Pittsburgh for the near future. The partnership announced that Malcolm "Mac" Prine, president and board chairman of home-building giant Ryan Homes Inc., would serve as the team's president and chief executive officer. Ryan Homes was one of a dozen or so groups involved in the partnership, which outbid a group that included Tanner. The Pirates skipper expressed disappointment at the time but said, "The final thing is the team is staying here." Tanner said he would talk to the new owner and that his future with the club would be "dictated by what the new owner says to me."[31] Within a week, Tanner was gone — a decision he described as mutual. "They didn't want me, I didn't want them," Tanner said. "I didn't want to come back. We've resolved the issue and I'm happy for that. They could have kept me on hold and I appreciate that he (Prine) didn't do that."[32] Stargell publicly expressed an interest in Tanner's old job as manager, but within two days of Tanner's departure, the Pirates announced that they had ruled out Stargell as a possible new skipper after the former slugger met with interim GM Brown. "He told me that he hoped someday to be ready but that, at present, he was not ready to manage," Brown said of Stargell. "He has not applied for the job and I would be amazed if he did."[33]

Within a week, Stargell had himself a new job — serving as first-base coach and specialized hitting instructor under Tanner, who agreed to a five-year contract to manage the Atlanta Braves. The first time Stargell would pull on a Braves jersey would be the first time he donned the uniform of another organization besides the Pirates. That fact was not lost on Stargell after the announcement became public. "I'd be lying if I said I didn't have mixed emotions, because I've been here for so many years," he told the *Atlanta Constitution* in an interview from his Pittsburgh home. "But I have the chance to be with someone I admire and respect, Chuck Tanner. I want to do everything I can to help him with a new organization. I had some other calls, but I wanted to stay with Chuck."[34] He told John Clayton of the *Pittsburgh Press* that leaving the Pirates was "like going through another divorce. The city and the people here mean a lot to me. It's a real love affair. It is something a grown man has to deal with. As I'm departing, I will take a towel with me and be loyal to Chuck Tanner, just like I was loyal to the Pirates."[35]

While Stargell was getting used to the idea of being something other than a Pirate, he received some good news — in late February 1986, Commissioner Peter Ueberroth meted out punishment to those involved in the previous year's Pittsburgh drug trial, suspending seven players, including Parker and Berra for a year, but allowing them to play if they donated 10 percent of their salaries to drug-prevention programs. Four other players were suspended for 60 days, but their suspensions would be held in abeyance if they followed specific guidelines issued by the commissioner.[36] At the same time, Ueberroth exonerated Stargell of any wrongdoing, saying that he was "wrongly accused" of giving amphetamines to players. In a written statement, Ueberroth said "there is no wrongdoing on his [Stargell's] part." When asked if that meant criminal wrongdoing, Ueberroth responded, "I mean any wrongdoing. Willie Stargell had no wrongdoing. I looked at it eight ways from Sunday and somebody was out of line."[37]

The next month, during spring training in Florida, Stargell was busy trying to get comfortable wearing that new jersey and working with his old boss, Tanner, who defended his decision to bring Stargell south. "They didn't want Willie in Pittsburgh," Tanner said. "On the last day of the season, I told him that he'd be with me. The new people there complained later that I took him. And I said I took Willie Stargell when he was unemployed in Pittsburgh. Now, he's my first-base coach."[38] Stargell told the media during spring training that even though he had expressed an interest in the Pirates' managing vacancy after Tanner left, deep down he knew he wasn't ready, based on his half-season experience as a base coach under Tanner in Pittsburgh. "I'm dumb enough to know you have to be qualified and need to spend time doing these things," he said. "I learned a lot last year." He said he got a different view of the game from the dugout and from watching Tanner manage. "It was like falling in love again," Stargell said. "I saw a part of the game that really intrigued me, got my curiosity going." Media members brought up the Pittsburgh drug trials and in particular Berra's claims that Stargell had provided him with amphetamines. "It was a tough year, and everybody tried to deal with it and go on with their lives," Stargell said. "The only thing that really hurt me [about Berra] was that here was a guy I had gone to war with, accomplished so much with. For him to say that was mind-boggling. I'll never understand that."[39]

The 1986 campaign was a season of firsts for Stargell and one of the more surreal ones took place on May 26, when he trotted from the Atlanta dugout to the first base coach's box at Pittsburgh's Three Rivers Stadium, wearing the Braves' uniform. His presence elicited a standing ovation from the crowd of 14,102. "I was absolutely moved," Stargell said later. "Embarrassed again. When you have a day like that, it's just tough to talk about. There isn't a word to describe that particular moment. I didn't know how to act. If I could have hugged every one of those fine people, I would have." Seeing as how that would have been impossible, Stargell instead tipped his cap and took a bow. He admitted it wasn't easy to go from the Pirates' black and gold to the Braves' red, white and blue color scheme. "I had to think about it a lot," he said. "I'll never forget what happened here. I'll never forget the Pirates or the people here. But life is all about growing, and experiencing new things, and that's what I'm doing."[40] Stargell said he would continue to root for the Pirates. "I enjoy those kids. That's what I enjoyed most about last season, working with those young guys. That, to me, is what coaching is all about. If you want to give something back to the game, you go to the young players and say, 'Here I am. I have a world of knowledge and I want to share it with you. Maybe I can help you enjoy your career as much or more than I did mine.' That's what I've tried to do."[41]

A little less than halfway through the season, Stargell talked once again about his managerial aspirations, saying that he had been getting exposure as a coach to several key facets of the game that would come into play as manager — personnel meetings, contract meetings, etc. "It is like getting the necessary education before you graduate from college, before going on about your career," he said. He addressed the idea that the upper levels of baseball management might not want a black manager and said he would be sad if that were indeed true. However, Stargell said he didn't believe that was the case because of the quality of people in baseball. "Once I get the qualifications for being a manager, should somebody tell me that because of the color of my skin they don't feel they should hire me ... I'm going to be real disappointed with the game because of the commitment I have made to it," he said. "I've studied the game from a player's standpoint long enough to know, though, that you really have to be color blind."[42]

Despite the optimistic start, all did not go well for the Braves in 1986, as they finished last in Tanner's first year as manager with a 72–89 record. The next year was even worse, as Atlanta fashioned a 69–92 mark, including an abysmal 27–53 road record. The 1987 season also was marked at the outset by inflammatory comments made by Al Campanis, vice president of player personnel for the Los Angeles Dodgers, who on April 6 appeared on ABC TV's *Nightline* to help observe the 40th anniversary of Jackie Robinson breaking baseball's color barrier. The visit ignited a firestorm, as Campanis essentially told a national audience that blacks might not be qualified to serve in high-level baseball positions. "I don't believe it's prejudice," Campanis said. "I truly believe that they may not have some of the necessities to be, let's say, a field manager, or perhaps a general manager." Campanis apologized for his remarks, but the Dodgers wasted little time in asking for — and receiving — Campanis's resignation. The episode also served as a launching point for scores of people to weigh in on whether blacks were receiving a fair shake when it came to being considered — let alone being hired — for high-level positions in baseball such as field manager and general manager. Ueberroth said he believed strongly in bringing more blacks to front office positions and that he would put his job on the line if necessary to improve the situation. "We have blatantly said baseball needs to improve [on blacks holding front-office jobs]," Ueberroth said on ABC's *Nightline* just two days after Campanis had appeared on the same show. "If we didn't intend to do something about it we would have ignored it. We're going to do something about it."[43]

Frank Robinson, the former Orioles Hall of Famer who became baseball's first black manager in 1975 with Cleveland, said Campanis merely "was saying what a lot of baseball people think, and I'm glad it's finally out in the open. Black people have to take hold and keep it out in the open. They have to make sure it just doesn't get swept under the rug. This is something I've felt for years and haven't been able to say because I had no proof. But now that's been said, it's out in the open." Madlock — Stargell's former Pirate teammate who by then had moved on to the Dodgers — said periodically people would talk about the lack of blacks in coaching and managing positions in football and baseball, but then the talk would go away. "I hope this time it can take it a little further and really get down to why there are not blacks in higher echelon jobs in professional sports," Madlock said.[44]

Two managerial vacancies occurred during the 1987 season, but Stargell — and every other potential black candidate — was bypassed for the jobs. Joe Morgan, Stargell's old acquaintance from the Bay Area, was upset that his pal was overlooked. Morgan said Stargell would be more effective than the vast majority of managers. "I know how good he is, how deserving he is, but ... maybe baseball doesn't deserve Willie Stargell," Morgan said of Stargell. "When he was playing, Willie Stargell was respected by every player. Every one.... All 599 other guys had respect for Willie Stargell, and there have been a lot of managers who've been hired the last couple of years you can't say the same thing about." Morgan expressed frustration at the pace at which baseball was moving to bring blacks into more meaningful positions — Campanis's statements notwithstanding. "When did Campanis make those remarks — April?" Morgan asked at the end of June. "Everybody's been saying, 'We're going to see change, we're going to change.' Well, I don't see any changes."[45] Stargell would not bring race into the issue, though. "Clubs have different needs at different times," he said. "Some are looking for a fiery manager at a given time. Others may be looking for a pitching-oriented manager. When the time comes that you fit the needs of a club, you'll get a fair appraisal."[46]

Campanis's remarks and the subsequent outcry prompted Stargell and several other minority players, former players, coaches and managers to band together and discuss the current state of affairs with regard to underrepresentation of minorities in baseball. During the next two years, the group — which became known as the Baseball Network and also featured the likes of Frank Robinson, Ralph Garr, Dusty Baker and Billy Williams — began meeting with the representatives of Major League Baseball to try to expedite the process of getting more blacks and minorities into meaningful positions both in the dugout and in front offices.

Ray Burris, who won more than 100 games in the big leagues as a pitcher during his 15-year career, was among those involved in the Baseball Network. Burris said the group's purpose was to make Major League Baseball aware of individuals who were interested in becoming a part of the game's decision-making process. Burris said Ueberroth showed a genuine interest in instigating some changes, and as a sort of pioneer in the area of improving minorities' chances of gaining a foothold in baseball outside the lines, Burris was pleased to be a part of the process. That's because, down the road, he hoped to work his way into a decision-making position within Major League Baseball. "With all the years I had played, I felt I had a lot to offer with regard to my knowledge of the game and the business side of the game," he said. Burris said the group went in with realistic expectations and so while the Baseball Network's efforts did not trigger a tidal wave of minority hiring, the group did make a difference — at least in Burris's estimation. "We had a lot of common ground, but we also had some disagreements and different beliefs and thought processes and we had to work through that," he said of those who participated. "It all started with a sharing of ideas and then we had to fine-tune things. We needed to determine exactly what we wanted to accomplish and that was how to get blacks in baseball positions. We knew we weren't going to start at the general manager position or start as an owner. Let's be real. But we knew we could start at some point in an organization and hopefully have the ability to elevate ourselves as time went on. That was our goal."[47]

Looking back some 25 years later, Burris said he believed the Baseball Network did make a difference. He pointed out successful managerial runs turned in by minorities such as Jerry Manuel, who piloted the Chicago White Sox to a division crown and four second-place finishes in a six-year stretch, and Dusty Baker — who led the Giants to the National League pennant in 2002 — as evidence that men of color have made their mark in high places. In the front office, Kenny Williams has had a solid run as the White Sox general manager, and Tony Regins enjoyed his share of success as the Los Angeles Angels of Anaheim's general manager from 2007 until he resigned in 2011. "When you look at baseball and the sporting world in general, there's been a lot of overall improvement, from managers to general managers to coaches to farm directors," Burris said. "You've had a lot of growth in these areas. But I would be a fool to think every club in major league baseball is going to hire a black to be a general manager. That isn't going to happen. So what is the percentage that is going to satisfy me? Or would satisfy a Willie Stargell? I don't know. But if there's one or two, that's better than none."

In addition to working with Ueberroth, the Baseball Network also met with Dr. Harry Edwards, a professor of sociology at the University of California, Berkeley, who was working with the commissioner's office. While Burris believed Ueberroth was sincere in his efforts to help increase minority representation in Major League Baseball, he wasn't as impressed with Edwards, perhaps best known for helping to organize a black boycott of the 1968 Olympics. "To me, he was very vague in his presentation to us," Burris said. "He never said point blank, 'Guys, this is where it's at.' It was all of the rhetoric of what he was about and what baseball was about. We didn't want a history of baseball. We had a history of baseball — we were part of that history. We didn't need history — we needed to know what we could do at that point to make things better and what his position was with the commissioner. I didn't feel comfortable with what he was saying. It's not that we were trying to discredit him, but we felt he was trying to discredit us." Edwards told the *Chicago Tribune* after a meeting in December 1987 that both sides were moving forward "with some urgency and dispatch. People will look back on this year as the beginning of something significant and important. Not just for baseball, but for American society." Edwards noted that minority hires in Major League Baseball had increased from 17 to 86 between April 17 and December 8 of that year. "But it's another thing to be able to look at this process down the line—three years, five years, eight years and see 300 jobs and the situation still going strong because there is a solid base and a solid structure for progress there."[48]

Burris said Stargell's role with the Baseball Network was a critical one, as he served on the group's executive board. "The thing I remember about Willie was his clear view on the mindset of baseball at that time," he said. "I think we all had an idea but he had a better idea from the things he'd had a chance to witness—the things he'd seen going through the Pirates organization." Burris said the Baseball Network was unable to remain intact because of scheduling and funding difficulties. "But for that short time, we were given the opportunity to have our voices be heard by the baseball establishment and the people we thought to be very important. We got a lot of press and a lot of awareness out of it. That awareness, I think, fueled over the long haul the opportunities for things to happen. I just wished we would have been able to stay in contact. But maybe that effort brought enough awareness at the time when things needed to be made aware of, so that people would start thinking about these things. If that's what happened, then we served our purpose in that particular arena."

Nine months after Campanis's bombshell statement, the topic of race in professional sport again seized the spotlight. This time, a television personality named Jimmy "The Greek" Snyder, a veteran oddsmaker who had worked for 12 years as a pro football analyst for CBS, said during a TV interview that blacks "got everything. If they take over coaching jobs like everybody wants them to, there's not going to be anything left for white people." CBS Sports fired Snyder the following day. Snyder's comments again raised the question as to whether professional sports was doing enough to further the cause of minorities. Stargell and his former teammate Bill Robinson told the *Pittsburgh Post-Gazette* that they didn't believe enough progress had been made since the Campanis incident and they doubted whether Snyder's comments would speed up the process of getting minorities involved in a more meaningful way in professional sports. "We're not the people doing the hiring and firing," Stargell said. "All you and I are doing is guessing. Every time a remark is made, they come to a minority and ask them what they think about it. I'd like to hear what some non-minorities have to say." Stargell likened Snyder's remarks to the ones Campanis made the previous April. "It's very difficult to understand people in the kind of position they're in saying what they're saying."[49]

CHAPTER 10

The Hall Calls — and So Does Home

WITH THE SUBJECT OF RACE in baseball still simmering during the winter of 1987-88, Willie Stargell received a call that would change his life. Shortly before 9 P.M. on the night of January 12, Jack Lang — the secretary/treasurer of the Baseball Writers' Association of America — called Stargell at his home in Stone Mountain, Georgia, to tell him he had been elected to the Baseball Hall of Fame and would be enshrined in the magical village of Cooperstown on July 31. "I'll be forever in your debt," Stargell told Lang, and then wept. He hugged his son, Willie Jr., and said, "I just wanted to play. I didn't go out there to be considered great. I just wanted to be consistent." Stargell became just the 17th player to be elected on the first ballot and the 200th player overall selected for enshrinement. He was named on 352 of the 427 ballots cast by 10-year members of the writers group, or 82.4 percent. Players needed to appear on 321 ballots — or 75 percent — to gain entry to the shrine. "The Hall of Fame was made for players like Willie Stargell," said Chuck Tanner, Stargell's boss with the Atlanta Braves and his former manager in Pittsburgh. "It couldn't be a Hall of Fame without Willie Stargell."[1]

Although Stargell was known perhaps most for his prodigious home runs — the shots that left Dodger Stadium, for example, or the monumental drives in Olympic and Veterans stadiums, that's not what he was most proud of. "Winning, knowing the formula for winning. That's what I'm proud of," he said. "The thing is you have to be daring, you have to take a chance. I can remember Roberto Clemente pulling me aside when I was young and telling me that I could do this or try to do it first. There is a formula for winning, but you have to be sincere about your commitment. Ability will get you there, but your mentality will sustain for any period of time."[2]

Stargell was asked the day before the Hall of Fame voting was announced if he'd thought about what it would be like to get the call. "There would be nothing to describe being in the presence of those immortal players," he said. "It's tough to imagine being with those people, people I've been in awe of, people like Ruth, Williams, Cobb, Wagner, Mays, Aaron." Still, he knew the very real possibility existed that he would not gain election, particularly given it was his first crack. He flashed back to his MVP voting snubs in 1971 and 1973. "I've learned not to get too excited about something that's out of my hands," Stargell said of the Hall of Fame voting. "If it doesn't happen, I'm just as proud to have been considered with all of those players."[3]

The day after his election, Stargell appeared in New York for a press conference, where he apologized to the media for his eyes looking "like two cherries in a glass of buttermilk. You think you're well equipped to handle the moment, but Mother Nature humbles you at the damndest times."[4] The next day, he appeared at a luncheon in Pittsburgh to celebrate his election to the Hall and received an unsolicited endorsement for his managerial aspirations from a somewhat unlikely source — Pirates manager Jim Leyland, who spent 11 seasons managing in the minor leagues before getting his big-league opportunity in Pittsburgh. Leyland said that while most men would need to spend time managing in the minor leagues before getting a big-league job, Stargell was the exception because of his knowledge of the game and his ability to relate to people. "Strategy is overrated," Leyland said. "The key to managing is that it's a people business. And I expect Willie Stargell will be a successful major-league manager in the near future." Leyland said he didn't know Stargell well but that he saw the way people in the game respected him. "There are a lot of players who are heroes to the fans," he said. "But I'm not sure there are many players who are heroes to other players. I think Willie Stargell is a hero to the players because of what he accomplished and what he stands for." Stargell talked a bit about managing, saying, "I don't see where the game is going to be a total stranger to me. I don't see where it will be all that different [than as a player or coach]. You surround yourself with good people. That makes it easier."[5]

Stargell's Hall of Fame election wasn't the only major development in his life during the winter of 1987-88. The Braves also announced that Stargell, who had served as a first-base coach his first two seasons in Atlanta, would be moving over to coach third base for 1988. Terence Moore, an Atlanta columnist, claimed that was even a more startling development than Stargell's Hall of Fame election because there had never been an American-born black to hold down that position in major league baseball history. Moore wrote that the Braves' decision "figures to change baseball's racist foundation. Finally. The reason Stargell has no black predecessors as third-base coaches is the same reason there are no black managers, no black pitching coaches, no black head coaches in the NFL, few black quarterbacks, centers, middle linebackers and middle infielders. Those are considered jobs for thinking men, and the prevailing powers throughout amateur and professional sports prefer the status quo." Stargell said when Tanner told him about the switch, his first reaction was that it was an honor — and a "unique challenge." He acknowledged that the move to third base was another step closer to him attaining his ultimate goal: serving as the manager of a big league club. But he said he was focusing only on putting all his strength and energy into his new coaching job. "When I've served my time at third base, hopefully I will have done well enough to have somebody offer me a managerial job. I don't have ants in my pants."[6]

He again alluded to his managerial aspirations when the club convened in West Palm Beach, Florida, for spring training in February. He said he viewed the third-base coaching job as a challenge he was eager to take on. "I know what the flip side of coaching third can be, but I look forward to it. I know I'm going to make mistakes, but I'm not afraid to make mistakes. I see this as a step on the ladder. The more I can learn, the more hands-on experience I can get, I will be more prepared to manage when I do go on to that." Tanner said he was seeking someone aggressive and smart to coach third base. "I want a third-base coach to think ahead, make the decisions early instead of standing there and hoping everything falls into place. It's a very responsible job. But Willie was a very responsible captain for me. He was a very responsible hitter in the clutch. The big thing is he has to be alert and in the game all the time. There are so many things you have to learn. Willie adjusted his whole career. He can adapt to this."[7]

But Tanner's grand plan — which ultimately called for Stargell to succeed him as manager if the former slugger hadn't already landed a job elsewhere — never materialized the way he'd drawn it up. First, there was an awkward return to Pittsburgh on May 20 — a return punctuated by a robust round of booing by Pirates fans when Stargell headed out to coach third base for the first time. The boos were in response to reports by the Pittsburgh media that Stargell had put the kibosh on the Bucs' bid to hold yet another night in his honor — which would have been the third such event since 1980. The Pirates had flown Stargell back to Pittsburgh in January to announce the ceremony, but the two sides could not agree on appropriate compensation and the event never happened. The *Pittsburgh Post-Gazette* reported that Stargell had told the Pirates that an expensive luxury car would be an appropriate gift. Douglas Danforth, the Pirates board chairman, did not address the car request but said, "It's very simple. We were unable to get together on terms. It was a misunderstanding. There are no hard feelings at all."[8]

Stargell related a slightly different version to *Press* columnist Gene Collier, saying he had no contact with the club from his firing in 1985 until early in 1988 when the Pirates proposed a third night honoring him. Stargell said he was convinced that if the Galbreath family had still owned the club, the two sides could have agreed on a suitable way to acknowledge his Hall of Fame election. He also said he found it "intriguing" the way the media made him out to be greedy. "It's as if they were waiting for an opportunity to unload on Willie," he said. "Maybe with feelings they've been harboring for some time." Collier, though, characterized Stargell and his agent's attempts to negotiate the terms and conditions of the failed "Willie Stargell Night" as "another sickening example of arrogance" and said that Stargell or his agent "actually listed the model of luxury car that should be involved." In retrospect, Stargell told Collier he would have been happy if the Pirates had merely acknowledged his pending trip to Cooperstown. "Just say one of our own is going into the Hall of Fame," Stargell said. "And then I'd tip my cap and that would be it."[9]

In addition to booing Stargell when he took the field that night, some of the crowd of 18,880 booed him again when a Stargell video clip was shown on the stadium scoreboard. Tanner was incensed at the crowd's reaction. He grabbed Stargell after the game and said plainly within earshot of the assembled media, "I want to apologize Willie, for the people who booed you. You never should have been a Pirate."[10] On Saturday, which would have been "Willie Stargell Night," the Pirates would not even flash the former slugger's image on the Three Rivers scoreboard—ostensibly because they wanted to spare the greatest slugger and one of the most beloved players in franchise history further booing.

Things quickly got worse for Stargell, Tanner and the Braves, who finished their weekend series with the Pirates at 12–27. After flying from Pittsburgh to Chicago following the final game of the three-game set on Sunday, Braves general manager Bobby Cox asked to see Tanner, Stargell and the two other coaches he brought from Pittsburgh—Skinner and Tony Bartirome, the old Bucco trainer and minor-league spring training camp mate of Stargell's—in the team hotel. After a three-hour meeting, all four were dismissed. Tanner was stunned at Cox's decision to replace him with Russ Nixon—the former third-base coach who was reassigned to an organizational post to allow Stargell to coach third base—in part because he believed the club was improving, despite its 12–27 record. "We were on a program to rebuild," said Tanner, who had never been forced out of a job during a season in his 18 years as a big league manager. "I wasn't the one to get it done because they didn't want me." Cox explained that it was simply time for a change. "It was the most difficult thing I've had to do in my life," he said. "Chuck was great about it, but we had to do something different."[11] Stargell, meanwhile, expressed surprise at the move because — like Tanner — he believed the Braves had been making progress although the club was just 153–208 under Tanner. "I can't sit here and tell you it's unfair," said Stargell, who noted he remained committed to becoming a manager. "When a team decides to make a change, then those are the consequences. I try not to dwell on bitterness. There's a reason for everything."[12] Two weeks later, team president Stan Kasten said that Stargell was offered a chance to remain with the Braves organization. When asked if Tanner had convinced Stargell to turn down the job offer, Kasten replied, "No comment."[13]

Stargell's next turn in the baseball spotlight came a little more than two months later, when his titanic presence energized the quaint New York Finger Lakes village of Cooperstown while there for the Hall of Fame induction ceremony on July 31. He eschewed a speech he had prepared for the crowd of 10,000 or so — many sporting Pirate gear — and instead chose to improvise. "I can only stand up here and say that you are looking at one proud individual," said Stargell, who went on talk about growing up in Alameda, California, and finding Pittsburgh to be a very special area. "It wasn't a fancy place," he said. "The people were real. If you did what was expected of you and worked hard, you could earn the respect of that town. To the young people, I want to say that I am living proof that hard work earns rewards. There are no shortcuts." Later, after the applause died down, Stargell talked about getting back into the game — his abrupt departure from the

On Hall of Fame induction day, July 31, 1988, Willie stands proudly with the plaque that guarantees him baseball immortality (courtesy National Baseball Hall of Fame Library, Cooperstown, New York).

Braves some two months earlier notwithstanding. "I'd like to give a lot back to baseball and I feel like I have a lot to give. I think I can contribute as a farm director, a director of player personnel, an assistant to a general manager or to a field manager, or as one of the game's ambassadors. Traveling abroad; I'd look forward to that."[14]

At least one member of the Pittsburgh media on hand for the induction ceremony referred to the bungled Willie Stargell Night earlier that summer. Tom McMillan, a columnist for the *Post-Gazette*, questioned how Pittsburgh fans should remember Stargell. "Should we remember him as sweet-sounding father figure who promotes 'humanistic endeavors,' preaches hard work, and, in a recent interview with a national newspaper, lashed out against materialism? Or should we remember him as a greedy former Pirate who heard about Willie Stargell Hall of Fame Night and wanted payment — specifically, a $70,000 car — in exchange for his participation? Should we remember him as the captain and spiritual leader of the 1979 World Series champions, leader of an astonishing Series comeback, co–MVP of the National League? Or should we remember him as the captain and spiritual leader of a team that would eventually find itself gutted in the most publicized drug scandal in the game's history?"[15]

While McMillan questioned Stargell's behavior and character at his Hall of Fame induction, one of his media counterparts in Atlanta, *Atlanta Journal-Constitution* columnist Roy S. Johnson, used the opportunity to urge the Braves to bring Stargell back to the organization. "The Braves could use Willie Stargell," Johnson wrote. "As much as Russ Nixon has been able to accomplish in his frustrating effort to steady the sinking Braves, they could use him, badly.... They could use his knowledge, his experience, his love of the game." Johnson referred to Stargell's induction speech, where he noted that he wanted to "give something back to baseball because you've given so much to me." The Braves, Johnson wrote, "could use it all."[16]

Four months later, long after the balls and bats of another season had been put away, the Baseball Network reconvened, this time in Atlanta during baseball's annual winter meetings, to renew the call for greater minority representation. They listened while Commissioner Ueberroth said minority employment in Major League Baseball had risen from 2 percent to 10 percent in two years — and then listened when home run king Henry Aaron — the Braves' director of player development — described Ueberroth's speech as "the same old bull, just dressed up a bit." But Stargell said he was pleased that Ueberroth had reaffirmed a commitment to minorities. "We have some real areas that we need to expound on, decision-making areas," Stargell said. "I'm excited there's a commitment because with a commitment in due time something will happen. As far as results, we have a long way to go." After Ueberroth spoke, members of the Baseball Network huddled for more than an hour with representatives from the commissioner's office. Stargell called the meeting "very good, really impressive. We all sort of joined hands and reaffirmed our commitment to work together on this thing."[17]

While Stargell remained on the outside looking in, his exile period wouldn't last much longer. In February, 1989, he agreed in principle to return to the Braves as a roving instructor. The arrangement called for Stargell to split his time at spring training between the Braves' major and minor league camps, where his duties would include motivation and outfield instruction. Cox listed hitting instruction among Stargell's responsibilities and indicated a willingness to let Stargell free-lance a bit when it came to his assignments, in part to allow Stargell to take advantage of the additional visibility that his recent Hall of Fame induction provided. "He doesn't work for anybody else," Cox said of Stargell. "Willie fits in well with our people and is a great asset."[18] Stargell would go on to spend another eight productive seasons with the Atlanta organization, working his motivational magic and providing hitting tips for many of the players who would go on to great success with the Braves — players like Ron Gant, Ryan Klesko, David Justice and a sure-fire Hall-of-Famer-in-waiting, Chipper Jones. He served in several capacities, including roving minor-league hitting instructor and special assistant to scouting director Chuck La Mar. Later he was named special assistant for player personnel.

Cox said Stargell was a huge asset to the Braves organization, even if much of his work took place behind the scenes. "Just for our players to be around a guy like that, the motivation he gave the players and the hitting tips — Willie was tremendous. He was great with the younger guys — he put his heart and soul into it. He was a good guy to listen to. It didn't have to be about hitting all the time — he'd talk about other stuff. But I liked Willie as a hitting instructor. He would talk mechanics and the mental parts and spreading the ball around the field a little bit. I loved Willie."[19]

Even while in Atlanta, Stargell admitted to keeping close tabs on his old ballclub after the Pirates turned the corner and became serious contenders in 1990. "I've been checking on the scores, keeping up with them," Stargell said in May of that season. "I consider this like an old relationship. The Pirates were my girlfriend. It got to the point where we had to go our separate ways, but I have a lot of fond memories. That's where I learned how to win and about motivation. So they'll always be special for me. It's nice to see they're doing well again."[20] Things got sticky the following season, when Stargell's current and former organizations squared off in the playoffs. "I'm rooting for the Braves, but I remember the Pirates," Stargell said while helping groom future Braves at the club's fall Instructional League camp in Florida. "Let's put it this way. If the Braves don't win, I hope the Pirates do." That would be the first of two straight years when the Braves and Pirates would meet in the National League Championship Series, with the winner advancing to the World Series. In the first go-round, Atlanta prevailed in a tight seven-game series that featured four one-run games, including three that ended in scores of 1–0. The 1992 matchup featured an even more dramatic conclusion, as the Pirates took a 2–0 lead into the bottom of the ninth inning of the seventh and decisive game, only to see the Braves rally for three runs—the last of which was scored by former Pirate Sid Bream when he narrowly beat Barry Bonds's throw home from left field on pinch-hitter Francisco Cabrera's single.

While Stargell certainly was interested in the fate of the big-league Braves, he seemed to get more enjoyment talking about what was coming down the Atlanta pipeline, in the minor league system. After all, he'd been in on the ground floor, helping the Braves rise from years of mediocrity, including a worst-to-first bolt in 1991. "This is no accident," he said of the Braves' success heading into the 1991 postseason and added that the good times were just beginning. "The minor league system is in great shape, too," he said. "We haven't seen the last of the Braves." Stargell proved prophetic; the franchise would go on to win an unprecedented 14 consecutive division titles, a string that ended in 2005. He said he liked staying in the background, working with the Braves' minor-leaguers. "I enjoy talking hitting with the young players from the neck up. I like teaching them winning hitting and thinking."[21]

The players who came through the Braves' system remembered the things that Stargell told them as they made their way up the ladder. "He was very smart—and intelligent about the game—along with being a great talent," said Gant, who used to wear a mantra that Stargell had given him—"I Will—I Can—I Am"—under the brim of his cap. "One of the things he told me was that if you get into a slump, you should go down to the [batting] cage, turn the machine on and just bunt 50 balls. Don't swing—just bunt 50 balls. Then turn the machine off, go in and eat a sandwich and you'll get yourself out of that slump. Sure enough, I was in one of those slumps and I did the 50 balls, went back and went 3-for-4 with two home runs that night. Willie was part of the reason why I stayed out of those long, extended slumps."[22] Klesko, who finished his 16-year big league career with 278 home runs, credited Stargell with making a huge difference in his approach early on. "I used to sit and talk with him for hours," he said in 1997. "I didn't know how to hit the ball the other way. I owe almost everything I've done hitting-wise to him. Before I got to the big leagues, Willie was my main guy."[23]

In a 2010 interview, Chipper Jones said that one of things Stargell told him was to swing the heaviest bat he could. "He knew I'd develop as a power hitter," he said. "I was 6–3, 180 pounds then, but I'm 6–3 200 now. If you swung a heavy bat, even when a pitcher jammed you, you could still muscle a ball to the outfield for a single. Or, if you hit it square, you could hit it out of the ballpark." Jones said Stargell's advice was always simple but smart. One such message: slow feet, quick hands. "When your feet are quick, your hands are moving and you're not balanced. It puts you behind the fastball and ahead of the curveball. That's not the place you want to be." Stargell talked a lot about the mental approach to hitting. "How and when to lay off certain pitches — and how to look for certain pitches in certain situations." Jones said Stargell — who ranked number 7 all-time among major league baseball's career strikeout leaders with 1,936 whiffs — never talked much about going down on strikes. "A strikeout is the same as grounding out," Jones said. "You might feel a little better about yourself, but it's still an out." Jones said not everything that Stargell said applied directly to him because he was a different sort of hitter. "I was trying to go out there every day and hit .300 and he was more of a run-producer," he said. "But as a young player, I was a sponge. I soaked up everything from my hitting instructors — guys like Frank Howard and Willie Stargell. You'd be stupid not to. You'd take little bits of each one and see what applies to you. Maybe 50 percent of what Willie said applied to me."[24]

David Justice, who gained the reputation of being somewhat moody and who rubbed some people — including teammates — the wrong way, said Stargell tried to counsel him during his early years in the Braves' system. "Willie used to say you can break people up into three sections," Justice said late in the 1993 season. "One third will like you no matter what. One third are not going to like you no matter what. Then you've got a third just waiting to see. They're on the fence."[25]

While Stargell was enjoying his role as mentor/instructor with the Braves, his personal life took a major turn. On January 16, 1993, in Wilmington, North Carolina, the 52-year-old Stargell was married for the third time. His new bride was Margaret Weller, a 33-year-old crisis counselor. A story that ran December 27, 1991, on the front page of the *Wilmington Morning Star*'s local/state section related the tale of Stargell's engagement, saying that he hid a diamond engagement ring in the pocket of a coat that Weller had received from her parents for Christmas. "I had no idea," Weller said. "He kept saying, 'Will you?' I told my family I had to have some time to myself. I cried as I ran out of the room." Stargell did not officially propose until the next morning; he got down on his knees and asked Weller to marry him. "She makes me very happy," he said. "It took a lot of planning to pull it off. She was totally surprised." The couple had met three years earlier at a banquet in Raleigh, where Stargell was the guest speaker. Weller did not know much about Stargell, nor about baseball, but came to enjoy the game. Stargell said he was impressed with Weller's family background; her father was a retired postman and her mother a retired school administrative assistant. "Her parents are the epitome of what you want parents to be," Stargell said. "Everyone is warm and down to earth." According to the story, the couple was "shy" about talking about their relationship and their future and wanted a chance to break the news to friends and family before the media got involved.[26] The wedding took place in St. Paul's Episcopal Church in Wilmington with some 400 former teammates, friends and family members taking in the ceremony. Stargell said none of his accomplishments in baseball could compare to exchanging vows with Weller. "This is something much more personal," he said. "I regard it as something very sacred. You can always go into baseball and try to get a hit, but to me, this is just like two trees getting together and going out into the world to blossom."[27]

By 1994, Stargell's business card needed revision again — he was now serving as the Braves' special assistant to the director of scouting and the director of player personnel. The club had expanded Stargell's responsibilities each year and by '94 he was involved in all personnel matters at both the major- and minor-league levels. Stargell was asked just prior to the start of the 1994 season why he wasn't practicing his craft with his first franchise — the Pirates. "I've thought about what it might be like to be back there," he told the *Post-Gazette*'s Ron Cook. "But nobody has asked me." Cook recounted the Tanner firing in Pittsburgh, Tanner's bringing Stargell to Atlanta and the ill-fated "Willie Stargell Night" in 1988. Stargell denied that the day in his honor fell through because the Pirates failed to deliver a luxury sports car as he had demanded and said he was hurt by the media's portrayal of him as greedy. "They took the word of some unnamed source over mine," he said. "Baseball was never about money to me. It was about opportunity. I never had any serious bickering about money with the Pirates. I could have left several times as a free agent, but my loyalty was to the Pirates. I loved Pittsburgh." Stargell said the booing he received the night he took his spot in the third-base coaching box for the first time at Three Rivers Stadium, which precipitated Tanner's — and his own — firing by the Braves, didn't leave a lasting mark. "That one night doesn't ruin all the good memories I have of Pittsburgh," he said. "Not good memories, great memories."[28]

Later that year, while the Braves were preparing to play in their fourth of what would be 14 straight NL playoff series, Stargell paid a visit to the club's

Instructional League camp to work with a couple of the club's prospects. "We wanted Willie to put a few finishing touches on things," said Bobby Dews, an instructor and camp coordinator. "He works with them on what to expect in game situations — how to react in certain situations. He gives the kids a lot of confidence. He's a great motivator, having been such a great player. He takes his time with them and gives them respect."[29]

He wasn't just respectful to the players. As a roving hitting instructor, Stargell would make the rounds throughout the Braves' minor league system, stopping in the various towns that housed the organization's various affiliates. And when he showed up at those minor league ballparks, people knew about it. Mike Snee, who worked as the director of ticket sales for the Durham Bulls — the Braves' Class A club at the time — remembered Stargell trying to find some privacy in the press box, but that was usually a losing battle. "He'd get to breathe for a little while," he said. "If he went out in the daggone stadium, he'd be accosted. He'd try to find a place in the press box because he had a job to do. But throughout the course of the game, you'd have people coming to the office — they'd see him and it was, 'Is that Willie? Is that Willie?' Every now and then he'd go out and sign. He was the nicest guy. You'd see a big guy and think he was going to be kind of loud. But he was not. He was very low-key, gracious and soft-spoken. Lots of kids would run around the ballpark with broken bats or foul balls and they'd keep a bunch of this stuff and wait for Willie to come to town, and then try to get him to sign it. He'd always sign. He would never bat an eyelid."[30]

Stargell's impact on the Atlanta franchise, both as an instructor and in the scouting realm, was becoming well known, and the Braves brain trust was more than willing to acknowledge his contributions. "He makes a tremendous impression on young people, either the players he works with or the ones he meets," Braves general manager John Schuerholz said in March of 1995. "I think it is important that a guy [like Stargell] is not just a figurehead, but rather a productive member of the staff, as is the case with Willie." Stargell said he enjoyed working directly with young players on the field, but admitted that he also liked being involved in the scouting end of things. "There are a lot of things I'm equipped to get involved with," he said. "I offer my opinion about various things. Branching out has been good." Stargell said he would enjoy working as a minor league director and didn't rule out the idea of becoming a general manager. At that time, Atlanta's Bob Watson was the major leagues' lone black general manager. "I've got my feelers out," Stargell said. "If a farm director job or player personnel job came open for me, it would be great."[31]

In retrospect, those who worked with Stargell during his stay in Atlanta said he played no small role in the success the franchise had during the 1990s and into the 2000s. "We had a tremendous minor-league system at that time — we were blessed with great talent, which obviously the record will show," La Mar said. "And Willie had input on a lot of our young players who eventually ended up having long and productive careers at the major league level." La Mar said it's not uncommon for organizations to bring in retired stars and hire them as "special assistants" — almost in an honorary capacity, to keep them involved in the game. Stargell was no honorary assistant, though. And while he certainly appreciated being around the game, he took it seriously — and particularly when it came to teaching hitting. "I think he had more connection with the hitters than any other phase of the game," La Mar said. "He truly relished the mentality of a power hitter. That's who he was. I think most power hitters have that identity. It's an attitude. If you hit 500 home runs in the major leagues, it not only takes ability but it takes an attitude. I think Willie loved talking to our young men who showed some power potential in the organization. He really relished it. He was one of those guys who could win a young player over even if that player didn't know about his history. Those days, and even now, a lot of younger players didn't know the history of the game like we did as kids. Some of our guys had to look at the media guide to find out who Willie was. 'We Are Family?' What the heck is 'We Are Family?' But Willie never wore his success on his sleeve. He communicated with people like he'd never had a major league career. I think he gained their respect right off the bat by the type of person he was and how he treated those young players. Then they realized that not only did he know what he was talking about and they liked being around him, but this guy was pretty good. And he wasn't one of these guys who walked in and made this grand announcement — that you have to listen to me because I'm Willie Stargell. He was as humble a star as I've ever been around. He was truly the total package — you seldom see someone with that kind of career stay that humble and friendly to all of us who will never reach his heights in the profession. He was that good of a person to everyone in the Braves organization."[32]

Schuerholz, who arrived in Atlanta during the fall of 1990 as general manager, said that Stargell commanded plenty of attention and just as much respect among his players by simply being who he was — a thoughtful, quiet, perceptive person. "When he shared his views, whether they were to a player about how that player ought to personally approach his craft, or whether it was in a staff meeting sharing his opinion of a player and his potential and his ability, his strengths and weaknesses, he communicated very well," Schuerholz said. Unlike some naturally gifted and successful players who have a tough time connecting with those players who are less talented, Stargell seemed to be able to reach a broad spectrum of youngsters. That didn't just come naturally, either, Schuerholz said. "He was a guy who cared about the game — he knew the game and studied the game and he had played on winning teams, so he knew what winning environments had to be like, what work ethic and work culture was demanded by people who wanted to be part of a winning environment. And Willie did that in his own inimitable, gentle giant fashion."

Although Stargell had often voiced a desire to become a manager in the mid to late 1980s, Schuerholz said the two never talked about that. "He seemed to be one of those rare individuals who wasn't standing in one level of responsibility and looking upward at what his next step or goal might be. Instead, he focused on the job he had and he did it with pride, dignity and responsibility."[33]

Stargell wasn't the only Hall of Fame slugger employed by the Braves in the late 1980s and early 1990s. Aaron, who retired in 1976 as the game's career home run leader with 755, worked as Atlanta's vice president and director of player development for 13 years before becoming a senior vice president in 1989. Aaron said when the Braves fired Tanner and several of his coaches in 1988, the organization wanted to keep Stargell on board. "He was supposed to stay with the ballclub," Aaron said. "Chuck gave Willie the bad news about Chuck being fired and he thought Willie was going to be fired. But Willie was not going to be one of the ones fired. I know that to be true. I don't know what happened, but Willie got back with the Braves." Aaron said he and Stargell had "mountains of conversations" in the Braves spring training home of West Palm Beach, Florida, discussing the Braves organization and individual players. "Willie was in a class of his own when talking about talent. He knew talent, he knew how to coach and knew how to work in the front office. He could do it all. And he enjoyed it very much. He brought a lot to the game. He enjoyed being with the players, with the coaches. He could talk their language. It wasn't like he was a foreigner. He could talk baseball. And when he saw someone with a little talent, he could help." Part of that was because Stargell wasn't that far removed from his own big-league career, having retired in 1982. "He had a connection with older and younger players alike," Aaron said. "He could sit down with players who'd been in the game for 20 years and hold a good conversation, but then he could also sit down with someone like Ron Gant, just trying to make it in the big leagues, and bring something to that table, too."[34]

Tanner, who saw Stargell work with hitters both as a coach in Atlanta and as a player with the Pirates, said the key to Stargell's effectiveness as a hitting coach was that he "didn't try to make everybody hit like him. He tried to make them hit like they hit and get the best out of their swing, not his swing. He was a good hitting instructor and he helped a lot of guys." Tanner said he thought Stargell would have made an excellent manager, and that was all part of his plan. In both Pittsburgh and Atlanta, he would make Stargell sit near him in the dugout and tell him things about the game. "I was grooming him," Tanner said. "I would say, 'Willie, when the time comes, I'm going into the front office and you'll be the manager.'" Tanner had no doubt Stargell would succeed in that role. "He could communicate individually and collectively and he could chew their ass out if he needed to," he said. "He could give them hell his way and get his point across. He knew how to get to whoever the person was he was dealing with. And that's what you have to do to be a successful manager."[35]

Stargell never had the opportunity to manage — at any level. But his work in the Braves front office caught the attention of a new regime in Pittsburgh. A new ownership group headed by a young Californian named Kevin McClatchy bought the ballclub in 1996 for $92 million, and it wasn't long afterward that he began wondering why Stargell was no longer in the Pirate fold. McClatchy talked to Dick Freeman, the team's former president and chief operating officer, but still couldn't understand why the broken relationship hadn't been mended. "So I reached out to Willie," McClatchy recalled.[36] Cam Bonifay, whom the new Pittsburgh ownership had hired to serve as general manager, said one of the things he and McClatchy had talked about after he took the job was to get more former Pirates involved in the organization and particularly in the field operations side. "We wanted to help develop the 'Pirates way' of bringing back championships to Pittsburgh," Bonifay said.[37] Toward that end, the Pirates called Atlanta and asked permission to speak with Stargell and ask him to come back to the Pirates. Bonifay and McClatchy envisioned Stargell wearing multiple hats — going to spring training and evaluating some of the minor league players and also serving as a sounding board for what was going on at the major league level. McClatchy said Stargell was surprised that the club would contact him but excited at the prospect. McClatchy asked Stargell to visit in person to discuss the idea. "It was a very emotional meeting," McClatchy said. "I think he had felt a separation. Obviously it was a powerful moment — a tearful reunion to being asked to come back to the organization that he loved. It meant a lot to him — there was no hesitation on his part to come back once that offer was made. He wanted to be here."

McClatchy said it was important to mend that fence — and strengthen it — and bring Stargell back to the fold. "He was the identity of the organization in many ways," McClatchy said. "He helped with former players; he helped with fans. There was a presence. Getting Dave Parker back would not have evolved if Willie had not reached out to him." Stargell, officially hired as a senior adviser, also worked with the team's alumni organization and met with potential sponsors, trying to sell the concept of what would become PNC Park — a brand new Pirate playground that would rise from the banks of the Allegheny River on Pittsburgh's North Shore, a long Stargell poke from the now-departed Three Rivers Stadium. Stargell was effective in his new role, McClatchy said. "When Willie spoke, people would listen. There was no question that players respected him and would listen to anything he had to say. He was a first-ballot Hall of Famer." Pirates brass anticipated that Stargell's presence might have residual positive impacts off the field — and specifically in the black community. Although the club claimed that its minority attendance — pegged at 6.8 percent — had increased by 300 percent, it also looked to capture a more robust share, particularly considering more than one in four city residents was black. Steve Greenburg, the Pirates' vice president, said he hoped Stargell's return to the organization could translate to an upward tick at the gate among minority residents. "If it shows a prominent minority presence in Pirates baseball and in baseball in general, it's going to be a big plus," he said. McClatchy said he had spoken to some members of the black community, and they were very excited that the hiring of Stargell could help in that area. "But we have a lot more steps to take to get the black community back to the ballpark. I've done a lot of speaking there and a lot of our employees have been involved, but they need to see us there more and they need to know we'd like them here. I think part of it is that it's a little intimidating to go to a baseball game where 99 percent of the people are white."[38]

At a February 11, 1997, press conference announcing Stargell's return to the club, he said he was surprised when the Braves had told him that the Pirates had called to ask permission to talk with him. "I felt good, yet I felt kind of strange because I hadn't entertained it. I had almost forgotten about the idea of coming back." Bonifay was excited about the prospect of having Stargell around to help evaluate players at all levels of the system. "He will be a man that I will count on," Bonifay said. "He will be a man I will use in a lot of different ways." Stargell said one of the reasons he was willing to return to the organization was because it seemed committed to building a championship-caliber club. But he said that wouldn't be done quickly — just as it wasn't in Atlanta or in Cleveland, where the long moribund Indians franchise had been resurrected in the mid-'90s. There, he said, the organizations asked fans to be patient. "As a result, they have brand-new stadiums and great atmosphere within the community," Stargell said.[39]

Looking back nearly 15 years later, Bonifay said Stargell's role with the club was a meaningful one and his presence certainly was a boon to the organization. During spring training, Stargell would observe both major and minor league players and mingle with them to share what he had learned during his life in the game. "The amount of knowledge and the amount of information he gave our younger players, and the suggestions he made in the development of our younger and older players, was very positive," Bonifay said. "We were very happy to have him as a member of our staff. There's no question he had the background and knowledge to talk to our younger players about specific things they needed to become successful players. The knowledge of what it took to prepare to be a major-league player while still in the minor leagues — the things that have to be accomplished, the individual skill sets necessary to become an improved player. Those kinds of things were the most important aspects he offered our organization at the time." Although Stargell was nearly 60 by this time, he had no problem relating with younger players — and vice versa. "When it came to hearing his expertise, they were open and willing to listen," Bonifay said. "He had a very good way of talking to and relating to younger players. He was not overbearing. He could describe and teach and break things down in a very simple manner, without being over-mechanical. He had a very simplistic way of giving young players knowledge and being able to have them understand what he was saying. He was very good in that regard."

Smizik said it was apparent that the Pirates brass greatly appreciated Stargell's skills and his opinions. "I don't think he was a figurehead — I think he knew talent and Cam [Bonifay] had a lot of respect for Willie's opinion," he said. "And Willie got his role with the Pirates. He was a very perceptive baseball guy. Lots of times good hitters don't get the credit they deserve. Ralph Kiner had a brilliant knowledge of hitting. Hal McRae had a brilliant knowledge of hitting. I can't speak to Willie's days as a hitting coach but talking to him and knowing how people regarded him, his word was tremendous."[40] Frattare said Stargell's return in 1997 was a boon to the organization. Just to have him watch the younger players take batting practice was a major benefit. "He wasn't going to push himself on anybody because that wasn't his style," Frattare said of Stargell. "But he had an opportunity to sit on the bench and watch. And he knew how much the mental approach was important to players, particularly younger players trying to figure it out. His time was extremely memorable from that standpoint."[41]

In his first spring training with the club, Stargell said he just tried to pass along things that had been passed on to him. "It's nothing I invented," he said. "But it's things that I know work." He said he was looking for "uniqueness" and finding plenty of it. He compared it to the situation that existed when he first arrived in Atlanta. "They were struggling but they had a lot of young talent in the minor leagues. Same here. It's like being in Africa in one of those diamond mines. You see a rock that's all muddy, but it has a little tiny speck that's glittering and you know there's something there. It just takes somebody to get that prize jewel out and mold it so it can have the brilliance and color it should have."[42]

Once the season started, Stargell would spend stretches of four or five days with minor league teams, then meet with Bonifay and others to discuss his observations. He kept up this arrangement despite needing time to tend to some health issues that would worsen in the coming years and ultimately end his life in April 2001. Bonifay said Stargell was receiving treatment — including kidney dialysis — for medical issues from the time he returned to the organization in February 1997 until he stopped actively working for the club in late 2000. The Pirates gave Stargell all the time he needed for treatment whenever he would require it. "At certain times, he was physically unable to do certain things," Bonifay said. "But the times he was there and the times he felt well were the times we capitalized on the most." The treatments that Stargell required, Bonifay said, were just part of his schedule.

Word of Stargell's medical situation reached the media in the fall of 1999, and it was widely reported that he was battling serious health problems and had been hospitalized for three weeks. Team officials issued a statement attributed to Stargell in which he thanked his "well-wishing fans for their concern after hearing of my hospitaliza-

After returning to the Pirates organization in January 1997, Willie enjoyed working with youngsters on the finer points of hitting, among other subjects (courtesy Pittsburgh Pirates).

tion. I have, in fact, been in the hospital for three weeks for management of a recent illness." In the same statement, Stargell refuted media reports that he would be hospitalized for at least three more weeks and said he was expected to be discharged within a few days.[43]

In February 2000, a Pittsburgh media outlet reported that Stargell had undergone minor surgery in Wilmington, and that he was expected to attend spring training later that month. In March, while visiting the Pirates' spring training complex in Bradenton, Associated Press reporter Alan Robinson wrote that "for a 60-year-old man who nearly died only a few months ago, Stargell looks very much alive, very much in charge, very much in control." Stargell concurred, saying, "I haven't felt this well in a long time." Robinson wrote that although Stargell had been undergoing kidney dialysis for several years, it was an infected finger—not the kidney issues—that caused him to be hospitalized for six weeks the previous fall. The infection set in after Stargell accidentally cut himself in his kitchen and did not immediately seek treatment. Ultimately a portion of the finger had to be amputated. Although Stargell had not regained his strength—he relied on a golf cart to get around the Pirates' minor-league complex in Bradenton—he hadn't lost his touch when it came to evaluating talent. "Willie Stargell knows baseball," Bonifay said.[44]

Bonifay said Stargell kept working for the Pirates, and his input continued to be appreciated. "He was always evaluating and I always asked him for his evaluations and his opinions—what he saw from different players," Bonifay said. "I thought he had a very good feel for it. He pointed out things—development issues—in certain players that had to be addressed." Bonifay said Stargell's front-office skills were such that if his health had not deteriorated, he would have remained an important part of the Pirates organization for many more years, serving as a mentor for younger players. Bonifay said he didn't believe Stargell's effectiveness would have diminished over time and that he would have remained relevant to this day. "One thing you'll find is that the Hall of Fame transcends every generation," Bonifay said. "Without question, he was not only a Hall of Fame player but a Hall of Fame individual the way he approached people, how he put them at ease about who he was and what he had to offer. It could be the next generation or three generations down the road and he would have had relevance in terms of what he had to offer." That's because, in the end, baseball is not a game of change, Bonifay said. "Outsiders may view it that way, but not the players themselves. It's still a game of 60 feet, 6 inches and 90-foot bases. That has not changed, pitchers have not changed, hitters have not changed and the ability to do that on a consistent basis is what separates those very good ones from those who do not have very good careers."[45]

Stargell's involvement in the organization grew smaller as the 2000 season went along when his health took a turn for the worse. "It was really a struggle for him and his family," Bonifay said. "He spent a lot of time at home at the end of the 2000 season." Stargell returned to town for the final home series of the 2000 season — the last games ever to be played at Three Rivers Stadium, which was to be replaced the following campaign by PNC Park. On September 29, the Pirates announced that a 12-foot bronze statue of the slugger would be built near the left-field entrance to PNC Park on Federal Street. He joined former teammate Clemente and Honus Wagner as the only members of the then-114-year-old franchise to have statues made in their honor, although World Series hero Bill Mazeroski would join those ranks in 2010. At a press conference announcing the statue, Stargell fought back tears, saying, "I'm overwhelmed, but I'm also thankful. All I wanted to do was play ball." However, he added that now that the statue was in the works, "You'd catch hell taking it away from me. It's special, very special."[46]

The statue's base was to be constructed of stainless steel and granite and was to include a "Stargell Star" that featured his signature. The base also includes the quote from Stargell regarding his initial impression of Pittsburgh, coming through the Fort Pitt Tunnel with Bob Veale, on the way in from Columbus in 1962: "Last night, coming in from the airport, we came through the tunnel and the city opened up its arms and I felt at home."

Local sports media member Stan Savran said the press conference announcing the Stargell statue was one of the last times he saw Willie. "I did a long TV interview with him about that," he said. "I have a picture of the two of us doing the interview — I still have it on my bulletin board. He was truly moved — he was moved to tears. That's how touched he was that they were going to build a statue and put it out in front of PNC Park. Willie was really overcome with emotion."[47] At the press conference, Stargell reflected on what it was like to spend his entire playing career in one uniform and talked about how much he valued and respected that uniform. In fact, he said that never once in his career did he toss the Pirate uniform on the floor. "That's how particular I was," he said.[48]

McClatchy recalled visiting Stargell in the hospital to look at some photographs that were to be used as a model for his statue. McClatchy said Stargell told him, "I want a picture that shows me just before I was about to hit the shit out of the ball."

On the night of September 29, Stargell received a standing ovation from the Three Rivers crowd of more than 40,000 — and both dugouts — and spoke before the game. "Lots of wonderful things have happened in this stadium," he said. "I'll never forget you." Stargell appeared much leaner than he had been

Willie holds an imaginary bat as he scrutinizes a model of the 12-foot bronze statue that would be unveiled in early April 2001 as the Pirates got set to open their new PNC Park on Pittsburgh's North Shore (courtesy Pittsburgh Pirates).

in years, due to his health issues. He would not discuss those issues specifically, saying it was a "personal matter." But he said he no longer was required to receive regular dialysis treatments and that the infection that had dogged him earlier was no longer an issue. "I've been given the green light to travel," Stargell said. "My destiny is up to me. I do have a lot of fight in me."[49]

Two days later, the Pirates played their final game at Three Rivers, losing to the Cubs 10–9 in front of a sellout crowd of 55,351— the largest regular-season crowd in club history. About 30 minutes after the game, the Pirates paid their final tribute to the stadium. More than 20 retired players were on hand to say goodbye to the old yard, which at one time was considered state-of-the-art but had been relegated to irrelevancy by the advent of new baseball-only parks like Baltimore's Camden Yards. Tekulve, the old submarining right-hander, took the mound and current catcher Jason Kendall stood near the area of home plate. But Tekulve wouldn't be delivering the final pitch. Instead, the voice of the Pirates late public address announcer, Art McKennan, introduced Stargell, and the sellout crowd erupted. Stargell was helped to the mound, where he was embraced by his former manager Tanner and ex-teammates including John Candelaria, Manny Sanguillen, Grant Jackson and Nellie Briles, and then made his final pitch.[50]

Several of Stargell's former teammates were unable to attend the final game, including Oliver, who had a prior engagement. But he had a chance to see portions of the ceremony on the news later that night and was chilled by the sight of his mentor, whose health was deteriorating. "When I saw him, I just said, 'Wow — it won't be too much longer,'" Oliver recalled.[51] Another former teammate who was not at Three Rivers that night regretted his absence. "I wish I'd been there because I had something really important to say to Willie," said Bob Priddy, who had played with Stargell in the lowest of the minor-league rungs some 40 years earlier. "I would have said, 'Hey, Willie, isn't it amazing that at one time in your baseball career, they wouldn't even let you sleep in the same hotel as us or eat in the same restaurants as us — you couldn't go to the same toilets as us or drink out of the same water fountains. And now they're building a statue for you. Ain't that something?'"[52]

CHAPTER 11

"We Kiss You Goodbye"

SPIRITS WERE SOARING as the spring of 2001 approached and when April rolled around, the Pirates prepared to move into brand new PNC Park, with Opening Day slated for April 9. Two days earlier, the Pirates unveiled the 12-foot, one-ton statue of Stargell, coiled and ready to unleash his powerful swing in front of the left-field entrance to the park on Federal Street. The club said that Stargell was not feeling well enough to make it to the unveiling ceremony and was home in Wilmington. "It's a great day," Pirates owner Kevin McClatchy said, "but it's not 100 percent great, because my friend isn't here." McClatchy said the Pirates planned to have an official dedication sometime during the summer when Stargell's health improved enough for him to attend. However, the club wanted to unveil the statue in time for the April 9 home opener.[1]

Several hundred fans attended the April 7 unveiling, including Mike Schwab, an ambulance driver from Greenfield and a Pirates season-ticket holder. "He was my childhood idol," Schwab said of Stargell. "I hope he can make a full recovery. I was born in 1970 and when I met him, I had him sign his 1970 baseball card for me." Several Pirate luminaries attended the unveiling, including Tanner and even Vera Clemente, the widow of the Pirates legendary right fielder. Susan Wagner, the statue's sculptor, said she used old photographs and film of Stargell as well as vintage uniforms and bats to craft the statue, which took her a year to complete at the Polich Artworks Foundry in upstate New York. Tanner approved of the final product. "That's just how he held the bat!" he exclaimed.[2] Schwab, meanwhile, couldn't contain his emotion. "I can't say much," he said. "It's beautiful."[3] Tanner, too, was almost moved to tears. "Time goes so fast," he said as he walked away from the statue. "Why won't time stand still so we can still watch Willie play?"[4]

Fans like Schwab who idolized Stargell were the rule, rather than the exception, in Pittsburgh. He might have been the most beloved figure in the city's sports history until Mario Lemieux came along with the NHL Penguins. As such, Stargell was the recipient of thousands of letters from fans during his 21-year playing career. The Pirate offices maintain copies of some of those letters as well as the responses that Stargell provided. Tom O'Toole, who lived in North Braddock, sent Stargell a letter in October 1973 thanking him for a photograph that the slugger had sent to a Kenny Condon. O'Toole's letter included a lucky Irish coin. "I don't know what it is, but it is straight from Ireland and I understand it is a lucky piece.... May this coin bring you good luck and keep your confidence in yourself."

Robert Curran, of Snyder, New York, wrote that same season and asked Stargell if he had some sort of a musical tune in mind when he stood in the batter's box and windmilled his bat prior to the pitcher's delivery. "I have no 'tune' in mind in doing the exercises I go through when I step into the batter's box," Stargell wrote. "The muscles in my arm have a tendency to tighten up when I'm waiting for the pitch, so I move my arms to relax before the pitcher throws the ball." Near the end of Stargell's career, Carol Senger Korynta wrote Pirates public relations director Joe Safety on behalf of her grandmother, Annie Senger, who at 90 years of age was a devoted Pirates fan and in need of "a little cheer to her day." Stargell responded, in his graceful handwriting: "Dear Mrs. Senger, It has come to my attention that you are one of America's biggest Pirate fans. I sure hope that you will continue to lend us your support and devotion. After winning the championship in 1979 and then coming up short last year, I know which one I like the best! We have every intention of reclaiming the championship in 1981 and we will need your continued support to do it. My very best wishes to you and may God Bless you! Warmly, Willie Stargell."

In some cases, Stargell did more than just write letters to fans — he forged friendships with them. Ned Sokoloff was in his early 30s when he came to know Stargell through his relationship with Stargell's attorney, David Litman. Sokoloff was given access to Stargell behind the scenes — riding with Stargell in the latter's white Rolls Royce at spring training in Bradenton, serving as the official photographer during the first Willie Stargell Day in 1980, coming and going through the Pirate clubhouse. "Those years were like magic to me," Sokoloff said in a 2008 interview. "Willie was a living legend but if you knew him like I knew him, he was like a normal guy. He made me feel like I belonged. I can't imagine what it must have been like to be a celebrity. When he walked into [Litman's] law firm, all the girls in the office would get out of their seats to take a peek at him. Just to gaze upon him. But behind it all, he had to deal with life just like everyone else. He had family issues, financial situations just

A 12-foot bronze statue honoring Willie was unveiled to the public just days before the opening of PNC Park in Pittsburgh—the same day that the slugger died (courtesy Pittsburgh Pirates).

like everyone else. He was so involved with things. He had a lot going on with his sickle cell anemia foundation—he was dealing with all this charity work. He had 15 plates spinning."[5]

Sokoloff was among thousands of season-ticket holders who turned out on the morning of April 9, 2001, for the much-anticipated opening of PNC Park. But the day would be a bittersweet one for all involved—fans, players, front office workers and anyone else with a soft spot in their heart for the Pirates. Stargell, the mountain of a man who so many times carried the team on his back and willed them to win with the force of his personality and the whoosh of his left-handed swing, died just after midnight—12:23 A.M.—at New Hanover Regional Medical Center in Wilmington. He had suffered a stroke in his brain stem, which resulted from complications of long-standing high blood pressure, heart failure and kidney failure. Stargell's physician, Dr. James McCabe, said that Stargell—who had been on dialysis since 1996—had been admitted to the hospital on February 23 and was recovering from gall bladder surgery when his health deteriorated. "He fought a courageous battle against heart failure and high blood pressure for the past four years with the help of a team of nephrologists, physicians, highly skilled nurses and rehab specialists," McCabe said in a statement released by the hospital. "Despite our best efforts, he suffered an acute stroke and died peacefully this morning with his wife and family at his side." McCabe said Stargell suffered from hypertension and that it affected not only his kidneys and heart, but the blood vessels in his brain. "So it becomes a multi-organ problem, as it did with Willie, despite the care he received, and the care he took of himself."

McCabe said more than two years before Stargell's death, hypertension had led to damage of the blood supply to Stargell's bowel, and so part of it was removed in an operation at the University of Pittsburgh Medical Center. Given Stargell's other health issues, the surgery was risky, and McCabe said Stargell nearly died. "To this day, I consider it a miracle that he survived," he said.[6] McCabe said in a hospital press release that Stargell was receiving dialysis treatments three times a week and while that is a difficult regimen for many, Stargell "just adjusted, accepted it as 'it's part of my life, and I'm going to make the best of it.'" McCabe said Stargell's athleticism certainly helped him through the last four years of his life, as did being in good shape and exercising. "I suspect he fought battles all of his life, and he approached this the same way," McCabe said. "He just had this charisma that it would be okay."

Frances Weller, the sister of Stargell's wife, Margaret, issued a statement on behalf of the family through the New Hanover Health Network. "While the world has lost a hero, the Weller family has lost a friend. And certainly Margaret has lost her best friend." Frances Weller called Stargell "the finest human being I've ever known. And my sister was very lucky to have been married to a man like Willie. Those who were fortunate enough to get to know Willie were blessed. In the last few months, Willie didn't want to give up. It was as though his life went into extra innings. But this morning, the lights went out in his stadium."

The news reached Pittsburgh in a heartbeat; McClatchy had been on the phone with Margaret Weller twice that night. When McClatchy got word that Stargell had passed, he contacted Bonifay. "It kind of reverberated through the organization," Bonifay recalled. "The opening of the ballpark was some-thing that the city of Pittsburgh was looking forward to and we were very hopeful Willie was going to be able to come to that opening. It was a day of mixed emotions. It was a beautiful opening on a beautiful day in Pittsburgh, which is sometimes hard to get at that time of the year. Sunny skies, a brand new place and the sadness of knowing that one of our great ones had passed away. The mental and emotional dilemma of going through that day was one

I'll never forget. Chuck Tanner and I talked about it as we walked around the new ballpark and walked up to Willie's statue. It was a sad day and a happy day all in one."

Blass, Stargell's former teammate and later a Pirate broadcaster, recalled the death of another Hall of Fame Pirate when he heard the news about Stargell's passing. "When we heard about [Roberto] Clemente's death at 4 o'clock in the morning, I went to Willie's house," Blass said. "I'm not sure where to go this morning."[7]

The tributes began pouring in for Stargell, and they continued flowing for weeks. On the day he died, scores of fans gathered at Stargell's statue, having their photographs taken and leaving flowers and other items at the foot of the 12-foot bronze structure. A placard sitting near the base of Stargell's left foot read, "We kiss you goodbye," referring to Prince's famous home run call on Pirates broadcasts through much of Stargell's career. "He was probably my first baseball hero growing up," said Glenn Winegardner, 39, of Gaithersburg, Maryland. "Pops was the man, all through the '70s. He was the Pittsburgh Pirates. He epitomized the Pirates."[8]

Several of the 2001 Pirate players talked about Stargell's presence within the organization. "Every word out of his mouth, you listened to," said the catcher Kendall, whose father, Fred, spent 12 seasons in the big leagues and had specifically told his son to soak in as much of Stargell's wisdom as he could. "That was the type of aura he had about him. He taught me a lot about the game." Kendall admitted that the excitement of opening the new ballpark, coupled with the news of Stargell's death, made for a most unusual day. "It's really strange — it's a weird feeling," he said. Pirates manager Lloyd McClendon said Stargell had encouraged him to apply for the managerial job, telling him that he had all the necessary ingredients to become a big-league skipper. "So much of Willie is inside of me," McClendon said on Opening Day. "There is so much passion and love for the game that he instilled in me."[9] McClendon, whose team lost that home opener 8–2 to Cincinnati, said that he and Stargell talked a lot — and many times it wasn't about the current game. "We would talk about how the game had changed so much for young black players, the wonderful opportunities it presents for minorities today. Willie had a lot to do with that. I'm here today because of him in a lot of ways."[10] McClendon said he would remember many things that Stargell told him, but maybe the most important thing he heard Stargell say was, "Respect the game, but have fun."[11]

Savran recalled that Opening Day as a "horribly sad day. I remember going to the TV studio and doing a long pregame show, then I went to the office next to PNC Park and that's when I found out. It put a terrible, somber mood on the entire day. I remember standing in front of the Pirate dugout doing this pregame show and I remember hearing an audible gasp go through the crowd when they announced it. It was terribly sad. Lanny Frattare was conducting the ceremony — they had a tribute prepared. The Pirates knew how ill he was, but I did not. I remember Lanny's voice breaking as he was reading that stuff."[12] Savran said he and other media members were aware that Stargell had been hospitalized and was dealing with some serious health issues "but I don't know that any of us knew how serious. And I don't think any of us knew he was near death."

From the other side of the country, where Stargell spent the bulk of his boyhood learning the game, more tributes came. Morgan, the East Bay native who was overlooked by the Pirates as an amateur and traded by the Houston Astros before going on to have a Hall of Fame career with the Reds, called Stargell "a very special individual, not just a great baseball player. No one disliked Willie Stargell. He was a player's player and the greatest teammate ever, from what I hear from his teammates. One of the things lacking in my life is that I was never his teammate." Morgan called Stargell "the greatest leader of men I ever knew."[13]

At Encinal High School, where the football and baseball facilities are both named in Stargell's honor, word of his death hit the Jets baseball team hard. "He's real big to us," senior pitcher Jason Rivera said. "When you come out here every day and see the Willie Stargell [Field] sign, it's something to be proud of. To see that sign every day just motivates us." Shortstop Nick Loy said the team looked up to Stargell. "We respect him a lot."[14]

Four days after Stargell's death, some 400 people gathered at his funeral at St. Paul's Episcopal Church in Wilmington. Many of his friends and former teammates were in the church and continued on to the burial ceremony at Oleander Memorial Gardens. Former Pirates catcher Manny Sanguillen, who was crushed when Clemente — his best friend — died in 1972, wore Stargell's number 8 jersey to the services. "I don't know what I'm supposed to do now," Sanguillen said. "I'm so sad. I've lost my two best friends. Willie and Roberto. What am I going to do now?"[15] Morgan, who would deliver the eulogy, said he wanted to see Stargell during the last months of his life, but that Stargell told him not to come to Wilmington. "He said, 'No — I'm fine.' He never did tell me how ill he was. He didn't want anyone to know. I really believe he didn't want anyone to see him deteriorate. He wanted you to remember him as he once was. My memories are still of the Willie Stargell I knew because I didn't see him deteriorating at the end. Looking back, I should have gone. But by the same token, I have the memories he wanted me to have. I don't know if I was right or I was wrong there."[16]

Ed Ott, the former catcher with the '79 championship team, said he had seen Stargell during his final spring training in Bradenton "and I probably wish I hadn't. I hardly recognized him. I had a friend of mine with me — he was my coach in Allentown. We went over to Pirate City and I asked if Willie was there. He had just come back from a doctor's appointment — it didn't even look like him — but I introduced him to my friend. Later I thought to myself, 'I wish I hadn't seen him.' Instead of that big burly guy with the great smile, I have the image of him just coming off dialysis and not at his best. It was your basic day and night."[17] Oliver said he had kept in touch with Stargell throughout his illness and would call him a couple of times a month right up until the end. "I'd say, 'Wilver — how you feeling, man?' He'd call me 'Chief' — and he'd say, 'God's looking out for me. Still hangin' tough.' He'd never give you any indication anything was wrong with him. He didn't complain, although as a friend you knew things were going on that were not positive. But he tried to stay upbeat. And he was upbeat all the way up to the end."[18] Bartirome, the former Pirate trainer, said Stargell didn't want anyone pitying him in his final months. "Whatever came about, he was going to take it like the man that he was. He didn't want people to know anything. For him — a big, strong guy — to get sick like that, it was heartbreaking. You never think of a guy like that being sick."[19]

Garner said when he learned that Stargell was ill, he made it a point to go see him. "He was not looking good — his color was not good," he said. "I felt bad about it and I tried to stay in touch. But Willie never wanted you to do anything out of sympathy. You had to be very careful — he would avoid you if he even thought that was what you were doing. He was a very rare individual."[20] Jackson, known as "Buck" to his teammates on the '79 title team, said he ran into Stargell at Detroit Metro Airport one day after he returned to the Pirates organization and did not recognize him. "I saw a guy sitting there sweating bullets," Jackson said. "I walked over to him and said, 'Sir, sir — are you all right?' He lifted his head and I saw it was Willie. He said, 'Buck, I don't feel good at all.' He was going back to Wilmington to find out what the problem was."[21]

Tanner said the players who knew Stargell best would be hit the hardest on the day he was laid to rest. "He was like a shepherd with his sheep," Tanner said. "He touched everyone he ever met." Blass, who never forgot Stargell for his standup support during the right-hander's decline and ultimate departure from the game, said, "I was at Clemente's funeral and now I'm going to be at Willie's. You always think the best people are going to live forever. This just doesn't seem right."[22] Parker, who had his ups and downs with the Pirate organization and with Stargell, made it to Wilmington for the funeral and served as a pallbearer. "I felt like I had to be here because he was like a father to me."[23] It wasn't just his former teammates who were touched. Across the country, in San Diego, San Francisco Giants manager Dusty Baker — who played against Stargell while with the Dodgers and Braves — remembered him as "the universal man. If we wanted to send someone to Mars or Venus to show the best of the human race, Willie would be the guy."[24]

Two days later, back in Pittsburgh's Hill District, other folks remembered Stargell and the impact he had on their neighborhood 30 years earlier. They talked about his long-ball prowess or meeting him on the street or the work he did for various charities. And they talked chicken. "We used to have transistor radios when he came up to bat," recalled Butch Smith. "When he hit a home run, 'Spread Chicken on the Hill with Will.' People came out of the woodwork." Ruth White, who had worked with Stargell during her stint as director of the Sickle Cell Society, remembered Stargell as a major help to the cause. "Anytime I needed something and asked him, he'd say, 'I'll try to do it, Miss White.' He helped us become what we've become — a viable society where patients are able to get the help they need. Something they didn't get before Willie."[25]

The next day, upward of 1,000 people packed St. Mary of Mercy Church in Pittsburgh for yet another memorial service. On the altar was a cross made of flowers, and a single black-and-white photograph of Stargell was on display. The Reverend Donald Wuerl, bishop of the Catholic Diocese of Pittsburgh, was among the clergy taking part in the service. While noting the sadness of Stargell's death, Wuerl said Stargell's passing was an opportunity to celebrate and remember his life. "The community relived the memories and highlights of a life that touched us all," he said. "He was more than an extraordinary player. He was a good person." Oliver, who had asked Stargell to serve as his best man at his wedding many years earlier, was among three people who delivered eulogies. "Willie Stargell," Oliver said, "was a winner in every aspect of the word."[26] Blass remarked about Stargell's physical stature, calling him a "big man. He had to be a big man to contain that enormous heart."[27] Tanner said Stargell had the heart of a lion — not to mention a cannon for a throwing arm — and dancing feet. "He had fun and he was funny. He was the strongest of men, the greatest of heroes." Tanner then looked upward and added, "I'm hoping to manage you again someday."[28]

CHAPTER 12

The Real Family

A SIDE FROM HAVING TO CHANGE POSITIONS a time or two, prove to a couple of managers that he could hit left-handed pitching, battle a nagging
weight problem and put up with perhaps more than his share of injuries,
Willie Stargell sailed through his major-league career relatively unscathed on
the baseball diamond.

His adult life off the diamond, though, had more than a few challenges.
Two of his three marriages ended in divorce. Two of his five children were
born to women to whom Stargell was not married. He was the subject of a
controversial book, in which his off-field exploits were chronicled by a writer
and photographer who were given surprisingly open access during the 1973
season. He was accused by two teammates of providing amphetamines, an
accusation that later was found to have no substance by baseball's commissioner. He watched helplessly as his second wife, Dolores, battled for her life
after suffering a near-fatal brain aneurysm, then had to endure the media
reports of the couple's separation and ultimate divorce just a few years later.
Yet after his divorce from Dolores he remained on relatively good terms with
her. The same could be said of his post-marital relationship with his first
wife, Lois. And all five of his children remained a major part of his life until
the very end. Family — just as it was important to the 1979 Pirates — was one
of the pillars upon which Stargell built his life.

One of the family members closest to Stargell was his sister, Sandrus
Collier. Although technically Stargell's half-sister — they shared the same
mother, Gladys, but had different fathers — Stargell never thought of Sandrus
as anything but his sister. Ten years younger than her famous brother, Collier
had an up-close-and-personal view of the Hall of Famer during his teenage
years, and much of his adult life as well. She remembers Willie the ballplayer
had a persona that was different from Willie the brother or Willie the family

man. "With his family, he was more down to earth. And in baseball, he was more focused. I mean, you never messed with him during baseball season. Don't ask him to go anywhere, don't ask him to do too much of anything because he had to focus on baseball. And if they were in the playoffs or anything, forget it. It's strange — you look at the person as a family member, not as a baseball player. You want him to be interested in what's happening in your life — 'There are things going on in my life, too,' I'd say. But he'd say, 'Oh, I wish I could, but I can't.' I didn't understand it when I was younger. Once I got older, then I could understand where he was coming from."[1]

Collier's earliest memories of her brother were from his days at Encinal High School, back in Alameda, California. As an older brother, Willie treated her well — at least until his friends came over. "Then I was the pain-in-the-butt little sister," she said. She can remember Stargell getting set to head off to his first spring training with the Pirates early in 1959. She and her parents took him to the airport, and her mother, Gladys, was nervous because her son was about to get on an old propeller-style airplane; this was in the days before jet engines were the rule. Collier said a local clergy member — a Reverend Bailey, who had large church in Oakland — was boarding the plane as well and because Gladys knew the reverend, she felt better about seeing her son off. Collier had no idea at that time exactly what her brother was up to. "I just thought he was going somewhere," she said. "I think it didn't hit me that he was playing baseball until his name started showing up in books or sports magazines or sports papers."

By the time Collier turned 12 or so, her brother had reached the big leagues and it was then that it really hit home — her brother was a baseball player. When the Pirates made their West Coast road trips, Collier and her parents would go watch them play at San Francisco's Candlestick Park. And often times Stargell would bring teammates over to the family home in East Oakland after the games. "I remember when he first made it to the major leagues," Collier said. "I think every relative we had showed up." Baseball was a familiar pastime for Percy and Gladys, as one of Percy's cousins played in the old Negro Leagues. Gladys began following the Pirates when Stargell made the club, but mostly she was focused on one player. "All she really cared about was Willie Stargell," Collier said. "She wanted the Pirates to do well, but as far as she was concerned, there was only one player on that team." Collier said her mother's favorite announcer in the major leagues was the Dodgers' Vin Scully because Scully referred to Stargell by his given name — Wilver — rather than Willie.

Collier, who became an elementary school teacher, understood baseball and enjoyed the game, and she would take her students on field trips to

Candlestick Park because some of them never had the experience of seeing a game in person. "And I loved going to the games." She spent parts of her summers traveling with her brother when he would make his West Coast road trips, going to Los Angeles and San Diego. He was protective of his younger sister even when she was plenty old enough to make her own decisions. "I wasn't allowed to date baseball players," she said. "Willie was very firm with them — he'd say, 'You cannot date my sister. Don't even look at her twice.' I tried, but they would go, 'Oh no, you are Stargell's sister — you are hands-off.' And I used to ask him why and he said, 'I know what ballplayers are like and you're not going to be involved in that.' I hated it. When he finally said I could, I wound up being older than all of them. And he said, 'Good — that's just how I planned it.'"

As she grew older, Collier spent plenty of time with her brother back east during the season. She enjoyed visiting with Willie's wife, Dolores, and when Dolores suffered her brain aneurysm in 1976, Collier spent more than a month with the family while Dolores was undergoing rehabilitation therapy in Harmarville, a suburb of Pittsburgh. "It was very hard for Willie to concentrate on baseball that year, what with the kids and him having to go out to Harmarville," Collier said. A year or so later, Stargell asked his sister if she would give up her teaching job and consider relocating to Pittsburgh permanently to help him with his sickle cell foundation. "I looked at him like he was crazy. I said, 'You're sick aren't you?' It took me a year to think about it and I said, 'I'll give it a try.' I gave myself five years." Ultimately, Collier would get married and she would end up living the next 10 years in Pittsburgh, helping to run the Willie Stargell Foundation before financial issues forced its closure in 1984. "It was the right time to be there," Collier said of her time in Pittsburgh, which included the 1979 "We Are Family" championship and all the good times that came with it. "It seemed like once I got there, things just fell into place for him," she said. She ran interference for her brother, helping whenever he needed it. She never regretted moving to Pittsburgh because it benefited both her and her brother. "I think it really helped, especially during all that World Series madness," she said. "You can always move somewhere and it doesn't work out, but for me, something just clicked. I would not give up that time for anything. I really enjoyed the experience." The Pirates — and Stargell's — triumph in the 1979 World Series paid huge dividends for Stargell's sickle cell foundation and his endorsement opportunities. "We were inundated with phone calls — people came out of the woodwork," Collier said. "We had some things lined up before the World Series, but once people realized who they had, they capitalized on that."

Relocating from California to Pittsburgh wasn't easy at the outset for

Collier. She experienced what she called "culture shock" at first. For one thing, she had never been to Pittsburgh in the winter before. So she didn't know how to drive in the snow and ice. In fact, she didn't know how to walk in the snow and ice, either. "My husband said, 'You better stand in the window and watch how people are walking' and that's basically what I did," she said. "You take short steps — you do not take long steps or think you can go running in the snow. And driving? That really took me a while. But after that first year, I could handle anything."

Collier said she helped Willie with a number of charitable endeavors, including delivering food baskets to those in need. She used to think she had grown up in poverty, but one year on Christmas morning, she experienced something that put her childhood in the proper perspective. "This one family had plastic on their windows, some of the windows were cracked and there were eight or nine people living in this room," she said. "And I remember coming out of that house and sitting in my car crying. My husband looked at me and said, 'You thought you were poor? That was poor.' Growing up in Oakland, I wasn't privileged. But both my parents worked and provided for us, although we didn't always get what we wanted. But to see what I saw that day, it really changed how I thought about things from that point on. I think I did a little growing up when I moved to Pittsburgh."

Collier said when she was younger, Stargell was more like a father figure to her than a brother. She had a serious asthma problem and was sick much of the time, and can remember her brother taking care of her or making sure she was okay. "I think he used to hate it, too, sometimes," she said. "He was the big brother but he was also a secure person that I could feel safe with." Collier said Stargell was there to help her with her adjustment to Pittsburgh, too. She came to him once early in the process and he provided some needed advice. "I told him, 'Okay, Willie, I can't handle this.' He said, 'I experienced this, too, when I first left home. It's going to hit you in about six months and then you're going to be okay.' So that father figure always remained with me."

The tables were turned some 20 years later when Stargell's health began to fail. "Then I became the mother figure," she said. Stargell would call Sandrus, or ask his third wife, Margaret Weller Stargell, to call Sandrus and ask for her to come." It was difficult in the beginning because I was going through a divorce and had to find someone to watch my son and call in my teaching job," she said. "Lots of times I'd get calls on Saturday and I'd need to be there that night. I couldn't drive that far in the middle of the night, so I'd have to fly. But I'd go. And lots of times I'd stay in the hospital. I noticed the reversal of roles. And I remember my mother always saying, 'Make sure you take care of your brother.'"

Collier said her brother's involvement in the sickle cell foundation reflected what he saw his role and purpose to be. "He just wanted to help people," she said, "and to be there for the community. The community loved him — the whole town loved him because of what he would do, whether it was helping out in baseball clinics or making sure kids were off the street."

Collier said her brother didn't express many regrets, even though he played in an era when salaries paled in comparison to those just years later. Stargell's annual salary information is available for several years; court records filed in conjunction with his divorce from Dolores indicated that he earned $289,233.52 for his Most Valuable Player season in 1979 and then $416,908, $269,778 and

Willie taking it easy during a cold winter day in Pittsburgh (courtesy of Sandrus Collier).

$336,218 for his final three big-league seasons. Earlier salary figures were not available, but in *Out of Left Field,* Stargell's attorney, Litman, referred to an offer of $165,000 that GM Joe Brown made for the 1974 season. Still, those figures pale in comparison to what players earn today and even what players took home shortly after Stargell left the game. "We talked about the fact that he was on the cusp of the big salaries and he said it would have been nice," Collier said. "I think he had the opportunity to get more, but he chose to take benefits vs. the big-buck salary because he didn't feel like bucking the system. There were people who told him he could have gotten more after the Comeback Player of the Year [in 1978] and the MVP season in 1979, and he could have. But he chose not to. I think he was comfortable. I don't think he had any regrets."

Collier said that while Stargell was always there for his family and was plenty active in the community, he was also his own man in the true sense of the word. "Willie was one of those who would do what he wanted to," she said. "It wasn't anything wrong or dangerous. But if he felt like going to Aruba today, he would pack up and go. And he'd say, 'I'll see you when I get back.' Those kinds of things. He was very comfortable with just being Willie the person. I don't want to say he had a premonition of his death, but I think he lived his life to the fullest, the way he wanted to. Not that he beat his own drum. He'd do things in the norm, but I think he just enjoyed life. It was the simple things in life he enjoyed, too, not something that was very extravagant."

Although Stargell liked the freedom to come and go, Collier remembered her brother embracing the role of fatherhood. "He loved the kids and he loved taking them places. When they were small and he was home in the winter, wherever he would go, he would feel his kids should go, or he would do things that included the kids. They just had a good time — you could see it in their smiles."

Collier said Stargell never talked to her about issues related to racism when he was in the minor leagues; after all, when he was 19 she was only 9. But she believes the experiences he had in Alameda and the Bay Area helped him negotiate those stormy seas. "He knew growing up in California that there were good people in the world. He was in a different place and he knew if he was going to be playing baseball, he was going to have to experience this. I think what Jackie Robinson went through played a big part in helping him manage to survive all that. That's when Willie started reading a lot and that helped him get over those types of things."

Years later, when Stargell left Pittsburgh and headed for Atlanta, Collier said she believed he never wanted to go. "He really felt he was going to get something with the Pirates," she said. "Then when Chuck Tanner left, he went because Chuck asked him to go. That helped a lot. He liked it in Atlanta — he could have stayed there. But he also missed Pittsburgh. Pittsburgh has something about it; you stay there for a while and it takes a piece of you." Returning to Pittsburgh prior to the 1997 season was like "coming home" for Stargell, his sister said. "He was no longer a player, but he was still loved and respected. He still had things to offer to the younger guys, and he really loved coaching the younger ones and scouting for them. I've heard guys in passing say how much they learned from him. They respected him. And he was fair and respectful to them. I think that made a difference to a lot of players."

Collier said she became aware of her brother's medical problems right after he married Margaret, in January 1993. Collier was aware of Stargell's high blood pressure; he had been treated for that issue since late in his playing days. In those days, team personnel would provide Stargell with the proper medication, Collier said, but after he retired — and especially after he left Pittsburgh — he wouldn't always take that medication. "I wasn't around anymore so I wasn't there, Johnny on the spot," she said. "He had to do it himself. I think he just forgot that he needed to do this until one day he had to take a physical and all these things came out. One thing led to another after he got married." Collier said she believes Stargell's travel schedule as a minor-league instructor might have played a role in his deteriorating health because it was not easy getting direct flights into and out of Wilmington. "You could be stuck in Charlotte for three to five hours at a time," she said. Then there was Stargell's appetite, which — like many other aspects of his life, was in a Hall of Fame category. "His weight issue was a family tradition," Collier said. "He liked good food — gourmet food — and wine. There were certain things he wasn't supposed to eat, but he would say, 'I'm going to die with something — I might as well enjoy my ride.' And we'd all say, 'Don't say that.' His illness was very hard for all of us because he would always bounce back. But the last time he didn't bounce back. The last time I saw him, which was a week before he passed, I just knew it. It wasn't the same anymore. He had actually stopped talking. He couldn't talk."

Collier said her brother's decision to marry for the third time caught her — and other family members — off-guard. "I think he was at a point in his life where he was tired of coming home from road trips and being by himself," she said. "It was kind of a surprise for us, but it was a nice, pleasant surprise."

Before there was Margaret Weller, there was Dolores Parker. And before Dolores Parker there was Lois Beard. Her family lived just a few blocks from the Stargell family in East Oakland, and she and Stargell began dating at Encinal High School in the late 1950s and remained together through Stargell's early years in the Pirates' organization. The two eventually were married on May 14, 1962, but the wedding did not occur without some drama involved. At the same time Lois was pregnant with the couple's first daughter, Wendy, Stargell also had fathered another daughter, Precious, with a woman named Brenda Joyce Hyde. Lois, who later remarried after her divorce from Stargell and is known as Lois Booker, believed Stargell's growing celebrity status — after all, he was an up-and-coming, handsome professional ballplayer — made people want to get close to him. Not that she was terribly understanding about it. "I told him, 'You got yourself in this dilemma, what are you going to do?'"[2] Stargell wasn't sure Hyde's baby was his — a California court ruled in 1964 that Precious Wilbern Vernel Stargell was indeed Stargell's daughter — and because he had a longstanding relationship with Lois, the two were married. Stargell also provided monthly support for Precious — who was born less than a month after Wendy, in 1962 — and in fact Precious spent plenty of time with Wendy, Lois and Willie. "I still tease her when I call," Lois said of Precious. "I always say, 'This is your other mother calling.'" What could have been a heated or at least terribly awkward situation remained more than civil in part due to the approach that Willie and Lois took. "We always tried to keep things light and Wilver had a great sense of humor — that's something we all have," she said. "Rather than get upset, we tried to keep things together and remember our purpose." In fact, Lois said, all of Stargell's children — he had another daughter, Dawn, with a third woman and two more children with his second wife, Dolores — were one big happy family for the most part. Even the various mothers of Stargell's children corresponded regularly with one another and got along well throughout Stargell's life. Lois said it was not at all unusual for Precious and Wendy to spend time together. "Precious would take Wendy to the movies or take her to lunch or dinner when she'd come out for the summer to be with her mother and my mother," she said. "I'm big on family and I thought everyone in the family should know each other and know their history."

Stargell and Lois parted ways following the 1964 season, although the divorce did not become final until early in 1966. Lois said that even after Stargell remarried in November of 1966, it was not uncommon for Wendy to spend part of the summers at the Stargell home in Pittsburgh. And Lois said Wendy also would visit Dawn and her mother in Atlanta from time to time. "We have what you would call a really extended family," Lois said. "It all worked out well between Wilver and me because we concentrated on taking care of Wendy, keeping in touch and staying positive." Lois recalled an incident in a Los Angeles court house where she and Stargell were involved in a hearing pertaining to Wendy's child support. "We were going back and forth in the courtroom with the lawyers but when we went outside in the hallway, we were talking about where we were going to meet later," Lois said. "My attorney said to me, 'I don't understand — you're in there battling about Wendy's benefits and then you come out here and it's, "How's your mother?" "How's *your* mother?" But that's the way we were raised. You still have a mission as far as taking care of your child. You still have family. Sometimes people get a divorce and they want to divorce everything. But I think you should stay positive. You can't have too much love."

Lois said Stargell's death at the age of 61 hit her extremely hard, despite the fact that they had been divorced for more than three decades. "It was a life shut out too quickly," she said. "I think he just pushed himself too much and it seemed like he just wore out. Even when he was playing he was always having surgery — one year he had surgery on both knees. He would just not stop and try to rehabilitate them. Sixty-one is so young. I knew he was sick, but sometimes he'd get sick and then he'd get well. But this time ... I was really surprised." Lois recalled a trip she made back to Oakland from her southern California home in 2009 and it all flashed back to her — school dances, baseball practice, young love in bloom. "All of a sudden you think to yourself, 'He's not dead.' But he is dead. You can't believe it. Someone you've known since you were 14 and now you're 66. That's a long time. Not only were we friends, we were boyfriend and girlfriend and husband and wife."

Stargell's outgoing, positive personality and his love of music — and particularly dancing — is largely what attracted Lois back at Encinal High School. So it only made sense that dancing played a role in the first meeting between Dolores Parker and Stargell back in 1962. Not even 18 yet, Parker was attending a fashion show put on by Ebony magazine at Soldiers and Sailors Memorial Hall in Pittsburgh when she first saw Stargell. Having just returned from his winter league stint in the Dominican Republic, Stargell had taken a shine to a Latino model and the two of them danced most of the night away. "I was so upset — I kept waiting for him to dance with me," Dolores said in an interview conducted online for *High & Tight*, a blog by Jimmy Scott, in 2010.[3] Finally, late in the evening, Stargell asked Dolores to dance. "I said, 'No — definitely not," she said. A day or two later, Dolores saw Stargell's picture in one of the Pittsburgh newspapers — it was a story about some surgery that Stargell was scheduled to have — and she felt badly because she thought she had treated him poorly at the fashion show. Dolores, who did not even know Stargell was a professional athlete the night she met him, went to visit him in the hospital and brought him some flowers. And he asked if she'd go out with him when he finished his hospital stay. The two began a serious relationship after Stargell separated from Lois. "He originally said he'd never get married again," Dolores told Scott. "He'd just gotten a divorce — he wasn't even thinking about getting married. But I was."[4]

The two got engaged and then he sent for her to come to California after the 1966 season. On November 19, 1966, near Nevada's scenic Lake Tahoe, the two exchanged vows and Dolores Parker became Dolores Stargell. But being married to a ballplayer was not easy, in part because of the schedule. "He was gone a lot," she told Scott. "The guys are gone so much. You don't really have a husband. He's married to the city. Devoted to the game. I thought you got married to your husband and he'd come home for dinner every night." But that's not the life of a ballplayer or his spouse. Instead, players normally head into work in the afternoon for a night game and don't get home until midnight or close to it. And then there were long road trips that would keep

Stargell away for days at a time. Dolores did not care for the schedule. "I thought, 'This isn't so great," she said. "I have a marriage but I don't have a husband. I was raising my kids on my own. He was never there."

Dolores and Willie enjoyed going out in the early days in Pittsburgh, but it wasn't long before Stargell's celebrity status began working against the couple. As his fame grew, so did the difficulty in going out in public. One time, Dolores asked Willie to take the family to Kennywood Park — a well-known local amusement park — because the Stargells had never been there before. All was going well until a young boy noticed that Stargell was in the park. "Before I knew it, a thousand people were standing around us," Dolores said. People crowded Stargell, pressing him for his autograph. "That was the first time and the only time we went to the amusement park together," she said.

Dolores said her husband truly enjoyed playing in Pittsburgh, despite being a Californian for the most part. He appreciated the fact that the fans pulled for him and he liked to help other Pittsburgh athletes get acclimated to the city when they first arrived. "Everybody kind of looked up to him," she said. "That's why they called him Pops. When Franco [Harris] came into town, he liked to lead him around and show him the ropes. That was kind of fun for him." And he definitely enjoyed hosting people as well. "We had the best parties," she said. "Will was a party guy. We always had something fun going on, whether it was a party in a Chinese restaurant or he'd cook on the wok."

Willie and Dolores set up their first home in Pittsburgh in an apartment near Highland Park, then a few years later moved to a house in the suburb of Penn Hills with young son, Wilver Jr., who was born in 1967. Then, after daughter Kelli was born in 1969, the family moved to a bigger home in Point Breeze. Dolores characterized her husband as a caring and loving father but said his many commitments in Pittsburgh — even during the off-season — made him somewhat of an absentee father at times. "He was very much the humanitarian," she said. "He always wanted to go into the depressed areas and help. On Christmas Eve, he and his friend would buy turkeys out of his own pocket and distribute them. And he did a lot of work for sickle cell. He was always occupied, doing something to help someone." The drawback, though, was that he wasn't always around to help with the little things at home. Dolores recalled an incident when Willie Jr. was playing ball and trying to put on an athletic supporter for the first time. He wasn't sure if it went on over his shorts or under them and he came to ask his mother. "Willie was probably out teaching at a baseball camp," she said. "When he was home, he still wasn't home. He'd play golf in the morning. Everybody was pulling at

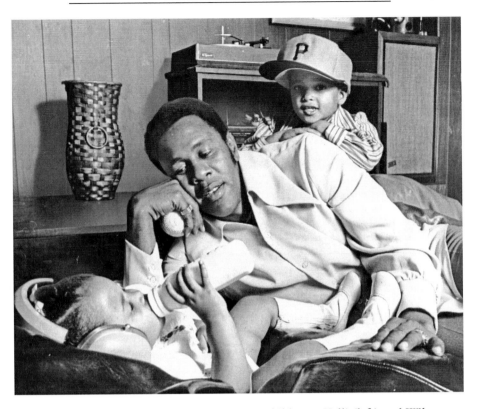

Willie relaxes at home with his two youngest children — Kelli (left) and Wilver Jr. (courtesy The Associated Press).

him every which way. He was out helping kids, helping people. He would do all kinds of things. And then there was the banquet circuit. In the off-season, he was around, but I never could find him."

Being married to a professional athlete — particularly a young, attractive and powerfully built athlete — also had its disadvantages in that other women would go to great lengths to be with Stargell. "It was always there — there was always someone hanging on," she said. "It was a lot in my face." Dolores said she and Willie "kind of, sort of" talked about the women — known as groupies or "baseball Annies." She said she took the attitude that "whatever he does on the road is his business; just don't let it get back home." She said her husband "wasn't an angel before I met him, so why should I expect him to be one now? I had no idea what was going on when they were on the road and I didn't want to know. People tried to get into his room. Some got in and some didn't. It was a very vulnerable time."

Both she and Willie discussed some of the difficulties of married life in the controversial book, *Out of Left Field*. Dolores even had plans to write her own book, which she tentatively titled, *The Glamorous Life of the Ballplayer's Wife*. "I don't really know Willie that well," she said in *Out of Left Field*.[5] "I used to try and figure him out, but Willie is a very secretive person. Very private. He keeps things from me. I don't think he is hiding anything or covering up. It's just his personality." Stargell, who admitted in the controversial book that he didn't give his family enough support, said he learned that love is "communication and understanding and trust. When there's a problem, and one's mind is going in one direction while the other's flying away, you've got to find a happy medium. Dee and I are working toward a better understanding."[6]

But the Stargells' marital relationship took a turn for the worse following Dolores's medical problems, which started on May 24, 1976, when she suffered an aneurysm and worsened when she had a stroke. She was in a coma for six weeks and then spent six months in rehabilitation, trying to regain use of her paralyzed left side. She said the experience not only affected her physically — she walked with a limp and had to use a cane and "old lady" shoes to help her with her stability — but left her confused, and she believes that contributed to the downfall of their marriage. "My comprehension was just shot, pretty much," said Dolores, who today serves on the board of directors for the Joe Niekro Foundation, established to aid in the research and treatment of aneurysm patients and families. "I was jealous of him, I think. I needed him to be more attentive at that time, which he wasn't, I guess." She said her husband was there for her while she was in the hospital but when he wasn't as responsive while she was in rehab, she began to get suspicious. And Willie, she said, "didn't reassure me that everything was cool. And if he did, I didn't remember. All of that helped to tear the marriage down. I became pretty unstable with my thinking."

Dolores sought to end the marriage and the two separated, living in their own homes just minutes apart from one another for several years before the divorce became final in September, 1983 — about a year after Stargell retired as a player. Like many children caught in the middle of marital discord, Willie Jr. and Kelli did not want to see the couple go their separate ways. Dolores said young Willie was angry at her for years over her wanting to end the marriage and ultimately moved to Atlanta and lived with his father. Mother and son — he was actually known as Son-Son to those close to him in his younger days — have since mended their fences.

In a deposition related to the divorce, Stargell talked about Dolores's recovery from her stroke. He said the specialists at the Harmarville rehabilitation center were able to motivate her by "infuriating" her. "When they got her mad enough, she just went from zero back to practically one hundred in less than a year's time," Stargell said. "She has shown in that particular case that she has a tremendous amount of drive."

When the attorney asked Stargell if he had anything else to add, he replied, "She's a hell of a woman."

Dolores and Willie remained on good terms for the most part following their divorce until Willie married for the third time. She said she and Margaret have "no relationship" and that Stargell's third wife — who turned down repeated requests to be interviewed — "did not care for me at all. But I could care less. I don't have anything against her or anyone else. She was like 30 years younger than me. She was just a kid and I'm a mature lady. I don't fret over stuff like that."

Stargell and Margaret did not have children. Wilver Jr. was Stargell's only son among his five children and while Willie Jr. was given his father's name, he didn't carry on the tradition. He and his wife, Nicole, chose to name their sons Cody and Dakota rather than pass on the name Wilver. "I figured maybe, just maybe, they might want to name one of their own kids after their grandfather and make him the third," he said. "They could do it like that." Willie Jr. said the name is a burden of sorts. "It's like, you know what, I'm going to use my name as I got it, but I don't think I want to put that on my child," he said. "I want them to grow up with the legacy of Willie Stargell being their grandfather, but I also want them to be able to do it on their own, at the same time."[7]

Willie Jr. tried to shield his own sons as well as his daughter, Cheyenne, from their grandfather's legacy when they were growing up and playing Little League baseball and other sports. One time, Cody came up to the plate in a Little League baseball game and started to windmill his bat, just like his famous grandfather. "The coach asked me, 'Did you teach him how to do that?'" Willie Jr. said. "Everyone in the stands is looking at him and saying, 'He's his grandfather.' And we're like, 'What is he doing? We better talk to him about not swinging the bat like that.' Our children didn't know who he was. But the other kids on the team and their families knew. And they were in awe that they had Willie Stargell's grandchildren on the team."

Willie Jr. said he first became aware that his father was different from most dads when he was about 7 years old. He was going to Three Rivers Stadium and hanging out during practices and games. After the games would end, he would go into the clubhouse and meet his dad, and they would walk through the tunnel and out onto the field, as Stargell would park his car in a lot beyond center field. "One of my first memories is doing that walk every day," Willie Jr. said. "The tarp would be out already. If it was windy, the tarp would have those big air bubbles and I'd go running out over the tarp, knocking the air bubbles down. Some of the best memories I have was of taking that walk out to center field."

The center-field exit was one way that Stargell avoided the throngs of autograph seekers, although some savvy fans caught on to the strategy and would be waiting for him and other players to emerge there. "They'd still be out there and they'd be running at him, 'Willie, Willie, can I get your autograph?'" Willie Jr. recalled. "I'm just walking next to him, looking up at my dad, stars in my eyes, on the other side of this partition and saying, 'Wow, I just can't believe all these kids my age — and even older adults — are calling for my dad. He'd walk over and sign some autographs and then say, 'Okay, we gotta go.' Then we'd jump in the car and head on to the house. That was awesome. We'd have nice little father-son conversations. I'd say like, 'Nice home run' or something like that as we were riding home. It was fun."

Stargell never brought his on-field problems home to the family. "Bad games to him weren't really bad games," Willie Jr. said. "And if they were, he never talked about it. It was more like, it was still a game. Even if they lost, he was still having fun. Of course it mattered if they won. But if they lost, it wasn't like, 'Oh, my God.' It wasn't like that at all. Lots of people can't differentiate between winning and losing. They're always striving to win. But it's a game. You have to understand you're going to lose some time. You're not going to win every game. When you're out there in the field, you're going to make an error. Being a hitter you're going to strike out or pop out — you're not always going to get a hit. For him, he was trying to hit it out of the park. Kiss it goodbye."

That was the way that Prince, the Pirates' radio and television voice, would send off each Stargell home run — a call that brought a smile to young Willie's face back in the day. "I loved when [Prince] would say that," he said. "My dad would be at bat and they'd be talking about him — Stargell this and Stargell that — then you'd hear the crack of the bat and it would be, 'back, back ... kiss it goodbye.' And I'd be, 'Yeahhhh!' I didn't care where I would be — I would just go totally crazy. Every time my dad hit a home run, it was amazing."

Young Willie made several road trips with his dad; he fondly recalled a visit to Chicago's Wrigley Field, where he got to play in the ivy that climbed the outfield wall — one of the park's trademark features. Only boys — no girls — were permitted to make those road trips. But young Kelli did break her own barriers of sorts when she burst into what had been an all-male Pirates clubhouse one day.

Willie Jr. was 12 years old during the magical 1979 "We Are Family" season, when the Sister Sledge hit was blaring through the Three Rivers Stadium sound system and "Pops" Stargell was handing out his famous "Stargell Stars" to his teammates for deeds well done. "We had rolls of stars at the house," the younger Stargell recalled. "I'm grabbing them, taking them to my friends at school — cutting them off, and I'm like, 'Okay, 50 cents a star!' My friends loved those stars. That whole season was just phenomenal. Especially when it came down to the playoffs and the World Series. I didn't get to go to Baltimore, but I was home watching the games diligently, talking to him every night after the games. And when they won, it was just crazy. During the Series, we would always go to the airport and pick them up. Back then, you could go all the way to the terminal and wait for passengers. So we're there waiting for Dad to come out. Fans want autographs left and right — I always loved the rides, going or coming back from the stadium or the airport."

Stargell's celebrity status only increased with his performance in that '79 Series and the flip side of that was that he was even more in demand than before. "It did take him away from us," Willie Jr. said. "But we were already programmed to be used to that type of situation. Not that it was a good thing that he was being taken away. But that was the lifestyle he had to have by being a celebrity and a superstar. You're going to be away from your family a lot. In ways it helped and in ways it hurt. It hurt in the way where we didn't get all the quality time we should have had as kids. He loved playing baseball and that was his passion. So in order for him to be as good as he was at it, he had to give more than 100 percent. And that took away from family times sometimes."

Celebrity did have its perks, though; for example, the family was able to travel to Hawaii in the off-season following the '79 World Series run for the ABC television show "Superteams," staying in a high-rise hotel on the island of Maui for 10 days. The show brought players and their families from four teams — the Pirates, Baltimore Orioles, Pittsburgh Steelers and Los Angeles Rams — together for some televised competitions. There were other trips, including one memorable deep-sea fishing trip to Mexico which father and son made as part of a contest sponsored by a major rod/reel manufacturer for which Stargell had done some promotional work. That morning, before the group headed out to sea, young Willie gorged himself at breakfast and when the boat hit the water, his stomach took a turn for the worse — and he ultimately lost his breakfast overboard. "I was about 12 or 13 — it was so funny," he said. "My dad is like, 'Yeah, have whatever you want for breakfast. Have some more sausage.' Knowing that I'm not supposed to eat. He was laughing and I'm like, 'Thanks, Dad.'"

At home, the slugger was an attentive father who looked for opportunities to teach his children a lesson. One time, Stargell got wind that Kelli was experimenting with smoking cigarettes and told both her and Willie Jr. that if they wanted to smoke, they should try smoking with him. So he bought some cigars and cigarettes — and Tab soda — and they all sat down and smoked for half the evening. The kids spent most of the time coughing and choking — and feeling nauseated. They don't smoke to this day. "It was her idea," Willie Jr. said of Kelli. "I didn't want to smoke anything. But I had to because it was a 'one for all, all for one' type of thing in our house. I got so sick, dizzy-like sick, I wanted to throw up. And he's like, 'Well, taste it with some Tab.'"

While Stargell certainly had no difficulty providing for his family during his playing days, the transition from player to retired player, particularly before he got the call from Cooperstown in January 1988, provided some financial challenges. Stargell's divorce file, which included an entry dated November 4, 1983, indicated Stargell was earning $40,000 in salary from the Pirates in 1983 — his first retirement year. It was a far cry from his final salary as a player — $336,218, in 1982, and an even steeper decline from the $416,908 he took home during the 1980 season. Stargell did list other income in the divorce documents — $900 from Willie Stargell Inc. in 1983, $10,000 from services rendered to Jiffy Foods, $47,333 from promotional and advertising work for Koolvent Aluminum products, $46,429 from Champale in 1982 and 1983 and $42,000 from HSE in 1983 — but that didn't come close to matching his final salary as a player. And it wasn't as though Stargell had squirreled away thousands; a different court document, dated May of 1984, indicated that he had a less than $2,900 combined in four separate bank accounts.

Willie Jr. said he believed his father was disappointed the Pirates didn't offer him a front-office position in the late 1980s after he worked for the team for several years following his retirement as a player. He said his dad never talked about being a field manager but said that if he'd been given a chance, he would have been a successful one. "He had a lot to teach," Willie Jr. said. "He definitely went before his time because there were a lot more lessons to learn from my father." Willie Jr., who attended Johnson & Wales University in Miami, where he studied culinary arts for two years and worked for years in the restaurant industry in and around Atlanta, said after his father got involved in the scouting/instructing/player development end of the business, he took to it very quickly. "I know he loved looking at the young guys coming up — that was one of his other passions. To help them and to teach those kids the different things they needed to come up in the game then because it was totally different from when he came up in the '60s. There was a lot he wanted to show them, to teach those guys."

Epilogue

MORE THAN A DECADE HAS PASSED since Willie Stargell died, but his impact is felt by scores of those he left behind — family, friends, former opponents and countless fans who watched him windmill his bat and send baseballs flying to the upper reaches of stadiums across America. His legacy also includes the Willie Stargell Foundation Inc., whose mission is to provide funds to support kidney disease research and treatment for those afflicted with kidney disease, according to its website. Stargell's name also is associated with the dialysis center at Wilmington, North Carolina–based New Hanover Regional Medical Center, which was renamed "The Willie 'Pops' Stargell Dialysis Center" in 2006 in recognition of a generous gift made in Stargell's memory. According to the foundation website, Stargell spent the last five years of his life receiving dialysis treatments and he wanted others who needed similar treatments to receive it in a "comfortable and relaxed setting."[1]

Margaret Weller Stargell, Stargell's widow, serves as the president of the foundation's board of directors. The foundation's work is ongoing; in 2012, the group awarded $50,000 in grants — $5,000 each to the UNC and Duke Kidney Transplant Outreach Programs, $10,000 to the DaVita Kidney Emergency Fund, and $30,000 to the New Hanover dialysis center that bears Stargell's name. The foundation's major fundraiser is a golf tournament held each November; the 2012 tournament was the 10th annual.

* * *

Stargell also reentered the public consciousness in a major way in the summer of 2012 when the U.S. Postal Service unveiled a 45-cent First-Class Forever stamp in his honor. Also featured on the new stamps were Joe DiMaggio, Larry Doby and Ted Williams. The unveiling of the stamps coincided with the annual Baseball Hall of Fame Weekend celebration in Cooperstown,

N.Y., and events commemorating the new stamps also took place in New York, Cleveland, Boston and Pittsburgh.

Weller Stargell, contacted by the *Pittsburgh Post-Gazette* at her home in Wilmington, said she loved the stamp design, which depicts Stargell in a late–1970s era "We Are Family" gold shirt, in his batting stance. "I think it's Willie," she said. "It's vibrant. He comes to life on that. It is an extraordinary honor for an extraordinary human being. To know he will be on a forever stamp to be remembered for years to come is overwhelming, and it warms my heart."[2] Steve Blass said he was thrilled to hear of the stamp honoring his long-time teammate "and I wish Willie was here and we could have a glass of wine together. He goes beyond just being a great ball player."[3]

Stephen Kearney, executive director of stamp services for the U.S. Postal Service, told the *Post-Gazette* that Stargell's inclusion in the stamp group was recommended by the Citizens Stamp Advisory Committee, a group that reviews 40,000 suggestions a year for new stamps. After the stamps were unveiled to the public, the Postal Service launched a campaign on August 8 that it called "8 on 8" — encouraging fans to mail eight letters to their friends and family using the Stargell stamp. "Willie's amazing ability and appeal connected with people in Pittsburgh and the nation throughout his Hall of Fame career," Joe Meimann, the Pittsburgh postmaster, said in a press release issued by the Postal Service. "Now his image can once again connect people together by sending his stamp on a letter to friends and loved ones."

* * *

Stargell's image likely won't disappear when the commemorative stamps do. A Pittsburgh resident named Gregory Gibson Kenney will see to that. Kenney, a professionally trained actor who operates an organization known as Educate Us Productions, uses a theatrical setting to bring historical figures to life for school groups and other gatherings. Among the historical figures Kenney portrays is Stargell, whom he tried to emulate while growing up in the city. "He was left-handed and I'm left-handed," Kenney said of Stargell. "Playing pickup baseball, as you do as a kid, he was always my guy."[4]

Stargell met Kenney while the latter was re-enacting part of the life of Stargell's former teammate, Clemente, at a Pittsburgh Pirates fan festival and the two had a chance to talk. The conversation resulted in a 30-minute presentation that takes audiences into Stargell's life as a young child all the way until his retirement as a player in 1982. "I try to include little pieces of history that folks would never know about," Kenney said. "That's what the program is all about." Kenney said the program doesn't just look at the high points of Stargell's life. He mentions the struggles that the slugger went through during the 1971 World Series, for example. Although Stargell never got to see Kenney perform the program, several members of Stargell's family had a chance to take it in during a presentation at the Clemente Museum in Pittsburgh. "The family loved it so I think he would approve," Kenney said.

Even though it's been more than 30 years since Stargell last swung his mighty Louisville Slugger, Kenney believes the former slugger remains relevant due to his own unique story. "Everyone might not know his story but they know about 'We Are Family,'" Kenney said. "It's a great experience and everyone who watches it takes something from it and can put it into their own lives. For Willie, the lesson is that hard work and determination will get you there every single time. It's all about working hard — dreams don't come true without hard work. We can tell our kids that they can be anything they want to be, but sometimes we leave out the fact 'if you're willing to work hard.' The message is, don't be afraid to put in the time and you'll see results."

Chapter Notes

Chapter 1

1. Willie Stargell and Tom Bird, *Willie Stargell: An Autobiography* (New York: Harper & Row, 1984), 14–15.
2. Ibid., 27.
3. Ibid., 31.
4. Nick Cabral, in discussion with the author, June 2008.
5. Joe King, in discussion with the author, June 2008.
6. Curt Motton, in discussion with the author, June 2008.
7. Robert Earl Davis, in discussion with the author, June 2009.
8. Anthony "Lil" Arnerich, in discussion with the author, July 2010.
9. William Patterson, in discussion with the author, August 2007.
10. George Read, in discussion with the author, June 2008.
11. Lois Beard Booker, in discussion with the author, August 2009.
12. Paul Meyer, "Star Power," *Pittsburgh Post-Gazette,* January 13, 1988, 11.
13. Al Abrams, "Willie Stargell for MVP," *Pittsburgh Post-Gazette,* September 20, 1973, 23.
14. "Hot-hitting Willie Stargell No Longer Speaking Softly," *Eugene Register-Guard*/Associated Press, June 27, 1971, B8.
15. Dan Donovan, "The Stargell Way," *Pittsburgh Press,* May 20, 1974, 23.

Chapter 2

1. Ron Brand, in discussion with the author, June 2010.

2. Preston Bruce, in discussion with the author, June 2011.
3. Gene Alley, in discussion with the author, June 2008.
4. Vic Roznovsky, in discussion with the author, May 2010.
5. Dick Doepker, in discussion with the author, June 2011.
6. Bob Priddy, in discussion with the author, May 2010.
7. Cornell Law School. "Civil Rights." Legal Information Institute.
8. Roy McHugh, "On the Hill, Will," *Sport,* October 1964, 106.
9. Lois Beard Booker, in discussion with the author, August 2009.
10. Bryan Miller, "Eating Out, from the Minors to Montrachet," *New York Times,* September 21, 1988, C1.
11. Edvins Beitiks, "Gun at His Head Put Stargell on Path to Manage," *San Francisco Examiner,* June 30, 1987, F1.
12. George Read, in discussion with the author, June 2008.
13. Rex Johnston, in discussion with the author, June 2009.
14. Gene Alley, in discussion with the author, June 2008.
15. Rudy May, in discussion with the author, May 2010.
16. Joe Morgan, in discussion with the author, June 2010.
17. Joe L. Brown, in discussion with the author, June 2010.
18. Steve Blass, in discussion with the author, July 2009.
19. Bob Veale, in discussion with the author, June 2010.

20. Les Biederman, "Pirates May Trade for Outfield Help," *Pittsburgh Press,* March 26, 1962, 14.

Chapter 3

1. Bill Virdon, in discussion with the author, May 2010.
2. Bob Skinner, in discussion with the author, May 2010.
3. Les Biederman, "Road Jinx Ruining Giants," *Pittsburgh Press,* September 17, 1962, 26.
4. Bob Friend, in discussion with the author, August 2009.
5. "Both Stargell, Savage Ready," *Pittsburgh Courier,* April 20, 1963, A8.
6. Lindy McDaniel, in discussion with the author, June 2010.
7. Les Biederman, "Pirate Bats Feast on Braves' Hurling," *Pittsburgh Press,* June 18, 1963, 28.
8. Steve Blass, in discussion with the author, July 2009.
9. Ed Rumill, "Pirates 'Too Left-Handed,'" *Christian Science Monitor,* March 10, 1964.
10. Al Abrams, "Sidelights on Sports," *Pittsburgh Post-Gazette,* July 8, 1964, 18.
11. Bill Jenkinson, *Baseball's Ultimate Power* (Guilford, Connecticut: Globe, 2010), 155–159.
12. Al Abrams, "Sidelights on Sports," *Pittsburgh Post-Gazette,* July 24, 1964, 16.
13. Joe L. Brown, in discussion with the author, June 2010.
14. Frank Finch, "'Big D' and Dodgers Star(gell) Struck," *Los Angeles Times,* June 25, 1965, III-1.
15. Les Biederman, "Stargell & Co. Deflate Dodgers," *Pittsburgh Press,* June 25, 1965, 27.
16. Les Biederman, "Stargell Shows He's a Hustler all the Way," *Pittsburgh Press,* July 14, 1965, 60.
17. Charley Feeney, "Stargell's Bat Streaks Pirates Past Astros," *Pittsburgh Post-Gazette,* June 6, 1966, 43.
18. McHugh, "On the Hill, Will," 107.
19. Ron Santo, in discussion with the author, June 2010.
20. Ric Roberts, "Bucs Sure to Set Precedent," *Pittsburgh Courier,* February 25, 1967, 12.
21. Les Biederman, "Mrs. Stargell's Cooking Too Good," *Pittsburgh Press,* March 1, 1967, 87.
22. Charley Feeney, "Roamin' Around," *Pittsburgh Post-Gazette,* June 1, 1967, 31.

23. Charley Feeney, "Stargell's Weight, Average Rise Happily," *Pittsburgh Post-Gazette,* August 18, 1967, 8.
24. Gene Clines, in discussion with the author, May 2010.
25. "Johnson Orders Out Troops; Dozen Cities Hit by Violence," *Pittsburgh Post-Gazette,* April 6, 1968, 1.
26. "City Lifts Curfew but Keeps Guard Up," *Pittsburgh Press,* April 10, 1968, 1.
27. Robert Johnson, "Fires, Looting Most Obvious," *Pittsburgh Press,* April 10, 1968, 1.
28. Charley Feeney, "Pirates Tout Stargell as Season Opens," *Pittsburgh Post-Gazette,* April 10, 1968, 30.
29. Richard Dozer, "Cubs Routed, 13–6; Stargell of Pirates Hits 3 Home Runs," *Chicago Tribune,* May 23, 1968, 3–1.
30. Ed Rumill, "Stargell Escapes from the Shadows," *Christian Science Monitor,* June 20, 1968, 6.
31. Les Biederman, "Morale Soars on Stargell's Home Run Spree," *Pittsburgh Press,* May 23, 1968, 43.
32. Tony Bartirome, in discussion with the author, August 2009.

Chapter 4

1. Joe L. Brown, in discussion with the author, June 2010.
2. Report of the President's Commission on Campus Unrest (Washington, D.C.: U.S. Government Printing Office, 1970).
3. Steve Blass, in discussion with the author, July 2009.
4. Bob Veale, in discussion with the author, June 2010.
5. Bob Smizik, "Stargell's 'Fowl Ball' Shoots Down Astros," *Pittsburgh Press,* April 21, 1970, 30.
6. Bill Christine, "Stargell Hits Roof, Pirates Win," *Pittsburgh Press,* April 26, 1970, 4–1.
7. Roy Blount Jr., "This Big Man Is the Cool Man," *Sports Illustrated,* October 5, 1970, 17–18.
8. Brady Keys, in discussion with the author, July 2011.
9. Charley Feeney, "Ellis Fires No-Hitter Against Padres, 2–0," *Pittsburgh Post-Gazette,* June 13, 1970, 10.
10. Bill Christine, "No-Hit Ellis Knows About Pressure," *Pittsburgh Press,* June 13, 1970, 6.
11. Bob Smizik, "Ellis: I Pitched No-Hitter on LSD," *Pittsburgh Press,* April 8, 1984, D1.

12. Roy Blount Jr., "No Disgruntlements Round Here," *Sports Illustrated,* August 10, 1970, 18–19.

13. Paul Lukas, "The Pirates Great Uniform Revolution," *ESPN.com,* July 29, 2010.

14. Phil Musick, "Bing Gets Bang Out of it … So Do Fans," *Pittsburgh Press,* July 17, 1970, 21.

15. Roy McHugh, Strangers in Paradise," *Pittsburgh Press,* July 17, 1970, 20.

16. Robert Voelker, "48,846 Fans Open New Stadium," *Pittsburgh Post-Gazette,* July 17, 1970, 1, 4.

17. Bill Christine, "Reds, Stargell Profit in Opener," *Pittsburgh Press,* July 17, 1970, 20.

18. Charley Feeney, "Reds Christen 3 Rivers, Nip Bucs, 3–2, before 48,846," *Pittsburgh Post-Gazette,* July 17, 1970, 16.

19. Bill Christine, "Buc Avalanche Buries Braves," *Pittsburgh Press,* August 2, 1970, 4–1.

20. Bill Christine, "Stargell's Blast Whips Mets," *Pittsburgh Press,* August 10, 1970, 24.

21. Ibid.

22. Jimmy Jordan, "Injuries Helped Mold Champs, Says Danny," *Pittsburgh Post-Gazette,* September 28, 1970, 24.

23. Bill Christine, "Pirates Make Exit Without Excuses," *Pittsburgh Press,* October 5, 1970, 39.

24. Blount, "This Big Man Is the Cool Man," 17–18.

25. Charley Feeney, "Ghetto Work Intrigues Willie Stargell," *The Sporting News,* August 10, 1968, 16.

26. Merv Rettenmund, in discussion with the author, May 2010.

27. Jim "Mudcat" Grant, in discussion with the author, June 2010.

28. Jim O'Brien, *New York Post.*

29. "Of Course Pop Is Getting Older, But the Pirates Know He's Getting Better, Too," *People,* December 12, 1979, 78.

30. www.sicklecellsocietypgh.org, accessed July 19, 2011.

31. Lacy J. Banks, "Big Heart: Willie Stargell Voices Concern for People as Well as Pennants," *Ebony,* October 1971, 132.

32. Bill Christine, "Think Victory in Spring — Stargell," *Pittsburgh Press,* March 22, 1971, 25.

33. Bill Christine, "Pirates Pennant Timber and Murtaugh Knows It," *Pittsburgh Press,* April 5, 1971, 29.

34. Phil Musick, "Cold Remedy," *Pittsburgh Press,* April 22, 1971, 57.

35. Charley Feeney, "Stargell, Not June,

Busting Out All Over," *Pittsburgh Post-Gazette,* April 22, 1971, 26.

36. Musick, "Cold Remedy," 57.

37. "Stargell Sets Record Pace," *Pittsburgh Press,* April 23, 1971, 50.

38. Marino Parascenzo, "Stargell Beats All Sorts of Deadlines," *Pittsburgh Post-Gazette,* April 28, 1971, 22.

39. Feeney, "Stargell, Not June, Busting Out All Over," 26.

40. Steve Blass, in discussion with the author, July 2009.

41. Bruce Kison, in discussion with the author, May 2010.

42. Nellie King, in discussion with the author, July 2009.

43. Blount, "This Big Man is the Cool Man," 17–18.

44. Gene Clines, in discussion with the author, May 2010.

45. Al Oliver, in discussion with the author, August 2009.

46. Sam Nover, in discussion with the author, July 2010.

47. Tony Bartirome, in discussion with the author, August 2009.

48. Dick Young, "How Stargell's Saigon Visit Made Him a Better Hitter," *New York Daily News,* June 24, 1971.

49. Roy McHugh, "Stargell Costing Fans," *Tuscaloosa (Ala.) News,* July 23, 1971, 7.

50. "Stargell: You Can't Think Homers," *Newark Star-Ledger,* July 13, 1971.

51. Banks, "Big Heart: Willie Stargell Voices Concern for People as Well as Pennants," 133.

52. Bob Smizik, *The Pittsburgh Pirates* (New York: Walker and Co., 1990), 162.

53. Howie Evans, "Stargell Takes Another Roundtrip," *Black Sports,* August 1971.

54. Nelson "Nellie" King, *Happiness Is Like a Cur Dog* (Bloomington, Indiana: Author House, 2009), 256.

55. Bruce Markusen, "Cooperstown Confidential," September 1, 2006, accessed July 15, 2012.

56. Joe L. Brown, in discussion with the author, June 2010.

57. Bill Christine, "Pirates Douse Cards for East Title," *Pittsburgh Press,* September 23, 1971, 42.

58. Phil Musick, "Giants Take Defeat Hard," *Pittsburgh Press,* October 6, 1971, 81.

59. Phil Musick," Pirates Win Gamble — And Title," *Pittsburgh Press,* October 7, 1971, 37.

60. "Our Bucs Are No Bums," *Pittsburgh Press,* October 15, 1971, 30.

61. Roy McHugh, "Some Kind of Bunt," *Pittsburgh Press,* October 13, 1971, 71.

62. Bill Christine, "Orioles Feel the Pinch (by May)," *Pittsburgh Press,* October 14, 1971, 33.

63. Robert Voelker, "Delirium Grips City As Bucs Win," *Pittsburgh Post-Gazette,* October 18, 1971, 1.

64. Bob Smizik, "A Vote for Willie," *Pittsburgh Press,* November 24, 1971, 38.

65. Smizik, *The Pittsburgh Pirates,* 162.

Chapter 5

1. Bill Christine, "Murtaugh May Quit if Bucs Win," *Pittsburgh Press,* October 16, 1971, 6.

2. Charley Feeney, "Virdon is Ready to Manage Pirates," *Pittsburgh Post-Gazette,* November 24, 1971, 20.

3. Al Abrams, "Sidelights on Sports," *Pittsburgh Post-Gazette,* November 24, 1971, 20.

4. Bill Virdon, in discussion with the author, May 2010.

5. Bob Smizik, "Wild Pitch Capsizes Bucs, Wrecks Dynasty," *Pittsburgh Press,* October 12, 1972, 42.

6. Charley Feeney, "The End," *Pittsburgh Post-Gazette,* October 12, 1972, 21.

7. Pat Livingston, "Pirates Go Out with the Heads High," *Pittsburgh Press,* October 12, 1972, 42.

8. Trudy Labovitz, "Roberto's Charities Go Unacclaimed," *Pittsburgh Post-Gazette,* January 1, 1973, 30.

9. Charley Feeney, "The Great Roberto Died Caring for Others," *Pittsburgh Post-Gazette,* January 2, 1973, 14.

10. Hal Bodley, "Death of 'Pops' Leaves Gaping Hole," *USA Today,* April 10, 2001.

11. Bruce Kison, in discussion with the author, May 2010.

12. Bob Smizik, in discussion with the author, July 2010.

13. Bob Smizik, "Pirate Switch No Shock to Virdon," *Pittsburgh Press,* September 6, 1973, 25.

14. Pat Livingston, "Most Difficult Decision in 35 years — Brown," *Pittsburgh Press,* September 6, 1973, 25.

15. Bruce Kison, in discussion with the author, May 2010.

16. Tony Bartirome, in discussion with the author, August 2009.

17. Al Oliver, in discussion with the author, August 2009.

18. Bob Veale, in discussion with the author, June 2010.

19. "Willie No. 8? Writer Admits He 'Goofed,'" *Pittsburgh Post-Gazette,* November 22, 1973, 98.

20. Ira Miller, "Rose Jumps for Joy, Willie Just Jumps," *Beaver County* (Pa.) *Times,* November 21, 1973, B1.

21. Steve Blass, in discussion with the author, July 2009.

22. Susan Hall, in correspondence with David Litman, March 14, 1973.

23. Bill Christine, "Stargell's 'Bland' Book Turns Out to be a Sizzler," *Pittsburgh Post-Gazette,* August 10, 1974, 6.

24. David Blasband, in correspondence with William Guilfoile, August 28, 1974.

25. Bob Smizik, "Stargell Pumps New Life Into Bucs," *Pittsburgh Press,* October 9, 1974, 61.

26. Jerry Reuss, in discussion with the author, June 2010.

27. Mike Littwin, "Willie Stargell: Fun-loving Chief of a Merry Crew," *Los Angeles Times,* August 30, 1979, H1.

28. Dave Parker, in discussion with the author, May 2010.

29. Bob Smizik, "The Bucs Stop Here," *Pittsburgh Press,* October 8, 1975, 53.

30. "Begged to Stay On, Fired Prince Says," *Pittsburgh Press,* October 31, 1975, 1.

31. Nelson "Nellie" King, in discussion with the author, July 2009.

32. Anthony Cotton, "Fine, Like Good Wine," *Sports Illustrated,* August 20, 1979, 49.

33. Two Continents press release, July 1976.

34. Vito Stellino, "Stargell Book Finally Hits Print," *Pittsburgh Post-Gazette,* June 24, 1976, 12.

35. Bob Adelman and Susan Hall, *Out of Left Field* (New York: Two Continents Publishing Group, 1976), 59.

36. Bob Smizik, "It May Take Two to Fill Joe L's Shoes," *Pittsburgh Press,* September 30, 1976, 42.

37. "Willie No Manager," *Pittsburgh Press,* October 9, 1976, 6.

38. John Clayton, "Finley Gets Way, Bucs Get Tanner," *Pittsburgh Press,* November 6, 1976, 6.

39. "Pirates' Bob Moose Killed," *Ellensburg* (Wash.) *Daily Record,* October 11, 1976, 5.

40. Bob Smizik, "Pirates Punch Out 8–7 Decision over Philadelphia," *Pittsburgh Press,* July 9, 1977, A6.

41. Russ Franke, "Pirates Hurting, Stargell on Disabled List," *Pittsburgh Press*, August 4, 1977, B7.

42. Jim Brosnan, "Willie Stargell Heart and Soul of the Pirates," *Boys Life*, March 1981, 6.

43. Russ Franke, "Stargell Turns on the Power," *Pittsburgh Press*, May 21, 1978, D1.

44. Charley Feeney, "Bucs Dead, Funeral Date Pending," *Pittsburgh Post-Gazette*, August 7, 1978, 11.

Chapter 6

1. Dan Donovan, "Madlock Provides Another Good Bat," *Pittsburgh Press*, June 29, 1979, B6.

2. Dan Donovan, in discussion with the author, June 2010.

3. Phil Musick, "Stargell's Brilliance Drives Pirates to Top," *Pittsburgh Post-Gazette*, October 1, 1979, 9.

4. Tony Bartirome, in discussion with the author, August 2009.

5. Greg Brown, in discussion with the author, June 2010.

6. Lanny Frattare, in discussion with the author, June 2010.

7. Chuck Johnson, "Beloved 'Pops' Dies at 61," *USA Today*, April 10, 2001.

8. Chuck Greenwood, "Stargell's Stars Honored Top Plays of '79," *Sports Collectors Digest*, April 10, 1998.

9. Ed Ott, in discussion with the author, June 2010.

10. Dave Parker, in discussion with the author, May 2010.

11. Phil Garner, in discussion with the author, May 2010.

12. Don Robinson, in discussion with the author, August 2009.

13. Bert Blyleven, in discussion with the author, August 2008.

14. Steve Nicosia, in discussion with the author, August 2009.

15. Rudy May, in discussion with the author, May 2010.

16. Harding Peterson, in discussion with the author, May 2010.

17. Don Robinson, in discussion with the author, August 2009.

18. Dan Donovan, "Managing Interests Stargell," *Pittsburgh Press*, October 3, 1979, F1.

19. Jim Rooker, in discussion with the author, August 2009.

20. Chuck Tanner, in discussion with the author, July 2009.

21. Marino Parascenzo, "Phillie Fans Conceding NL East to Bucs," *Pittsburgh Post-Gazette*, August 13, 1979, 17.

22. Musick, "Stargell's Brilliance Drives Pirates to Top," 9.

23. Phil Musick, "Stargell Makes Life Sweet for Candy, Bucs," *Pittsburgh Post-Gazette*, October 3, 1979, 37.

24. Dan Donovan, "Series-Bound Pirates Sweep Reds," *Pittsburgh Press*, October 6, 1979, A4.

25. Charley Feeney, "And Now, the World Series," *Pittsburgh Post-Gazette*, October 6, 1979, 1.

26. Phil Musick, "Stargell Takes Spot Next to Mom and Flag," *Pittsburgh Post-Gazette*, October 6, 1979, 6.

27. Dan Donovan, "Pirates Confident Despite 5–4 Loss," *Pittsburgh Press*, October 11, 1979, C1.

28. Phil Garner, in discussion with the author, May 2010.

29. Littwin, "Willie Stargell: Fun-loving Chief of a Merry Crew," H1.

30. Dan Donovan, "Bungling Bucs Fall Behind Orioles," *Pittsburgh Press*, October 13, 1979, A4.

31. Pat Livingston, "Tekulve Still No. 1 in Tanner's Book," *Pittsburgh Press*, October 14, 1979, D1.

32. Dan Donovan, "Tanner Picks Rooker as Today's Starter," *Pittsburgh Press*, October 14, 1979, D2.

33. Phil Musick, "Rooker Survives on Guts," *Pittsburgh Post-Gazette*, October 15, 1979, 11.

34. Ken Nigro, "Bucs Win, 4–1, to Capture Series," *Baltimore Sun*, October 18, 1979, C1.

35. Alan Goldstein, "McGregor Got Ball Too Low on Stargell," *Baltimore Sun*, October 18, 1979, C6.

36. Jack Mann, "Stargell's Message Has Kept Pirates Together," *Washington Star*, October 18, 1979.

37. Ibid.

38. "Stargell the Ageless Wonder," *Ellensburg* (Wash.) *Daily Record*, October 19, 1979.

39. Sandrus Collier, in discussion with the author, August 2010.

40. Dave Anderson, "Pops Hit One for 'The Family,'" *New York Times*, October 18, 1979, D17.

41. Phil Musick, "Invincible Willie Hit by a Cold," *Pittsburgh Post-Gazette*, October 19, 1979, 13.

42. Dan Donovan, "Willie, 'Family' Win It All," *Pittsburgh Press*, October 18, 1979, 1.

43. Anderson, "Pops Hit One for 'The Family,'" D17.

44. William Allan Jr., "25,000 Fans Roar Welcome to Their Pirates," *Pittsburgh Press,* October 19, 1979, 1.

Chapter 7

1. Phil Musick, "Day for Wonderful Willie," *Pittsburgh Post-Gazette,* October 26, 1979, 9.

2. Richard Rottkov, "Madison Ave. Finds Stargell a Red Hot Advertising Property," *The News World,* January 11, 1980, B13.

3. "Writers Who Ignored Stargell Tell Why," *Lewiston* (Idaho) *Morning Tribune,* October 14, 1979, C2.

4. Charley Feeney, "MVP First: Stargell, Hernandez Tie," *Pittsburgh Post-Gazette,* November 14, 1979, 15.

5. Dan Donovan, "No Gripes from Willie," *Pittsburgh Press,* November 14, 1979, D1.

6. Franco Harris, in discussion with the author, August 2011.

7. Donovan, "No Gripes from Willie," D1.

8. Russ Franke, "Pirates Take Over First by a Nose," *Pittsburgh Press,* July 21, 1980, B5.

9. Dan Donovan, "Pittsburghers to Thank 'Captain Willie' Today," *Pittsburgh Press,* July 20, 1980, D2.

10. John Clayton, "Parker Feeling Mighty Low after Assault with Battery," *Pittsburgh Press,* July 21, 1980, B5.

11. Donovan, "Pittsburghers to Thank 'Captain Willie' Today," D2.

12. Carrie Seidman, "Stargell: A Leader's Ordeal," *New York Times,* September 18, 1980.

13. Chuck Tanner, in discussion with the author, July 2009.

14. Sam Nover, in discussion with the author, July 2010.

15. Grant Jackson, in discussion with the author, August 2009.

16. Bob Smizik, in discussion with the author, July 2010.

17. Greg Brown, in discussion with the author, June 2010.

18. Dan Donovan, "Pirates Can Relax, Willie's Injury Minor," *Pittsburgh Press,* March 4, 1981, D1.

19. "Stargells Separate," *Pittsburgh Post-Gazette,* April 11, 1981, 12.

20. Dan Donovan, "Willie Still Ailing; Tiant Called Up," *Pittsburgh Press,* August 12, 1981, D1.

21. "End Is Near — Stargell," *Pittsburgh Post-Gazette,* September 23, 1981, 11.

22. Charley Feeney, "Stargell Says Report Premature," *Pittsburgh Post-Gazette,* September 24, 1981, 7.

23. Charley Feeney, "Stargell to Return," *Pittsburgh Post-Gazette,* December 22, 1981, 20.

24. Dan Donovan, "Pinch Homer Tonic for Stargell, Pirates," *Pittsburgh Press,* July 1, 1982, C1.

25. Charley Feeney, "Stargell HR Wins for Pirates, 3–2," *Pittsburgh Post-Gazette,* July 22, 1982, 26.

26. Russ Franke, "Old Stargell's Bat Still Has Some Pop," *Pittsburgh Press,* July 22, 1982, C1.

27. Bill Stieg, "Love Feast," *Pittsburgh Post-Gazette,* September 7, 1982, 13.

28. Pittsburgh Pirates press release, September 1982.

29. Stan Savran, in discussion with the author, June 2010.

30. Barry Wilner, "Stargell Party, Fete Successful," *Kentucky News Era,* September 7, 1982, 18.

31. Dave Smith, "Stargell: Someone Special," *Pittsburgh Press,* October 4, 1982, C1.

32. Paul Jayes, "Stargell Pops a Single in his Last Time At Bat," *Pittsburgh Post-Gazette,* October 4, 1982, 18.

Chapter 8

1. ESPN Classic, April 13, 2001.

2. Paul Meyer, "Star Power," *Pittsburgh Post-Gazette,* January 13, 1988, 11.

3. Jerry Crasnick, "Historian Says Cat's Measurement is Fair," *Denver Post,* June 2, 1997, C7.

4. Claire Smith, "Galarraga's Big Blast Recalls Clouts of Old," *New York Times,* June 3, 1997, PB11.

5. Charley Feeney, "Stargell Homer, Ribant Arm Edge Reds, 2–1," *Pittsburgh Post-Gazette,* July 10, 1967, 21.

6. Roy McHugh, "Sisk Silences Mets — And Critics," *Pittsburgh Press,* October 13, 1971, 47.

7. "Stargell's 542-foot Homer New Major Record," *Pittsburgh Courier,* July 15, 1967, 11.

8. "It's No Secret ... Willie Buries Phils," *Pittsburgh Press,* April 14, 1969, 32.

9. Bill Christine, "Stargell Blast Icing on Victory Cake," *Pittsburgh Press,* August 20, 1969, 73.

10. Joshua Pahigian and Kevin O'Connell, *The Ultimate Baseball Road Trip: A Fan's Guide*

to Major League Stadiums (Guilford, Connecticut: Lyons Press, 2004), 81.

11. Bill Christine, "Pirates Win Despite Rash of Goof-ups," *Pittsburgh Press,* July 17, 1969, 35.

12. Phil Musick, "Stargell Leads Pirates Bombing," *Pittsburgh Press,* August 6, 1969, 68.

13. Ross Newhan, "Apollo 12? Stargell's Blast Flattens Dodgers," *Los Angeles Times,* August 6, 1969, C1.

14. Vincent Bonsignore, "Stargell a Legend at Dodger Stadium," *Los Angeles Daily News,* April 10, 2001, S1.

15. Musick, "Stargell Leads Pirates Bombing," 68.

16. Todd Shubin, in discussion with the author, August 2010.

17. Bob Hunter, "Bombs Away at Big O," *Los Angeles Herald Examiner,* April 10, 2001, D5.

18. Allan Malamud, "Dodgers Win Home Run Duel," *Los Angeles Herald Examiner,* May 9, 1973, D1.

19. Ross Newhan, "Dodgers Beat Bucs, 7–4; Wilver Drives Ball Out of Stadium," *Los Angeles Times,* May 9, 1973, G1.

20. Malamud, "Dodgers Win Home Run Duel," D1.

21. Jim Murray, "Stargell's Wrong Bid," *Los Angeles Times,* July 11, 1973, III-7.

22. Joe L. Brown, in discussion with the author, June 2010.

23. Richard Cohen, *A Team for the Ages: Baseball's All-Time All-Star Team* (Guilford, Connecticut: Lyons Press, 2004), 162.

24. Ron Santo, in discussion with the author, June 2010.

25. George Langford, "Cub Woes Continue; Pirates Get 8 in 4th; Rip Cubs, 10–0," *Chicago Tribune,* May 31, 1971, C1, 6.

26. Jenkinson, *Baseball's Ultimate Power,* 155–159.

27. Ibid.

28. Ken Mandel, "Stargell's Star a Lasting Tribute," *MLB.com,* June 25, 2003.

29. Frank Fitzpatrick, "Blast from the Past," *Philadelphia Inquirer,* June 30, 2003, C6.

30. Mandel, "Stargell's Star a Lasting Tribute."

31. Paul Hagen, "It Still Gives us the Willies, 32 Years Later; Stargell's Poke to 600 Level Left its Mark on Vet," *Philadelphia Daily News,* June 25, 2003, 82.

32. Mandel, "Stargell's Star a Lasting Tribute."

33. Russ Franke, "Stargell Turns on the Power," *Pittsburgh Press,* May 21, 1978, D1.

34. Rudy May, in discussion with the author, May 2010.

35. Jerry Reuss, in discussion with the author, June 2010.

36. Wayne Twitchell, in discussion with the author, May 2010.

37. Ron Taylor, in discussion with the author, June 2010.

38. Phil Niekro, in discussion with the author, June 2010.

39. Bob Smizik, "Willie's 'Upper' Cut Decks Gentry, Braves, 3–1," *Pittsburgh Press,* June 1, 1973, 33.

40. Charley Feeney, "Stargell's Bolt Shatters Gentry's Gem, 3–1," *Pittsburgh Post-Gazette,* June 1, 1973, 10.

41. Smizik, "Willie's 'Upper' Cut Decks Gentry, Braves, 3–1," 33.

42. "Stargell's 'Called Shot' the Real Deal," *Seattle Times,* May 1, 2001.

43. Dwight Jaynes, in discussion with the author, July 2010.

44. Mike Brown, "Stargell's Magic Moment Inspires Doubleday Crowd," *The* (Oneonta, N.Y.) *Star News,* August 5, 1980, 12.

45. Bob Walk, Pirates radio broadcast, April 10, 2012.

Chapter 9

1. Robert Freeman, in discussion with the author, June 2010.

2. Joseph Schwantner, in discussion with the author, June 2010.

3. Jane Blotzer, "Stargell Hits a Homer in his Concert Debut," *Pittsburgh Post-Gazette,* January 17, 1983, 21.

4. Ibid.

5. David Effron, in discussion with the author, June 2010.

6. Carl Apone, "Stargell Scared but Ready for Concerts Honoring King," *Pittsburgh Press,* January 12, 1983, B10.

7. "Stargell Brings Determination to Stage," *Syracuse Post-Standard,* January 11, 1990, Lifestyle section.

8. Andrew Druckenbrod, "Willie Stargell, PSO Team Up for 'Lincoln,'" *Pittsburgh Post-Gazette,* September 30, 2000, B10.

9. Willie Stargell, "Yes, I Am Ready," *Parade,* April 3, 1983, 10.

10. "Schweiker Supports Sickle Cell Anemia Program," *Pittsburgh Courier,* November 13, 1971, 2.

11. "A Gift of Hope."

12. Neddie Hollis, in discussion with the author, June 2010.

13. Ed Blazina and Ed Bouchette, "Stargell Foundation Strapped," *The* (Greensburg, Pa.) *Tribune-Review,* June 8, 1982.

14. John Golightly, "Halt Fund-Raising, State Orders Group Formed by Stargell," *Pittsburgh Post-Gazette,* June 9, 1983, B4.

15. Peter Mattiace, "Willie Stargell Foundation May Fold," *Gettysburg Times,* July 3, 1982, 15.

16. Bohdan Hodiak, "Stargell Dissolves Sickle Cell Foundation," *Pittsburgh Post-Gazette,* January 4, 1984, 6.

17. "Hard Times Close Stargell Foundation," *Pittsburgh Press,* January 3, 1984, B8.

18. Noreen Heckmann, "The Marketing of Willie Stargell," *Pittsburgh Press,* May 31, 1983, D1.

19. Ibid.

20. Ibid.

21. "Work for Willie," *Indiana* (Pa.) *Gazette,* July 26, 1988, 22.

22. "Palmer's 6 Shutout Innings Pace O's," *Miami Herald,* March 19, 1983, D4.

23. "Stargell Named Minors Coach," *Pittsburgh Press,* October 22, 1984, D2.

24. Mark Purdy, "Manager in the Making," *Gannett News Service,* March 12, 1980.

25. Bob Hertzel, "When There's a Will…," *Pittsburgh Press,* March 29, 1985, C1.

26. Bob Hertzel, "Stargell Will Coach First Base for Pirates," *Pittsburgh Press,* June 14, 1985, C1.

27. Ron Cook, "Guiding Force," *Pittsburgh Press,* June 15, 1985, C1.

28. Gary Pomerantz, "Once the City of Champions, Pittsburgh is a Troubled Town," *Washington Post,* June 30, 1985, D1.

29. Mark Asher, "Stargell, Madlock Named in Drug Trial Testimony," *Washington Post,* September 11, 1985, B1.

30. Jan Ackerman and Carl Remensky, "Parker: Buc Captains Gave Pills," *Pittsburgh Post-Gazette,* September 13, 1985, 1.

31. Jon Schmitz, "Deal for Pirates Reached," *Pittsburgh Press,* October 2, 1985, 13.

32. Charley Feeney, "Pirates, Tanner: A Mutual Split," *Pittsburgh Post-Gazette,* October 8, 1985, 36.

33. Bob Hertzel, "Pirates Manager Won't Be Stargell," *Pittsburgh Press,* October 9, 1985, C3.

34. Gerry Fraley, "Tanner Hires Stargell as Braves Coach," *Atlanta Journal-Constitution,* October 15, 1985.

35. John Clayton, "Stargell Goes to Work for Tanner," *Pittsburgh Press,* October 15, 1985, C1.

36. Curt Holbreich, "22 Players Hit with Baseball's Drug Penalties," *Pittsburgh Press,* March 1, 1986, 1.

37. "No Wrongdoing on Stargell's Part," *Pittsburgh Press,* March 1, 1986, A6.

38. Joseph Durso, "Atlanta Gets Tanner's Cheery Style," *New York Times,* March 23, 1986, S6.

39. Gerry Fraley, "No More 'Willies' for Braves Now?" *Atlanta Journal-Constitution,* March 2, 1986, D6.

40. Chris Mortensen, "Stargell Gets Rousing Ovation Upon Return to Pittsburgh," *Atlanta Journal-Constitution,* May 27, 1986, D5.

41. Ron Cook, "Stargell's Return Gives Fans Reason to Stand and Cheer," *Pittsburgh Press,* May 25, 1986, D6.

42. Hal Hayes, "Coaching Will Expose Me to Areas That I Need to Know About," *Atlanta Journal-Constitution,* June 21, 1986, D2.

43. Paul Sullivan, "Robinson's Daughter: Mom Not Shocked on Campanis," *Chicago Tribune,* April 10, 1987, 4–3.

44. Tim Liotta, "Campanis Comments, Resignation Spark Discussion," *Fredericksburg* (Va.) *Free-Lance Star,* April 9, 1987, 15.

45. Beitiks, "Gun at His Head Put Stargell on Path to Manage."

46. Ed Hinton, "Stargell Wants to Manage — Not to be a Black Manager," *Atlanta Journal-Constitution,* July 10, 1987, E3.

47. Ray Burris, in discussion with the author, June 2011.

48. Fred Mitchell, "Edwards: Minorities are Moving Forward," *Chicago Tribune,* December 8, 1987, 3–4.

49. Chuck Finder, "Black Coaches Want Action, Not Talk," *Pittsburgh Post-Gazette,* January 19, 1988, 25.

Chapter 10

1. Bob Hertzel, "Stargell Makes 'Hall' Hit First Time Up," *Pittsburgh Press,* January 12, 1988, C1.

2. Ibid.

3. Gerry Fraley, "Stargell Awaits Hall of Fame Announcement," *Atlanta Journal-Constitution,* January 12, 1988, D1.

4. Jack O'Donnell, "'Pops' Stargell: One Jump from Being Called 'Skip,'" *Beaver County* (Pa.) *Times/New York Daily News,* January 14, 1988, B1.

5. Paul Meyer, "Leyland Endorses Stargell for Manager," *Pittsburgh Post-Gazette,* January 15, 1988, 13.

6. Terence Moore, "With Stargell, Blacks in Baseball Finally Getting to Third Base," *Atlanta Journal-Constitution,* January 16, 1988, C3.

7. Gerry Fraley, "New Role as Braves Third-Base Coach Demands Being in Tune with Manager," *Atlanta Journal-Constitution,* March 13, 1988, D26.

8. Steve Halvonik, "225 Chamber Members Honor Stargell," *Pittsburgh Post-Gazette,* May 21, 1988, 12.

9. Gene Collier, "Spotlight Curdles Stargell's Weekend," *Pittsburgh Press,* May 22, 1988, D1.

10. "Boos Bother Braves' Tanner," *Pittsburgh Post-Gazette,* May 21, 1988, 12.

11. Gerry Fraley, "Braves Fire Tanner, Four on His Coaching Staff," *Atlanta Journal-Constitution,* May 23, 1988, A1.

12. Mark Bradley, "Hurt Tanner Says: 'I Managed Great,'" *Atlanta Journal-Constitution,* May 24, 1988, E1.

13. Roy S. Johnson, "Chuck Was Very Hurt … It Was Difficult for Him," *Atlanta Journal-Constitution,* June 5, 1988, D1.

14. Gene Collier, "Hall of Famer Stargell's Search for Job a Bust," *Pittsburgh Press,* August 1, 1988, D1.

15. Tom McMillan, "The Call of Fame," *Pittsburgh Post-Gazette,* August 1, 1988, D1.

16. Roy S. Johnson, "Braves Need 'Boxcar Willie,'" *Atlanta Journal-Constitution,* August 2, 1988, D1.

17. Darryl Maxie, "Minority Hiring: Majors Balking?" *Atlanta Journal-Constitution,* December 6, 1988, 1.

18. Joe Strauss, "Stargell to be Instructor for Braves," *Atlanta Journal-Constitution,* February 9, 1989, D3.

19. Bobby Cox, in discussion with the author, August 2010.

20. Jeff Schultz, "Avast! Pirates on the Plunder Once More," *Atlanta Journal-Constitution,* May 19, 1990, E1.

21. Greg Boeck, "Stargell Has Ties to Both Teams," *USA Today,* October 17, 1991, C3.

22. Ron Gant, in discussion with the author, August 2010.

23. "Braves Notes," *Augusta* (Ga.) *Chronicle,* May 13, 1997.

24. Chipper Jones, in discussion with the author, August 2010.

25. Joe Strauss, "Glimpses of Justice," *Atlanta Journal-Constitution,* September 21, 1993, E1.

26. Andrea Shaw, "Stargell Pops the Question; Local Woman Says Yes," *Wilmington* (N.C.) *Morning Star,* December 27, 1991, B1.

27. "Morning Briefing," *Pittsburgh Post-Gazette,* January 18, 1993, C2.

28. Ron Cook, "Stargell Teaches Lessons Learned," *Pittsburgh Post-Gazette,* April 1, 1994, C1.

29. I.J. Rosenberg, "While Big Leagues Take Recess, Braves' School Still in Session," *Atlanta Journal-Constitution,* October 9, 1994, E4.

30. Mike Snee, in discussion with the author, August 2010.

31. I.J. Rosenberg, "Stargell Makes Impression from Field to Front Office, *Atlanta Journal-Constitution,* March 15, 1995, C7.

32. Chuck LaMar, in discussion with the author, July 2010.

33. John Schuerholz, in discussion with the author, May 2011.

34. Henry Aaron, in discussion with the author, August 2011.

35. Chuck Tanner, in discussion with the author, July 2009.

36. Kevin McClatchy, in discussion with the author, September 2007.

37. Cam Bonifay, in discussion with the author, June 2010.

38. Gene Collier, "Stargell's Pull Could Push Fans Back to Ballpark," *Pittsburgh Post-Gazette,* February 12, 1997, B1.

39. Bob Smizik, "Pops is Home," *Pittsburgh Post-Gazette,* February 12, 1997, B1, 6.

40. Bob Smizik, in discussion with the author, July 2010.

41. Lanny Frattare, in discussion with the author, July 2010.

42. Paul Meyer, "In Stargell's New Role with the Pirates, the Eyes Have It," *Pittsburgh Post-Gazette,* March 30, 1997, C5.

43. "Stargell Plans to Go Home Soon," *Atlanta Journal-Constitution,* September 3, 1999, D5.

44. Alan Robinson, "Stargell Dodges Death, Returns to Pirates," *Los Angeles Times,* March 26, 2000.

45. Cam Bonifay, in discussion with the author, June 2010.

46. Robert Dvorchak, "Frozen in Time," *Pittsburgh Post-Gazette,* September 30, 2000, D1.

47. Stan Savran, in discussion with the author, June 2010.

48. Dvorchak, "Frozen in Time," D1.
49. Ibid.
50. Bob Smizik, "Fitting Finale," *Pittsburgh Post-Gazette,* October 2, 2000, C1.
51. Al Oliver, in discussion with the author, August 2009.
52. Bob Priddy, in discussion with the author, May 2010.

Chapter 11

1. Dan Gigler, "Stargell's Image Forever Cast in Bronze Outside," *Pittsburgh Post-Gazette,* April 8, 2001.
2. Ibid.
3. Ibid.
4. "Statue Honoring Stargell Unveiled at PNC Park," *Beaver County* (Pa.) *Times,* April 8, 2001.
5. Ned Sokoloff, in discussion with the author, May 2008.
6. Anita Srikameswaren, "Long History of High Blood Pressure Cited as the Main Cause of Stargell's Death," *Pittsburgh Post-Gazette,* April 10, 2001, A8.
7. Gene Collier, "Numbers Couldn't Measure the Man," *Pittsburgh Post-Gazette,* April 10, 2001, A1, 8–9.
8. Jonathan Potts, "'Pops' Epitomized Pirates," *Pittsburgh Tribune-Review,* April 10, 2001.
9. Rob Biertempfel, "Players, Officials, Fans React to Stargell's Death," *Pittsburgh Tribune-Review,* April 10, 2001.
10. Ron Cook, "Pirates' Family Mourns Death of Beloved Pops," *Pittsburgh Post-Gazette,* April 10, 2001, C1.
11. Paul Meyer, "Foli Leads Celebration of Stargell's Life," *Pittsburgh Post-Gazette,* April 10, 2001, C5.
12. Stan Savran, in discussion with the author, June 2010.
13. John Shea, "Windmill Swing in Steel Mill Town," *sfgate.com,* April 10, 2001.
14. Jonathan Okanes, "Stargell's Death Felt in East Bay," *Contra Costa* (Calif.) *Times,* April 10, 2001, C1.
15. Ron Cook, "Remembering Willie: A Journey's End," *Pittsburgh Post-Gazette,* April 14, 2001, C1.
16. Joe Morgan, in discussion with the author, June 2010.
17. Ed Ott, in discussion with the author, June 2010.

18. Al Oliver, in discussion with the author, June 2010.
19. Tony Bartirome, in discussion with the author, August 2009.
20. Phil Garner, in discussion with the author, May 2010.
21. Grant Jackson, in discussion with the author, August 2009.
22. Cook, "Remembering Willie: A Journey's End," C1.
23. Millard Ives, "A Final Goodbye," *Wilmington* (N.C.) *Sunday Star-News,* April 15, 2001, A1.
24. Lyle Spencer, "Stargell Death Leaves Void in Baseball, Life," *Riverside* (Calif.) *Press Enterprise,* April 13, 2001, C1.
25. Chuck Finder, "Finder on the Web: A Community Mourns the Man More than the Athlete," *Pittsburgh Post-Gazette,* April 17, 2001.
26. Johnna Pro, "A Stellar Tribute," *Pittsburgh Post-Gazette,* April 18, 2001, A1.
27. "Stargell Remembered at Service," *New Pittsburgh Courier,* May 5, 2001, 1.
28. Pro, "A Stellar Tribute," A1.

Chapter 12

1. Sandrus Collier, in discussion with the author, August 2010.
2. Lois Beard Booker, in discussion with the author, August 2009.
3. Dolores Stargell, online interview conducted for *Jimmy Scott's High & Tight,* accessed May 2012.
4. Ibid.
5. Adelman and Hall, *Out of Left Field,* 65.
6. Ibid., 69.
7. Willie Stargell Jr., in discussion with the author, August 2010.

Epilogue

1. Willie Stargell Foundation, Willie "Pops" Stargell Dialysis Center, http://www.williestargellfoundation.org/dialysis.php, accessed August 14, 2012.
2. Diana Nelson Jones, "Willie Stargell to Appear on Postage Stamp," *Pittsburgh Post-Gazette,* August 26, 2011.
3. Ibid.
4. Gregory Gibson Kenney, in discussion with the author, May 2012.

Bibliography

Abrams, Al. "Sidelights on Sports." *Pittsburgh Post-Gazette,* July 8, 1964.
_____. "Sidelights on Sports." *Pittsburgh Post-Gazette,* July 24, 1964.
_____. "Sidelights on Sports." *Pittsburgh Post-Gazette,* November 24, 1971.
_____. "Willie Stargell for MVP." *Pittsburgh Post-Gazette,* September 20, 1973.
Ackerman, Jan, and Carl Remensky. "Parker: Buc Captains Gave Pills." *Pittsburgh Post-Gazette,* September 13, 1985.
Adelman, Bob, and Susan Hall. *Out of Left Field.* New York: Two Continents, 1976.
Allan, William, Jr. "25,000 Fans Roar Welcome to Their Pirates." *Pittsburgh Press,* October 19, 1979.
Anderson, Dave. "Pops Hit One for 'The Family.'" *New York Times,* October 18, 1979.
Apone, Carl. "Stargell Scared but Ready for Concerts Honoring King." *Pittsburgh Press,* January 12, 1983.
Asher, Mark. "Stargell, Madlock Named in Drug Trial Testimony." *Washington Post,* September 11, 1985.
Banks, Lacy J. "Big Heart: Willie Stargell Voices Concern for People as well as Pennants." *Ebony,* October 1971.
"Begged to Stay On, Fired Prince Says." *Pittsburgh Press,* October 31, 1975.
Beitiks, Edvins. "Gun at His Head Put Stargell on Path to Manage." *San Francisco Examiner,* June 30, 1987.
Biederman, Les. "Morale Soars on Stargell's Home Run Spree." *Pittsburgh Press,* May 23, 1968.
_____. "Mrs. Stargell's Cooking Too Good." *Pittsburgh Press,* March 1, 1967.
_____. "Pirate Bats Feast on Braves' Hurling." *Pittsburgh Press,* June 18, 1963.
_____. "Pirates May Trade for Outfield Help." *Pittsburgh Press,* March 26, 1962.
_____. "Road Jinx Ruining Giants." *Pittsburgh Press,* September 17, 1962.
_____. "Stargell & Co. Deflate Dodgers." *Pittsburgh Press,* June 25, 1965.
_____. "Stargell Shows He's a Hustler All the Way." *Pittsburgh Press,* July 14, 1965.
Biertempfel, Rob. "Players, Officials, Fans React to Stargell's Death." *Pittsburgh Tribune-Review,* April 10, 2001.
Blasband, David. In correspondence with William Guilfoile. August 28, 1974.
Blazina, Ed, and Ed Bouchette. "Stargell Foundation Strapped." *The* (Greensburg, Pa.) *Tribune-Review,* June 8, 1982.
Blotzer, Jane. "Stargell Hits a Homer in His Concert Debut." *Pittsburgh Post-Gazette,* January 17, 1983.

Blount, Roy, Jr. "No Disgruntlements Round Here." *Sports Illustrated,* August 10, 1970.
_____. "This Big Man Is the Cool Man." *Sports Illustrated,* October 5, 1970.
Bodley, Hal. "Death of 'Pops' Leaves Gaping Hole." *USA Today,* April 10, 2001.
Boeck, Greg. "Stargell Has Ties to Both Teams." *USA Today,* October 17, 1991.
Bonsignore, Vincent. "Stargell a Legend at Dodger Stadium." *Los Angeles Daily News,*
    April 10, 2001.
"Boos Bother Braves' Tanner." *Pittsburgh Post-Gazette,* May 21, 1988.
"Both Stargell, Savage Ready." *Pittsburgh Courier,* April 20, 1963.
Bradley, Mark. "Hurt Tanner Says: 'I Managed Great.'" *Atlanta Journal-Constitution,* May
    24, 1988.
"Braves Notes." *Augusta Chronicle*/Morris News Service, May 13, 1997.
Brosnan, Jim. "Willie Stargell Heart and Soul of the Pirates." *Boys Life,* March 1981.
Brown, Mike. "Stargell's Magic Moment Inspires Doubleday Crowd." *The* (Oneonta, N.Y.)
    Daily Star, August 5, 1980.
Christine, Bill. "Buc Avalanche Buries Braves." *Pittsburgh Press,* August 2, 1970.
_____. "Murtaugh May Quit if Bucs Win, *Pittsburgh Press,* October 16, 1971.
_____. "No-Hit Ellis Knows About Pressure." *Pittsburgh Press,* June 13, 1970.
_____. "Orioles Feel the Pinch (by May)." *Pittsburgh Press,* October 14, 1971.
_____. "Pirates Douse Cards for East Title." *Pittsburgh Press,* September 23, 1971.
_____. "Pirates Make Exit Without Excuses." *Pittsburgh Press,* October 5, 1970.
_____. "Pirates Pennant Timber and Murtaugh Knows It." *Pittsburgh Press,* April 5, 1971.
_____. "Pirates Win Despite Rash of Goof-ups." *Pittsburgh Press,* July 17, 1969.
_____. "Reds, Stargell Profit in Opener." *Pittsburgh Press,* July 17, 1970.
_____. "Stargell Blast Icing on Victory Cake." *Pittsburgh Press,* August 20, 1969.
_____. "Stargell Hits Roof, Pirates Win." *Pittsburgh Press,* April 26, 1970.
_____. "Stargell's 'Bland' Book Turns Out to Be a Sizzler." *Pittsburgh Post-Gazette,* August
    10, 1974.
_____. "Stargell's Blast Whips Mets." *Pittsburgh Press,* August 10, 1970.
_____. "Think Victory in Spring — Stargell." *Pittsburgh Press,* March 22, 1971.
"City Lifts Curfew but Keeps Guard Up." *Pittsburgh Press,* April 10, 1968.
Clayton, John. "Finley Gets Way, Bucs Get Tanner." *Pittsburgh Press,* November 6, 1976.
_____. "Parker Feeling Mighty Low after Assault with Battery, *Pittsburgh Press,* July 21,
    1980.
_____. "Stargell Goes to Work for Tanner." *Pittsburgh Press,* October 15, 1985.
Cohen, Richard W. *A Team for the Ages: Baseball's All-Time All-Star Team,* Guilford, Con-
    necticut: Lyons Press, 2004.
Collier, Gene. "Hall of Famer Stargell's Search for Job a Bust." *Pittsburgh Press,* August 1,
    1988.
_____. "Numbers Couldn't Measure the Man." *Pittsburgh Post-Gazette,* April 10, 2001.
_____. "Spotlight Curdles Stargell's Weekend." *Pittsburgh Press,* May 22, 1988.
_____. "Stargell's Pull Could Push Fans Back to Ballpark." *Pittsburgh Post-Gazette,* February
    12, 1997.
Cook, Ron. "Guiding Force." *Pittsburgh Press,* June 15, 1985.
_____. "Pirates' Family Mourns Death of Beloved Pops." *Pittsburgh Post-Gazette,* April 10,
    2001.
_____. "Remembering Willie: A Journey's End." *Pittsburgh Post-Gazette,* April 14, 2001.
_____. "Stargell Teaches Lessons Learned." *Pittsburgh Post-Gazette,* April 1, 1994.
_____. "Stargell's Return Gives Fans Reason to Stand and Cheer." *Pittsburgh Press,* May 25,
    1986.
Cornell Law School. "Civil rights." Legal Information Institute.
Cotton, Anthony. "Fine, Like Good Wine." *Sports Illustrated,* August 20, 1979.

Crasnick, Jerry. "Historian Says Cat's Measurement is Fair." *Denver Post,* June 2, 1997.
Donovan, Dan. "Bungling Bucs Fall Behind Orioles." *Pittsburgh Press,* October 13, 1979.
_____. "Madlock Provides Another Good Bat." *Pittsburgh Press,* June 29, 1979.
_____. "Managing Interests Stargell." *Pittsburgh Press,* October 3, 1979.
_____. "No Gripes from Willie." *Pittsburgh Press,* November 14, 1979.
_____. "Pinch Homer Tonic for Stargell, Pirates." *Pittsburgh Press,* July 1, 1982.
_____. "Pirates can Relax, Willie's Injury Minor." *Pittsburgh Press,* March 4, 1981.
_____. "Pirates Confident Despite 5-4 Loss." *Pittsburgh Press,* October 11, 1979.
_____. "Pittsburghers to Thank 'Captain Willie' Today." *Pittsburgh Press,* July 20, 1980.
_____. "Series-Bound Pirates Sweep Reds." *Pittsburgh Press,* October 6, 1979.
_____. "The Stargell Way." *Pittsburgh Press,* May 20, 1974.
_____. "Tanner Picks Rooker as Today's Starter." *Pittsburgh Press,* October 14, 1979.
_____. "Willie, 'Family' Win it All." *Pittsburgh Press,* October 18, 1979.
_____. "Willie Still Ailing; Tiant Called Up." *Pittsburgh Press,* August 12, 1981.
Dozer, Richard. "Cubs Routed, 13-6; Stargell of Pirates Hits 3 Home Runs." *Chicago Tribune,* May 23, 1968.
Druckenbrod, Andrew. "Willie Stargell, PSO Team Up for 'Lincoln.'" *Pittsburgh Post-Gazette,* September 30, 2000.
Durso, Joseph. "Atlanta Gets Tanner's Cheery Style." *New York Times,* March 23, 1986.
Dvorchak, Robert. "Frozen in Time." *Pittsburgh Post-Gazette,* September 30, 2000.
"End is Near — Stargell." *Pittsburgh Post-Gazette,* September 23, 1981.
ESPN Classic, April 13, 2001. espn.go.com/classic/s/2001/0409/11700699.html.
Evans, Howie. "Stargell Takes Another Roundtrip." *Black Sports,* August 1971.
Feeney, Charley. "And Now, the World Series." *Pittsburgh Post-Gazette,* October 6, 1979.
_____. "Bucs Dead, Funeral Date Pending." *Pittsburgh Post-Gazette,* August 7, 1978.
_____. "Ellis Fires No-Hitter Against Padres, 2-0." *Pittsburgh Post-Gazette,* June 13, 1970.
_____. "Ghetto Work Intrigues Willie Stargell." *The Sporting News,* August 10, 1968.
_____. "MVP First: Stargell, Hernandez Tie." *Pittsburgh Post-Gazette,* November 14, 1979.
_____. "Pirates Stargell. "Pirates Tout Stargell as Season Opens." *Pittsburgh Post-Gazette,* April 10, 1968.
_____. "Pirates, Tanner: A Mutual Split." *Pittsburgh Post-Gazette,* October 8, 1985.
_____. "Reds Christen 3 Rivers, Nip Bucs, 3-2, before 48,846." *Pittsburgh Post-Gazette,* July 17, 1970.
_____. "Roamin' Around." *Pittsburgh Post-Gazette,* June 1, 1967.
_____. "Stargell Homer, Ribant Arm Edge Reds, 2-1." *Pittsburgh Post-Gazette,* July 10, 1967.
_____. "Stargell HR Wins for Pirates, 3-2, *Pittsburgh Post-Gazette,* July 22, 1982.
_____. "Stargell, Not June, Busting Out All Over." *Pittsburgh Post-Gazette,* April 22, 1971.
_____. "Stargell Says Report Premature." *Pittsburgh Post-Gazette,* September 24, 1981.
_____. "Stargell to Return." *Pittsburgh Post-Gazette,* December 22, 1981.
_____. "Stargell's Bat Streaks Pirates Past Astros." *Pittsburgh Post-Gazette,* June 6, 1966.
_____. "Stargell's Bolt Shatters Gentry's Gem, 3-1." *Pittsburgh Post-Gazette,* June 1, 1973.
_____. "Stargell's Weight, Average Rise Happily." *Pittsburgh Post-Gazette,* August 18, 1967.
_____. "The End." *Pittsburgh Post-Gazette,* November 12, 1972.
_____. "The Great Roberto Died Caring for Others." *Pittsburgh Post-Gazette,* January 2, 1973.
_____. "Virdon Is Ready to Manage Pirates." *Pittsburgh Post-Gazette,* November 24, 1971.
Finch, Frank. "'Big D' and Dodgers Star(gell) Struck." *Los Angeles Times,* June 25, 1965.
Finder, Chuck. "Black Coaches Want Action, Not Talk." *Pittsburgh Post-Gazette,* January 19, 1988.
_____. "Finder on the Web: A Community Mourns the Man More than the Athlete." *Pittsburgh Post-Gazette,* April 17, 2001.

Fitzpatrick, Frank. "Blast from the Past." *Philadelphia Inquirer,* June 30, 2003.

Fraley, Gerry. "Braves Fire Tanner, Four on His Coaching Staff." *Atlanta Journal-Constitution,* May 23, 1988.

_____. "New Role as Braves Third-Base Coach Demands Being in Tune with Manager." *Atlanta Journal-Constitution,* March 13, 1988.

_____. "No More 'Willies' for Braves Now?" *Atlanta Journal-Constitution,* March 2, 1986.

_____. "Stargell Awaits Hall of Fame Announcement." *Atlanta Journal-Constitution,* January 12, 1988.

_____. "Tanner Hires Stargell as Braves Coach." *Atlanta Journal-Constitution,* October 15, 1985.

Franke, Russ. "Old Stargell's Bat Still Has Some Pop." *Pittsburgh Press,* July 22, 1982.

_____. "Pirates Hurting, Stargell on Disabled List." *Pittsburgh Press,* August 4, 1977.

_____. "Pirates Take Over First by a Nose." *Pittsburgh Press,* July 21, 1980.

_____. "Stargell Turns on the Power." *Pittsburgh Press,* May 21, 1978.

"A Gift of Hope." The Willie Stargell Foundation.

Gigler, Dan. "Stargell's Image Forever Cast in Bronze Outside." *Pittsburgh Post-Gazette,* April 8, 2001.

Goldstein, Alan. "McGregor Got Ball Too Low on Stargell." *Baltimore Sun,* October 18, 1979.

Golightly, John. "Halt Fund-Raising, State Orders Group Formed by Stargell." *Pittsburgh Post-Gazette,* June 9, 1982.

Greenwood, Chuck. "Stargell's Stars Honored Top Plays of '79." *Sports Collectors Digest,* April 10, 1998.

Hagen, Paul. "It Still Gives us the Willies, 32 Years Later; Stargell's Poke to 600 Level Left its Mark on Vet." *Philadelphia Daily News,* June 25, 2003.

Hall, Susan. In correspondence with David Litman, March 14, 1973.

Halvonik, Steve. "225 Chamber Members Honor Stargell." *Pittsburgh Post-Gazette,* May 21, 1988.

"Hard Times Close Stargell Foundation." *Pittsburgh Press,* January 3, 1984.

Hayes, Hal. "Coaching Will Expose Me to Areas That I Need to Know About." *Atlanta Journal-Constitution,* June 21, 1986.

Heckmann, Noreen. "The Marketing of Willie Stargell." *Pittsburgh Press,* May 31, 1983.

Hertzel, Bob. "Pirates Manager Won't Be Stargell." *Pittsburgh Press,* October 9, 1985.

_____. "Stargell Makes 'Hall' Hit First Time Up." *Pittsburgh Press,* January 13, 1988.

_____. "Stargell Will Coach First Base for Pirates." *Pittsburgh Press,* June 14, 1985.

_____. "When There's a Will...." *Pittsburgh Press,* March 29, 1985.

Hinton, Ed. "Stargell Wants to Manage — Not to be a Black Manager." *Atlanta Journal-Constitution,* July 10, 1987.

Hodiak, Bohdan. "Stargell Dissolves Sickle Cell Foundation." *Pittsburgh Post-Gazette,* January 4, 1984.

Holbreich, Curt. "22 Players Hit with Baseball's Drug Penalties." *Pittsburgh Press,* March 1, 1986.

Hunter, Bob. "Bombs Away at Big O." *Los Angeles Herald Examiner,* May 9, 1973.

"It's No Secret ... Willie Buries Phils." *Pittsburgh Press,* April 14, 1969.

Ives, Millard. "A Final Goodbye." *Wilmington* (N.C.) *Sunday Star-News,* April 15, 2001.

Jayes, Paul. "Stargell Pops a Single in His Last Time At Bat." *Pittsburgh Post-Gazette,* October 4, 1982.

Jenkinson, Bill. *Baseball's Ultimate Power: Ranking the All-Time Greatest Distance Home Run Hitters.* Guilford, Connecticut: Globe Pequot Press, 2010.

Johnson, Chuck. "Beloved 'Pops' Dies at 61." *USA Today,* April 10, 2001.

Johnson, Robert. "Fires, Looting Most Obvious." *Pittsburgh Press,* April 10, 1968.

Johnson, Roy S. "Chuck Was Very Hurt ... It Was Difficult for Him." *Atlanta Journal-Constitution,* June 5, 1988.
_____. "Braves Need 'Boxcar Willie.'" *Atlanta Journal-Constitution,* August 2, 1988.
"Johnson Orders Out Troops; Dozen Cities Hit by Violence." *Pittsburgh Post-Gazette,* April 6, 1968.
Jones, Diana Nelson, "Willie Stargell to Appear on Postage Stamp." *Pittsburgh Post-Gazette,* August 26, 2011.
Jordan, Jimmy. "Injuries Helped Mold Champs, Says Danny." *Pittsburgh Post-Gazette,* September 28, 1970.
King, Nelson. *Happiness Is Like a Cur Dog.* Bloomington, Indiana: Author House, 2009.
Labovitz, Trudy. "Roberto's Charities Go Unacclaimed." *Pittsburgh Post-Gazette,* January 1, 1973.
Langford, George. "Cub Woes Continue; Pirates Get 8 in 4th; Rip Cubs, 10–0." *Chicago Tribune,* May 31, 1971.
Liotta, Tim. "Campanis Comments, Resignation Spark Discussion." *The Free Lance-Star* (Fredericksburg, Virginia), April 9, 1987.
Littwin, Mike. "Willie Stargell: Fun-loving Chief of a Merry Crew." *Los Angeles Times,* August 30, 1979.
Livingston, Pat. "Most Difficult Decision in 35 years — Brown." *Pittsburgh Press,* September 6, 1973.
_____. "Pirates Go Out with Heads High." *Pittsburgh Press,* October 12, 1972.
_____. "Tekulve Still No. 1 in Tanner's Book." *Pittsburgh Press,* October 14, 1979.
Lukas, Paul. "The Pirates Great Uniform Revolution." *ESPN.com,* July 29, 2010.
Malamud, Allan. "Dodgers Win Home Run Duel." *Los Angeles Herald Examiner,* May 9, 1973.
Mandel, Ken. "Stargell's Star a Lasting Tribute." *MLB.com,* June 25, 2003.
Mann, Jack. "Stargell's Message Has Kept Pirates Together." *Washington Star,* October 18, 1979.
Markusen, Bruce. "Cooperstown Confidential." September 1, 2006.
Mattiace, Peter. "Willie Stargell Foundation May Fold." *The Gettysburg Times/*Associated Press, July 3, 1982.
Maxie, Darryl. "Minority Hiring: Majors Balking?" *Atlanta Journal-Constitution,* December 6, 1988.
McHugh, Roy. "On the Hill, Will." *Sport,* October, 1964.
_____. "Sisk Silences Mets — And Critics." *Pittsburgh Press,* June 8, 1967.
_____. "Some Kind of Bunt." *Pittsburgh Press,* October 13, 1971.
_____. "Stargell Costing Fans." *Tuscaloosa News/*Newspaper Enterprise Association, July 23, 1971.
_____. "Strangers in Paradise." *Pittsburgh Press,* July 17, 1970.
McMillan, Tom. "The Call of Fame." *Pittsburgh Post-Gazette,* August 1, 1988.
Meyer, Paul. "Foli Leads Celebration of Stargell's Life." *Pittsburgh Post-Gazette,* April 10, 2001.
_____. "In Stargell's New Role with the Pirates, the Eyes Have It." *Pittsburgh Post-Gazette,* March 30, 1997.
_____. "Leyland Endorses Stargell for Manager." *Pittsburgh Post-Gazette,* January 15, 1988.
_____. "Star Power." *Pittsburgh Post-Gazette,* January 13, 1988.
Miller, Bryan. "Eating Out, from the Minors to Montrachet." *New York Times,* September 21, 1988.
Miller, Ira. "Rose Jumps for Joy, Willie Just Jumps." *Beaver County* (Pa.) *Times/*United Press International, November 21, 1973.
Mitchell, Fred. "Edwards: Minorities Are Moving Forward." *Chicago Tribune,* December 8, 1987.

Moore, Terence. "With Stargell, Blacks in Baseball Finally Getting to Third Base." C3. *Atlanta Journal-Constitution*, January 16, 1988.

"Morning Briefing." *Pittsburgh Post-Gazette*, January 18, 1993.

Mortensen, Chris. "Stargell Gets Rousing Ovation Upon Return to Pittsburgh." *Atlanta Journal-Constitution*, May 27, 1986.

Murray, Jim. "Stargell's Wrong Bid." *Los Angeles Times*, July 11, 1973.

Musick, Phil. "Bing Gets Bang Out of It ... So Do Fans." *Pittsburgh Press*, July 17, 1970.

_____. "Cold Remedy." *Pittsburgh Press*, April 22, 1971.

_____. "Day for Wonderful Willie." *Pittsburgh Post-Gazette*, October 26, 1979.

_____. "Giants Take Defeat Hard." *Pittsburgh Press*, October 6, 1971.

_____. "Invincible Willie Hit by a Cold." *Pittsburgh Post-Gazette*, October 19, 1979.

_____. "Pirates Win Gamble — And Title." *Pittsburgh Press*, October 7, 1971.

_____. "Rooker Survives on Guts." *Pittsburgh Post-Gazette*, October 15, 1979.

_____. "Stargell Leads Pirates Bombing." *Pittsburgh Press*, August 6, 1969.

_____. "Stargell Makes Life Sweet for Candy, Bucs." *Pittsburgh Post-Gazette*, October 3, 1979.

_____. "Stargell Takes Spot Next to Mom and Flag." *Pittsburgh Post-Gazette*, October 6, 1979.

_____. "Stargell's Brilliance Drives Pirates to Top." *Pittsburgh Post-Gazette*, October 1, 1979.

Newhan, Ross. "Apollo 12? Stargell's Blast Flattens Dodgers." *Los Angeles Times*, August 6, 1969.

_____. "Dodgers Beat Bucs, 7–4; Wilver Drives Ball Out of Stadium." *Los Angeles Times*, May 9, 1973.

Nigro, Ken. "Bucs Win, 4–1, to Capture Series." *Baltimore Sun*, October 18, 1979.

"No Wrongdoing on Stargell's Part." *Pittsburgh Press*/Scripps Howard News, March 1, 1986.

O'Brien, Jim. *New York Post*, April 26, 1971.

O'Donnell, Jack. "'Pops' Stargell: One Jump from Being Called 'Skip.'" *Beaver County* (Pa.) *Times/New York Daily News*, January 14, 1988.

"Of Course Pop is Getting Older, But the Pirates Know He's Getting Better, Too." *People*, December 24, 1979.

Okanes, Jonathan. "Stargell's Death Felt in East Bay." *Contra Costa Times*, April 10, 2001.

"Our Bucs Are No Bums." *Pittsburgh Press*, October 15, 1971.

Pahigian, Joshua, and Kevin O'Connell. *The Ultimate Baseball Road Trip: A Fan's Guide to Major League Stadiums*. Guilford, Connecticut: Lyons Press, 2004.

"Palmer's 6 Shutout Innings Pace O's." *Miami Herald*, March 19, 1983.

Parascenzo, Marino. "Phillie Fans Conceding NL East to Bucs." *Pittsburgh Post-Gazette*, August 13, 1979.

_____. "Stargell Beats All Sorts of Deadlines." *Pittsburgh Post-Gazette*, April 28, 1971.

"Pirates' Bob Moose Killed." *Ellensburg* (Wash.) *Daily Record*, October 11, 1976.

Pittsburgh Pirates press release, September 6, 1982.

Pomerantz, Gary. "Once the City of Champions, Pittsburgh Is a Troubled Town." *Washington Post*, June 30, 1985.

Potts, Jonathan. "'Pops' Epitomized Pirates." *Pittsburgh Tribune-Review*, April 10, 2001.

Pro, Johnna A. "A Stellar Tribute." *Pittsburgh Post-Gazette*, April 18, 2001.

Purdy, Mark. "Manager in the Making." Gannett News Service, March 12, 1980.

Report of the President's Commission on Campus Unrest. Washington, D.C.: U.S. Government Printing Office, 1970.

Roberts, Ric. "Bucs Sure to Set Precedent." *Pittsburgh Courier*, February 25, 1967.

Robinson, Alan. "Stargell Dodges Death, Returns to Pirates." *Los Angeles Times*/Associated Press, March 26, 2000.

Rosenberg, I.J. "Stargell Makes Impression from Field to Front Office," *Atlanta Journal-Constitution*, March 15, 1995.

_____. "While Big Leagues Take Recess, Braves' School Still in Session." *Atlanta Journal-Constitution,* October 9, 1994.

Rottkov, Richard. "Madison Ave. Finds Stargell a Red Hot Advertising Property." *The News World,* January 11, 1980.

Rumill, Ed. "Pirates 'Too Left-Handed.'" *Christian Science Monitor,* March 10, 1964.

_____. "Stargell Escapes from the Shadows." *Christian Science Monitor,* June 20, 1968.

Schmitz, Jon. "Deal for Pirates Reached." *Pittsburgh Press,* October 2, 1985.

Schultz, Jeff. "Avast! Pirates on the Plunder Once More." *Atlanta Journal-Constitution,* May 19, 1990.

"Schweiker Supports Sickle Cell Anemia Program." *Pittsburgh Courier,* November 13, 1971.

Seidman, Carrie. "Stargell: A Leader's Ordeal." *New York Times,* September 18, 1980.

Shaw, Andrea. "Stargell Pops the Question; Local Woman Says Yes." *Morning Star* (Wilmington, N.C.), December 27, 1991.

Shea, John. "Windmill Swing in Steel Mill Town." *sfgate.com,* April 10, 2001.

Sickle Cell Society of Pittsburgh. *wwwsicklecellsocietypgh.org,* accessed July 19, 2011.

Smith, Claire. "Galarraga's Big Blast Recalls Clouts of Old." *New York Times,* June 3, 1997.

Smith, Paul. "Stargell: Someone Special." *Pittsburgh Press,* October 4, 1982.

Smizik, Bob. "The Bucs Stop Here." *Pittsburgh Press,* October 8, 1975.

_____. "Ellis: I Pitched No-Hitter on LSD." *Pittsburgh Press,* April 8, 1984.

_____. "Fitting Finale." *Pittsburgh Post-Gazette,* October 2, 2000.

_____. "It May Take Two to Fill Joe L's Shoes." *Pittsburgh Press,* September 30, 1976.

_____. "Pirate Switch No Shock to Virdon." *Pittsburgh Press,* September 6, 1973.

_____. "Pirates Punch Out 8–7 Decision over Philadelphia." *Pittsburgh Press,* July 9, 1977.

_____. *The Pittsburgh Pirates.* New York: Walker & Company, 1990.

_____. "Pops Is Home." *Pittsburgh Post-Gazette,* February 12, 1997.

_____. "Stargell Pumps New Life Into Bucs." *Pittsburgh Press,* October 9, 1974.

_____. "Stargell's 'Fowl Ball' Shoots Down Astros." *Pittsburgh Press,* April 21, 1970.

_____. "A Vote for Willie." *Pittsburgh Press,* November 24, 1971.

_____. "Wild Pitch Capsizes Bucs, Wrecks Dynasty." *Pittsburgh Press,* October 12, 1972.

_____. "Willie's 'Upper' Cut Decks Gentry, Braves, 3–1." *Pittsburgh Press,* June 1, 1973.

Spencer, Lyle. "Stargell Death Leaves Void in Baseball, Life." *Riverside* (Calif.) *Press Enterprise,* April 13, 2001.

Srikameswaren, Anita. "Long History of High Blood Pressure Cited as the Main Cause of Stargell's Death." *Pittsburgh Post-Gazette,* April 10, 2001.

"Stargell Brings Determination to Stage." *The* (Syracuse, N.Y.) *Post-Standard,* January 11, 1990.

"Stargell Named Minors Coach." *Pittsburgh Press,* October 22, 1984.

"Stargell Plans to Go Home Soon." *Atlanta Journal-Constitution,* September 3, 1999.

"Stargell Remembered at Service." *New Pittsburgh Courier,* May 5, 2001.

"Stargell Sets Record Pace." *Pittsburgh Press,* April 23, 1971.

"Stargell the Ageless Wonder." *Ellensburg* (Wash.) *Daily Record/*United Press International, October 19, 1979.

"Stargell: You Can't Think Homers." *Newark Star-Ledger,* July 13, 1971.

Stargell, Willie. "Yes, I Am Ready." *Parade,* April 3, 1983.

Stargell, Willie, and Tom Bird. *Willie Stargell: An Autobiography.* New York: Harper & Row, 1984.

"Stargell's 542-foot Homer New Major Record." *Pittsburgh Courier,* July 15, 1967.

"Stargell's 'Called Shot' the Real Deal." *Seattle Times,* May 1, 2001.

"Stargells Separate." *Pittsburgh Post-Gazette,* April 11, 1981.

"Statue Honoring Stargell Unveiled at PNC Park." *Beaver County* (Pa.) *Times,* April 8, 2001.

Stellino, Vito. "Stargell Book Finally Hits Print." *Pittsburgh Post-Gazette,* June 24, 1976.

Stieg, Bill. "Love Feast." *Pittsburgh Post-Gazette,* September 7, 1982.

Strauss, Joe. "Glimpses of Justice." *Atlanta Journal-Constitution,* September 21, 1993.

_____. "Stargell to Be Instructor for Braves." *Atlanta Journal-Constitution,* February 9, 1989.

Sullivan, Paul. "Robinson's Daughter: Mom Not Shocked on Campanis." *Chicago Tribune,* April 10, 1987.

Voelker, Robert. "48,846 Fans Open New Stadium." *Pittsburgh Post-Gazette,* July 17, 1970.

_____. "Delirium Grips City as Bucs Win." *Pittsburgh Post-Gazette,* October 18, 1971.

Walk, Bob. Pittsburgh Pirates broadcast, KDKA-FM/93.7 The Fan, April 10, 2012.

"Willie No Manager." *Pittsburgh Press,* October 9, 1976.

"Willie No. 8? Writer Admits He 'Goofed.'" *Pittsburgh Post-Gazette,* November 22, 1973.

Willie Stargell Foundation. Willie "Pops" Stargell Dialysis Center. http://www.willies-targellfoundation.org/dialysis.php, accessed August 14, 2012.

Wilner, Barry. "Stargell Party, Fete Successful." *Kentucky New Era*/Associated Press, September 7, 1982.

"Work for Willie." *Indiana* (Pa.) *Gazette,* July 26, 1988.

"Writers Who Ignored Stargell Tell Why." *Lewiston* (Idaho) *Morning Tribune*/Associated Press, October 14, 1979.

Young, Dick. "How Stargell's Saigon Visit Made Him a Better Hitter." *New York Daily News,* June 24, 1971.

Index

Numbers in **bold italics** indicate pages with photographs